USING ECONOMETRICS:
A Beginner's Guide

USING ECONOMETRICS:
A Beginner's Guide

Henry J. Cassidy

Professorial Lecturer
Virginia Polytechnic Institute and
    State University
Graduate Economics Program in
    Northern Virginia

and

Director, General Research Division
Office of Policy and Economic Research
Federal Home Loan Bank Board

Reston Publishing Company, Inc.
A Prentice-Hall Company
Reston, Virginia

Library of Congress Cataloging in Publication Data

Cassidy, Henry J
  Using econometrics.

  Includes index.
  1. Econometrics.   2. Regression analysis.
I. Title.
HB139.C37   330′.028   80-27774
ISBN 0-8359-8135-5

Editorial/production supervision and interior design
by Barbara J. Gardetto

10 9 8 7 6 5 4 3 2 1

Printed in the United States of America

To Susan, Laura, Michael, and Jessica

Contents

Preface

This book is a nontheoretical presentation of the principles of econometric theory. Its objective is to acquaint potential users with the basic concepts of econometrics and, in particular, regression analysis, without the relatively severe mathematical training and sophistication that is usually required. The book is aimed at undergraduates, beginning graduate students, and the economics professional. For many executives today, the utility they derive from modern econometric analysis is severely impaired because of their lack of understanding of the technique of regression analysis.

This text offers a new organization and scope for econometrics. It serves as a "how-to-do-it" manual for regression analysis. The aim is to develop skills and insight sufficiently to permit novice researchers to conduct their own regression analyses and to read and understand regression analyses. The book was designed as an introductory text for students in the Master's Program at Virginia Polytechnic Institute and State University, Graduate Economics Program for Northern Virginia, but it is also intended for undergraduate students.

Even though brief explanations are given, it is assumed that the reader understands the basic propositions of economics, including concepts such as elasticity measures, demand and supply curves, production functions, and some aggregate relationships such as the consumption function. The statistical background is developed as needed in the text in the context of the regression model, the differential operator of calculus is not used, and the text avoids the usual manipulations with calculus and statistical operators. Usually, students who are familiar with the concepts of statistics (and calculus) do much better, other things equal, than the others. If anything should be a prerequisite, it is courses in statistics and algebra.

The text is designed to make the reader a regression *user*, not a theoretical econometrician. To achieve this end efficiently and economically, a number of features characterize and distinguish the approach of this book.

- There are no proofs of the various propositions, although algebraic manipulations of various regression models are presented. An understanding of the properties of the various estimators is stressed, but derivations of estimating formulas and proofs of the properties of estimators need be of no concern to regression users.

- All the required statistical concepts are introduced and explained in the context of the linear regression model.

- Differential and Integral Calculus is not employed.

- The multivariate regression model is introduced in Chapter 1. There is only a short section dealing strictly with the bivariate (one regressor) regression model. The simple model, however, is used throughout the text whenever it is sufficient to demonstrate the points made.

- Learning by doing is highly recommended. Chapter 1 presents an overview of the basic ''mechanical'' elements of multiple regression analysis and suggests a project for students to complete as they work their way through the book.

- Model development is stressed early on, in Chapter 2, and is discussed apart from any discussion of estimating techniques. This early treatment is intended to assist students in formulating their own regression models.

- Monte Carlo simulations are used to introduce notions of expected value, dispersion, inference, and hypothesis testing, in the context of the regression model; and to demonstrate the effects of various specification errors and the consequences of suggested remedies. In a sense, the Monte Carlo simulations are used as a substitute for the mathematical proofs found in most texts.

- The emphasis is on structural equations, since they comprise the cause-and-effect propositions of economics, and systems of equations are emphasized.

- The emphasis is on simplicity in model formation and estimation. The reader is warned that many of the fancier econometric approaches amount to ''curve fitting'' and should be used with caution.

The emphasis of the text is on the application of regression analysis to inference and hypothesis testing. The topics are geared to first-time regression users. However, the book goes beyond the rudimentary mechanics of regression analysis in that it stresses, through the use of Monte Carlo simulations, the consequences for inference and hypothesis testing of making various kinds of specification errors.

A Teacher's Guide has been developed to accompany the text. It consists of teaching hints as well as questions and answers for each chapter. These questions may constitute homework problems, especially if the students are not assigned a regression project during the course. The Teacher's Guide also contains a suggested syllabus and hints on topics for the regression project. A few proofs are presented that do not appear to be available elsewhere. A separate document contains the documentation for the computer programs, written in Fortran, that were used to conduct the Monte Carlo experiments. Please write Reston Publishing Company for a copy of the Teacher's Guide, and for the program documentation. The program documentation is available to students at a nominal charge.

In all my econometrics courses, I have found vue-graphs or flip-charts of the equations an invaluable teaching aid. It saves my concentration to make the necessary points and emphases, instead of expending my energy writing continuously on the blackboard. It also makes teaching econometrics less of an exhausting chore. I have constructed vue-graphs that essentially outline my classroom discussion, with key words and all the equations, tables, and graphs in the text, put together in a form that aids in the smooth flow of the classroom discussion. I have also video taped the important sections of the text. These video tapes are geared especially for the professional economist who wants to take a self-taught course in econometrics. For information as to the availability and cost of the vue-graphs and the video tapes, and how to get tape copies of the computer programs, write to the author, 3100 N. Oakland Street, Arlington, Virginia 22207.

The list of people who have assisted me along the way is indeed long, and to those people I give my thanks. In particular, however, I would like to thank Professor David Meiselman for his continuing support of the project, financially and morally; Art Bruckheim and Tony Virgilio, for programming and Art for assistance with Chapter 7 (the ARIMA analysis); and to many people for editing and typing assistance, including Michael Bloom, Glenda Brooks, and Kim Brooks. A special note of thanks is due Professor Harry Kelejian and Dr. Richard B. Hoffman, who very thoroughly reviewed earlier drafts; Professor Barry Falk, who contributed to Chapter 7; and Professor P.A.V.B. Swamy, who helped me with the ridge regression analysis of Chapter 11. I especially thank my students, whose suggestions, comments, and corrections over the years are reflected in this book.

Henry J. Cassidy

1 Overview of Regression Analysis

1.1 Usefulness of Regression Analysis

1.1.1 Usefulness of Economics

Economics is a study of human behavior. Human beings are depicted as economic actors, each of whom plays out one or more roles in the process of attempting to satisfy human wants. The major categories of actors are entrepreneurs, households, and government. Entrepreneurs in a free-enterprise system make decisions about which scarce resources are to be used to produce which goods and services. Households make decisions about which goods to consume, given a set of choices of goods and their prices. Households also offer labor services to entrepreneurs for the purpose of producing goods and services. Governments make decisions affecting various aspects of the production, distribution, and consumption of goods and services.

Economists attempt to understand the whole process of satisfying wants and to understand all the elements of the process. As in the study of any phenomenon, the ultimate purpose of understanding it is to make it work better, to be able to suggest remedies when something goes wrong, or to make it operate differently (viewed as "better" by those making the changes). The suggestions of economists are aimed primarily toward those people whose decisions can make a difference in the way the production, distribution, and consumption process operates, namely, the entrepreneurs and government officials. For example, producers may use economic analysis to decide which products to produce and how to price them; or the government may decide to alter the allocation of wealth, income, or goods and services or to change the levels of aggregate income, employment, and prices by using its powers to tax, spend, and commandeer people and goods.

1

1.1.2   Usefulness of Econometrics

A very notable characteristic of economists is the disparity of views on how economic processes do or should operate. One of the major purposes of econometrics is to defend or refute alternative theories through the use of quantitative evidence. Once affirmative quantitative evidence has been assembled, it can be used to forecast or predict economic outcomes. The usefulness of accurate forecasting and prediction can be readily appreciated, because the costs of not achieving the decision-maker's desired results can be very high: bankruptcy for the entrepreneur and political upheaval for the government official.

Econometrics attempts to quantify the economic processes. The processes are described in terms of relationships. For example, consumer demand for a particular commodity is actually a relationship between the amount demanded and its price, the prices of complementary and substitute goods, and income. This relationship is called a *function*. The productive process is also a function: output depends on the quantity of factors of production (broadly classified as capital, labor, and raw materials) employed; this particular relationship is called a *production function*.

Economists make forecasts of *variables*. Examples are sales, profits, Gross National Product, taxes, interest rates, and the inflation rate. Some variables are under the direct control of decision-makers. Entrepreneurs can set the prices on the goods they produce, and the government can set the tax rate. These variables that are under the control of decision-makers are called *policy parameters*. Relationships or functions involving policy parameters are thus of special interest to econometricians because it is here that the ultimate payoff is achieved. Prediction is a type of forecasting in which one variable—most likely a policy parameter—is varied to assess how the variable of interest, such as sales or tax revenues, responds, while the other relevant variables are held at specified levels. Sometimes economic theory can be used to predict outcomes, whereas econometrics offers a quantitative estimate of the outcome and provides a technique for holding other variables constant.

The components of econometric analysis are (1) the relationships or functions or, more generally, the economic *models* of human behavior, (2) the data on the variables that are needed to quantify the models, and (3) the quantification of the models. Only the first and third components are explored in this book. In fact, the development of various quantification techniques is what the *science* of econometrics is all about.

1.1.3   Alternative Approaches to Quantification

There are many approaches to quantification, and selecting the appropriate one is the *art* of econometrics. Just as there are alternative economic theories, there are alternative quantification techniques. In general, there are three broad categories of quantification techniques, (1) descriptive statistics, (2) nonparametric techniques, and (3) parametric techniques. Descriptive statistics are various displays of the data, and they attempt to give an intuitive understanding of the relationships without actually quantifying them. Often, they are a useful adjunct to quantified relationships. Nonparametric techniques explore the *degree* of relationship between variables in a function, as contrasted to parametric techniques, which show the amount by which one variable is expected to change if one or more other variables in the relationship change by given amounts. While descriptive statistics and nonparametric techniques are often useful, they do not have the power of the parametric techniques that is so useful for prediction.

1.1.4 Objectives of the Text

There are many parametric techniques, including factor analysis and discriminant analysis. The econometric technique explored in this book is *regression analysis*. The following section presents an overview of regression analysis. The basic—and rather mechanical—elements of regression analysis are presented. The reader is expected to learn how to specify a regression model in terms of the relationships among variables and what the regression technique is supposed to do. The final section of this chapter presents an overview of the steps in applying regression analysis. For a classroom situation, it is suggested that the student specify a regression model at this point; this is the first step of a term project in applied regression analysis.

The major objective of this text is to teach the techniques of regression analysis. Upon completion, the student should be able to formulate, test, evaluate, and u regression models and also be able to read, understand, and evaluate critically arti or reports containing regression analyses. The importance of critical evaluation be stressed too strongly. The *limitations* of regression analysis must be fully per and appreciated by anyone attempting to use the findings of regression an Missing data or data inaccurately measured, incorrect formulation of the re ship(s), poor choice of estimating technique, or improper testing procedure— these problems imply that predictions from regression analyses need to be v with some suspicion. Unfortunately, these kinds of problems are extremely co in applied regression analysis. In many cases, regression analysis is simply no to provide the proper type of testing of relationships or predictions. This tex designed to highlight the limitations of regression analysis as well as to demonstr how to use the technique.

This text attempts to provide the minimum set of regression tools and understa ing that economists need to perform successful empirical research on a wide range economic propositions. The emphasis in this text is on the interpretation and appl cation of the techniques of regression analysis. Because the computer accomplis all the arithmetic and data manipulation required, there is no need for the regress user to be able to prove analytically the mathematical propositions that form the of econometrics. An understanding of the regression tools can be achieved wit having to investigate the mathematical derivations. An analogy can be drawn t tomobile mechanics: they must be able to understand the functioning of the m nisms of a car in order to diagnose faults and to repair them, but they do not have to be aware of the engineering formulas that were employed in designing the various mechanisms. This text attempts to serve as a guide to building, estimating, evaluating, and using regression models; diagnosis of faults and finding appropriate remedies play an essential role in this process. The reader will learn that, just as with a car, a faulty diagnosis can be costly, and therefore, suggested repairs should be considered very carefully. The purpose of this text is to make the reader a "regression mechanic," one who employs the tools of regression analysis but does not invent or design them—more advanced texts are written for that purpose. But just as car mechanics cannot repair cars unless they understand how they work, neither can regression mechanics build and repair regression models unless they understand the fundamental operations of the technique. This text attempts to supply that understanding without the advanced mathematical detail.

1.2   The Regression Analysis Technique

This section presents a bare-bones outline of the general method of performing single-equation regression analysis. Only the major points are discussed in order to give the reader a brief overview of the mechanics. Chapter 2 discusses model development, usually the most difficult exercise in all of regression analysis. If the regression model is correctly and fully specified, estimation becomes a much simpler chore. There are almost always data problems, but these problems are truly secondary to the correct specification of the theoretical model itself. Thus, before the mechanics of estimation are outlined in Chapter 3, the theoretical aspects of model building are explored in Chapter 2.

Chapter 4 presents what is known as the "classical model." The classical model is composed of a standard set of assumptions; Chapters 6 through 9 deal with estimating equations when some of those assumptions are violated. Chapter 10 extends the notions of hypothesis testing, the fundamentals of which must be introduced early (in Chapter 5). Chapter 11 presents a summary of the material of this text (emphasizing the "artistic" elements of applied regression analysis) and presents a few extensions of regression analysis.

1.2.1   Dependent and Independent Variables

Regression analysis is a statistical technique that attempts to "explain" or "predict," in the form of a single empirical equation, movements in one variable, the dependent variable (or "regressand"), as a function of the movements in a set of variables, called the independent variables (or "regressors"). Regression analysis is a very natural statistical tool for economics because most economic propositions can be stated in single-equation functional form: quantity demanded (regressand) is a function of price, income, prices of substitute and complementary goods, etc. (regressors); aggregate consumption (regressand) is a function of disposable income, price expectations, etc. (regressors); output (regressand) is a function of capital and labor inputs (regressors).[1]

---

[1] Often, there are several related economic propositions that, when taken as a group, suggest a system of regression equations. An example is a two-equation model of supply and demand; usually, these two equations must be considered together instead of separately. These models are discussed in Chapters 2 and 9.

The main body of economics is concerned with cause-and-effect propositions: if the price of a good increases by one unit, then the quantity demanded decreases on average by a certain amount, depending on the elasticity of demand (defined in Section 2.2.1); if aggregate disposable income increases by a billion dollars, then aggregate consumption increases by a certain amount, depending on the marginal propensity to consume; if the quantity of capital employed increases by one unit, then output increases by a certain amount, depending on the marginal productivity of capital. All these propositions pose an if-then, or *causal*, relationship that logically postulates a "dependent" variable having movements that are causally determined by movements of a number of specified "explanatory" variables. The *behavior* of a given economic group or entity is explained by the causal propositions of economics: the economic entities are households for the demand and aggregate consumption functions; and whereas production functions are of a technical, or engineering, type, they depict behavior patterns of entrepreneurs, or producers.

The purpose of regression analysis in economics is to quantify and use the behavioral relationships postulated by economic theory: to quantify magnitudes such as the elasticity of demand, the marginal propensity to consume, and the marginal productivity of capital. In many cases, verification or rejection of an economic proposition is the desired end product of the regression analysis, in which case the precise quantification of the magnitude of the coefficients in the relationship is not the goal. In other cases, the purpose of regression analysis is to forecast the value of the dependent variable, given assumed or predicted values of the regressors. The same general statistical approach is used in all cases, but the emphasis on the various steps of regression analysis differs according to the purpose of the regression analysis.

Because regression analysis can be used to quantify the behavioral relationships of economic theory, it forms the basis for most of the empirical research carried out in economics. Although other statistical tools are used and may be more appropriate for certain applications, for most economists, regression analysis is the primary statistical technique that is used.

1.2.2   The Single-Equation, Linear Regression Model

The single-equation, linear regression model, in its simplest form, may be written as:

$$Y_i = \beta_0 + \beta_1 X_i + \epsilon_i \qquad i = 1, 2 \ldots, n \qquad (1.2.1)$$

where

Y_i = the ith observation on (or of) the *dependent variable* or *regressand*,

X_i = the ith observation on the *explanatory* or *independent* variable, also called the *regressor*,

ϵ_i = the ith observation on the *error* or *disturbance* term,

β_0 and β_1 = the *regression coefficients*, and

n = the number of observations.

A fuller writing of the regression model (equation 1.2.1) is as n equations, one for each observation, as follows:

$$Y_1 = \beta_0 + \beta_1 X_1 + \epsilon_1$$
$$Y_2 = \beta_0 + \beta_1 X_2 + \epsilon_2$$
$$Y_3 = \beta_0 + \beta_1 X_3 + \epsilon_3$$

.

.

.

$$Y_n = \beta_0 + \beta_1 X_n + \epsilon_n$$

That is, the regression model is assumed to hold for each observation.

As an illustration, suppose Y_i is aggregate consumption in year i and X_i is aggregate disposable income in year i; so the regression equation represents the simplest of the (Keynesian) aggregate consumption functions. Figure 1.2.1 is a graphical illustration of this function; the dots represent observed pairs of X and Y, and, in the sample, there are n such observational pairs. A given level of income (X) is postulated to cause or determine a given level of consumption (Y) in a simple, linear manner. "Linearity" refers to the fact that the regression relationship $AVG(Y_i) = \beta_0 + \beta_1 X_i$ shown in Figure 1.2.1 is a straight line. The notation "$AVG(Y_i)$" is used to show the distinction between the regression equation 1.2.1 and the straight line shown in the graph. The difference is that the error term ϵ_i is omitted in the straight-line representation of the regression relationship.

The error term ϵ_i is included in the regression relationship (equation 1.2.1) because actual, observed values of Y_i very likely do not all fall on a straight line. For example, if income is \$2.0 trillion for the fifth observation in the data set (i.e., $X_5 = 2.0$; in Figure 1.2.1, the observed value X_5 is shown on the horizontal axis) and the

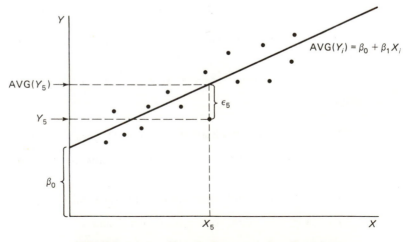

FIGURE 1.2.1   Simple Consumption Function

regression coefficients are $\beta_0 = 0.1$ and $\beta_1 = 0.8$, then the computed value of consumption for the fifth year would be $\beta_0 + \beta_1 X_5 = 0.1 + 0.8\,(2.0) = \$1.7$ trillion. The interpretation of this $1.7 trillion figure is that, *on average*, $1.7 trillion in consumption can be expected each time an income level of $2.0 trillion is observed; hence the use of the AVG notation. In period 5, however, the actual, observed level of consumption (Y_5) may be $1.5 trillion. In another period, such as the tenth year in the sample, income may be $2.0 trillion again, but this time consumption may be $1.8 trillion. Regression relationships are able to show only the *average* or *expected* level of consumption for each level of observed income, which for this fifth observation is shown by the average regression relationship $\text{AVG}(Y_5) = \beta_0 + \beta_1 X_5$. The equation cannot predict without error the actual, or observed, level of consumption in each period. In the example, the error in the fifth period, written as ϵ_5, is the $1.5 trillion of consumption observed less the level of consumption that is expected, $1.7 trillion, or $ $-\,0.2$ trillion.

An error term is always present for regression equations. In the consumption function example, consumption may have been less than expected in period 5 because of uncertainty over the future course of the economy, causing consumers to save more and to consume less than they on average would if the uncertainty did not exist. Another reason for the error in period 5 may be that the consumption function attempts to portray the behavior of people, and there is an element of unpredictability in human behavior; that is, just by chance households consumed less than they were expected to on average. A third reason for the error may be that the *observed* amount of consumption in period 5 may have been different from the *actual* level of consumption due to some error (such as sampling error) in the measurement of consumption in the National Income Accounts. A fourth reason for the error may be that the true relationship is not exactly linear as was assumed. Any of these reasons can explain the error between the observed values of Y_i and the values expected from the hypothesized linear relationship, $\text{AVG}(Y_i)$.

The expression $\beta_0 + \beta_1 X_i$ is called the *deterministic* part of the regression equation. It indicates what the expected level of consumption is for any given value of X_i. Notationally, the deterministic part of the equation is written as in Figure 1.2.1:

$$\text{AVG}(Y_i) = \beta_0 + \beta_1 X_i \qquad\qquad (1.2.2)$$

The part of equation 1.2.1 that distinguishes it from the deterministic part (equation 1.2.2) is the error term, ϵ_i. This part of the regression equation is called the *stochastic* or *random* part. It is always included because the observed value of Y_i is very unlikely to be the same as the regression-line value $\text{AVG}(Y_i)$.

The coefficient β_0 is called the "constant term" or the "Y-intercept." In Figure 1.2.1, it is the expected value of Y_i when X_i is zero. The coefficient β_1 is called the "slope" coefficient. It shows the increase in the average or expected value of Y_i caused by an increase in X_i of one unit (e.g., one trillion dollars). In other words, it shows the response of the expected value of Y_i to *changes* in X_i. Since being able to predict changes in the dependent variable if X_i changes is the essence of quantifying behavioral relationships, most of the emphasis in regression analysis is on slope coefficients such as β_1.

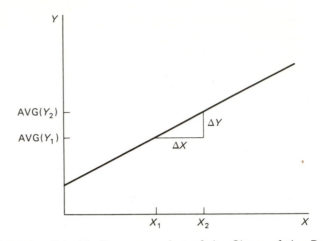

FIGURE 1.2.2 Graphic Representation of the Slope of the Regression Line

Figure 1.2.2 is a graphic interpretation of the slope of the regression line. If X were postulated to increase from X_1 to X_2, the value of Y predicted from the regression line would increase from Y_1, the level associated with X_1, to Y_2, the level associated with X_2. For linear (i.e., straight-line) models, the response in the predicted value of Y due to the change in X, i.e., the slope, is measured as:

$$\frac{AVG(Y_2) - AVG(Y_1)}{X_2 - X_1}$$

When Δ is used to denote the change in the variables (and Y is used instead of $AVG(Y)$), the slope coefficient can be represented as:

$$\beta_1 = \frac{\Delta Y}{\Delta X}$$

Some readers may recognize this as the "rise" (ΔY) divided by the "run" (ΔX), which refers to the directions in the graph by which the changes in Y and X are measured.

Variables other than income are likely to affect the level of consumption. If the interest rate is relatively high, people may save more and consume less, or if uncertainty about recession is rampant, consumption may be curtailed. If we define

X_{i1} = the ith observation on disposable income,

X_{i2} = the ith observation on the interest rate, and

X_{i3} = the ith observation on an index of consumer uncertainty over recession,

then all three variables can be expressed as determinants of Y in a *multiple linear regression model*:

$$Y_i = \beta_0 + \beta_1 X_{i1} + \beta_2 X_{i2} + \beta_3 X_{i3} + \epsilon_i \qquad (1.2.3)$$

There are now four coefficients, three "slope" coefficients, β_1, β_2, and β_3, and a constant term β_0. In the single-regressor model used earlier, there were only two coefficients. The single-regressor model is sometimes called the "simple" or "bi-variate" model. Now, the deterministic part of the equation is the expression $\beta_0 + \beta_1 X_{i1} + \beta_2 X_{i2} + \beta_3 X_{i3}$. For example, if $X_{5,1}$ (read as the fifth observation on the first regressor, income) is \$2.0 as before, $X_{5,2}$ is 13.0 percent, $X_{5,3}$ is 0.9 (an index), $\beta_0 = 0.2$, $\beta_1 = 0.8$, $\beta_2 = -0.0001$, and $\beta_3 = -0.0002$, then the expected or average value of consumption is

$$\text{AVG}(Y_1) = 0.2 + 0.8(2.0) - 0.0001(13) - 0.0002(0.9) = 1.80 \qquad (1.2.4)$$

Notice that the expected value of consumption for period 1 is 1.8 instead of the 1.7 obtained from the simple model. Notice also that β_0 is different, 0.2 instead of 0.1. There is no particular reason for β_1 to be the same in both models because the interpretation of β_1 differs in each model. In the simple model, β_1 shows the increase in the expected value of Y_i for a one-unit increase in income, called X in the simple model. In the multiple regression model, β_1 is the increase in the expected value of consumption for a one-unit increase in income, called X_1, *holding the interest rate* (X_2) *and consumer expectations* (X_3) *constant at some specified levels*. Being able to account for other factors in describing the bivariate relationship between Y and X_1 is the tremendous advantage that the multiple regression model has over the simple model.

The error term in the multiple regression model (equation 1.2.3) has the same interpretation as in the simple model. To summarize, the error term is required because:

1. usually, the many minor influences on Y are omitted from the relationship,

2. human response always contains an element of unpredictability,

3. the variables in the relationship might not be measured exactly, and

4. the true deterministic relationship might not be exactly linear.

Often the expression "Y is regressed on X_1, X_2, X_3" is used to indicate a multiple regression function, with Y being the dependent variable and the X's being the *explanatory* variables or regressors. The regressors are also often called *independent* variables. Also, it is often said that "Y is explained by X_1, X_2, and X_3" to convey the notion of the causality implied by the multiple regression equation.

The general multiple regression model with K regressors is written as:

$$Y_i = \beta_0 + \beta_1 X_{i1} + \beta_2 X_{i2} + \cdots + \beta_K X_{iK} + \epsilon_i \qquad i = 1, 2, \ldots, n \qquad (1.2.5)$$

With time series models the subscript i denoting the observations is usually written as t to denote time. It also does not matter if, e.g., X_{i1} is written as X_{1i}. Often, the observational subscript (i or t) is deleted entirely, and the reader is expected to understand that the relationship holds for each observation in a sample. (In the general model, some textbooks include the constant term β_0 in the value of K by writing the deterministic part of the equation as $\beta_1 + \beta_2 X_{i2} + \beta_3 X_{i3} + \cdots + \beta_K X_{iK}$. Note that X_{i1} is then deleted; in fact it is the "variable" of the constant term β_1, taking on the value of unity: β_1 times 1, which equals β_1. Some texts also write $\beta_0 X_0$ instead of β_0, where X_0 equals unity.)

1.2.3 The Estimated Regression Model

The bivariate model (equation 1.2.1) portrayed in Figure 1.2.1 is assumed to be the *true* regression model, yet it is a figment of our imaginations, having been invented in our minds using economic theory. A consumption function is assumed to be quite real, but it is never observed in practice. Only the X, Y observational pairs (the dots in Figure 1.2.1) are observed. From this sample of observations, researchers attempt to *infer* the magnitudes of the regression parameters β_0 and β_1. The regression coefficients are often called *parameters* to connote the fact that their magnitudes are never observed in practice. All that are observed are *estimates* of these parameters, computed in some way from the X, Y observations.

Given the set of observations as in Figure 1.2.1, if we visually drew a straight line through the scatter of points, we likely would draw a line very similar to the true regression line that is drawn there. But because of the error term that produces the observed values along with the deterministic portion of the equation, in some X, Y samples we may not be so lucky. Figure 1.2.3 demonstrates a particular sample of observations on X and Y that come from the same true regression model shown in Figure 1.2.1. As can be seen, the Y observations for the low values of X are, on average, below the regression line, and those for high values of X are generally above it. This pattern could have occurred just by happenstance, or it could have occurred because the estimation was carried out incorrectly. This pattern was selected to show that drawing a straight line through these points—which is essentially what computer programs do to estimate regression equations—produces a line quite different from the true regression line. Unfortunately, estimated regression lines different from the true line are the rule and not the exception. The estimated line is shown as the dashed line in Figure 1.2.3.

What is observed in practice, then, is not the parameters β_0 and β_1, but estimates of them, denoted as $\hat{\beta}_0$ and $\hat{\beta}_1$. The expression

$$\hat{Y}_i = \hat{\beta}_0 + \hat{\beta}_1 X_i \qquad (1.2.6)$$

is thus the applied, empirical counterpart to the regression line

$$\text{AVG}(Y_i) = \beta_0 + \beta_1 X_i .$$

The term $\hat{Y}_i$ indicates that a sample value of X_i is multiplied by the estimated slope $\hat{\beta}_1$ and added to the estimated constant term $\hat{\beta}_0$ to calculate the *estimated, computed, calculated,* or *fitted value* of Y_i. As may be seen in Figure 1.2.3, the computed value of Y for the sixth observation, $\hat{Y}_6$, lies on the estimated (dashed) line, and it differs from the observed value of Y, Y_6. The difference between the calculated and observed value of Y is called the *residual*, and it is defined and computed as:

$$e_i = Y_i - \hat{Y}_i \qquad (1.2.7)$$

The residual is somewhat like the error term, which is defined as:

$$\epsilon_i = Y_i - \text{AVG}(Y_i) \qquad\qquad (1.2.8)$$

Both the residual and the error term show deviations from the observed value of Y_i, but the residual shows the deviations from the *estimated* regression line, whereas the error term shows the deviations from the true regression line, and to reiterate, the estimated regression line likely differs from the true line. The error term, like the parameters β_0 and β_1, is never observed in practice; the residual is observed and measured whenever a regression line is fit or estimated (by the computer) to a sample of X, Y pairs.

The definitions of the residual and error term of equations 1.2.7 and 1.2.8 hold as well for the multiple regression model. Since the true, unobserved multiple regression model was written above as equation 1.2.5, the observed, estimated multiple regression model is written here for completeness:

$$Y_i = \hat{\beta}_0 + \hat{\beta}_1 X_{i1} + \hat{\beta}_2 X_{i2} + \cdots + \hat{\beta}_K X_{iK} + e_i \qquad i = 1, 2, \ldots, n \qquad (1.2.9)$$

A discussion of how the coefficient estimates are obtained is deferred until Chapter 3.

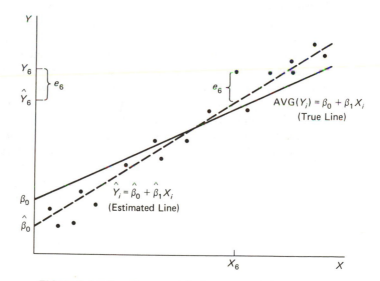

FIGURE 1.2.3 True and Estimated Regression Lines

1.2.4 Evaluation of the Estimated Model

Once the data on Y and the X's are obtained and the computer produces estimates of the coefficients, the researcher must evaluate the results. There are two general aspects of this evaluation process: an examination of how well the regression line as a whole "fits" the data and an inquiry into whether the estimated coefficients conform to the *a priori* expectations held by the researcher before the data were collected and the estimates computed.

In practice, alternative regression models are usually specified, estimated, and compared. Alternative models may be those that contain different sets of regressors. There is considerable danger in estimating alternative models because the final estimated equation selected from all the equations estimated depends on which alternative models were estimated and tested (see Section 6.4). Nevertheless, such exploratory research appears to play a large and important role in applied regression analysis. The usual justification for estimating alternative models is essentially that, since the data contain the information of the true regression model, the researcher should be able to discern the appropriate model from the inappropriate ones by comparing various statistics of the alternative estimated equations. Thus, evaluating regression results is a valuable exercise in itself, but it is often an essential step in exploratory research to select one formulation of the regression model over another.

1.2.4(a) How Well Does the Regression Line Fit the Data?

An estimated regression equation should be capable of "predicting" the sample observations of the dependent variable Y with some degree of accuracy. That is, the $\hat{Y}_i$'s of equation 1.2.6 should be "close to" the actual values of the sample Y_i's. A comparison of these values is appropriate in order to determine the overall adequacy of the regression equation, which was estimated using the sample values of the Y_i's. In many applications, the $\hat{Y}$'s are not very close to the observed Y's, causing the researcher to question the adequacy of the hypothesized regression model.

Various statistical measures are used to assess the degree to which the $\hat{Y}_i$'s approximate the corresponding sample Y_i's. All these measures are based on the degree to which the regression equation "explains" the values of Y_i better than the naive predictor, its sample mean, denoted as $\overline{Y}$. The sample mean requires no knowledge of the values of the X's or of the estimated coefficients. All measures of the estimated equation's overall goodness of fit to the Y's focus on the deviations from the mean, $Y_i - \overline{Y}$ $(i = 1, \ldots, n)$. Econometricians focus on the squares of the deviations added up, or summed, over all observations. This computed quantity is usually called the "total sum of squares," or "SST" in most econometric texts, and is written as:

$$\text{SST} = \sum_{i=1}^{n} (Y_i - \overline{Y})^2 \qquad (1.2.10)$$

(The Appendix to this chapter provides an explanation of the summation notation Σ.) It is easy to see that without the squaring, positive and negative deviations, though quite large in absolute value, could cancel each other out and give rise to a very small sum of the deviations of Y_i from its mean $\overline{Y}$. And formulating equation 1.2.10 in terms of the sum of the absolute value of the deviations turns out to be inconvenient mathematically. Thus, how well the regression line "explains" the sum of squared deviations from the mean of the sample values of Y forms the basis for the various measures of the overall adequacy of the estimated regression equation.

From equation 1.2.7, the actual value of Y_i is identically equal to the estimated value of Y_i, $\hat{Y}_i$, plus the residual, e_i (because the residual is defined as the difference between Y_i and $\hat{Y}_i$). Thus, equation 1.2.10 may be written as:

$$\sum_i (Y_i - \bar{Y})^2 = \sum_i [(\hat{Y}_i - \bar{Y}) + e_i]^2$$

$$= \sum_i (\hat{Y}_i - \bar{Y})^2 + \sum_i e_i^2 + 2\sum_i (\hat{Y}_i - \bar{Y}) e_i \qquad (1.2.11)$$

For the estimating techniques dealt with in this text, the last term of equation 1.2.11 equals zero. Thus, a basic identity arises, from which most of the measures of the overall goodness of fit are derived:

$$\sum_i (Y_i - \bar{Y})^2 \qquad = \qquad \sum_i (\hat{Y}_i - \bar{Y})^2 \qquad + \qquad \sum_i e_i^2 \qquad (1.2.12)$$

| Total Sum of Squares (SST) | Regression Sum of Squares (SSR) | Error Sum of Squares (SSE) |

This basic equation says that the total sum of squares of the deviations in Y_i relative to its mean—which the estimated regression equation is to explain—can be decomposed into two components: the sum of squares of the deviations of the fitted values of Y_i, i.e., $\hat{Y}_i$, from the sample mean of Y, i.e., $\bar{Y}$; and the sum of the squares of the residuals. This decomposition is usually called the "decomposition of variance" or the decomposition of the squared deviations of Y_i from its mean.

Figure 1.2.4 illustrates the decomposition of variance for the simple regression model. All estimated values of Y_i lie on the estimated regression line $\hat{Y}_i = \hat{\beta}_0 + \hat{\beta}_1 X_i$. The sample mean of Y is denoted by the horizontal line at $\bar{Y}$. The total deviation of the actual value of Y_i from its sample mean value is decomposed into two components, the deviation of $\hat{Y}_i$ from the mean and the deviation of the actual value of Y_i from the fitted value $\hat{Y}_i$. Thus, the first component of equation 1.2.12 measures the amount of

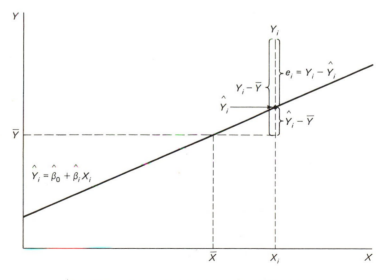

FIGURE 1.2.4   "Decomposition of Variance"

the squared deviations of Y_i from its mean that are "explained" by the regression line. In Figure 1.2.4, the fitted regression line has a fitted value $\hat{Y}_i$ that lies closer to the value of Y_i than does $\bar{Y}$, thus "explaining" in a purely empirical sense a portion of the squared deviations of Y_i from its mean. This component of the total sum of squared deviations is attributable to the fitted regression line, and it is appropriately called the "regression sum of squares," or "SSR."

The SSR is the "explained" portion of the total sum of squares. The "unexplained" portion, that is, unexplained in an empirical sense by the estimated regression equation, is the deviation of Y_i from the fitted value $\hat{Y}_i$, called the residual. The sum of squares of the residuals is called the "error sum of squares" or "SSE." (In actuality, the "errors" are unobservable, but, since the term "residual sum of squares" would have to be denoted "SSR," quite obviously this symbol cannot be used twice.)

Thus, the basic identity, equation 1.2.12, decomposes the squared deviations of Y_i from its mean into two components, the explained (SSR) and the unexplained (SSE) components. The measures of the overall statistical fit of the estimated equation usually involve a comparison of these two components.

Coefficient of Determination, R^2. The coefficient of determination, R^2, is simply the ratio of the explained portion (or one minus the ratio of the unexplained portion) to the total sum of squares:

$$R^2 = \frac{SSR}{SST} = 1 - \frac{SSE}{SST} = 1 - \frac{\Sigma\, e_i^2}{\Sigma(Y_i - \bar{Y})^2} \qquad (1.2.13)$$

The higher R^2 is, the higher is the degree of the overall fit of the estimated regression equation to the sample data. That is why measures of this type are called "goodness of fit" measures. Since SST, SSR, and SSE are all positive (or at least not negative, being *squared* deviations), R^2 must lie in the interval

$$0 \leqslant R^2 \leqslant 1 \qquad (1.2.14)$$

Thus, a value of R^2 close to unity shows a "good" overall fit, whereas a value near zero shows a failure of the estimated regression equation to explain the values of Y_i any better than could be explained by the sample mean $\bar{Y}$.

Figures 1.2.5 through 1.2.7 demonstrate some extremes. Figure 1.2.5 shows that X and Y are related in a curvilinear fashion but not in a linear one. Thus, the fitted regression line might be $\hat{Y} = \bar{Y}$, and the estimated linear regression can do no better than the sample mean to estimate Y_i on the basis of X_i. The explained portion SSR $= 0$, and the unexplained portion SSE equals the total squared deviations SST; thus, $R^2 = 0$. In this case, the residuals are large relative to the deviations in Y from its mean, implying that a regression line is not useful in describing the relationship between X and Y.

Figure 1.2.6 shows a relationship between X and Y that can be quite adequately "explained" by a linear regression equation: the value of R^2 is 0.95. Figure 1.2.7 shows a perfect fit, $R^2 = 1$. Such a fit implies that *no estimation* is required; the relationship contains no error term and is thus completely deterministic. In fact, estimated equations with R^2's close to unity should be viewed with suspicion: they very

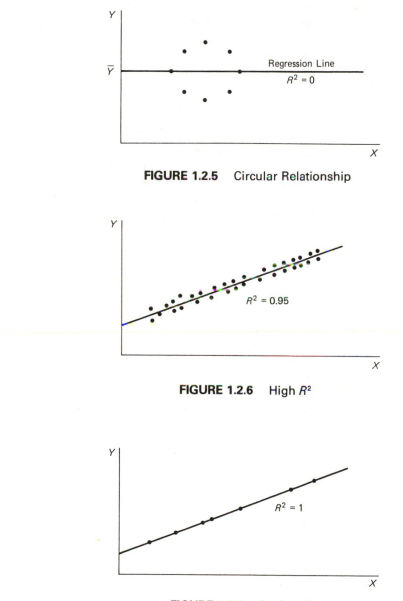

FIGURE 1.2.5   Circular Relationship

FIGURE 1.2.6   High R^2

FIGURE 1.2.7   Perfect Fit

likely do not "explain" the movements of the dependent variable Y in terms of the causal proposition advanced. Rather, they may simply be the result of "spurious correlation," a high degree of statistical fit caused, for example, by common trends, an omitted variable that causally explains both the dependent and the independent variables, or by a near identity among the variables.

The F-Ratio. While the R^2 is a heuristic measure of the overall degree of fit, a slightly modified version is a "statistical test" of the overall degree of fit of the estimated equation. The term "statistical test" is explained in Chapter 5; but for the application here, it can be briefly defined as a procedure by which the researcher can accept or reject the estimated equation based on its ability to explain the total sum of squares. The following is a rather mechanical explanation of how to use the F-ratio.

The F-ratio is defined as:

$$F = \frac{\text{SSR} / (K)}{\text{SSE} / (n - K - 1)} \qquad (1.2.15)$$

Thus, the F-ratio is the ratio of the explained to the unexplained portions of the total sum of squares, adjusted for the number of regressors (K) and the number of observations (n). When the value of F is "high," the estimated regression equation "statistically" provides an adequate explanation of the overall deviations in Y_i from its mean. If the computed value of the F-ratio is greater than a "critical value" found in the table of F-values (see the Statistical Tables at the end of the text), then the overall fit of the equation is declared to be statistically acceptable; otherwise, it is not acceptable.

As an example of the mechanical application of this procedure, assume that there are three regressors $(K = 3)$ and 25 observations $(n = 25)$. Also assume a 5-percent level of significance; for now, the level of significance can be explained as follows. On the basis of the test, the researcher may declare the statistical fit of the estimated regression relationship to be adequate when, in fact, the true (theoretical) regression model indicates that such a fit should not have been obtained because the movements in the error term are large, on average, relative to the movements in Y_i produced by the deterministic portion of the regression equation. But this chance of an error of inference occurs, on average, only 5 percent of the time the regression procedure is attempted. The 5-percent figure is the selected "level of significance."

The F-tables are shown for 1- and 5-percent levels of significance (statistical tables A-2 and A-3, respectively). From the 5-percent level of significance table, the "critical value" of F may be found. The appropriate column in this table is selected on the basis of the "numerator degrees of freedom," K, or 3 in this illustration. (Note that the numerator of the F-ratio (equation 1.2.15) is divided by K.) The appropriate row in the F-table is selected on the basis of the "denominator degrees of freedom," $n - K - 1$, or $25 - 3 - 1 = 21$ in this case. (Note that the denominator of equation 1.2.15 is divided by $n - K - 1$.) Thus, from the table, the critical value of the F-ratio is 3.07. This critical value of F indicates that the regression equation is "statistically significant," i.e., that its overall fit to the data is adequate statistically, when the computed F from equation 1.2.15 usually supplied by the computer regression package is greater than the critical value 3.07.

"Adjusted" or "Corrected" R^2, or $\bar{R}^2$. One of the problems with the R^2 measure is that adding another regressor can never decrease the value of R^2 because the SST is the same (the dependent variable has not changed) and all the estimating techniques ensure that adding a variable will not reduce the deviations of Y explained by the original regressors. The problem with adding another variable the inclusion of which is not clearly indicated by theory is that it requires the estimation of another

coefficient. This lessens the "degrees of freedom," or the excess of the number of observations over the number of parameters estimated, $n-K-1$. The greater the degrees of freedom, the more reliable,[2] or accurate, the estimates are likely to be (see Section 1.3.5). Thus, the measure $\overline{R}^2$ was invented to incorporate into the R^2 measure the fact that a degree of freedom is lost as another regressor is added. It is defined as:

$$\overline{R}^2 = 1 - \frac{\text{SSE}/(n-K-1)}{\text{SST}/(n-1)} \qquad (1.2.16)$$

The $\overline{R}^2$ can decrease if an additional regressor is added to the equation. However, the $\overline{R}^2$ measure is only one of a number of factors that should be considered when deciding whether a regressor should be added. As is stressed in Chapter 6, theoretical considerations are most important, and what the inclusion of the regressor does to the other estimated coefficients should be examined.

The Standard Error of the Equation (SEE). The "standard error of the equation" (SEE) is defined as:

$$\text{SEE} = \left[\frac{\text{SSE}}{n-K-1} \right]^{1/2} \qquad (1.2.17)$$

The SEE is the estimated standard deviation of the disturbance term. It is an absolute measure of the unexplained deviations of Y from its mean. The SEE is measured in the same units (e.g., dollars) as the dependent variable. However, when its absolute value is presented by itself, it is difficult to interpret; therefore, the mean value of Y is usually also presented in the documentation, and the standard error is often stated relative to the sample mean $\overline{Y}$: SEE/$\overline{Y}$. This is a type of "coefficient of variation," which shows the degree of variability of the error term relative to the mean value of the dependent variable. If the standard error is large relative to $\overline{Y}$, the equation is usually deemed unsatisfactory. The absolute and relative measures of SEE serve as heuristic indicators of the dispersion in the unexplained portion of the deviations in Y, in much the same manner as the R^2 does.

1.2.4(b) How Well Do the Coefficient Estimates Conform to a Priori Expectations?

In the linear regression model, the "slope" coefficients, the coefficients of the regressors, are interpreted as the change in the average value of Y_i upon (or "with respect to") a unit change in X_{ik}, holding all the other regressors and the error term constant. Notationally:[3]

---

[2] As shown in Section 4.2.2, the estimates have lower "variance."

[3] The Δ notation of equation 1.2.18 is normally shown as ∂, the "partial differential operator" of calculus. Those familiar with calculus should substitute ∂'s in their text for Δ's whenever the latter are used. The Δ implies a change in a variable; in this case, $\Delta \text{AVG}(Y_i)/\Delta X_{ik}$ is a change in the average value of Y_i caused by a small (or unit) change in X_{ik}, holding all other variables in the equation constant. That is, the regression equation can be written in difference form (ignoring the error term) as:

$$\Delta Y_i = \beta_1 \Delta X_{i1} + \beta_2 \Delta X_{i2} + \cdots + \beta_K \Delta X_{iK}$$

The constant term disappears because its "variable," unity, cannot change. This equation says that changing all the X's by some given amount causes Y to change in the manner described by the equation. All regressors but X_1, e.g., being held constant implies that $\Delta X_{i2} = \Delta X_{i3} = \cdots = \Delta X_{iK} = 0$. Thus, the equation becomes $\Delta Y_i = \beta_1 \Delta X_{i1}$, and the interpretation of β_1 is $\Delta Y_i / \Delta X_{i1}$, the change in Y_i given a change in X_{i1}

$$\beta_k = \frac{\Delta AVG(Y_i)}{\Delta X_{ik}} \qquad k = 1, 2, \ldots, K \qquad (1.2.18)$$

Given this interpretation, two primary questions are asked of the estimated coefficients: are the signs and magnitudes "correct"? and are the coefficients different from zero?

Are the Signs and Magnitudes "Correct"?   Economic theory usually indicates what the signs of the coefficients should be, either positive or negative, and sometimes indicates the magnitudes of the coefficients. The first concern, then, is whether the estimated coefficients are of the expected signs. If any one of the coefficients fails to pass this initial examination, the entire equation is suspect, and repairs of some kind are necessary. The theory that underlies the equation may be incorrect so that the model is not specified correctly, the measurement of the variables may be faulty, or one or more variables may not have enough variation in the sample to verify the *a priori* expectations (because economists usually cannot control their experiments but must take whatever empirical observations are available). The correction of any of these types of regression maladies, if possible, is the responsibility of the applied researcher.[4]

Are the Coefficients Different from Zero?   If a coefficient β_k is zero, the regressor X_k is not a relevant variable and should not be included in the regression equation. A statistical test, the "t-test," was designed to examine whether the sample data do or do not indicate that a regression coefficient is zero. The rather mechanical use of the t-test is explained here, while Chapter 5 provides a fuller explanation of its use. The "t-statistic" on which this test is based is computed as:

$$t_k = \frac{\hat{\beta}_k}{s_{\hat{\beta}_k}} \qquad k = 1, 2, \ldots, K \qquad (1.2.19)$$

where $s_{\hat{\beta}_k}$ is the estimated "standard error" of $\hat{\beta}_k$, as computed by the computer regression program. Suffice it here to say that alternative estimates of β_k are obtained with different samples. The residuals from the estimated equation are used to infer what the possible dispersion of these alternative estimates of β_k could be, and $s_{\hat{\beta}_k}$ is an empirical measure of the possible dispersion of $\hat{\beta}_k$.

A "high" value of t_k, in absolute value, indicates that the estimated coefficient is statistically different from zero. The critical value of t can be found in the "t-

---

holding all the other regressors and the error term constant. By definition, β_1 is interpreted as a "slope" coefficient. In the simple regression model, there are no other variables to hold constant, and the slope is the degree of "slant" to the regression line.

A number of rules that depend on the functional form of the equation have been developed in calculus to compute the change in one variable in response to a change in another. The reader is not required to perform these operations, only to interpret them once performed (in a "cookbook" fashion). Thus, the reader does not have to know calculus, but throughout the text he or she should interpret the Δ symbol as explained here, except in Section 2.4 on dynamic models.

[4] Advanced readers will note that a sequential mode of operation is intimated here. Usually, such a mode is a practical necessity, although it makes estimation and hypothesis testing more difficult. See Section 6.4.2 on "Stepwise Procedures."

distribution'' table, statistical table A-1 at the end of the text. Using a 5-percent (one-sided) level of significance and 21 as the degrees of freedom (the degrees of freedom are $n-K-1$, where $n = 25$ and $K = 3$), the critical value of t is 1.72. Thus, a calculated value of the t-statistic greater than 1.72 (in absolute value) shows that the estimated coefficient is statistically different from zero.

It is not necessary that the t-statistic for each of the estimated coefficients be different from zero in order for the equation to be acceptable. But it is usually necessary that those variables of special theoretical importance have statistically significant coefficients.

The reader should be warned that these are the bare-bones, even *ad hoc*, procedures and are presented here only to indicate the basic mechanics. The main part of this text shows that one must be very careful during the entire estimation procedure. The student is encouraged to undertake a regression project in conjunction with this book. At this point, the student should state which variable is selected as the dependent variable and should state which variables ''explain'' or ''determine'' the values of the dependent variable. For each postulated regressor, the student should tell a story about the effect that the regressor is expected to have on the dependent variable and, in this way, state what the expected signs of the regression slope coefficients are.

1.3   Steps in Applied Regression Analysis

This section presents an overview of the steps used in applied regression analysis. The relative emphasis and effort expended on each step varies from researcher to researcher, but normally all the steps have to be taken in order to achieve a successful completion of the estimating procedure. The steps are presented in the proper sequence of their execution. It is very important that this sequence be followed. Special note should be taken of the relatively large amount of effort required *before* the data are collected.

1.3.1   Specify the Theoretical Regression Model

The most important step in applied regression analysis is the *specification of the regression model*. Specification includes the following components:

1. Specifying which variables are to be included as regressors.

2. Specifying what the signs (or magnitudes) of the coefficients should be.

3. Specifying how the variables should be measured.

4. Specifying the functional (mathematical) form of the equation.

5. Specifying the type of error term in the equation.

6. Specifying interrelationships between the equation of direct interest and related equations.

A regression equation is "specified" when each of these elements is appropriately treated. The emphasis in this text is on estimating "behavioral" equations, equations describing the behavior of various economic entities. Nonbehavioral equations are equations that do not need to be estimated. Two types of equations that do not need to be estimated are identities and equilibrium conditions. These equations should be included in the analysis of related behavioral equations, and methods to accomplish this are shown at various points in the text.

Each of the elements of specification is determined primarily on the basis of economic theory, not on the basis of the results of an estimated regression equation. Thus, the "correct" specification of the model is the logical first step in regression analysis and is the most crucial. A mistake in any of the six elements of specification results in what is called a "specification error." Of all the kinds of mistakes that can be made in applied regression analysis, specification error is usually the most disastrous in terms of the usefulness of the estimated equation. Thus, the more effort put into applying economic theory at the beginning of a project, the more satisfactory the regression results are likely to be. Chapter 2 discusses alternative ways that a regression model may be specified, and various elements of specification are discussed throughout the text.

1.3.2 Review the Literature

Before developing the theoretical model too deeply—and certainly before estimating it—the researcher should review the scholarly literature. The most convenient method is: (1) to obtain the latest issues of the *Journal of Economic Literature* (this journal has the title and author of most books and major journals classified by subject and by journal), (2) to look for several recent articles related to the selected topic, (3) to find and read them, and (4) to trace back in the literature, if appropriate, the articles that are referenced.

The purpose of reviewing the literature is to economize on one's time and effort, because someone else may have already examined the topic of interest sufficiently to permit the researcher to use the results generated. The researcher may disagree with the approach or assumptions used by the authors or may want to adopt their theoretical model to a different data set. In any event, any further work now has one or more points of reference in the literature. Researchers should not have to "reinvent the wheel": they can start their investigation where the literature left off. Take advantage of the effort invested by previous researchers/authors: this is what the "March of Science" is all about. Of course, the need for complete documentation dictates that full credit or blame be given to the appropriate authors. Therefore, any research paper (such as the suggested term project) should begin with a comment on why the previous research was faulty, why it did not go far enough, or why its methodology can be used on a closely related problem.

1.3.3 Select the Variables

Selection of the dependent variable is determined by the purpose of the regression analysis; it is the variable to be "explained" by the regressors. Selection of regressors is based on *causality*: a regressor is selected because it is a causal determinant of the dependent variable; on the basis of theory, it is expected to explain at least part of the variation in the regressand. The technique of regression analysis shows which variables are *correlated* with the dependent variable, after accounting for other regressors. The technique does not *prove* economic causality. Whenever researchers use regression analysis to infer causality, they implicitly assume that the statistical correlation corroborates their theory, which focuses on causality. In reality, the theory is *never proven* by statistical correlation; rather, the statistical correlation, if found, can be said to *not disprove* the theory. An estimated regression can add another piece of evidence that a theory is not incorrect; but just as the example does not prove the rule, regression results do not verify the theory. The regression results are necessarily based on only a sample of all observations that could possibly be generated by a given theory, and it is not scientifically correct to make generalizations based on an examination of just a sample.

There are dangers in specifying too many or too few regressors. The attempt should be made to specify only the "relevant" explanatory variables, those variables that are expected on the basis of theory to assert a "significant" influence on the dependent variable. Variables suspected to have virtually no effect should be excluded, unless their possible effect on the dependent variable is of some particular (e.g., policy) interest.

In a demand equation for a consumption good that "explains" the quantity demanded, the price of the product and consumer income or wealth are necessary variables on the basis of economic theory. Economic theory also indicates that complementary and substitute goods are important; therefore, the researcher may select as regressors the prices of these complements and substitutes. But immediately the problem arises of which complements and substitutes to select. Of course, selection of the "closest" complements and substitutes is appropriate, but how far beyond a few should one go? At the theoretical level, the choice of the number and kind of substitutes and complements is made on the basis of judgment. It is possible to use the estimated regression equation to indicate which goods to include, but there are enough problems in estimating a regression equation that the resolution of these issues at the theoretical level should be given a high priority.

When researchers make the judgment, for example, that only the prices of two other goods need to be included, they are said to impose their "priors" (i.e., *a priori* information), or their "working hypotheses" on the regression equation. Imposition of such priors is a common practice that economizes on the number and kind of hypotheses that the regression equation has to examine. The only danger is that the prior is wrong to the extent that it will diminish the usefulness of the estimated regression equation. Each of the priors should be explained in detail by the researcher. In addition, a useful part of the documentation of the regression project is an analysis of the likely consequences if the priors are incorrect.

The dependent variable may be thought of as having a coefficient of unity. *Normalization* refers to the selection of the variable in the equation the coefficient of which is unity, i.e., selecting the left-hand variable. In a supply and demand framework, either price or quantity could be the left-hand variable since they are mutually determined. In some cases, theory may be helpful in the normalization of an equation. For example, if a demand (or supply) equation is thought to be inelastic, as in Figure

1.3.1, then it is appropriate to have quantity as the dependent variable. Since its price may or may not be a relevant variable in "explaining" the demand for the good, having price as the dependent variable under such circumstances makes little sense. An example of an inelastic demand curve is the demand for a narcotic drug by habitual users. Another example is the demand for a factor of production that constitutes only a minor share of the total cost of production. In this case, the expectation of the inelasticity of demand for the good is reinforced if it is believed that the demand for the final product is not very elastic.

Similarly, if a supply (or demand) curve is thought to be highly elastic, as in Figure 1.3.2, then price is the appropriate dependent variable because the function may or may not change much as the quantity supplied changes (over the relevant range of observation).

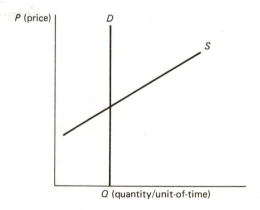

FIGURE 1.3.1   Demand not a Function of Price

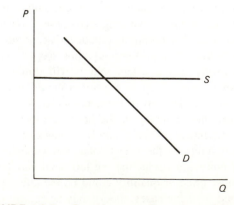

FIGURE 1.3.2   Supply not a Function of Quantity

1.3.4   Specify the Signs of the Coefficients

In the demand equation for a final consumption good, the quantity demanded (Q_D) is expected to be inversely related to its price (P) and the price of a complementary good (P_C), and directly related to consumers' income (Y) and the price of a substitute good (P_S). In implicit functional form, which is usually the first step in the written development of a regression model, the relation is expressed as:

$$Q_D = f(\overset{-}{P}, \overset{+}{Y}, \overset{-}{P_C}, \overset{+}{P_S}) \qquad (1.3.1)$$

The signs above the variables indicate the sign of the respective regression coefficient in a linear model, e.g., the coefficient of P is expected to be negative. This is simple notation that has become increasingly popular. (The sign is also referred to as the "sign of the partial derivative" of Q_D with respect to P. This terminology is derived from differential calculus, as discussed in footnote 3, page 17.)

In many cases, the basic theory is commonly understood so that no documentation discussing why the signs are as stated need be provided. However, if any controversy surrounds the selection of an appropriate sign, the researcher should document the controversy or the opposing forces at work and the reasons for hypothesizing a positive or negative coefficient. Alternatively, if theory does not suggest an unambiguous sign, then a question mark may be placed above the respective variable. For example, if the variables in the demand equation are measured in real terms, theory may not be clear whether (actual or expected) inflation has a separate effect on demand. If the researcher wants to examine this, the implicit functional form may be written as:

$$Q_D = f(\overset{-}{P}, \overset{+}{Y}, \overset{-}{P_C}, \overset{+}{P_S}, \overset{?}{INF}), \qquad (1.3.2)$$

where INF is a variable measuring inflation.

(As one of the by-products of the computer age and the multivariate model, variable names are often presented as a series of capitalized letters and numbers, which serve as a mnemonic device to represent the variable in a logical way. After the symbols are explained, readers can usually understand the symbols without having to refer to a glossary of terms. However, a glossary of terms should be provided by the researcher whenever the number of variables becomes large, such as more than seven, to pick an arbitrary cut-off point.)

1.3.5   Collect the Data

After at least a preliminary specification of the regression model, data collection may begin. This step may be done before, during, or after the method of estimation is selected. Usually, the development of the theoretical model and the selection of the estimating technique are on-going processes as new thoughts come to mind. Typically, the theoretical model never really jells in one's mind until all aspects of the problem are investigated. Often, inductive reasoning applies as the researcher examines the data and begins to see patterns or relationships that were not thought of originally. Also, when the regression results turn out different from what was expected, which happens more often than not, the primary avenue of inquiry should be to rethink the theoretical basis of the model.

However, the researcher should avoid adjusting the theory to fit the data, thus introducing "researcher bias." The advice given here is for the researcher to "walk the fine line" between making appropriate and inappropriate adjustments to the model. Selecting between appropriate and inappropriate modifications is one of the artistic elements in applied regression analysis.

1.3.5(a) Degrees of Freedom.

The general rule is the more observations the better. Ordinarily, the researcher takes all the observations that are readily available. Even if a number of computations are necessary to quantify a variable, the onus is on the researcher to explain why laziness prevented quantification for as many observations as were available. The technique of regression analysis imposes the constraint that all the variables have the same number of observations. Of course, they all should have the same frequency (monthly, quarterly, annual, etc.) and time period (except for lagged variables—see Section 2.4). Very often, the frequency selected is determined by the availability of data. However, if, for example, just one variable prevents the frequency from being quarterly because it is available only annually, often the researcher will make linear or nonlinear quarterly interpolations (i.e., estimates of the value of the variable between observed values) of that variable.[5] If it is a slow-moving variable such as total population, such an approach may be adequate. However, all data manipulations as well as the data sources must be fully documented. When there is much to explain, the documentation is usually relegated to a "data appendix." If the data are not generally available or are available only after considerable computation, the data are often included in this appendix.

The reason it is preferred to have as many observations as possible concerns the concept of "degrees of freedom." Consider fitting a straight line to two points on an X,Y coordinate system, as in Figure 1.3.3. Such a curve-fitting exercise can be done *mathematically* without error. Both points lie on the line, and there is no *estimation* of the coefficients involved. The two points determine precisely the two parameters, the intercept and the slope. Estimation takes place when a straight line is fit to three or more points that were generated by some process that is not exact. The excess of

---

[5] Given an annual data series, quarterly estimates are usually interpolated linearly or exponentially (using the geometric mean). Let X_0 and X_4 be the two observed annual data points one year apart between which it is desired to interpolate the quarterly numbers. The two procedures are as follows:

	Linear	Exponential
Adjustment Factor a:	$a = \dfrac{X_4 - X_0}{4}$	$a = \frac{1}{4}\ln(X_4/X_0)$

$$\begin{cases} \hat{X}_1 = X_0 + a \\ \hat{X}_2 = X_0 + 2a \\ \hat{X}_3 = X_0 + 3a \end{cases} \qquad \begin{cases} \hat{X}_1 = X_0 e^a \\ \hat{X}_2 = X_0 e^{2a} \\ \hat{X}_3 = X_0 e^{3a} \end{cases}$$

The exponential interpolation is usually used when the data series appears to be growing according to an exponential trend (see Section 2.2.2). For more extensive data manipulations or "massaging," see Michael D. Intriligator, *Econometric Models, Techniques, and Applications* (Englewood Cliffs, NJ: Prentice-Hall, 1978), pp. 67–70. This text covers *interpolation* as shown above; *extrapolation*, which involves applying the same types of formulas to project data points outside the observed range; *splicing*, which refers to connecting two related series each of which is available for only a portion of the time period (usually, the first time series is divided by a constant that ensures that the two series connect without an unnecessary blip in the combined series); and *smoothing*, which involves seasonal, trend, or cyclical adjustments.

the number of observations (three) over the number of parameters to be estimated (in this case, the intercept and slope) is called the "degrees of freedom."

All that is necessary for estimation is a single degree of freedom, as in Figure 1.3.4. The desire to increase the degrees of freedom by increasing the number of observations derives from the notion of *precision*. The more points on the X,Y coordinate system that were generated from the same process, the more likely it is that pure chance will have less of an effect on the parameter estimates. That is, the more observations there are, the less likely it is that the purely random component will affect inferences about the deterministic portion of the equation, which is the portion of primary interest.

This results from the fact that for every large positive error, there is more likely to be an offsetting large negative error when the number of observations is large. With only three points, the random element is not given the opportunity to provide such offsetting observations.

In technical terms, greater precision from more degrees of freedom means that the variance of the estimator of each parameter becomes smaller. (The notion of

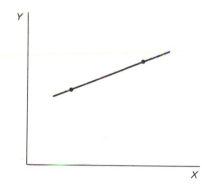

FIGURE 1.3.3   Mathematical Fit of Line to Two Points

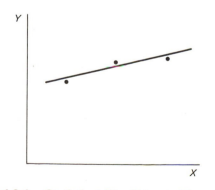

FIGURE 1.3.4   Statistical Fit of Line to Three Points

variance is developed in detail in Chapter 4; however, at this point, it may be noted that variance is a measure of the degree of dispersion of a random variable about its central tendency, i.e., its mean. The variance of an estimator increases if the observations tend to deviate more from the true regression line.) Thus, greater degrees of freedom results in more precise, or reliable, estimates of the parameters. In addition, statistical tests of hypotheses, such as the t- and F-tests discussed in Section 1.2, explicitly account for the degrees of freedom and are more precise (actually, more "powerful") the greater the degrees of freedom. Therefore, the researcher becomes less likely to make an error of inference as the degrees of freedom increase (see Chapter 4).

Why, then, do we not see more daily or weekly models? Shortening the frequency would appear to be an easy method of increasing the degrees of freedom. The basic reason such short time periods are unusual is that, with these short periods, the random component of the equation becomes very dominant, and the underlying economic forces are not given enough of a chance to show themselves or to work themselves out. In a demand and supply context, for example, the supply may be more of a "day" supply curve if the good is perishable (i.e., priced to sell regardless of its marginal cost), demand may be influenced by rapidly shifting expectations of prices and sales that may not be quantifiable, or market equilibrium may not be achieved each period. Thus, a daily or weekly model is likely to have so much "noise" that the fundamental relationship cannot be reliably estimated. Furthermore, selection of the appropriate time interval should be based to a large extent on the "interval of adjustment," i.e., the time period during which the relevant decisions are made. For example, since changes in automobile styles usually take place once a year, constructing a weekly model of this decision process would not be appropriate.

A comment on functional form is appropriate here. With three points, as in Figure 1.3.4, a second degree polynomial in X would fit the points exactly. In general, an nth degree polynomial fits $n + 1$ points exactly, in a deterministic relationship. Fitting $n + 1$ points with an $n - 1$ degree polynomial gives one degree of freedom, but it highlights the dangers of such curve-fitting devices. First, it is just one step away from mathematical determination; but second, the slope coefficient (the change in Y with respect to a unit change in X) is positive and negative over different ranges of X, something the theory is very unlikely to postulate. (See the discussion in Section 2.2 in which it is stressed that the functional form of the equation should reflect the theory.) Most polynomials have this second, very serious problem.

1.3.5(b)   Units of Measurement.

Does it matter if a variable is measured in dollars or in millions of dollars? Does it matter if the measured variable differs consistently from the true variable by 100 units? It does not matter in terms of the regression analysis; it only matters in interpreting the magnitude of the coefficients. Consider, for example, a measured variable X' that differs from the "true" value X in a linear way:

$$X_i' = a + bX_i \qquad (1.3.3)$$

where a and b are known (or unknown but fixed) constants. The regression equation

$$Y_i = \beta_0' + \beta_1' X_i' + \epsilon_i \qquad (1.3.4)$$

upon substitution for the measured X', is in actuality:

$$Y_i = (\beta_0' + \beta_1' a) + \beta_1' b X_i + \epsilon_i \qquad (1.3.5)$$

or

$$Y_i = \beta_0 + \beta_1 X_i + \epsilon_i \qquad (1.3.6)$$

where

$$\beta_0 = \beta_0' + \beta_1' a \qquad (1.3.7)$$

and

$$\beta_1 = \beta_1' b \qquad (1.3.8)$$

The factor a only alters the intercept term, which usually is not of much importance. Thus, adding 100 to all observations of a regressor does not change the interpretation of the regression. What is important is that the change in Y (ΔY) should be the same for a unit change in X as well as in X'. From equation 1.3.6:

$$\Delta Y = \beta_1 \Delta X \qquad (1.3.9)$$

But from equation 1.3.3, $\Delta X = \Delta X'/b$; thus, using equation 1.3.8, equation 1.3.9 can be written as:

$$\Delta Y = \beta_1 \Delta X = (\beta_1' b)(\Delta X'/b) = \beta_1' \Delta X'$$

Thus, the values of ΔY is the same regardless of which form of X is used, so changing the units of measurement of X does not alter the basic interpretation of the regression equation.

In summary, the multiplicative factor b does change the slope coefficient but only by the exact amount to compensate for the change in the units of measurement of X. If X were measured in billions of dollars instead of in dollar terms, holding Y the same, for example, the estimated slope coefficient would automatically increase by a factor of a billion.

This result implies that, in general, the magnitude of the coefficients are *arbitrary* because a scale change alters them and what scale is selected is arbitrary. The only cases in which the magnitudes of the coefficients are not arbitrary is when both the dependent and independent variable are assumed to be measured in the same units (as in a consumption function so that the coefficient of income, the marginal propensity to consume, can be assumed to be between zero and unity) or when the variable is measured in a functional form that keeps the interpretation of the slope coefficient the same. The latter usually only holds for the change of scale factor b and not for a nonzero value of the additive factor a. For example, if X is multiplied by b in the following equation:

$$Y_i = \beta_0 + \beta_1 \log(bX_i) + \epsilon \qquad (1.3.10)$$

where log refers to the logarithm of the expression in parentheses, only the constant term is altered, which is not of much concern:

$$Y_i = (\beta_0 + \beta_1 \log b) + \beta_1 \log X + \epsilon \qquad (1.3.11)$$

Similarly, the elasticity of Y with respect to X in a linear equation (see Section 2.2 for a discussion of this concept) is the same as long as the additive factor equals zero:

$$\eta_{Y,X}' = \beta_1' \frac{X'}{Y} = \frac{\beta_1}{b} \frac{bX}{Y} = \beta_1 \frac{X}{Y} = \eta_{Y,X} \qquad (1.3.12)$$

Also, the t-statistic is invariant (i.e., does not change in magnitude) with changes in the units of measurement; so are the R^2, $\overline{R}^2$, and the F-statistic. Thus, in this important respect (hypothesis testing), the units of measurement do not matter. Furthermore, it can be shown that the units of measurement of the dependent variable likewise do not alter the interpretation of the regression equation (except, as above, in interpreting the magnitude of the regression coefficients).

1.3.6 Estimate

The choice of the appropriate estimating technique is the general subject of this text. The ordinary least-squares technique, discussed in Chapter 3, is generally a technique that can be usefully applied for exploratory purposes. Where alternative techniques appear to be appropriate, they should be used and the empirical estimates compared. If one wants but a single estimated equation—which surprisingly may not be necessary—then the alternatively estimated equations have to be evaluated very carefully and judgment applied for a choice to be made.

One of the first tasks to be performed, even before looking at the estimated coefficients, is to check the data. Since estimation and data transformations are usually done on the computer, obtain a printout of the data set exactly as it was used in the regression estimation. Check one or two values of any variables that were transformed. If these values are correct, it can be assumed that the computer did not make any mistakes on the rest of the observations. Also, obtain a printout or a plot of the residuals and look for "outliers." An outlier is a large (positive or negative) residual that lies outside the range of the rest of the residuals. Looking for outliers is a very economical way to look for transcription errors, which often occur when preparing data for the computer. Examine the data for Y_i and all the regressors for the outlier observations. If the data are correct, such an examination may be used inductively to create new variables or functional forms that might appropriately explain the outliers.

1.3.7 Evaluate Results

After checking the data for errors, examine the signs and magnitudes of the coefficients, the t-statistics, and the overall measures of fit, as outlined in Section 1.2. A "Regression Mechanic's Checklist," presented in Section 11.3, outlines the usual steps to be taken at this point.

Regression results are rarely what one expected. Usually, additional model development is required, or alternative estimating techniques are called for. Be sure to reevaluate the model and to make any necessary changes before jumping into fancy regression "fix-up" routines. Sometimes these routines are methods of improving the overall measures of goodness of fit or some other statistic while playing havoc with the attainment of reliable estimates of the parameters of the appropriate model.

1.3.8 Document Results

A standard format is usually used to present estimated regression results, such as

$$\hat{Y}_i = 1.451 \quad + \quad 2.073X_{1i} \quad + \quad 2.900X_{2i}$$

$$(3.11) \qquad\qquad (7.89) \qquad\qquad\qquad (1.3.13)$$

$$\overline{R}^2 = 0.75 \qquad SEE = 21 \qquad \overline{Y} = 310.2$$

$$DW = 1.87 \qquad \text{Frequency: Quarterly} \quad \text{Period: 1964:I–1981:IV}$$

The numbers in parentheses are t-statistics. (Alternatively, they can be standard errors, but which statistics are shown should be stated in the documentation.) The DW is the Durbin-Watson statistic (discussed in Chapter 7). For cross-section data (see Section 2.5), the entire last row should be replaced by the number of observations. The subscript i denoting the observations may be deleted, or a subscript t may be used to denote time-series observations. Even though some computer regression programs present statistics to eight "significant" digits, the reported statistics should be carried out to only three or four places, and t-statistics should at most be carried to two decimal places. Unless the variables have been defined in a glossary or a table, short definitions of them should be presented along with the equations.

If there are a series of estimated regressions equations, then tables may be established providing all the relevant information from each of them.

One of the important parts of the documentation is the explanation of the model, the assumptions, and the procedures and data used. The written documentation must contain enough information so that the entire study can be exactly *replicated* (save for rounding errors) by some other researcher on the basis of the documentation alone. Just as in medicine, the "March of Science" can march on only when each step has been confirmed by others. Honest mistakes do happen, and the only way to protect against them is by full and honest documentation. In many scholarly journal articles, for the sake of brevity, authors state that they will send copies of the data or provide a special computer program to anyone interested. But otherwise, complete written documentation is the rule. Usually, one assumes that the reader knows basic econometrics. If this is not a valid assumption (e.g., if the paper is to be published in a popular journal), then there is not much point in presenting the estimated equation or even the theoretical equation.

Appendix to Chapter One: Understanding Summations

The Σ notation is read "the sum of." It is a shorthand arithmetic operator that indicates that the summation of a series of numbers is to be taken. Equation 1.2.10 is the first time that it is used in this text, involving the sum of squares of the observed deviations of Y_i from its sample mean, $\overline{Y}$:

$$\text{SST} = \sum_{i=1}^{n} (Y_i - \bar{Y})^2$$

The lower case letter i is called the index of the summation. The notation $i = 1$ below the Σ indicates that the index i is to take an initial value of unity, and the n above the Σ indicates that the final value of the index i is n. It is implicitly understood that the index i increases by one between its initial value (1) and its final value (n).

The quantity to the right of the Σ sign represents the numbers to be added together. In this case, this term is $(Y_i - \bar{Y})^2$. To put it all together, SST is defined as the sum over all observations $i = 1$ through $i = n$ of the quantity $(Y_i - \bar{Y})^2$. It is written as:

$$\text{SST} = (Y_1 - \bar{Y})^2 + (Y_2 - \bar{Y})^2 + (Y_3 - \bar{Y})^2 + (Y_4 - \bar{Y})^2 + (Y_5 - \bar{Y})^2$$

where the total number of observations, n, in this example is 5.

Often, the Σ notation is written simply as $\sum_{i}$, as in equation 1.2.11. The index i is shown explicitly, but, in the context of the analysis, it is made clear that the summation is over all observations $i = 1$ to $i = n$; thus, the "$=1$" and "n" are no longer written out. In fact, often the index i is not presented below the Σ sign if the context makes it clear what the summation is over (all observations). When there is any doubt, the full notation should be used.

Examples of the use of the Σ notation are presented throughout the text. When the initial observation is 2 instead of 1, then the notation should show it, such as:

$$\sum_{t=2}^{T} e_t^2$$

Here, the index is t, and it takes on values 2, 3, 4, . . . , $T-2, T-1, T$, where T is the total number of observations. This expression is equivalent to:

$$e_2^2 + e_3^2 + e_4^2 + \cdots + e_T^2$$

As another example, the single equation multiple linear regression model (equation 1.2.5) can be expressed in Σ notation. It is:

$$Y_i = \beta_0 + \sum_{k} \beta_k X_{ki} + \epsilon_i$$

In this expression there are two indexes, i and k, to reference the ith observation, and the kth regressor. For clarity, a k is placed below the Σ sign to denote that the summation is over the list of variables, not over the observations i. (The equation holds for each observation.) For clarity, $\sum_k \beta_k X_{ki}$ is written out as:

$$\beta_1 X_{1i} + \beta_2 X_{2i} + \cdots + \beta_K X_{Ki}$$

It is understood that the summation is up to $k = K$.

An infinite summation is written as

$$\sum_{i=1}^{\infty} \epsilon_i$$

where ∞ (infinity) means that there is no termination of values over which the index i runs. This expression can be written as $\epsilon_1 + \epsilon_2 + \cdots$, where the final $\cdots$ with no terminating symbol, such as ϵ_n, means an infinite number of them.

2 Alternative Regression Models

This chapter presents some of the major aspects of specifying, or building, the linear regression model. Since model specification is the most important and the first step in applied regression analysis, early attention is given to it in this text. Most econometric textbooks intersperse discussion of various aspects of model development with discussions of the special estimation problems they pose. This chapter mentions possible estimation problems that may arise and refers to the section of the text that addresses them.

The first section focuses on the measurement of variables. In some instances, theoretical considerations lead to specifying a variable in a special way. Two specific examples are cited: the user cost and the permanent income concepts. In other situations, the variable of interest may not be directly observable, and in yet other cases the variable may be qualitative in nature, such as whether or not a person has a Master's degree. The standard approaches to these situations are presented. These instances arise very often in applied regression analysis, so they are of particular importance.

The second section discusses alternative functional forms for the regression equation. Theoretical considerations usually dictate the form of the estimating equation. Graphical illustrations are presented of alternative functional forms, from which the researcher can select the most appropriate. The mathematical form corresponding to the graph is then found and can be used by the researcher in the regression analysis.

The third section discusses multi-equation models. These models are very common, and their application should be understood by even casual researchers. The classic supply and demand model is one of the most important of these multi-equation models.

The fourth section presents a number of dynamic time-series models. These are models of intertemporal relationships among variables and are commonly used in theoretical and applied research. Understanding dynamic models is essential to modern econometric model building. This is especially true of large-scale models of the aggregate economy.

The last section focuses on the interpretation of models estimated with cross-section data. Cross-section data differ from time-series data in that, at a single point in time, observations come from individual economic entities, such as households and firms. Usually, estimates from these data must be interpreted as showing the long-run behavior of the economic entities, as contrasted with the typically short-run behavior depicted by time-series data.

The appendix to this chapter discusses dominant variables, a situation that arises relatively infrequently in applied research. This is the situation in which a single regressor is so powerful in "explaining" the statistical movements of the dependent variable that other regressors are rendered statistically insignificant.

2.1 Measurement of Variables

2.1.1 Theoretical Specification of Variables

Theory is often used to determine the way variables should be measured. The researcher should hypothesize possible regression results and interpret them to see if their intended interpretation is achieved, based on the way the researcher has formulated the variables and the equation.

In many instances the actual measurement of variables is dictated by data limitations. For example, if the dependent variable is the quantity (or value) of television sets demanded per year, then the price variable should be measured as some average price *for each year*. It would be inappropriate, and possibly misleading, to measure the price of TV's as the price in any given month; a (weighted) average of price over the year would be more appropriate (usually weighted by the value of the TV's sold each month). Of course, if the equation is to include all TV sets sold in a year, then it would be appropriate to compute an aggregate price of TV's over all the various brands. In many instances of aggregations of this type, all the price data for the various brands may not be available, so data limitations lead the researcher to compromise and use the prices of one or a few of the major brands.

Note that, in theory, the concept of the supply of and demand for various aggregate commodities, such as TV's, is quite legitimate. The problem of computing the appropriate aggregate variables, however, is not straightforward, and the classical problems of index numbers and aggregation bias are likely to haunt the researcher. (These problems are beyond the scope of this text.) Typically, the researcher makes the best effort to compute the respective aggregate variables and then acknowledges that these problems are probably present. Usually, some heroic assumptions (or priors) enable the researcher to estimate the desired aggregate equation without having to estimate disaggregated equations, such as one equation for each brand of TV. Such a disaggregated approach may not be very economical and may be beyond the needs of the research project. Typically, obtaining satisfactory estimated equations for each of the separate brands is very difficult: incorrect or statistically insignificant signs of many of the coefficients are the likely results because of the difficulty of modeling and empirically estimating the disaggregated markets, in which many more factors (regressors) and random influences are present than at the aggregate level. (An example of this proposition is the research done by Ray Fair in applying a rather successful aggregate U.S. housing starts model to cities. The empirical results at the lower level of aggregation were a disaster, with low R^2's and many incorrect signs of the estimated coefficients. See Ray C. Fair, "Application of a Housing Model to SMSA Data," Federal Home Loan Bank Board Invited Research Working Paper No. 4, June, 1972.)

Another measurement issue was intimated in the TV example above. Since the composition of the market share, the size, and the quality of the various brands may change over time, it would make little sense to measure TV's demanded as the *number* of TV sets. The approach usually taken is to measure the variable in *value* or expenditure terms, under the assumption that value encompasses size and quality. Most often, it is best to state the variables in "real" terms: this is achieved by selecting the most appropriate price deflator, such as the Consumer Price Index or a particular Producer Price Index, and dividing the nominal value by it. Usually, selection of the appropriate deflator is not straightforward; often the selection is never questioned.

In addition, the price index may be adjusted for quality, in the form of a "hedonic" index.[1] Instead of adjusting the price index, the changes in quality can be implicitly accounted for by including in the equation the usual measure of price along with qualitative or dummy variables (see Section 2.1.3).

The economics literature contains two splendid examples of variables the measurement of which has been suggested by theory. Since their use is relatively common, they are presented at this point. The two variables are "user cost" and "permanent income." Each is discussed in turn.

2.1.1(a) User Cost.

Jorgenson[2] used neoclassical investment theory to obtain a measure of the cost of capital that could be used in investment equations. Prior to Jorgenson, the cost of capital—the price paid by entrepreneurs for capital equipment usage—was an elusive empirical concept. It is called user cost because it incorporates the period-by-period costs that apply to a user or a renter (if owned, an implicit renter) of capital equipment. If it is assumed that no expected price changes of the capital equipment occur, one of the forms of this variable is [3]

$$c_{t.} = q(r + \delta)\, \frac{(1 - k)\,(1 - u_t z)}{(1 - u_t)}$$

where

c_t = user cost of capital (period t), or the price or "rental rate" of capital services per unit of time;

[1] See Z. Griliches, "Hedonic Price Indexes for Automobiles: An Econometric Analysis of Quality Changes," Government Price Statistics, Hearings, U.S. Congress, Joint Economic Committee, 1961.

[2] See, for example, Dale W. Jorgenson, "Anticipations and Investment Behavior," in J. S. Duesenberry, et al., editors, *The Brookings Quarterly Econometric Model of the United States* (Skokie, IL: Rand McNally, 1965), pp. 35–94.

[3] Robert E. Hall and Dale W. Jorgenson, "Tax Policy and Investment Behavior," *American Economic Review*, June 1967, pp. 392–414. The formula is their equation (6) on p. 393.

q = cost of the capital equipment;

r = cost of capital, "the" interest rate, usually taken as a long-term government bond rate;

δ = rate of replacement or depreciation rate;

z = the "present value of the depreciation deduction on one dollar's investment;"[4]

k = the rate of the investment tax credit; and

u_t = the user's marginal tax rate.

Values of z have been computed for several methods of depreciation, for several assumed lifetimes of the capital equipment, and for several interest rates. Researchers merely need to look them up in the table supplied by Hall and Jorgenson.[5] For example, $z = 0.456$ for the sum-of-the-years'-digits method of calculating depreciation deductions, for an expected lifetime of the capital equipment of 25 years, and for an interest rate of 12 percent. What one usually does is assume a given method, life, and interest rate and use the computed (and tabled) value of z. Other than the original capital asset price (the amount of the expenditure on the equipment) and the tax parameters (the tax rates are usually taken as the assumed marginal rate or the average effective rate), only the depreciation rate δ needs to be supplied in the formula. For the depreciation rate, Hall and Jorgenson used 2.5 times the inverse of the lifetimes as stated in the tax code (Bulletin F).[6] For example, for manufacturing equipment, $\delta = 0.1471$ (an annual rate).

Jorgenson's formulation brings depreciation, taxes, an interest rate, and the cost of the equipment all into one variable on the basis of theory. Without this formulation, regression equations typically cannot show the effects of each of these factors separately. Using each of these factors as separate regressors is too "burdensome" for the estimated regression equations, with incorrect signs and statistically insignificant coefficients being the usual results.[7] Thus, this user cost variable is able to incorporate all the relevant factors, economizing on the degrees of freedom. It is now widely used in the estimation of various kinds of investment functions. Its use demonstrates the benefits of applying *a priori,* theoretical information in the development of regression models and, in particular, in the development of regressors.

2.1.1(b) Permanent Income.

Another example of using theory to formulate variables is permanent income. The concept, developed by Milton Friedman,[8] postulates that "permanent" income is the appropriately measured variable as a determinant of many kinds of consumption goods. Permanent income is an *ex ante,* theoretical construct that measures the family's ability to purchase goods and services over time, if the family can borrow and lend money to circumvent any cash flow problems. In particular, the permanent income hypothesis, as formulated by Friedman,

---

[4] Hall and Jorgenson, "Tax Policy," p. 393.

[5] Hall and Jorgenson, "Tax Policy," p. 395, Table 1.

[6] Hall and Jorgenson, "Tax Policy," p. 398.

[7] These results are due to multicollinearity and degrees of freedom problems.

[8] Milton Friedman, *A Theory of the Consumption Function* (Princeton, N.J.: Princeton University Press, 1957).

states that both income and consumption are composed of temporary (i.e., unexpected or random) and permanent components and that permanent consumption is a function of permanent income, the rate of interest, the ratio of property and nonproperty (i.e., human) income, and tastes and preferences (as determined in part by demographic factors and the relative variability of the temporary versus the permanent components).

In most applications of consumption functions, the measured value of consumption is the dependent variable, and permanent income is a regressor. In some applications, temporary income, defined as current income less permanent income, is also included as a regressor in order to assess the effect of unexpected changes in income on consumption.

Colin Wright[9] has suggested the following measurement of permanent income, $Y*$, for an aggregate, time-series analysis as a distributed lag of current income, Y:

$$Y_t^* = \beta \sum_{i=0}^{\infty} (1 - \beta + A)^i Y_{t-i}$$

where Y_t is current, observed income (usually in real terms); β is the weight that current income has in determining permanent income; and A is a trend term. In applications, A may be computed as the compound growth rate of Y. The value of β is selected as, thanks to Wright, somewhere in the range of 0.7 to 0.8 or possibly as high as 0.99, on an annual basis; for quarterly observations, a range of values of 0.33 to 0.73 has been found to be satisfactory.

For annual data with $A = 0.02$ and $\beta = 0.8$, permanent income is defined as:

$$Y_t^* = 0.8Y_t + 0.176Y_{t-1} + 0.04Y_{t-2} + \cdots$$

Since the weights (or coefficients) of current income fall off rapidly, only three (and possibly just two) years of current income data need to be used in constructing the permanent income measure. This is, of course, due to the selection of the values of β and A. Given A as computed from the data on current income, it may be appropriate to assume alternative values of β and to select a value for β that produces a measure $Y*$ that leads to the lowest standard error of the equation (SEE), where one regression equation is estimated for each measure of $Y*$. This procedure is appropriate only when the equation has been fully specified and no other "regression experiments" are attempted. (Also, the effect different $Y*$'s have on the other coefficients should be taken into account. See Section 6.4.1.) Usually, researchers assume a value for β that produces, to them, the most reasonable distributed lag of current income. As in all research, full documentation calls for spelling out the approach taken and an explanation of any priors that are assumed.

2.1.2 Proxies

Proxy variables are those that substitute for the theoretically desired variables when data on the desired variables are incomplete or missing altogether. For example,

---

[9] Colin Wright, "Estimating Permanent Income: A Note," *Journal of Political Economy*, September-October 1969, pp. 845–50.

the value of housing services is a variable that is not directly measured in the United States or elsewhere. Thus, one may use an estimate of the value of the housing stock as a proxy. The assumption is then usually made that the value of the housing stock is directly proportional to the value of housing services. Direct (or even indirect) proportionality is all that is required because the purpose of the regression analysis is to estimate the relationship of *changes* among variables, as opposed to being concerned about the absolute levels of the variables.

In general, then, a proxy variable is a "good" proxy when movements in it correspond in terms of relative magnitude to movements in the theoretically correct variable. Since the latter is unobservable, there is usually no deterministic way to examine the proxy's "goodness" directly; rather, the arguments why the proxy is or is not good need to be documented by the researcher. In some cases, proxies are admittedly of poor quality, but they are the only quantitative measures available and are used with the appropriate caveats being stated. Poor proxies and variables with large measurement errors constitute "bad" data. Bad data may lead the researcher to avoid the fancier estimating techniques because the empirical results would be too suspect. But the degree to which the data are "bad" is a matter of judgment, and it is up to the individual researcher to decide what to do with suspect data.

In fact, what may have started out as a regression project may be thwarted because of the lack of adequate data. In many cases, even the simplest of regression techniques may not be appropriate because the data are bad. Sometimes the data are measured with so much error that the researcher should probably only compose tables or graphs and make general inferences from these. (By the way, tables and graphs are generally very useful adjuncts to the documentation of regression equations.)

2.1.3 Qualitative or Dummy Variables

2.1.3(a) Simple Dummy Variables.   Some variables defy explicit quantification and can only be quantified in a qualitative manner. One of the most common ways such variables are quantified is by binary, or dummy variables. These variables take on only the values one or zero as some condition does or does not occur. This section is very important because dummy variables are used frequently in regression analysis, and they constitute a very powerful technique when used appropriately. The basic notions on how to construct and use these variables are presented first, and then some frequently used extensions are discussed.

As an illustration of the technique, suppose that Y_i represents the starting salary of the ith high school teacher, that this depends primarily on the type of degree earned, and that all starting teachers have either a B.A. or an M.A. An equation representing the relationship between earnings and the type of degree earned may be:

$$Y_i = \beta_0 + \beta_1 X_{i1} + \epsilon_i \qquad (2.1.1)$$

where

$$X_{i1} = \begin{cases} 1 \text{ if the } i\text{th person has an M.A.} \\ 0 \text{ otherwise} \end{cases} \qquad (2.1.2)$$

The variable X_{i1} thus takes on only values of zero or unity. The variable X_{i1} is called a dummy variable, or just a dummy. The term dummy probably comes from the dictionary definition referring to a person secretly acting for another. The dummy variable "acts for" or represents, in this case, the condition of having a Master's degree. Needless to say, the term has generated many a pun.

The coefficients of this regression equation are interpreted as follows:

(1) If the person has a B.A. only, X_{i1} is zero and, ignoring the error term,

$$Y_i = \beta_0 \qquad (2.1.3)$$

Since the coefficient β_0 applies to all beginning teachers, it is to be interpreted as the *average* level of earnings with a B.A. Since there are disparities in starting salaries, given a type of degree, a way to account for this would be to let $AVG(Y_i)$ stand for the *average* income level. Thus, equation 2.1.3. should be expressed as:

$$AVG(Y_i) = \beta_0 \qquad (2.1.4)$$

(2) If the person has an M.A., X_{i1} is unity, and

$$AVG(Y_i) = \beta_0 + \beta_1 \qquad (2.1.5)$$

Thus, $\beta_0 + \beta_1$ is interpreted as the average earnings level for a teacher with an M.A.

From these two equations, β_1 is interpreted as the *incremental* average earnings afforded by having the Master's degree as compared to the Bachelor's degree. This interpretation is important because it allows the researcher to formulate an expectation concerning the sign of β_1 prior to estimation. As was emphasized in Chapter 1 and is emphasized again in Chapter 5, being able to postulate the signs of coefficients is an essential step in regression analysis.

An alternative formulation of the regression model (equation 2.1.1) would be to define X_1 as:

$$X_{i1} = \begin{cases} 0 \text{ if the } i\text{th person has an M.A.} \\ 1 \text{ otherwise (i.e., has a B.A.)} \end{cases} \qquad (2.1.6)$$

That is, the conditions are turned around. In this case, β_1 would be interpreted as the incremental average earnings of a B.A. as compared to an M.A., and its sign would thus be expected to be negative. Since in this case β_1 is the incremental earnings of a B.A. over an M.A., it would be exactly the opposite sign—but of the identical absolute magnitude—of the β_1 in equation 2.1.1 above in which β_1 is the incremental earnings of an M.A. over a B.A. Since this is a mathematical quality of the analysis, this result is assured if the researcher estimated equation 2.1.1 two ways, using the two alternative definitions of X_1. The definitions of dummy variables are, in this sense, completely arbitrary; however, once they have been defined, only one interpretation can be placed on them. The interpretation should be assessed for reasonableness prior to estimation in order to save one the trouble of reestimating the equation to achieve a desired interpretation.

For each such dichotomous situation (i.e., B.A. and M.A.), only one variable is entered as a regressor. Beginners often make the mistake of including two variables. To continue the illustration for a demonstration of this error, define:

$$X_{i1} = \begin{cases} 1 \text{ if M.A.} \\ 0 \text{ if B.A.} \end{cases} \qquad (2.1.7)$$

$$X_{i2} = \begin{cases} 1 \text{ if B.A.} \\ 0 \text{ if M.A.} \end{cases} \qquad (2.1.8)$$

and formulate the model as:

$$Y_i = \beta_0 + \beta_1 X_{i1} + \beta_2 X_{i2} + \epsilon_i \qquad (2.1.9)$$

Such a model cannot be estimated because of *perfect multicollinearity* among the explanatory variables. Perfect multicollinearity is defined as an exact linear relationship among the explanatory variables. The "variable" associated with the intercept term is unity, a constant. This value, unity, is exactly equal to $X_1 + X_2$ for all observations:

$$1 = X_{i1} + X_{i2} \qquad (2.1.10)$$

because it is assumed that each starting teacher has either an M.A. or a B.A. and those with an M.A. are not counted among those with a B.A., by assumption.

The effect of perfect multicollinearity can also be demonstrated by evaluating equation 2.1.9. If a person has a B.A., then $\mathrm{AVG}(Y_i) = \beta_0 + \beta_2$; and if the person has an M.A., then $\mathrm{AVG}(Y_i) = \beta_0 + \beta_1$. Thus, three parameters, β_0, β_1, and β_2, are used to determine the average income levels of a B.A. and an M.A. With two conditions, only two parameters are needed to differentiate their beginning average salaries. The third parameter has no interpretation, and it cannot possibly be estimated; its value is arbitrary. Except for rounding error, computer regression programs will produce no output under these circumstances of perfect multicollinearity among some or all the regressors. Thus, one of the previous formulations should be used: to represent the two conditions, B.A. and M.A., only one dummy variable is used as a regressor.[10]

For an important extension, consider the case in which starting incomes also depend on whether the person has completed some of the requirements toward an M.A. Assume that the appropriate distinction is whether the person has half of the requirements completed. (Alternatively, three-fourths or some other fraction could be the appropriate cut-off point.) One might try to quantify this in a regression context as follows:

$$Y_i = \beta_0 + \beta_1 X_{i1} + \epsilon_i \qquad (2.1.11)$$

where

$$X_{i1} = \begin{cases} 1 & \text{if M.A.} \\ 0.5 & \text{if at least halfway toward an M.A.} \\ 0 & \text{if just B.A.} \end{cases} \qquad (2.1.12)$$

However, a formulation such as this usually imposes arbitrary constraints on the relationship between the various stages of completion of an M.A. To show this, the

---

[10] Suppressing the constant term (β_0) will eliminate this problem and is acceptable here. But to be consistent with the argument in Section 6.1 that the constant term should never be suppressed, this remedy is not suggested, and eliminating one of the dummies is.

equation is interpreted as:

If B.A.:

$$AVG(Y_i) = \beta_0 \qquad\qquad (2.1.13)$$

If half through the M.A.:

$$AVG(Y_i) = \beta_0 + 0.5\beta_1 \qquad\qquad (2.1.14)$$

If M.A.:

$$AVG(Y_i) = \beta_0 + \beta_1 \qquad\qquad (2.1.15)$$

Thus, β_1 is the incremental average earnings of a person with an M.A. compared to a B.A., as before, but the incremental average earnings of a person with half the M.A. completed is constrained by the model formulation to be *exactly half* the M.A. increment. (Compare equation 2.1.14 to equation 2.1.15.) This formulation may be retained only if one's priors are strong enough to make this assumption. Otherwise, a more general formulation, and the one usually preferred, would be

$$Y_i = \beta_0 + \beta_1 X_{i1} + \beta_2 X_{i2} + \epsilon_i \qquad\qquad (2.1.16)$$

where

$$X_{i1} = \begin{cases} 1 \text{ if M.A.} \\ 0 \text{ otherwise (half through or B.A.)} \end{cases} \qquad (2.1.17)$$

$$X_{i2} = \begin{cases} 1 \text{ if half through M.A.} \\ 0 \text{ otherwise (M.A. or just B.A.)} \end{cases} \qquad (2.1.18)$$

With two slope coefficients to estimate instead of just one as previously, the model is free to estimate the relative magnitudes of the incremental earnings for all three categories:

If B.A.:

$$AVG(Y_i) = \beta_0 \qquad\qquad (2.1.19)$$

If half through M.A.:

$$AVG(Y_i) = \beta_0 + \beta_2 \qquad\qquad (2.1.20)$$

If M.A.:

$$AVG(Y_i) = \beta_0 + \beta_1 \qquad\qquad (2.1.21)$$

Thus, the incremental average earnings of being half through the M.A. compared to a B.A. is β_2, and of having an M.A. compared to having a B.A. is β_1. On the theory that higher academic achievements confer higher average starting salaries, one would expect $\beta_1 > \beta_2 > 0$ (and, of course, $\beta_0 > 0$). The incremental average earnings of an M.A. as opposed to being only half through are

$$(\beta_0 + \beta_1) - (\beta_0 + \beta_2) = \beta_1 - \beta_2 \qquad\qquad (2.1.22)$$

The condition of a B.A. is not explicitly represented by a dummy variable in this formulation, and it is called the *omitted condition*. The omitted condition forms the basis against which the included conditions are compared. If one wanted to compare the incremental average earnings of the M.A. over just being half through the M.A., the model could have been structured to accommodate such a direct comparison (as opposed to using $\beta_1 - \beta_2$ above) by defining either half through or the M.A. as the omitted or base condition:

$$Y_i = \beta_0 + \beta_1 X_{i1} + \beta_2 X_{i2} + \epsilon_i \qquad (2.1.23)$$

where

$$X_{i1} = \begin{cases} 1 \text{ if B.A.} \\ 0 \text{ otherwise} \end{cases} \qquad (2.1.24)$$

$$X_{i2} = \begin{cases} 1 \text{ if half through the M.A.} \\ 0 \text{ otherwise} \end{cases} \qquad (2.1.25)$$

Then β_2 is the (negative) incremental average earnings of being half through an M.A. compared to having the M.A., and β_1 is the (negative) incremental average earnings of a B.A. versus an M.A. Thus, one would expect $\beta_1 < \beta_2 < 0$ and $\beta_0 > 0$ (β_0 is now the base earnings level of the omitted category, M.A.). As before, the same estimates of the effect of each level of academic achievement are obtained regardless of the way the model is formulated, but, by constructing the model appropriately, the effect of the condition of interest may be observed directly from the estimated coefficients without any manipulations. This is all the more important for hypothesis testing, which is discussed (with these models) in Chapter 10.

To review: (1) dummy variables are zero-one variables designed to represent a qualitative condition; (2) one less dummy variable is constructed than there are qualitative conditions; (3) for which condition the zero value stands is arbitrary, but once selected, there is a unique interpretation of the coefficient of the dummy; and (4) once set up, the signs of the coefficients can usually be determined *a priori*.

The reader may wonder, why the values zero and one? Suppose, in the first model (equation 2.1.1), that X_{i1} was defined as:

$$X_{i1} = \begin{cases} a \text{ if the } i\text{th person has an M.A.} \\ b \text{ if otherwise} \end{cases}$$

where a and b are some constants set by the researcher. Then the interpretation of equation 2.1.1 is as follows. If the person has only a B.A.:

$$\text{AVG}(Y_i) = \beta_0 + b\beta_1$$

If the person has an M.A.:

$$\text{AVG}(Y_i) = \beta_0 + a\beta_1$$

Thus, the incremental average earnings of an M.A. over a B.A. are:

$$\beta_0 + a\beta_1 - (\beta_0 + b\beta_1) = (a - b)\,\beta_1$$

Since the values of a and b were assigned by the researcher, the incremental effect can be computed. But nothing is gained, and the ease of the interpretation when X_1 was a zero-one dummy is lost. Thus, for ease in formulation and interpretation, researchers always use zero-one dummies.

Sometimes researchers use dummy variables to "account" for large deviations (residuals) in the fitted model, but such a practice amounts to curve fitting (because such variables are not suggested by theory) and should be avoided. Also, a zero-one dummy variable that has only a single observation that assumes a value of unity (or zero) and the rest zeroes (or ones) is to be avoided even if the variable is suggested by theory. Such a "one-time dummy" acts merely to eliminate that observation from the data set, and it artificially inflates the R^2. One would obtain exactly the same estimates of the other coefficients if that observation were deleted.[11]

In all the above illustrations of using dummy variables as regressors, little or no emphasis should be placed on the average effect on the dependent variable of the omitted condition. As noted, the average effect of the omitted condition becomes incorporated into the constant term of the equation, β_0, but, as explained in Section 6.1, estimates of β_0 are untrustworthy.

2.1.3(b)   Dummies for Seasonals and Trends in Time-Series Models.

Sometimes dummy variables are used to account for seasonal variation in the data; for example:

$$X_{t1} = \begin{cases} 1 \text{ in quarter 1} \\ 0 \text{ otherwise} \end{cases} \qquad (2.1.26)$$

$$X_{t2} = \begin{cases} 1 \text{ in quarter 2} \\ 0 \text{ otherwise} \end{cases} \qquad (2.1.27)$$

$$X_{t3} = \begin{cases} 1 \text{ in quarter 3} \\ 0 \text{ otherwise} \end{cases} \qquad (2.1.28)$$

in an equation:

$$Y_t = \beta_0 + \beta_1 X_{t1} + \beta_2 X_{t2} + \beta_3 X_{t3} + \beta_4 X_{t4} + \cdots + \beta_K X_{tK} + \epsilon_t \qquad (2.1.29)$$

where $X_4, X_5, \ldots, X_K$ are the other regressors and t indexes the quarterly observations. (Notice that three dummy variables are required to represent four seasons. In this formulation, β_1 shows the extent to which the mean value of Y differs from its mean value in the fourth quarter, the omitted condition. Similarly for β_2 and β_3.) This procedure may be used if Y or any of the other regressors $X_4, X_5, \ldots, X_K$ are not "seasonally adjusted" prior to estimation. Inclusion of a set of seasonal dummies "deseasonalizes" Y, and it also has the effect of deseasonalizing any of the other regressors that are not seasonally adjusted. Many scholars believe that the types of seasonal adjustment done prior to estimation, such as by the Census X-11 seasonal adjustment computer routine, distorts the data in unknown and arbitrary ways. Thus, they prefer to work with seasonally unadjusted data.

However, the implicit type of seasonal adjustment as carried out by the dummy variable approach above imposes the condition that the absolute amount of the seasonal variation (as indicated by β_1, β_2, and β_3) is the same throughout the data period, during which time the other variables may have doubled in size. Such an assumption is likely to be inappropriate and often is a type of "dimensional misspecification" (see Section 2.2.2). Thus, there is no perfect solution. Many researchers estimate their equations both ways: once with seasonally unadjusted data using the seasonal dummies

---

[11] It also biases the Durbin-Watson statistic (see Chapter 7) toward two. See Craig Swan and Henry J. Cassidy, "A Note on One-Time Dummies: Zero-One Dummy Variables Which Take on Only One Non-Zero Value," *Review of Business and Economics*, Spring, 1975, pp. 268–71.

as regressors and another time with seasonally adjusted data without the seasonal dummies. Often, the differences in the coefficients of $X_4, X_5, \ldots, X_K$, the coefficients of interest, are minimal, and no controversy develops. For most practitioners, using seasonally adjusted data is acceptable; the dummy variable approach may be used when at least one data series has not already been seasonally adjusted by someone else and the researcher wants to avoid the time and trouble of preseasonalizing the data.

Another preestimation procedure that is sometimes used is detrending the variables, done by regressing the variables on TIME and using the deviations from the fitted trend line. (TIME is any variable the current observation of which is always its previous observation plus one. For example, TIME is a variable taking the values 1, 2, 3, . . ., n for the n observations, or the values 1950, 1951, . . ., 1980—it makes virtually no difference which specific values are taken, as long as sequential observations differ by the same amount.) The idea is that if both Y and X show strong elements of trend, the regression of Y on X will reflect mainly the "spurious correlation" of the trend and will not reflect much of the causality from X to Y.

Another way to detrend the variables, however, is to use the raw values of Y and X and to add a TIME variable to the equation as another regressor: this implicitly detrends both Y and X.[12] The coefficient of TIME in this case represents the netting out of the trends in Y and X. Consequently, its estimated coefficient should be interpreted with this in mind. It is a favorite proxy for technological change in production functions or for changes in tastes over time in demand equations under the usually implicit assumption that these changes are smooth and increase by one each period. In a production function, a positive coefficient on TIME implies that output has, on average, increased during the sample period faster than would be indicated by the increases in the factors of production, thus indicating "neutral" technological change that is not related to the specific use of any input. As an explanatory variable, however, TIME really explains nothing in a causal as opposed to an empirical sense. The theoretical justification for including TIME is usually weak, and one should not rely on its theoretical interpretation when it usually plays the role of implicitly detrending all the variables in the equation. A major problem in relying on its coefficient estimate is that TIME will act as a proxy for omitted trendy variables, and its estimated cofficient will reflect its role as a proxy variable.

2.1.3(c)   Dummy Dependent Variables.   Researchers sometimes wish to examine the determinants (or causal factors) of a variable that is inherently qualitative. For example, they may want to predict whether an automobile will be purchased by a given household. The construction of a zero-one dummy variable is appropriate for such a dependent variable. Just set Y_i equal to unity if the purchase was made for the observations in the data set, which is assumed here to consist of a sample of households, and zero otherwise. As an exploratory exercise, it is usually worthwhile to employ the standard estimating technique (ordinary least squares—see Chapter 3) even

---

[12] For a general proof of these propositions, for seasonal dummies as well as TIME, see Ronald J. Wonnacott and Thomas H. Wonnacott, *Econometrics,* 2nd ed. (New York: John Wiley and Sons, 1979), pp. 447–51. Advanced students may want to prove this theorem for themselves for detrended variables.

though more refined estimating techniques are available (such as probit—see any advanced econometrics text).

In predicting values for Y_i given values of the regressors, one may obtain an estimated value Y_i of 0.35, for example. The interpretation is that given the values of the regressors, the *probability* of a purchase is 35 percent. Thus, estimated values of the dependent variable are interpreted as probabilities (here, of a purchase), even though the dependent variable took on only values of zero and unity in the data set. As a probability, any negative value of $\hat{Y}_i$ (such as $\hat{Y}_i = -1.3$) should be set equal to zero, and any value greater than unity should be set equal to unity. These possibilities are one of the reasons more refined estimating techniques may be appropriate if the direct estimation (the OLS technique) shows some promising results. However, the results from the more refined approaches might not differ from those of OLS, especially if there are many degrees of freedom.[13] By the way, one should expect a low R^2 with dummy dependent variables because $\hat{Y}_i$ is unlikely to equal Y_i, which is either zero or unity.

2.1.3(d) Multiplicative Dummies.

In the application of the simple dummy variable regressor, the constant term of the equations is shifted by the inclusion of dummy variables as regressors. (But note that the coefficient *estimates* of other regressors can also change by the inclusion of simple dummy variables.) This section shows how to use dummy variables to allow the slope coefficients to change according to some qualitative condition, as measured by a dummy variable. This extension of the dummy variable approach has a surprisingly wide range of applicability, and the material in this section is important in the discussion of hypothesis testing in Chapter 10.

Dummy variables can be used in a multiplicative fashion to form new variables that allow the slope coefficient to change according to the condition represented by the dummy variable. As an illustration, suppose the time needed to unload a shipment of goods from trucks (Y_i), called stop time, depends on the weight of the shipment (X_1), the number of pieces to be unloaded (X_2), and the volume (or amount of space) of the shipment (X_3).[14] The model is cross-sectional, consisting of observations each time a truck makes a pickup or a delivery. The term cross section means that the observations are not time-dependent in the chronological sense. (See Section 2.5.)

Suppose that the effect of the weight variable on stop time varies in some unknown, nonlinear fashion thought to be related to the weight of the shipment. One way to allow the regression equation to show the type of nonlinearity involved is to define the following dummy variable:

$$D = \begin{cases} 1 \text{ if weight} > w^* \\ 0 \text{ otherwise} \end{cases} \qquad (2.1.30)$$

where w^* is a constant assigned by the researcher, and then to define

---

[13] See John L. Goodman, Jr., "Is Ordinary Least Squares Estimation with a Dichotomous Dependent Variable Really That Bad?" Urban Institute Working Paper No. 216–23, September 1976.

[14] This example comes from Dabney T. Waring, Jr., and Henry J. Cassidy, "Determinants of Stop Time," *Transportation Journal,* Vol. 19, No. 1, Fall, 1979, pp. 50–61.

$$X_4 = DX_1 \qquad (2.1.31)$$

This multiplicative or "interaction" variable takes on the value of the weight of the shipment when the weight is above w^* and zero otherwise. The usefulness of this multiplicative variable can be seen in the following equation that may be used for estimation:

$$Y_i = \beta_0 + \beta_1 X_{i1} + \beta_2 X_{i2} + \beta_3 X_{i3} + \beta_4 X_{i4} + \beta_5 D_i + \epsilon_i \qquad (2.1.32)$$

The average value of Y_i is:

If weight $\leq w^*$:

$$\text{AVG}(Y_i) = \beta_0 + \beta_1 X_{i1} + \beta_2 X_{i2} + \beta_3 X_{i3} \qquad (2.1.33)$$

If weight $> w^*$:

$$\text{AVG}(Y_i) = (\beta_0 + \beta_5) + (\beta_1 + \beta_4) X_{i1} + \beta_2 X_{i2} + \beta_3 X_{i3} \qquad (2.1.34)$$

The interpretation of $\Delta \text{AVG}(Y_i)/\Delta X_{i1}$, the change in the average value of Y_i caused by a unit change in X_{i1}, holding the other variables constant, is:

If weight $\leq w^*$: $\qquad \beta_1$

If weight is $> w^*$: $\qquad \beta_1 + \beta_4$

From this, the coefficient β_4 represents the incremental effect on the slope of the highest weight bracket as compared to the effect of the lowest one. Thus, the type of nonlinearity of the effect of X_1 on Y may be examined by focusing by β_4.

Figure 2.1.1 shows the "partial" relationship between weight of the shipment and stop time that was the result of applying this approach. The other regressors in

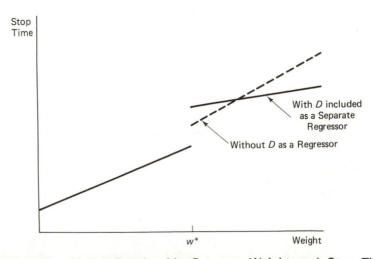

FIGURE 2.1.1 Partial Relationship Between Weight and Stop Time Using Dummy Variables (other regressors held at their mean values)

the equation are evaluated at their sample mean values in order to portray this partial relation holding the other regressors (and the error term) constant. The solid line indicates the result of estimating equation 2.1.32. As weight increases, holding the number of pieces and volume constant, the average stop time increases. Above weight w^* the stop time increases with increased weight, but at a slower rate (as indicated by the lower slope). (The fact that the stop time increased at w^* is of no particular importance; yet, as discussed below, this discontinuity would make such an equation impractical for various applications.)

The solid line shows a type of economy with respect to weight because stop time increases but at a lower rate for shipments that weigh more than w^*. The dashed line shows what the partial relationship between weight and stop time would be if the D variable were not included as a regressor along with the multiplicative term DX_1. As weight per shipment increases beyond w^*, the Y-intercept term changes if D is included as a separate regressor. But if D is not included, then the Y-intercept must be the same for both segments of the partial relationship. Thus, the type of economy alluded to would not be allowed to appear. In Figure 2.1.1, forcing a common intercept for both segments of the partial relationship by excluding D as a regressor implies that a *diseconomy* exists, compared to the economy found when D was included as a regressor. Without D, stop time increases at a *higher* rate beyond the critical weight w^* because it is forced to do so by the particular specification selected for the equation.

Since the inappropriateness of not including D as a separate regressor is very important, an alternative explanation of the consequences is presented here. The variable D in the sample may exhibit much more variability than the variable X_1, so that the multiplicative variable DX_1, without D as a regressor, may be primarily representing the condition for which $D=1$ (as weight being greater than w^*). Thus, the estimated coefficient of $X_4 = DX_1$, when D is not included as a regressor, primarily shows this effect, not the effect of the change in the slope coefficient of X_1. When D is included as a regressor, the coefficient of the multiplicative variable DX_1 is free to show the appropriate incremental change in the slope coefficient of X_1, if there is any. While there may be a high degree of collinearity between D and DX_1, the variable D should still be included. In fact, it should be included *because* of the high degree of collinearity. In such a case, if D were excluded, the coefficient of DX_1 is even more likely to show the effects of D itself and not the change in the slope coefficient of X_1.

A legitimate use of the R^2 measure (or the SEE) is to determine the level of w^*. If it is assumed that the equation is otherwise correctly specified, then a "search" routine can be applied. Various values of w^* are specified, the variable D is appropriately constructed, and the corresponding regressions are estimated for each of these values. The number of values of w^* specified depends on the degree of accuracy desired. The equation—and thus the value of w^*—is selected that yields the highest R^2. (The same general procedure was described in Section 2.1.1(b) to find the empirically appropriate definition of permanent income. See also Section 6.4.1.)

Recall that this analysis (which has been called an analysis with "jackknife" variables) may be exploratory. The researcher may want to use it to determine the shape of a continuous functional form that may be appropriate. In the particular example, using the square root of X_1 instead of X_1 itself may be adequate because it shows that stop time increases with weight, but at a decreasing rate. The square root of X_1 would replace X_1, D, and DX_1 if a continuous functional form were desired, for example for forecasting or for costing the loading and unloading of trucks in the present example. With the discontinuous functional form, a rather large change in stop time is inferred with shipments weighing 20,001 pounds as compared to 19,999 pounds (where $w* = 20,000$ pounds). Having a costing formula based on the estimated equation using the dummy variable would cause shippers to avoid weights just over 20,000 pounds. This problem is avoided with the continuous form. But if the empirical research is just to investigate the type of economies present, the dummy variable approach would be adequate as a final product.

If all the slope coefficients (and the intercept term) are allowed to assume different values for each weight (by including more interaction terms like the one used above, DX_1), then the single equation thus estimated produces estimates implicitly identical to those that could be produced by regressing Y on X_1, X_2, and X_3 estimated two times, once each for the data set exclusive to each specified range of weight. The researcher may want the single-equation approach, however, because the combined regression equation explicitly compares the coefficients for each range, e.g., providing explicit estimates of the differences, such as β_4 above. For a further explanation of this procedure, see Section 10.1.3 on the "Chow Test."

2.2   The Functional Form

This section presents alternative functional forms in "cookbook" fashion. The researcher should decide what theory suggests as the type of relationship between various regressors and the dependent variable, find that type of relationship in the graphs or the equations presented, and use the corresponding functional form. In this discussion, the error term plays a minor role. It is always shown but is assumed to be zero.

2.2.1   Linear Form

The linear regression model is linear in the parameters, but the variables themselves do not have to be linear. This distinction gives researchers the latitude to use alternative functional forms with the linear regression model. Theory and imposition of priors are used as guides to formulate various functional forms. This section discusses the linear form of the variables (i.e., Y regressed on $X_1, X_2, \ldots, X_K$).

The linear regression model is based on the assumption that all the slopes are constant:[15]

$$\frac{\Delta Y}{\Delta X_k} = \beta_k \qquad k = 1, 2, \ldots, K \qquad (2.2.1)$$

As a consequence of this assumption, the elasticities[16] are not constant:

---

[15] Throughout this section, the Δ notation will be used instead of the proper notation of calculus. Also, the *average* or *expected value* of Y with respect to a change in X_k is what is intended throughout, instead of the expressions such as $\Delta Y / \Delta X_k$. Readers may want to refer to Section 1.2.2 for a review of the interpretation of Δ in this text.

$$\eta_{Y,X_k} = \frac{\Delta Y/Y}{\Delta X_k/X_k} = \frac{\Delta Y}{\Delta X_k} \cdot \frac{X_k}{Y} = \beta_k \frac{X_k}{Y} \qquad (2.2.2)$$

The elasticities are usually computed at the means of the sample values for X_k and Y, given an estimate of β_k, to show a "representative" value of the elasticity in the basic linear model. If these two properties of the relationship are appropriate—or even if they provide a useful approximation—then the linear form of the variables is suggested.

The following sections suggest alternative forms for the variables: the exponential (logarithmic), semi-log, interaction terms, polynomial, inverse, combined, and inherently nonlinear forms.

2.2.2 Exponential Form

The researcher may specify that, contrary to the linear model, the elasticities and not the slopes are constant:

$$\eta_{Y,X_k} = \beta_k \qquad (2.2.3)$$

Given an assumption of a constant elasticity, one searches for the functional form that has this property, and it is the exponential form:

$$Y = e^{\beta_0} X_1{}^{\beta_1} X_2{}^{\beta_2} e^{\epsilon} \qquad (2.2.4)$$

(for the two-regressor model, where e is the base of the natural logarithms). A logarithmic transformation can be applied to make the equation linear in the coefficients:

$$\ln Y = \beta_0 + \beta_1 \ln X_1 + \beta_2 \ln X_2 + \epsilon \qquad (2.2.5)$$

Since $\Delta(\ln Y)/\Delta(\ln X_k)$ is interpreted as an elasticity[17] and it equals β_k, the condition of a constant elasticity is satisfied by this double-log equation. The interpretation of β_1 is, in this case, as follows: if X_1 changes by one percent while X_2 is held constant, Y changes by β_1 *percent*. In this equation, of course, the slopes do depend on the levels of the variables:

$$\frac{\Delta Y}{\Delta X_k} = \beta_k \frac{Y}{X_k} \qquad (2.2.6)$$

The log-linear form of equation 2.2.5 may be preferred over a linear form due to what is called "dimensional misspecification." In the linear form, a unit change in a regressor produces the same change in Y regardless of the level of Y, which may be inappropriate. For example, suppose Y is the time and savings account demand at banks and X_1 is the ratio of the rate paid on the accounts and the Treasury bill rate. It is likely that an increase in this ratio by one percent today will elicit more accounts than it would have 30 years ago when the level of such accounts was much lower.

---

[16] The elasticity shown in equation 2.2.2 is defined as the percentage change in Y for a unitary percentage change in X_k. The proportional (i.e., percent/100) changes are $\Delta Y/Y$ and $\Delta X_k/X_k$, and the ratio of the two yields the elasticity η_{Y,X_k}. Other regressors are held constant.

[17] This is because $\Delta(\ln Y) \simeq \Delta Y/Y$ and $\Delta(\ln X_k) \simeq \Delta(X_k)/X_k$, where $\simeq$ means "approximately equal to."

The log-linear form allows the absolute value of the current response to be much larger than the response was 30 years ago. According to the response equation 2.2.6, the numerator Y is larger today than 30 years ago while the denominator may be the same for both periods; thus, the response of Y to a unit change in X_1 is larger today than 30 years ago. In deciding whether this kind of error from a linear form is important, one should assess the extent of the range of values taken on by Y. If the range is large and the above logic applies, the log-linear form may be preferred.

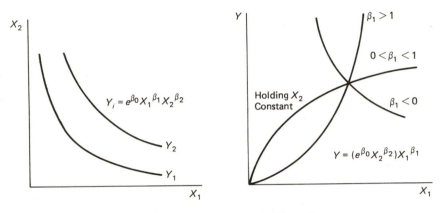

FIGURE 2.2.1   Exponential Function

Figure 2.2.1 is a graph of the double-log or exponential function (ignoring the error term). The panel on the left shows the economic concept of a production function or an indifference curve. Isoquants from production functions (and indifference curves from utility functions) show the substitutability between factors (goods) X_1 and X_2 to produce (yield) the same level of output (utility) Y. The right-hand panel shows the simple exponential function if X_2 is held constant. If X_1 was the only regressor, as in:

$$Y = \beta_0 X_1^{\beta_1}$$

then this equation would also be linear in the parameters (except the constant term) after a logarithmic transformation:

$$\ln Y = \ln \beta_0 + \beta_1 \ln X_1 = \beta_0^* + \beta_1 \ln X_1 \tag{2.2.7}$$

Since the constant term is usually not of special interest, this equation is ready for estimation (after adding an error term).

2.2.3   Semi-Log Form

The semi-log equation, another example of a nonlinear functional form that may be estimated using the linear regression model, may have as regressors logarithms of one or more of the independent variables. For example:

$$Y = \beta_0 + \beta_1 \ln X_1 + \beta_2 X_2 + \epsilon \tag{2.2.8}$$

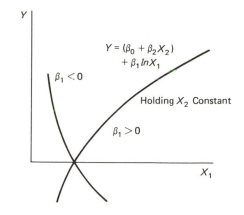

FIGURE 2.2.2 Semi-Log Function

In this case:

$$\frac{\Delta Y}{\Delta X_1} = \frac{\beta_1}{X_1} \tag{2.2.9}$$

and

$$\frac{\Delta Y}{\Delta X_2} = \beta_2 \tag{2.2.10}$$

Thus the partial effect (i.e., in equation 2.2.9, X_2 is assumed to be held constant) of X_1 on Y diminishes as X_1 increases, as shown in Figure 2.2.2. If X_1 changes by one *percent*, Y changes by $\beta_1/100$ *units*. The partial relationship (i.e., holding X_1 constant) of X_2 on Y is linear.

The elasticity of Y with respect to X_1 is

$$\eta_{Y,X_1} = \frac{\Delta Y}{\Delta X_1} \cdot \frac{X_1}{Y} = \frac{\beta_1}{Y} \tag{2.2.11}$$

which diminishes as Y increases.

Another type of semi-log equation is derived by taking logarithms of the following equation:

$$Y = e^{\beta_0 + \beta_1 X_1 + \beta_2 X_2 + \epsilon} \tag{2.2.12}$$

The transformed equation is:

$$\ln Y = \beta_0 + \beta_1 X_1 + \beta_2 X_2 + \epsilon \tag{2.2.13}$$

This model has neither a constant slope nor a constant elasticity. Its slope is:

$$\frac{\Delta Y}{\Delta X_k} = \beta_k e^{(\beta_0 + \beta_1 X_1 + \beta_2 X_2 + \epsilon)} = \beta_k Y \tag{2.2.14}$$

for $k = 1$ or 2. Thus, the slope is greater the higher the level of Y. The elasticity is:

$$\eta_{Y,X_k} = \frac{\Delta \ln Y}{\Delta X_k / X_k} = \beta_k X_k \tag{2.2.15}$$

If X_1 changes by one *unit*, Y changes by β_1 (times 100) *percent*, holding X_2 constant.

This type of exponential function is shown in Figure 2.2.3. The researcher should consider whether this type of relationship applies before using this kind of semi-log form. In general, simpler forms are preferred unless theory suggests the more complicated forms.

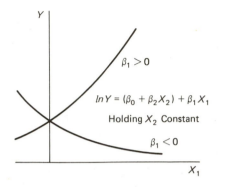

FIGURE 2.2.3   Exponential Function (Semi-Log in Y)

2.2.4   Interaction Terms

Another functional form that allows nonconstant slopes uses so-called "interaction terms," such as in the following equation:

$$Y = \beta_0 + \beta_1 X_1 + \beta_2 X_2 + \beta_3(X_1 X_2) + \epsilon \qquad (2.2.16)$$

The new variable, $X_1 X_2$, gives rise to the following interpretations of the slopes:

$$\frac{\Delta Y}{\Delta X_1} = \beta_1 + \beta_3 X_2 \qquad (2.2.17)$$

$$\frac{\Delta Y}{\Delta X_2} = \beta_2 + \beta_3 X_1 \qquad (2.2.18)$$

Thus, the change in Y with respect to one variable depends on the level of the other variable. In assessing empirical results of this equation, the researcher may find the estimate of β_3 to be of no particular interest; what is important are the signs and magnitudes of the various slopes (partial derivatives) over the relevant range of values of X_1 and X_2. When X_2 is held constant, Y is a linear function of X_1 (i.e., a straight line), so its graph is not drawn.

2.2.5   Polynomials

Polynomial expressions are often used if the slopes are expected to depend on the level of the variable itself. For example, in the second-degree polynomial (or quadratic) equation:

$$Y = \beta_0 + \beta_1 X_1 + \beta_2 X_1^2 + \beta_3 X_2 + \epsilon \qquad (2.2.19)$$

the slopes are:

$$\frac{\Delta Y}{\Delta X_1} = \beta_1 + 2\beta_2 X_1 \qquad (2.2.20)$$

and

$$\frac{\Delta Y}{\Delta X_2} = \beta_3 \qquad (2.2.21)$$

Thus, the first slope depends on the level of X_1. If this were a cost function, with Y being the average cost of production and X_1 being the level of output (at the firm level), then β_2 should be positive to assure that the cost curve is U-shaped. See Figure 2.2.4.

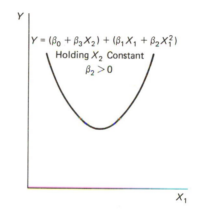

FIGURE 2.2.4   Quadratic Function

Polynomials are a curve-fitting device. In fact, any n observations can be fit to a regression curve exactly by a polynomial of degree n-1 (i.e., having as regressors $X_1, X_1^2, X_1^3, \ldots, X_1^{n-1}$). This regression relationship becomes a mathematical relationship, not a statistical one. The practicing econometrician should utilize the relevant economic theory to specify the model and the regression results to draw statistical inferences about the causal relationships among the variables, not simply "fit" the observed data to a curve. Thus, use of higher degree polynomials in regression analysis should be avoided. Furthermore, with polynomial regressors, the interpretation of the individual regressson coefficients becomes difficult, and the equation may produce unwanted results for particular ranges of X_1. For example, the slope for a third-degree polynomial may be positive over some of the range of X_1, then negative, and then positive again, when this may not be called for on the basis of theory. Even using the quadratic form imposes a particular symmetric shape (a U-shape or its inverse) to the partial effect. Some researchers use just the square of the variable and exclude from the equation its linear form, on the grounds that theory justifies a partial effect directly proportional to the level of the variable. Great care must be taken in developing one's priors to insure that the functional form will achieve exactly what is intended, and no more.

2.2.6 Inverse Form

The inverse or reciprocal functional form (in this case with respect to X_1) has some interesting features. It takes the form:

$$Y = \beta_0 + \beta_1\left(\frac{1}{X_1}\right) + \beta_2 X_2 + \epsilon \qquad (2.2.22)$$

The slopes are:

$$\frac{\Delta Y}{\Delta X_1} = \frac{-\beta_1}{X_1^2} \qquad (2.2.23)$$

and

$$\frac{\Delta Y}{\Delta X_2} = \beta_2 \qquad (2.2.24)$$

When β_1 is positive, the slope with respect to X_1 is negative and decreases in absolute value, approaching zero as X_1 increases. Hence, the partial relationship between X_1 and Y (holding X_2 constant) approaches $\beta_0 + \beta_2 X_2$ as X_1 increases (ignoring the error term). As shown in Figure 2.2.5, if β_1 is negative, the partial relationship intersects the X_1 axis at $-\beta_1/(\beta_0 + \beta_2 X_2)$ and slopes upward toward the same horizontal asymptote as when β_1 is positive.

2.2.7 Combinations of Functional Forms

Various combinations of the functional forms are possible. The form taken by X_1 may be different from the form taken by X_2, as was shown in most of the above examples. In addition, even Y may assume yet a different functional form. Remember that the researcher should attempt to specify the equation in such a way that the theory is represented in the best possible manner. If the theory is not clear, e.g., about the sign of the second partial derivative[18] or about asymptotes, the fancier functional forms may be just curve-fitting devices and should be avoided by the researcher.

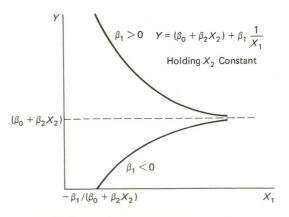

FIGURE 2.2.5 Reciprocal Function

Furthermore, the theoretical basis for any form other than the standard linear form should be based on theoretical grounds and should be well documented in the presentation of the regression project.

As an example of combined forms, the logarithmic-reciprocal form has some theoretical interest:

$$\ln Y = \beta_0 + \beta_1 \left(\frac{1}{X_1} \right) + \beta_2 X_2 + \epsilon \qquad (2.2.25)$$

The slopes are:

$$\frac{\Delta Y}{\Delta X_1} = \frac{-\beta_1}{X_1^2} Y \qquad (2.2.26)$$

$$\frac{\Delta Y}{\Delta X_2} = \beta_2 Y \qquad (2.2.27)$$

The partial relationship between Y and X_1 is particularly interesting for negative β_1. As shown in Figure 2.2.6, it starts at the origin and increases at an increasing rate, reaches a point of inflection, increases at a decreasing rate, and then approaches an asymptotic limit. Such a curve may be used to represent a learning curve or the market penetration of a new product.[19]

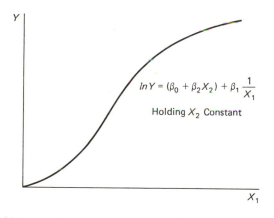

$$\ln Y = (\beta_0 + \beta_2 X_2) + \beta_1 \frac{1}{X_1}$$

Holding X_2 Constant

FIGURE 2.2.6   Logarithmic-Reciprocal Function

2.2.8   Inherently Nonlinear Forms

With advanced computer technology, the researcher should also not be bashful in hypothesizing nonlinear forms that cannot be transformed into a form that is linear

---

[18] The rate of change in the slope.

[19] For illustrations of these kinds of curves, see the two articles in *Technological Forecasting and Social Change*, 7, 1975, by M. O. Stern, R. U. Ayres, and A. Skapunka, "A Model for Forecasting the Substitution of One Technology for Another," pp. 57–59; and Devendra Sahal, "A Generalized Logistic Model for Technological Forecasting," pp. 81–97.

in the parameters. Estimation methods are now available to estimate equations such as:

$$Y = \beta_0 \beta_1^{X_1} X_2^{\beta_2} + \epsilon \qquad (2.2.28)$$

or

$$Y = \beta_0 + \beta_1 X_1^{\beta_2} + \epsilon \qquad (2.2.29)$$

The only major problem is that a technique to assess whether β_2, for example, is statistically different from zero in either of these nonlinear equations is not generally available to beginners. In these cases, beginners should rely on heuristic measures of the statistical reliability of an estimate (such as its standard error). An example of estimating nonlinear forms is given in Chapter 11.

2.2.9   Incomparable R^2's When Y Is Transformed

While the emphasis in applied regression analysis is usually on such things as the coefficient estimates and forecast intervals, it is worthwhile to note that, when the dependent variable is transformed from its linear form, the overall measure of fit, the R^2, no longer gives an appropriate indication of goodness of fit in terms of the original variable itself. For example, equation 2.2.13 has $\ln(Y)$ as its dependent variable and X_1 and X_2 as its regressors. As an alternative estimating equation, the researcher may regress Y on X_1 and X_2. A selection between the two equations should not be based on a comparison of the R^2's. The reason is that the total sum of squares (SST) of the dependent variable about its mean is different in the two formulations. In order to compare the equations on the basis of overall goodness of fit, the following procedure is suggested. Use the estimated equation in which $\ln(Y)$ is the dependent variable to generate the regression-line values for all n observations on $\ln(Y_i)$ and take the anti-log of each of these observations, which become the $\hat{Y}_i$'s of the equation. Then put these values into the R^2 formula. This R^2 is now directly comparable to the one computed for the equation in which Y was the dependent variable.

2.3   Multi-Equation Models

Most applications of econometrics do not involve just one equation. Quite often, there are identities among the variables that can be stated in the form of equations, and often there is dual causality, such as in a demand and supply framework, where the levels of price and quantity are determined simultaneously. In Section 2.3.2, it is shown how dual causality, or simultaneity, implies the existence of more than one equation. In general, all related equations should be specified even though the focus is limited to one equation. Very often, the other equations can and should be used to help estimate the coefficients of concern. But unless these other equations are specified, neither the researcher nor any reviewers of the research results have a firm basis on which to assess the reliability of the estimated equation or the potential usefulness of other equations in the estimation of the desired equation.

Two general types of multi-equation models are examined, those involving identities among the variables and those involving simultaneous equations models. These two types are encountered very frequently in regression analysis.

2.3.1 Identities Among the Variables

This section discusses two rather common types of situations in which identities among the variables indicate that alternative formulations of the regression model are identical, even though they look different. The first type involves the formulation of regressors, while the second involves the selection of the dependent variable.

2.3.1(a) Formulation of Regressors.

Many researchers formulate regressors in terms of differences in separate variables. For example, consider the public demand for savings accounts, the amount (quantity) of which is denoted by Q. The demand equation may be specified as:

$$Q = \beta_0 + \beta_1 Y + \beta_2 r + \beta_3 (r - r_c) + \epsilon \qquad (2.3.1)$$

where Y is a measure of income, r is the interest rate or the return paid on the account, and r_c is the rate on the closest competitive savings instrument, e.g., Treasury bills. Thus, the equation states that Q is a function of income, the interest rate paid on the investment, and the difference between its interest rate and the rate paid on the competing investment. However this model is implicitly identical to the following model:

$$Q = \beta_0' + \beta_1' Y + \beta_2' r + \beta_3' r_c + \epsilon \qquad (2.3.2)$$

In fact, the relationships among the two sets of coefficients are exact:

$$\begin{aligned} \beta_0' &= \beta_0 \\ \beta_1' &= \beta_1 \\ \beta_2' &= \beta_2 + \beta_3 \\ \beta_3' &= -\beta_3 \end{aligned} \qquad (2.3.3)$$

Since

$$\beta_2 r + \beta_3 (r - r_c) = (\beta_2 + \beta_3)\, r - \beta_3 r_c$$

the first formulation is equivalent to the second one. Since both equations are implicitly equivalent, neither form is preferred on a theoretical basis. Therefore, which one is chosen to estimate the coefficients is arbitrary.

If the interest rates move together, it may be difficult to distinguish the empirical series of observations on r and r_c. This is a special case of multicollinearity (or, between two variables, collinearity), in which an approximate linear combination exists among the regressors. With a high degree of collinearity, the movements in r and r_c resemble one another. As a consequence, the estimating technique is not able to compute with accuracy estimates of their individual effects on the dependent variable. Some researchers argue that the first formulation is preferable because, even though r and r_c are collinear, r and the composite variable $(r - r_c)$ are likely not to be collinear; thus, the collinearity problem disappears. Nonsense! The two approaches yield identical estimates of the slopes $\Delta Q/\Delta r$ and $\Delta Q/\Delta r_c$. Therefore, their implications are identical! However, if $(r-r_c)$ were used by itself, without r or r_c appearing as a separate regressor, then the collinearity problem is circumvented, but the interpretation of the equation changes. In particular, it is then assumed that r_c has just as much effect on Q as does r (in absolute value). This assumption may not be totally inappropriate if r_c can proxy for *all* alternative investments.

2.3.1(b)   Use of Identities in Selecting the Dependent Variable.   One
way that identities are useful is in deciding which variable should be the dependent variable. For example, should one estimate a consumption function as a consumption function or as a savings function? Since consumption and savings are related by the identity that they must sum to total income:

$$S + C = Y$$

as long as income is one of the regressors in each equation, it does not matter which variable, consumption or savings, is chosen as the dependent variable (assuming that the other variables remain the same). To illustrate, suppose one had to decide which of the following two equations to estimate:

$$C_t = \beta_0 + \beta_1 Y_t + \beta_2 C_{t-1} + \epsilon_{ct} \tag{2.3.4}$$

or

$$S_t = \delta_0 + \delta_1 Y_t + \delta_2 C_{t-1} + \epsilon_{st} \tag{2.3.5}$$

where C is consumption, S savings, Y income, and C_{t-1} is consumption lagged one period. Since $Y_t = C_t + S_t$, and $S_t = Y_t - C_t$, the savings equation may be written as:

$$Y_t - C_t = \delta_0 + \delta_1 Y_t + \delta_2 C_{t-1} + \epsilon_{st} \tag{2.3.6}$$

or

$$C_t = -\delta_0 + (1-\delta_1) Y_t - \delta_2 C_{t-1} - \epsilon_{st} \tag{2.3.7}$$

This is of the identical form as the consumption function, where the relationships among the coefficients are:

$$-\delta_0 = \beta_0$$
$$(1-\delta_1) = \beta_1$$
$$-\delta_2 = \beta_2$$

Thus, the two approaches are implicitly identical and the choice of either form is arbitrary. This in turn implies that applying the same estimating technique to both equations will yield identical estimates; namely

$$-\hat{\delta}_0 = \hat{\beta}_0$$
$$(1-\hat{\delta}_1) = \hat{\beta}_1$$
$$-\hat{\delta}_2 = \hat{\beta}_2$$

The R^2 is likely to be higher in the consumption equation than in the savings equation, but this is not a consideration in selecting the dependent variable. (The reason is that the sum of squares of the residuals is the same in each approach since the two approaches are implicitly identical, but the total sum of squares is greater for the consumption equation than it is for the savings function.) In general, the R^2 is not comparable among equations having different dependent variables, a point that was made in Section 2.2.9.

2.3.2 The Simultaneous Equations Model

Very often, the equation of interest is a "structural" equation that is part of a system of such equations. This type of equation attempts to describe the behavior of a single economic actor, such as households, when in fact this actor interacts simultaneously with other economic actors, such as producers. The behavior of each actor can be described by a regression equation, and the set of such behavioral equations forms a set of structural equations. It is extremely important to specify all such structural equations when attempting to estimate just one of them. This section discusses how to specify such a model, while Chapter 9 is devoted to their estimation.

The following three structural equations of supply and demand illustrate the basic notions of such models:

$$Q_t^D = \beta_0 + \beta_1 P_t + \beta_2 X_t + \epsilon_{Dt} \qquad \text{(Demand)} \qquad (2.3.8)$$

$$Q_t^S = \delta_0 + \delta_1 P_t + \delta_2 Z_t + \epsilon_{St} \qquad \text{(Supply)} \qquad (2.3.9)$$

$$Q_t^D = Q_t^S = Q_t \qquad \text{(Equilibrium Condition)} \qquad (2.3.10)$$

where Q^D and Q^S are the quantities demanded and supplied, respectively; P is the price; X is a demand variable, such as income; Z is a supply variable, such as the price of the major factor of production; ϵ_D and ϵ_S are the error terms for the demand and supply equations, respectively; the subscript t represents the time period; and the β's and δ's are the regression coefficients. The equilibrium condition (a behavioral equation but with no coefficients to estimate) may be substituted into the demand and supply equations, resulting in two equations in P and Q, the mutually dependent or *endogenous* variables:

$$Q_t = \beta_0 + \beta_1 P_t + \beta_2 X_t + \epsilon_{Dt} \qquad \text{(Demand)} \qquad (2.3.11)$$
$$Q_t = \delta_0 + \delta_1 P_t + \delta_2 Z_t + \epsilon_{St} \qquad \text{(Supply)} \qquad (2.3.12)$$

Price and quantity are mutually determined variables, and their market-clearing values are determined jointly by the interaction of these supply and demand forces, depicted as equations. This is called dual causality, or simultaneity, and the equations are called *simultaneous equations*. The variables involved in the dual causality are called *endogenous variables,* and those that are not are called the *predetermined*, or, in this case, *exogenous variables.* In this model X and Z are *exogenous.*

Suppose the equation that the researcher wants to estimate is the demand equation. This does not obviate the need for the researcher to write down the full model. As will be discussed in Chapter 9, the choice of the estimating technique that should be used to estimate the demand equation depends on, among other things, the type of supply equation in the structural model.

Each equation of the model is supposed to represent the actions of a single type of economic entity, whereas the entire set of equations is supposed to represent the interaction of these entities, usually in a market setting. There is another set of equations associated with each set of (the linear) structural equations that represents the solved, or *reduced-form,* equation set. Each equation in this reduced-form equation set has only one endogenous variable, and there are just as many reduced-form equations as there are endogenous variables (and structural equations). In the supply and demand model above, for example, Q is solved for in terms of X and Z, the exogenous variables, the values of which are determined outside the particular structure being examined. Likewise, P is solved for in terms of X and Z. (The reduced-form equations also contain error terms; these are ignored until Chapter 9.) Since X and Z affect demand and supply, respectively, the reduced-form equations for P and Q reflect the ''netting'' out of these opposing forces. In many cases, for example, when the focus is strictly on forecasting Q (or P), the researcher will simply want to use the appropriate reduced-form equation. As will be shown in Chapter 9, estimation of a reduced-form equation is much simpler than estimating a structural equation. However, even if the reduced-form equation is the appropriate choice of equations, the principle of full and complete documentation requires that the structural equations be specified, at least in implicit functional form. (If they are expressed in implicit functional form, the usual assumption is that the structural equations are linear. In this case, each reduced-form equation is linear and has as regressors all the exogenous and lagged endogenous variables in the entire structural system of equations. An example of a lagged endogenous variable is Q_{t-1}, the quantity demanded in the previous time period. It may be included as an additional regressor in the demand equation.)

In constructing a simultaneous equations model, the question invariably arises concerning the extent of the simultaneity. In the above example, the researcher may be tempted to make the input price, Z, endogenous. To do so would require adding another equation ''explaining'' Z, one describing the offering of services of the factor of production involved. And income X may be made endogenous, again by adding one or more equations to the model. Or a substitute good may be so closely related that its price and quantity may need to be determined (and its price included in the demand equation above) simultaneously with the determination of P and Q. The extent of the simultaneity is based on the intended purpose of the regression project and on the researcher's *priors*. Interactions deemed important by the researcher may have to be included in the simultaneous equations model by adding the appropriate equations, and equations are not supplied for interactions that are considered as ''given'' with respect to the model. Normally, for particular goods and services, the extent of the simultaneity is usually confined to the market directly at hand, such as the demand and supply of wheat; however, for more aggregative phenomena, such as explaining GNP or aggregate tax revenues, the extent of the simultaneity must be extended to include at least income and price-level determination. Two researchers can legitimately disagree about the necessary extent of the simultaneity: what is given and exogenous for one researcher is endogenous for another. There are statistical tests for the extent of simultaneity, but they are beyond the scope of this book.

(For each endogenous variable, an equation must be supplied, or else the simultaneous equations system cannot be solved for the values of the endogenous variables.

The equations do not have to be behavioral. For large models, researchers often count the number of equations to make sure it equals the number of endogenous variables.)

This section has introduced some basic notions about simultaneous equations models so that the student can begin to specify such a model. Section 2.4 covers an area that must at least be considered in all time-series models, dynamics.

2.4   Dynamic Models

In dynamic models, variables at different points in time are related to each other. This section attempts to provide the reader with an understanding of this important class of time-series models. Several of the more popular models are explained, while more complex models are left for advanced texts. The models discussed here are single-equation models, but they are frequently used in simultaneous equations systems. The following paragraphs describe the conceptualization of the dynamic process and situations in which such processes might arise, and then several standard types of dynamic models are presented.

Dynamic models can show the time path of variables from one static equilibrium level to another. A point of static equilibrium is one in which there is no tendency for any of the variables to change. Every variable is at peace, there are assumed to be no shocks to the behavioral system being examined: the error term is assumed to be identically zero and the exogenous variables are constant at such a point. When a shock comes, usually represented by a change in the level of one of the independent (actually, exogenous) variables, the static equilibrium is disturbed. The customary, standardized way to examine a dynamic model is to allow a specified exogenous variable to change by one unit. All other exogenous variables are held constant, as is the error term, and no future changes in the specified exogenous variable are allowed. Then the time path of the dependent variable resulting from this once-and-for-all type of shock is examined. It is expected that the dependent variable will deviate from its original static equilibrium level and move to a new static equilibrium level.

For most dynamic models, it takes several time periods before the new level materializes. It is the time path from one level of the variable to another that is the major concern to most researchers because, even if the estimation of the long-run, static equilibrium behavioral relationship is the goal, if the time-series data to be used for estimation have been generated from a dynamic process—and hence would be unlikely to represent equilibrium situations—ignoring the dynamics in the specification of the estimating equation would introduce error into the estimation process. That is to say, if the data had been generated by a process that is essentially dynamic, ignoring the dynamics in the estimation would likely introduce error of some kind or another (called specification error, in this case leaving out of the regression equation one or more relevant variables; specification error is discussed in Chapter 6).

The kinds of variables that are usually thought to exhibit dynamic behavior are "stock" variables, such as plant and equipment, machinery, and other physical assets. Quarterly and even annual time-series observations on such stocks are thought to show a continual process of adjustment to equilibrium because (1) it takes time to perceive what the new economic environment will turn out to be and to implement decisions once they have been made, and (2) information and transactions costs mitigate against hasty decisions. As new supply or demand conditions appear, entrepreneurs typically make continual adjustments in the amount of physical assets they control or own.

The adjustment is achieved by changes in the stock of the asset, which is called the "flow" of investment. The stock is the amount on hand, which can be measured only at a specified point in time, such as at the end of the year ("taking inventory"), whereas the flow of investment can only be measured over a period of time. By definition, the stock on hand at the end of the period is the amount of stock on hand at the beginning of the year *plus* net additions (or net investment). Net investment is defined as the total new stock purchased or put in place (which is gross investment) *less* economic depreciation. Economic depreciation is the actual physical wear and tear of the capital good during the time period, as opposed to accounting depreciation, which is the recorded depreciation on the accounting books for tax and reporting purposes. (The two types of depreciation are not likely to be the same dollar amount.)

Dynamic models that attempt to portray the adjustment to equilibrium are sometimes called stock-flow models. The term "putty-clay" has been used for such models to describe the fact that, for all practical purposes, new machinery can take almost any shape desired, like putty, but, once it is put in place as part of the stock, its form is permanent, like clay.

One of the most important reasons for a separate study of dynamic models is that the level of the stock of machinery on hand, e.g., a year from now, depends overwhelmingly on the amount of machinery in existence today, because most of the machinery on hand a year from now is also on hand today. Empirically, then, the intertemporal relationships of dynamic models are very important in "explaining" (in an empirical sense) the movements of stock variables. These relationships require special specifications of the regression equation.

Dynamic models have been applied to financial as well as to physical assets. The same logic applies although the speed of adjustment to similar shocks may be faster with financial assets. Dynamic models have even been applied to interest rates and other price variables under the assumption that such prices are "sticky" for institutional reasons. But prices normally adjust rather quickly, so dynamic models are usually inappropriate in studying their behavior.

Some of the more common dynamic models that are widely used in applied regression analysis are now presented. The reader should understand each one so that, when a particular situation arises in practice, the appropriate model can be selected and used in the applied research.

2.4.1 The Stock Adjustment Model

One of the most common types of dynamic models, and perhaps one of the more important ones because of its general applicability to a variety of situations, is motivated by the stock adjustment, or partial adjustment model. This model assumes that the *desired* level on some stock, say a particular capital good or some balance sheet item, Y^*, is determined on the basis of the values of one or more regressors, such as prices and interest rates:

$$Y_t^* = \beta_0 + \beta_1 X_{t1} + \beta_2 X_{t2} + \cdots + \beta_K X_{tK} + \epsilon_t \qquad (2.4.1)$$

This is a behavioral equation that describes the entrepreneurs' (or the households') process of determining the desired levels of Y. Without the disturbance term ϵ, the desired level of Y represents its static equilibrium level. Most often with stock items, such as machinery, there are costs involved in producing and delivering the item, and there are also costs in producing too many. In addition, there are often time lags involved, the amount of time between contemplating an order decision and putting the item in place. For these (and possibly other) reasons, an additional equation is specified that describes the dynamics of moving from one static equilibrium level to another.

For the stock adjustment model, the dynamic behavioral equation describes the attempt of the participants to narrow the gap between the actual and the desired levels of the stock. Because of the various costs involved, it is assumed that only a fraction of the gap can be adjusted in a single time period. Thus, the adjustment equation is written as:

$$Y_t - Y_{t-1} = \gamma(Y_t^* - Y_{t-1}) + \epsilon_{2t} \qquad (2.4.2)$$

where the stock is measured at the end of the period. In words, the actual change in the stock, on the left-hand side of the equation, is some positive proportion (γ) of the gap between the desired level of the stock (at time t) and the last-observed actual level (at time t-1), denoted as $(Y_t^* - Y_{t-1})$.

The parameter γ, which measures the *speed of adjustment*, is a positive fraction. A rapid adjustment is likely where the transactions costs and lag time involved in moving from one equilibrium level to another are low, and a slow adjustment is likely where these costs and lag time are high. For plant and heavy equipment and for housing, the transactions costs and lag time are likely to be high, so slow adjustment is expected, and γ should be close to zero; but for easily reproducible stock items with low per-unit costs, such as hand calculators, these costs (and usually the lag time) are low, so the adjustment is rapid, and γ should be close to unity. In fact, in the latter case, the stock adjustment equation is probably unnecessary, and the desired level of the stock, Y_t^*, may be nearly equal to the actual, observed level of the stock, Y_t. Thus, equation 2.4.1 can be estimated directly without concern over the dynamics.

A value of γ greater than unity implies that the gap between desired and actual levels of the stock is systematically overshot, which is implausible. A negative value of γ implies that the actual stock changes in the *opposite* direction from the gap between the desired and the beginning level of the stock, which also is implausible. Thus, γ should be between zero and unity (and it can equal unity but not zero because the latter implies that no adjustment takes place).[20] These considerations lead to the expectation that the estimated value of γ lies between zero and unity. If these expec-

---

[20] The model here is in terms of the *net* change in the level of a stock, or *net* investment as it is called. Some investment is required to maintain the stock, and this is called depreciation, or "economic depreciation." Thus, for γ to lie between zero and unity requires the assumption that the expenditures to maintain the capital equipment will be made. Some stock adjustment models add another term to the right-hand side of equation 2.4.2, namely the depreciation rate times Y_{t-1}, to represent this demand component for investment. Then the coefficient of adjustment, γ, is assured of being in the range zero to unity.

tations are not fulfilled by the regression estimates, the researcher should reexamine the model and possibly take another approach.

To reiterate, the stock adjustment model consists of two behavioral equations. The first is a type of static equilibrium statement of, for example, the demand for a stock item. The second describes the process of dynamic adjustment from one static equilibrium level to another.

Since the desired level Y^* cannot be observed, the estimation of the coefficients of each of the two equations is accomplished by a single, combined estimating equation derived as follows. Equation 2.4.2 may be written as:

$$\Delta Y_t = \gamma Y_t^* - \gamma Y_{t-1} + \epsilon_{2t}$$

where

$$\Delta Y_t = Y_t - Y_{t-1}$$

The right-hand side of equation 2.4.1 is then substituted for Y^*, which yields

$$\Delta Y_t = \gamma \beta_0 + \gamma \beta_1 X_{t1} + \cdots + \gamma \beta_K X_{tK} - \gamma Y_{t-1} + \epsilon_{3t} \qquad (2.4.3)$$

where

$$\epsilon_{3t} = \epsilon_{2t} + \gamma \epsilon_t$$

This equation can be estimated because all the variables are observable. The coefficient of the lagged stock variable is interpreted directly as (-1) times the coefficient of adjustment, γ. To show that equation 2.4.3 can be interpreted as a linear regression model, it may be written (and estimated) as:

$$\Delta Y_t = \delta_0 + \delta_1 X_{t1} + \cdots + \delta_K X_{tK} + \delta_{K+1} Y_{t-1} + \epsilon_{3t} \qquad (2.4.4)$$

where the newly labeled regression coefficients are

$$\delta_k = \gamma \beta_k \qquad \text{for } k = 0, 1, 2, \ldots, K$$
$$\delta_{K+1} = -\gamma$$

An estimate of the β_k can be obtained as $-\hat{\delta}_k / \hat{\delta}_{K+1}$, but usually the researcher does not need these separate estimates of the β_k's and can use 2.4.4 directly.

The coefficient of adjustment is of particular interest in that it describes the dynamic properties of the equation, as discussed above. On the basis of the theoretical adjustment equation, $0 < \gamma \leq 1$, there is postulated at least some nonzero adjustment, and overadjustment is not allowed. Thus, from the estimated equation one would insist that $-1 \leq \hat{\delta}_{K+1} < 0$. An estimate of δ_{K+1} near zero implies a very slow adjustment to desired levels, and an estimate of δ_{K+1} (or $-\gamma$) near minus one implies almost complete adjustment in a single period, which suggests a relatively costless adjustment process.

Since $\Delta Y_t = Y_t - Y_{t-1}$, the estimating equation 2.4.4 can be written equivalently in stock form as:

$$Y_t = \gamma \beta_0 + \gamma \beta_1 X_{t1} + \cdots + \gamma \beta_K X_{tK} + (1 - \gamma) Y_{t-1} + \epsilon_{3t} \qquad (2.4.5)$$

The only difference is that the coefficient of Y_{t-1} in this case is between zero and unity instead of between zero and minus one. Since these are equivalent equations, there is no need to select between them. As discussed in Section 2.3.1 in a similar circumstance, one should expect a higher R^2 using the stock variable instead of the flow variable as the dependent variable (because (a) the residual sum of squares is the same for both—i.e., the equations are "explaining" the same deviations—and (b) the total sum of squares for Y_t is greater than that for $(Y_t - Y_{t-1})$—the stock variable is measured in larger units than is the flow variable). But a higher R^2 is of no value because equation 2.4.5 yields the same implicit estimates as equation 2.4.4. Which one is selected for estimation is purely arbitrary.

Another dynamic model, the *adaptive expectations* model, also ends up with the same type of estimating equation as the stock adjustment model. Instead of Y being unobservable, X is unobservable, as in:

$$Y_t = \beta_0 + \beta_1 X_t^* + \epsilon_t \qquad (2.4.6)$$

where, for example, Y is the demand for a good and X^* is the expected (normal, optimum, permanent, or equilibrium) price of the good. Now, the formation of the X^* variable is required instead of the Y^* variable of the stock adjustment model:

$$X_t^* - X_{t-1}^* = \alpha(X_t - X_{t-1}^*) \qquad (2.4.7)$$

That is, the new expected level of X_t^* is formed by closing the gap partially between the observed X_t and the previous level of X^*. Thus, $0 < \alpha \leq 1$, and α is called the coefficient of expectations. Equations 2.4.6 and 2.4.7 are utilized to obtain an equation of the form of equation 2.4.5.[21] Other regressors in equation 2.4.5 come from supplying them as regressors to equation 2.4.6.

Equation 2.4.5 is applied in a variety of circumstances, and Y is often not a stock variable but rather a flow variable or a price variable. In particular, the *form* of equation 2.4.5 should be noted: the regressors include all the determinants of the desired or equilibrium level of Y (i.e., the X's) along with the *lagged value* of the dependent variable, which is included to represent the dynamic process of the adjustment from one equilibrium level to another. As is shown in Section 2.4.3, the lagged value of the dependent variable is the key to the dynamic time-series properties of this model. Without it, as long as the regressors all refer to the current time period, the dynamics are no longer present. Often, researchers with justification specify equation 2.4.5 directly such as according to the stock adjustment or adaptive expectations models. They specify equation 2.4.5 directly because they want to incorporate the kind of dynamic process that it embodies (as shown in Section 2.4.3).

2.4.2 The Distributed Lag Model

The stock adjustment model was presented first because it is used very frequently and it embodies the general concepts of dynamic models. This section presents a more general approach to dynamic models, the general class of which includes the stock adjustment model. This more general class of dynamic models is used to justify several

---

[21] For a derivation, see for example, Jan Kmenta, *Elements of Econometrics* (New York: MacMillan, 1971), pp.474–76.

alternative approaches for the specification of an equation that can be used for estimation, just as the two equations in Section 2.4.1, one for the desired level of the stock and the other for the stock adjustment process, lead to a single, dynamic equation that is used for estimation.

In its simplest form, the general model postulates a particular regressor X as having long-lasting effects on the dependent variable, such as in the following equation:

$$Y_t = \alpha + \beta_0 X_t + \beta_1 X_{t-1} + \beta_2 X_{t-2} + \cdots + \beta_m X_{t-m} + \epsilon_t \qquad (2.4.8)$$

where m is some positive integer selected by the researcher.

An example, which is known generally as time-series forecasting, is one in which a future value of a variable is forecast solely on the basis of its current and lagged values. Thus, Y_t could be X_{t+1} (read as X in time $t+1$, which is X one period from "now," that is, from time t). For example, X could be the aggregate price level; the equation would then be attempting to explain the price level of the next period as a *distributed lag* of current and past price levels. The coefficients β_0, β_1, etc., show the relative (and absolute) weights of the various lagged values of X as they "explain" the future value of X. The term distributed lag means that the relative weights are apportioned, or distributed, among the variables in such a manner that some variables are more important than others in determining Y_t (or X_{t+1} in this instance). As a general rule of thumb, it is usually thought that the more recent experience is likely to be more relevant in determining Y_t than is the experience long ago, because the experience long ago has lost its relevancy to the current situation. Thus, β_0, β_1, and β_2 collectively—while β_1 might be greater than β_0—are generally expected to be greater than, say, β_{10}, β_{11}, and β_{12} (in absolute value).

Many researchers do not wish to estimate this type of equation directly and instead use some indirect procedures. They avoid direct estimation because (1) there may not be enough observations relative to the number of parameters that need to be estimated, i.e., the degrees of freedom problem; or (2) the values of X and its lagged values may be collinear, which implies that the individual effect of any one of them, such as X_{t-j}, on the dependent variable could not be reliably estimated, i.e., the problem of multicollinearity.

Econometricians should reconsider their reluctance to estimate this equation directly. One should use one's priors to reduce the number of lagged terms as much as possible (that is, reduce the length of the lag, m), so that both problems are at least ameliorated. The fewer the number of regressors, the fewer the number of parameters to estimate and the fewer the variables that are collinear. In addition, the types of indirect estimation techniques usually employed impose a different set of priors, the validity of which may be questioned. This point is stressed in the presentation of these alternative estimating equations. Several of the more popular methods of estimating the distributed lag model indirectly instead of directly are described in Section 2.4.2 (a) and (b).

2.4.2(a)   Koyck (or Geometric) Lag.   One of the most common assumptions is that the effect of X diminishes in a geometric fashion the longer the lag is. This can be written as:

$$\beta_i = \beta_0 \, \lambda^i \qquad i = 1, 2, \ldots \qquad\qquad (2.4.9)$$

where

$$0 \leqslant \lambda < 1.$$

The effect of the assumption may be seen by substituting equation 2.4.9 for each slope coefficient in equation 2.4.8. The distributed lag equation becomes:

$$Y_t = \alpha + \beta_0 X_t + \beta_0 \lambda X_{t-1} + \beta_0 \lambda^2 X_{t-2} + \beta_0 \lambda^3 X_{t-3} + \cdots + \epsilon_t \qquad (2.4.10)$$

To make the point, this equation may be written as:

$$Y_t = \alpha + \beta_0 \, (X_t + \lambda X_{t-1} + \lambda^2 X_{t-2} + \cdots) + \epsilon_t \qquad\qquad (2.4.11)$$

Since it is assumed that λ is some positive fraction, each successive lagged term is weighted less than the previous term by that fraction λ. For example, if $\lambda = 0.2$, then equation 2.4.11 becomes

$$Y_t = \gamma + \beta_0 \, (X_t + 0.2X_{t-1} + 0.04X_{t-2} + 0.008X_{t-3} + \cdots) + \epsilon_t \qquad (2.4.12)$$

Thus, it is seen that successive lagged values have relatively less weight in determining the value of Y_t and that the distributed lag is of a particular shape. Figure 2.4.1 shows alternative relative weighting schemes based on different values of λ; notice that β_0 multiplies all the X's, so the relative weights are determined by the coefficients of the X_{t-j}'s in the parentheses of equation 2.4.11, starting with a relative coefficient of unity for X_t.

Researchers utilizing this approach estimate the magnitude of λ and then assess the estimate against their priors depending, on other things, whether the data employed were of a quarterly or an annual frequency. But equation 2.4.11 cannot be estimated directly (or easily) because of too many regressors (although the X terms beyond some point could be deleted for all practical purposes), and because of the restrictions

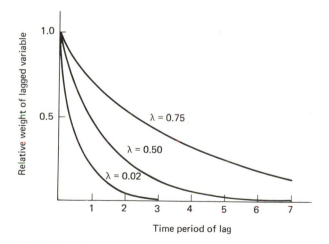

FIGURE 2.4.1   Geometric Weighting Schemes for Various λ's

imposed on the coefficients by equation 2.4.9. The following manipulations of this equation are used to derive an equation that is usually estimated. Multiply both sides of equation 2.4.11 by λ and lag it once (i.e., substitute $t-1$ for t in every instance that it appears in equation 2.4.11). The following equivalent equation is derived:

$$\lambda Y_{t-1} = \lambda\alpha + \beta_0(\lambda X_{t-1} + \lambda^2 X_{t-2} + \cdots) + \lambda\epsilon_{t-1} \qquad (2.4.13)$$

Subtract this from equation 2.4.11 to yield the equivalent equation:

$$Y_t - \lambda Y_{t-1} = \alpha(1-\lambda) + \beta_0 X_t + \epsilon_t - \lambda\epsilon_{t-1} \qquad (2.4.14)$$

which may be rewritten as

$$Y_t = \alpha' + \beta_0 X_t + \lambda Y_{t-1} + \eta_t \qquad (2.4.15)$$

where

$$\eta_t = \epsilon_t - \lambda\epsilon_{t-1}$$

and

$$\alpha' = \alpha(1-\lambda)$$

This, then, becomes the estimating equation. It appears simpler in form, and the two parameters β_0 and λ can be estimated directly. But it also contains a problem. As is discussed in Chapter 9, in order to apply a single-equation estimating technique to any equation, all regressors should be independent of the error term. Since Y_t and ϵ_t are directly correlated (because movements in Y correspond to movements in ϵ), Y_{t-1} and ϵ_{t-1} are correlated too. Thus, Y_{t-1} and η_t are correlated because η_t contains ϵ_{t-1}. Thus, application of a single-equation estimating technique suffers from what is known as simultaneous equations bias. So the researcher may be better off estimating the distributed lag model directly. (In this instance, even though equations 2.4.8 and 2.4.15 appear to be mathematically equivalent, they are not. The assumption of equation 2.4.9 was used in deriving the latter, thus restricting the coefficients. Also, the error terms are different, and equation 2.4.8 assumes a finite length of lag, whereas equation 2.4.15 assumes an infinite lag structure.)

The stock adjustment model is a type of Koyck distributed lag model in which the lag effects decrease in geometric fashion. The Koyck equation 2.4.15 is equivalent in form to the stock adjustment equation 2.4.5, except for the other regressors of equation 2.4.5. These other regressors could be added to equation 2.4.8 or to equation 2.4.15 directly, so the two approaches can be used to provide the same estimating equations. The justification is up to the researcher for the commonly used estimating equation 2.4.15. The usual choices are the stock adjustment, adaptive expectations, or the Koyck lag model.

2.4.2(b)   Almon, or Polynomial Distributed Lag (PDL).   A technique that has been very common since the mid-1960's is the PDL. It also involves the imposition of priors on the shape of the distributed lag coefficients, but of a different form than those imposed by the Koyck lag. In particular, the PDL assumes that the lag coefficients are shaped in the form of a polynomial:

$$\beta_k = \sum_{j=0}^{p} \lambda_j k^j = \lambda_0 + \lambda_1 k + \lambda_2 k^2 + \cdots + \lambda_p k^p \qquad k = 0, 1, \ldots, m \qquad (2.4.16)$$

That is, instead of the steadily declining weights on the lagged exogenous variable implied by the geometric distributed lag, the PDL allows a freer form for the weights, in the general shape of a polynomial. The polynomial is in k, the particular lag being considered, with k going from zero (no lag) to m, the maximum lag originally specified by the researcher in the general distributed lag model, equation 2.4.8. The parameter p, also supplied by the researcher, is called the degree of the polynomial. Essentially, the procedure involves fitting a polynomial of degree p to $m+1$ observations (the $m+1$ coefficients to estimate). For example, suppose the lag portion of the general distributed lag model were $\beta_0 X_t + \beta_1 X_{t-1} + \beta_2 X_{t-2}$, in which case $m = 2$. There are three parameters to estimate, β_0, β_1, and β_2. These are the three "observations" on which a polynomial is to be fit. At most, a second-degree polynomial ($p=2$) can be used to estimate three points; so, at most, the PDL is specified as $\beta_k = \lambda_0 + \lambda_1 k + \lambda_2 k^2$ for k equal to 0, 1, and 2. For this (maximum) formulation, there are also three λ parameters to estimate, λ_0, λ_1, and λ_2; therefore, enforcing this kind of PDL results in exactly the same estimates as the direct estimation of the distributed lag equation. The power of the PDL—and simultaneously its limitations—comes because the form of the PDL usually selected conserves on the number of estimates that are required by forcing constraints on the PDL estimation. One such constraint would be to force the degree of the polynomial to be less than m, such as $p = 1$, in which case $\beta_k = \lambda_0 + \lambda_1 k$ and there are only two λ's to estimate, λ_0 and λ_1, instead of three β's. How the procedure does the estimation is of no particular concern to regression users. What is important is to understand *what* it does.

Figure 2.4.2 shows several possible patterns for the β's, from the direct estimation of the distributed lag and from two hypothesized PDL's. The reason the PDL gives a different pattern than direct estimation of the distributed lag (here it is assumed that there are only the current values and four lagged values of the exogenous variable X) is that the number of coefficients estimated in the PDL is less than the number of

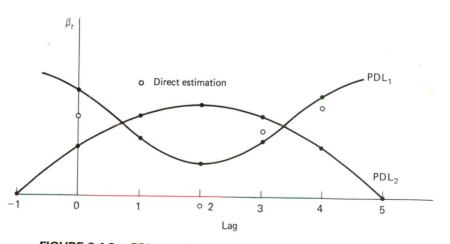

FIGURE 2.4.2   PDL and Direct Estimation of a Distributed Lag

coefficients estimated directly: for the PDL there are $p + 1$ λ's to estimate, and for the direct estimation there are $m + 1$ β's to estimate. The researcher selects the values for p and m. As noted above, if p is set equal to m, then the two approaches will yield the same set of β's; the two approaches are then mathematically equivalent. Note that p cannot be set greater than m; that would be fitting a pth degree polynomial to less than $p + 1$ points. Usually, p is set less than m, saving on the number of parameters to be estimated, i.e., saving on degrees of freedom.

The researcher can also impose priors (in the form of constraints) on the shape of the coefficient lag structure: PDL_1 in Figure 2.4.2 may be a third-degree polynomial, whereas PDL_2 may be a second-degree polynomial. Also, the researcher can impose the condition that in period -1—the period before any effect of X on Y occurs—or in period $m + 1$ (period 5 here), or both, the β's are zero (as for PDL_2). This, in essence, supplies additional points for estimation purposes beyond the $m + 1$ points assumed above. There is usually intuitive appeal that β_{m+1} is zero (called the "far" constraint) because the effect of X on Y is suspected to go to zero after the lag period specified by m is over.

However, what is wrong with this technique is that selection of p and the imposition of these "zero constraints" at either the near or far end of the lag are rather arbitrary. Thus, the resulting PDL estimates have an element of arbitrariness to them. Using a PDL becomes tantamount to curve fitting for its own sake, a practice to be avoided, especially by the casual researcher. PDL's may be used, but only with "heavy" (i.e., deeply believed) priors and with caution. Unfortunately, such heavy priors are rarely given in the literature when the PDL is used. Readers can only infer that the researchers estimated many different PDL equations until they found, *likely by chance*, the one that showed what they wanted the estimated equation to show. This can hardly be called scientific research; it is more the imposition of the researcher's priors on the data.

2.4.3 Time Profiles, or Signature of the Lag

The most important theoretical consideration with dynamic models prior to estimation is the "time profile" of the equation, in which the researcher systematically investigates the period-by-period and overall responses to exogenous shocks. The results of such an investigation should at least be summarized in the researcher's documentation of all dynamic models, and the estimated equation should be checked for conformity to the hypothesized time profile. (Readers with some familiarity with dynamic models may want to skip to the general model, Section 2.4.3(c). The intervening material explains how dynamic models work from the ground up.)

An important aspect of dynamic models is the long-term, static equilibrium impacts of changing exogenous variables. The long-run impacts are of interest in themselves, and the cumulative period-by-period effects are usually stated as a percentage of the long-term effect, as a standardized way of describing the time profile. How to investigate the long-run effects is shown in this section.

Two different dynamic models are used here in Sections 2.4.3(a) and (b) to demonstrate the standardized approach toward analyzing the time profile of dynamic models involving both the long- and short-run effects. For both these models, a

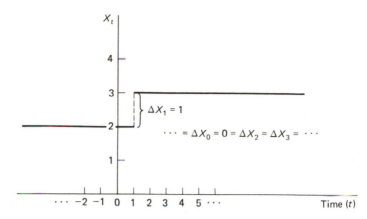

FIGURE 2.4.3 Standardized (Unit) Change in X_t at Time $t = 1$ for an Analysis of the Time Profile of Y_t

standardized method is used to "shock" them, thus starting the dynamic process of adjustment. Figure 2.4.3 illustrates the time path of an exogenous regressor, X, for the standardized analysis. For all time periods prior to time $t = 1$, X_t is assumed to be constant at a given level (the specific value of which is not important). Notationally, before $t = 1$, the change in X_t is zero, or $\Delta X_t = 0$. (The Δ notation here means the change in X from period $t-1$ to t or $\Delta X_t = X_t - X_{t-1}$. It does not mean the partial differential operator of calculus as in the interpretation of the slope coefficients.)

In the standard procedure, at time $t = 1$, X_t is incremented by one unit. (The one unit is in terms of whatever the units of measurement of X are, such as dollars or bushels.) The use of a single unit of X simplifies the analysis. Thus, by assumption, $\Delta X_1 = 1$, where the subscript indicates the particular time period, i.e., $\Delta X_1 = X_1 - X_0$. After X_t rises to its new level (one unit higher), it is assumed to remain at that new level thereafter, to avoid complicating the analysis. Thus, ΔX_t for $t = 2, 3, \ldots$ is assumed to be zero. This type of change in X_t is called a once-and-for-all change in X_t.[22]

To illustrate the analysis, we use two dynamic models. The first one is the general distributed lag model, equation 2.4.8, except that X enters with only two lagged values. The second one is the other general type of distributed lag model, the one with a lagged value of the dependent variable as a regressor. After these two illustrations, a more general model combining both illustrations is presented.

2.4.3(a) First Illustration: X Lagged Twice.
For the first illustration, the equation is assumed to contain X lagged just twice:

$$Y_t = \alpha + \beta_0 X_t + \beta_1 X_{t-1} + \beta_2 X_{t-2} + \epsilon_t \qquad (2.4.17)$$

---

[22] There is another type of standardized analysis that increases X_t by one unit each and every period starting with $t = 1$. In essence, this approach is equivalent to the one suggested here, but it is repeated an infinite number of times, for $t = 2, 3, 4, \ldots$.

This equation is written in terms of *changes* in the variables since such changes are the *raison d'etre* of dynamic models. The following manipulations derive the desired "change" equation.

Equation 2.4.17 holds for all time periods t, so substituting $t-1$ for t yields the equivalent equation:

$$Y_{t-1} = \alpha + \beta_0 X_{t-1} + \beta_1 X_{t-2} + \beta_2 X_{t-3} + \epsilon_{t-1} \qquad (2.4.18)$$

Subtracting equation 2.4.18 from equation 2.4.17 yields the equivalent equation:

$$\dot{Y}_t - Y_{t-1} = \beta_0(X_t - X_{t-1}) + \beta_1(X_{t-1} - X_{t-2}) + \beta_3(X_{t-2} - X_{t-3}) + \epsilon_t - \epsilon_{t-1} \qquad (2.4.19)$$

Finally, this equation may be written simply as:

$$\Delta Y_t = \beta_0 \Delta X_t + \beta_1 \Delta X_{t-1} + \beta_2 \Delta X_{t-2} + \Delta \epsilon_t \qquad (2.4.20)$$

Notice that the constant term α has dropped out of the first-difference equation 2.4.20. That is, the constant term is unimportant when it comes to analyzing changes in Y_t emanating from changes in X.

Period-by-Period Standard Analysis. Now to the standardized analysis. The assumption is that the only thing that causes Y_t to change is a once-and-for-all change in X_t at time $t = 1$. Thus, the error term is assumed to be identically zero for this analysis, so $\Delta \epsilon_t$ also equals zero for all time periods. The regressor X_t changes as was shown in Figure 2.4.3. Figure 2.4.4 shows how Y_t changes over time according to equation 2.4.20, given the specific changes in X_t and the specific values for purposes of illustration of

$$\beta_0 = 3, \quad \beta_1 = 2, \quad \text{and} \quad \beta_2 = -3$$

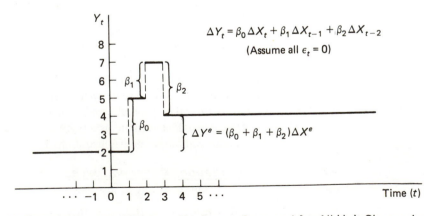

FIGURE 2.4.4 Time Profile of Y_t from a Once-and-for-All Unit Change in X_t:

$$Y_t = \alpha + \beta_0 X_t + \beta_1 X_{t-1} + \beta_2 X_{t-2} + \epsilon_t$$

(i.e., the Signature of the Distributed Lag)

Prior to $t = 1$, Y_t is assumed to be in static equilibrium at some level determined by the equilibrium level of X (shown in Figure 2.4.3). For example, according to the general equation 2.4.17, if $\alpha = -2$ and the equilibrium value of X_t is 2 before $t = 1$ (denoted as $X^e = 2$), then the equilibrium value of Y_t before $t = 1$ is

$$Y^e = -2 + 3(2) + 2(2) - 3(2) = 2.$$

Note that, in equilibrium, $X_t = X_{t-1} = X_{t-2} = X^e$.

(Also note that e denotes equilibrium values, not natural logarithms.) For the dynamic analysis, the specific level of Y prior to the change in X is of no particular importance. Thus, the analysis now focuses on the difference equation 2.4.20. Given the unit change in X_1, X_t rises from 2 to 3 and remains there. The effect on Y_t is shown by substituting $t = 1$ in equation 2.4.20. It becomes, at $t = 1$:

$$\Delta Y_1 = \beta_0 \Delta X_1 + \beta_1 \Delta X_0 + \beta_2 \Delta X_{-1} \tag{2.4.21}$$

(Again, and throughout the analysis, all ϵ_t terms are assumed to be zero.) Since X_t did not change prior to $t = 1$, ΔX_0 and ΔX_{-1} are both zero, and it is assumed that $\Delta X_1 = 1$ to standardize the analysis; ΔY_1 becomes:

$$\beta_0(1) + \beta_1(0) + \beta_2(0) = \beta_0$$

If $\beta_0 = 3$, Y_1 is shown in Figure 2.4.4 to increase over its initial equilibrium level of 2 to a new level in $t = 1$ of 5.

For time $t = 2$, substitute $t = 2$ in equation 2.4.20 to obtain:

$$\Delta Y_2 = \beta_0 \Delta X_2 + \beta_1 \Delta X_1 + \beta_2 \Delta X_0 \tag{2.4.22}$$

Since it is assumed that X_t changes only at $t = 1$, $\Delta X_2 = 0$, $\Delta X_0 = 0$, and, as before, $\Delta X_1 = 1$. Thus, ΔY_2 is evaluated as:

$$\Delta Y_2 = \beta_0(0) + \beta_1(1) + \beta_2(0) = \beta_1$$

Given $\beta_1 = 2$, the level of Y_2 is shown in Figure 2.4.4 to be 2 more than Y_1, or $Y_2 = 7$. Similarly, for time $t = 3$:

$$\Delta Y_3 = \beta_0 \Delta X_3 + \beta_1 \Delta X_2 + \beta_2 \Delta X_1 = \beta_0(0) + \beta_1(0) + \beta_2(1) = \beta_2 \tag{2.4.23}$$

In this example, β_2 is negative, -3, so $\Delta Y_3 = -3$, and the value of Y_3 is 3 less than Y_2, or $7-3 = 4$.

At $t = 4$,

$$\Delta Y_4 = \beta_0 \Delta X_4 + \beta_1 \Delta X_3 + \beta_2 \Delta X_2$$

The once-and-for-all change ΔX_1 has dropped out of the equation; thus, $\Delta Y_4 = 0$, and all subsequent values of $\Delta Y_t = 0$. No further effects on Y occur after $t = 3$ for the particular distributed lag model used for this illustration. The entire time path of Y_t shown in Figure 2.4.4 is called the standardized time profile of Y_t; it is also called the signature of the distributed lag.

The Long-Run Effect. Since X changed just once, in period 1, the change in X_1 also represents the equilibrium change in X, as X went from equilibrium level 2 to 3. This is denoted as ΔX^e. In Figure 2.4.4, Y went from an initial equilibrium level of 2 to a final equilibrium level of 4 for a "long-run" change of 2. The new level is just the cumulative result of the three changes in Y caused by the once-and-for-all change in X. The new equilibrium level of Y may be determined directly from equation 2.4.20 by setting all changes in X to the equilibrium change in X, or

$$\Delta Y^e = \beta_0 \Delta X^e + \beta_1 \Delta X^e + \beta_2 \Delta X^e = (\beta_0 + \beta_1 + \beta_2) \, \Delta X^e$$

Since $\Delta X^e = 1$, the new equilibrium level of Y is:

$$\beta_0 + \beta_1 + \beta_2 = 3 + 2 - 3 = 2$$

over the initial equilibrium level.

In this illustration, the two essential elements of a dynamic model have been shown: (1) the process of adjustment—the values Y_1, Y_2, and Y_3 as compared to Y_0 and as compared to the total equilibrium change—and (2) the total equilibrium effect of a once-and-for-all change in X—the value of Y_3 as compared to Y_0.

2.4.3(b)   Second Illustration: Lagged Dependent Variable.   The second illustration also focuses on these two essential elements of analysis for dynamic models. The second illustrative dynamic model is:

$$Y_t = \alpha + \beta X_t + \gamma Y_{t-1} + \epsilon_t \tag{2.4.24}$$

This is of the same form as equation 2.4.5, which was derived from the stock adjustment model, except here there is only one exogenous regressor, X. This equation is also the same as the Koyck distributed lag model equation 2.4.15. Thus, this illustration has wide applicability. As in the first illustration, the first-difference equation, assuming all $\epsilon_t = 0$, is:

$$\Delta Y_t = \beta \Delta X_t + \gamma \Delta Y_{t-1} \tag{2.4.25}$$

Period-by-Period Standard Analysis.   The standard once-and-for-all change in X (as shown in Figure 2.4.3) is still assumed. Assume that Y is in equilibrium before time $t = 1$, as before, and that the analysis starts at time $t = 1$. Substitute 1 for t in equation 2.4.25:

$$\Delta Y_1 = \beta \Delta X_1 + \gamma \Delta Y_0 \tag{2.4.26}$$

Since $\Delta Y_0 = 0$ (because we start from the analysis from equilibrium) and $\Delta X_1 = 1$:

$$\Delta Y_1 = \beta(1) + \gamma(0) = \beta$$

For the illustration, assume $Y_0 = 2.0$ and $\beta = 1$. Then as shown in Figure 2.4.5:

$$\Delta Y_1 = \beta \Delta X_1 = (1)(1) = 1$$

For $t = 2$, equation 2.4.25 becomes

$$\Delta Y_2 = \beta \Delta X_2 + \gamma \Delta Y_1 \tag{2.4.27}$$

Now ΔX_2 is zero, and the effect of X on Y comes only through the lagged term in equation 2.4.24. That is, ΔY_1 was found to be β; this value now enters the right-hand side of equation 2.4.27 as a determinant of ΔY_2. So:

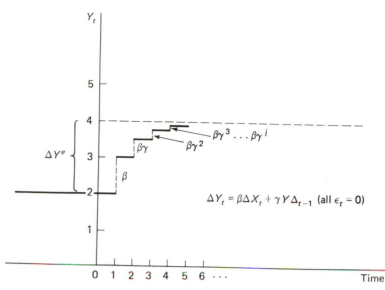

FIGURE 2.4.5 Time Profile of Y_t from a Once-and-for-All Unit Change in X_t: $Y_t = \alpha + \beta X_t + \gamma Y_{t-1} + \epsilon_t$

$$\Delta Y_2 = \beta(0) + \gamma(\beta) = \gamma\beta$$

Given $\gamma = 0.5$ and $\beta = 1$:

$$\Delta Y_2 = (0.5)\,(1.0) = 0.5$$

As shown in Figure 2.4.5, the value of Y increases from 3 to 3.5 in period 2.

For time $t = 3$, equation 2.4.25 becomes:

$$\Delta Y_3 = \beta \Delta X_3 + \gamma \Delta Y_2 \qquad (2.4.28)$$

Since $\Delta X_3 = 0$ and ΔY_2 was just found to be $\gamma\beta$, $\Delta Y_3 = \beta(0) + \gamma(\gamma\beta) = \gamma^2\beta$, or 0.25. For $t = 4$, $\Delta Y_4 = \gamma^3\beta = 0.125$; and $\Delta Y_5 = \gamma^4\beta = 0.0625$ and so on. The increments in Y become smaller and smaller, as long as γ is positive but less than unity. If γ is negative, then the increments of Y are successively of opposite sign, although they too become smaller in absolute value. If γ is greater than unity in absolute value, the increments become larger in absolute value. Thus, it is ordinarily assumed that $-1 < \gamma < 1$, so that a new equilibrium value exists. (This result is called a "stable solution.") Note that the stock adjustment and Koyck lag models imposed the more restrictive condition that $0 \leqslant \gamma < 1$.

The Long-Run Effect. It turns out that the equilibrium value of Y is 4 in this illustration and that the equilibrium value of the change in Y is $\Delta Y^e = 2$. This is shown below for a more general model. But note that Y_t never actually reaches 4 because, for each successive period, the distance between Y_t and Y^e is halved (the value of γ) to obtain the value of Y_{t+1}. In the extreme (or limit), as t approaches infinity, Y_t approaches Y^e, i.e., Y_t gets minutely close to Y^e.

2.4.3(c)   A General Model.   A more general dynamic model is:

$$Y_t = \beta_0 + \beta_1 X_t + \beta_2 X_{t-1} + \gamma_1 Y_{t-1} + \gamma_2 Y_{t-2} + \epsilon_t \qquad (2.4.29)$$

This equation is fairly general in the sense that it includes an exogenous variable (X) lagged once and the dependent variable Y lagged twice. Fewer lags, such as in the stock adjustment model, are analyzed by setting one or more of the coefficients, such as β_2 or γ_2, equal to zero. (Some readers may recognize this as a second-order difference equation. In fact, the following procedure could be replaced by an analysis of the path to equilibrium using the differencing calculus.)

The Long-Run Effect.   First, the long-run, static equilibrium model implied by equation 2.4.29 will be derived and discussed, and then the period-by-period dynamics will be examined. A general procedure for finding the long-run, equilibrium solution value of Y to a change in the long run, equilibrium value of an exogenous variable is to let all variables take on their long-run equilibrium solution values, set the error term to zero, and then shock the equilibrium value of any one of the exogenous variables by one unit and solve for the resulting change in the equilibrium value of Y. Thus, the first step is to let:

$$Y_t = Y_{t-1} = Y_{t-2} = Y^e,$$

$$X_t = X_{t-1} = X^e;$$

where Y^e denotes the equilibrium value of Y, and X^e equals the equilibrium value of X. Also, in equilibrium the error term is assumed to be zero. Enforcing these constraints follows from the definition of an equilibrium: no variable has a tendency to change. Make these substititions (and gather coefficients of X^e and Y^e), and equation 2.4.29 becomes:

$$Y^e = \beta_0 + (\beta_1 + \beta_2)X^e + (\gamma_1 + \gamma_2)Y^e \qquad (2.4.30)$$

Solve for Y^e:

$$Y^e = \frac{\beta_0}{1 - (\gamma_1 - \gamma_2)} + \left[\frac{(\beta_1 + \beta_2)}{1 - (\gamma_1 + \gamma_2)} \right] X^e \qquad (2.4.31)$$

Since the entire term in brackets is interpreted as a single coefficient of X^e in an equation linear in X^e, the long-run change in Y^e to a unit change in X^e is:

$$\frac{\Delta Y^e}{\Delta X^e} = \frac{(\beta_1 + \beta_2)}{1 - (\gamma_1 + \gamma_2)} \qquad (2.4.32)$$

(Of course, for this solution to be finite, $(\gamma_1 + \gamma_2)$ must not equal unity. Additional conditions are explained in footnote 23.)

Numeric Example.   A numeric example of this procedure is as follows. Suppose one had estimated the equation as:

$$Y_t = 3.5 + 0.8X_t + 0.6Y_{t-1} + 0.2Y_{t-2} + e_t \qquad (2.4.33)$$

(Notice that the estimate for β_2 is zero.) According to equation 2.4.32, the long-run static equilibrium response in Y to a once-and-for-all unit change in X is:

$$\frac{(0.8 + 0)}{1 - (0.6 + 0.2)} = \frac{0.8}{0.2} = 4.0$$

This long-run response may be stated as an elasticity, usually evaluated at the sample means: 4.0 times $(\overline{X}/\overline{Y})$. (The researcher should tell the reader that the elasticity was computed at the sample means.)

The Standard Time Profile.   Now the dynamic profile, or time profile, of the equation is investigated, and for illustrative purposes the estimated equation 2.4.33 is employed. For analysis, the equation can be written equivalently in first-difference form:

$$\Delta Y_t = 0.8\Delta X_t + 0.6\Delta Y_{t-1} + 0.2\Delta Y_{t-2} + \Delta e_t \qquad (2.4.34)$$

The method of deriving this equation was illustrated in deriving a similar equation in Section 2.4.3(a), equation 2.4.20. Notice that the constant term cancelled out in the operation. The focus on changes in the variables is appropriate because the dynamic analysis is concerned with the movements in variables from one period to the next.

To reiterate the points developed in the above illustrations, researchers normally use the standardized approach to examine the dynamic properties of such equations. It is assumed initially that the variables are in a state of static equilibrium, with no tendency to change. Thus, to start the analysis, all the first differences—the changes in the variables—are assumed to be zero. Another assumption is employed in order to focus on the deterministic portion of the equation: the error term and, in equation 2.4.34, the residual are assumed to be zero throughout the analysis.

The standard analysis also assumes that one of the exogenous variables (or the constant term) changes once-and-for-all by one unit. That is, X increases by one unit to a new level and remains at that new level throughout the remaining analysis. This "shock" starts the dynamic properties of the model in motion. The change in X is assumed to take place in the first period, so ΔX_t is then unity; its value is zero thereafter. (And ΔX_{t-1} in the original model is thus zero the first period—since $\Delta X_t = 0$ prior to $t = 1$, under the assumption of equilibrium—unity in the second period, and zero thereafter.)

Table 2.4.1 demonstrates the standard analysis of our assumed equation. In period 0, prior to the shock, all variables are assumed to be in equilibrium, so their first differences are zero. In the first period, $\Delta X_t = 1$, described as the "initial shock" to the dynamic system. After period 1, there are no new shocks, so $\Delta X_t = 0$, but $\Delta X_{t-1} = 1$ for period 2, based on the initial (period 1) shock.

Thus, the columns labeled "exogenous variables" can be filled out before examining the dynamic process. The remaining columns, however, can be completed only as the period-by-period responses of the dependent, or endogenous, variable ΔY_t are evaluated. In this illustration, there are two "lagged endogenous variable" terms, ΔY_{t-1} and ΔY_{t-2}. These become the major source of the dynamic properties of the model, since the effect on the dependent variable of ΔX_t is over after the first period. As shown for period 0, their initial values are zero under the assumption of starting from equilibrium.

The last three columns are the ones of eventual interest. From the model, period-by-period values of ΔY_t are computed (as done below), and these are accumulated to

TABLE 2.4.1

Time Profile for $Y_t = 3.5 + 0.8X_t + 0.6Y_{t-1} + 0.2Y_{t-2} + e_t$

Coefficients		Exogenous Variables		Lagged Endogenous Variables		Endogenous (Dependent) Variable		Cumulative ΔY_t	
									As a Percent of
		ΔX_t	ΔX_{t-1}	ΔY_{t-1}	ΔY_{t-2}			Period by-Period	Long-run Change
	Period	0.8	0	0.6	0.2	ΔY_t			
(Equilibrium)	0	0	0	0	0	0		0	0
(Initial Shock)	1	1	0	0	0	0.8		0.8	20%
(No New Shocks)	2	0	1	0.8	0	(.8) (.6)=.48		1.28	32%
	3	0	0	.48	0.8	(.48) (.6)+ (.8) (.2)=.448		1.73	43%
	4	0	0	.448	.48	(.448) (.6)+ (.48) (.2)=.365		2.09	52%
	5	0	0	.365	.448	(.365) (.6)+ (.448) (.2)=.309		2.40	60%
	6	0	0	.309	.365	(.309) (.6)+ (.365) (.2)=.258		2.66	66%
	.	.	.	.	.	.		.	.
	.	.	.	.	.	.		.	.
	.	.	.	.	.	.		.	.
	∞	0	0	0	0	0		4	100%

measure the cumulative change in Y from period 1 to any period of interest j. This cumulative change is compared to the total, long-run response of Y to a once-and-for-all change in X. The cumulative change in Y is 4 in the numeric example. Accumulating over an infinite number of periods, the cumulative change in Y will equal the long-run, static equilibrium change, in this case 4, assuming that it is possible for a new equilibrium level of Y to be reached. (There may be cycles for some models, for example, so that Y never converges to a given value.)

The changes in Y are obtained as follows. For period 1, $\Delta X_t = 1$, while the rest of the regressors equal zero. Thus:

$$\Delta Y_t = (0.8)(1) = 0.8$$

This magnitude becomes Y_{t-1} for period 2 ($\Delta Y_{t-1} = Y_{t-1} - Y_{t-2}$, which equals, for $t = 2$, $Y_1 - Y_0 = \Delta Y_1 = 0.8$). Since the coefficient of ΔX_{t-1} is zero, the only non-zero element on the right-hand side of the equation is:

$$0.6\Delta Y_{t-1} = (0.6)(0.8) = 0.48.$$

which is the value of ΔY_t for period $t = 2$. In period 3, $\Delta Y_{t-1} = 0.48$ (ΔY_{t-1} is, for $t = 3$, $\Delta Y_2 = 0.48$ from the third-to-the-last column); and $\Delta Y_{t-2} = 0.8$ (ΔY_{t-2} is, for

$t = 3$, $\Delta Y_1 = 0.8$). Thus, the change in Y in period 3 (ΔY_3) comes from two sources:

$$0.6 \; \Delta Y_{t-1} + 0.2 \; \Delta Y_{t-2} = (0.6)(.48) + (0.2)(0.8) = 0.448$$

Notice that the successive ΔY's are getting smaller and smaller. This is due to the particular values of the coefficients in this illustration. A good exercise for the student is to specify other values for the coefficients and to carry out the analysis. (This also makes a good test question.) Depending on the coefficient values, the successive values of ΔY can oscillate, dampen much faster or slower, or increase in magnitude. Discovering the type of time path is what this analysis is all about. The researcher must then assess the reasonableness of the particular time path, possibly respecifying the model if the estimated equation yields time paths that are ruled out by theory or one's priors.

The results of such an analysis are usually documented by reference to (1) the long-run impact of X on Y, in this case 4 units of Y per unit change in X; and (2) an adequate description of the dynamic process. For example, the documentation of the example equation of Table 2.4.1 could read as follows. "Twenty percent of the long-run effect of X on Y is achieved in the first quarter (or year or whatever), with Y slowly but steadily (without oscillation) approaching the equilibrium level. At the end of 4 quarters, 52 percent of the adjustment has taken place." Whenever the path to equilibrium is not smooth, a table should be included consisting of the last column of Table 2.4.1, supplied with a label such as: "Quarter-by-Quarter Cumulative Changes in Y in Response to a Once-and-for-All Change in X, Expressed as a Percentage of the Total Equilibrium Change in Y."

Notice that ΔY_t is never zero; there always is some "lingering over" of Y in ΔY_{t-1} and ΔY_{t-2}. But as time approaches infinity, ΔY_t approaches zero. The cumulative change in Y of 4 was taken from the long-run, static equilibrium analysis, as was the 100 percent adjustment shown in the table, since the analysis was carried out far enough to show that the ΔY's converge to zero as time approaches infinity. For equations showing oscillations in Y, the analysis may have to be carried out further, until the pattern is clearly discernible.[23]

2.5   Cross-Section Models

Quite often in applied regression analysis, the observations come from a cross section instead of a time series. In a cross section, the units of observations are from the same point in time and refer to individual economic entities, such as households or firms (or partial aggregates, such as observations pertaining to cities). Often, the model must be constructed differently depending on whether time-series or cross-section data are used. The primary difference is that cross-section data typically do not show

---

[23] Except for some initial, temporary pattern, the ultimate pattern of the standard adjustment process depends on the magnitudes of the coefficients of the lagged dependent variables, γ_1 and γ_2. The graph

(Continued on following page)

dynamic behavior. The emphasis of this section is on constructing and interpreting cross-section models. The usual (though not universally accepted) interpretation is that a model using cross-section data portrays long-run behavior.

In order to infer the conclusions of the previous paragraph, a housing model is developed using annual time-series data. Then the necessary modifications are made to the model in order to apply it to cross-section data: The model becomes a cross-sectional one. Then the cross-section model is likened to a time-series model applied to decennial data. Finally, the case is made for the long-run interpretation of the estimates from the cross-sectional model, followed by a warning against interpreting cross-sectional results in a dynamic sense. Mention of the indeterminate interpretation of pooled cross-section—time-series estimates and a summary conclude the section.

---

below shows the ultimate pattern of the solution in a qualitative way. The term cycles does not necessarily imply regularity; it only refers to oscillations or fluctuations of one kind or another in the sequential values of ΔY_t. Four general patterns are identified. Two are stable and two are explosive, implying that the values of ΔY_t eventually go to zero or to (plus or minus) infinity, respectively. Each of these is divided into two categories, depending on whether or not cycles are ultimately evident. The dynamic patterns specified do not apply to the borders or to where γ_1 or γ_2 are zero.

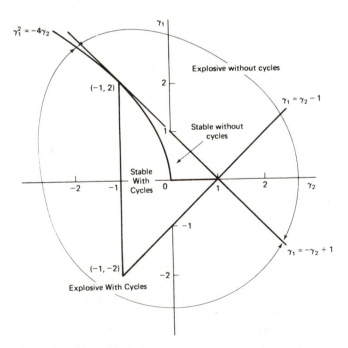

Qualitative Solution Patterns for

$$\Delta Y_t = \beta_1 \Delta X_t + \beta_2 \Delta X_{t-1} + \gamma_1 \Delta Y_{t-1} + \gamma_2 \Delta Y_{t-2}$$

Adapted from William J. Baumol, *Economic Dynamics,* 3rd ed. (New York: Macmillan, 1970) p. 221, Figure 32.

2.5.1 An Annual Time-Series Model

As an illustration, consider the following annual time-series model for the per-household demand for housing services in the United States:

$$\frac{Q_t}{HH_t} = f(\overset{-}{P_t}, \overset{+}{Y_t/HH_t}, \overset{+}{F_t}) \qquad (2.5.1)$$

where

Q	=	the demand for housing services (measured as the real, or deflated, market value of the stock of houses),
HH	=	number of households,
P	=	price per unit, such as an adaptation of Jorgenson's user cost [see Section 2.1.1(a)],
Y	=	aggregate permanent income [see Section 2.1.1(b)],
F	=	average family size, and
t	=	a subscript designating time.

Thus, the demand for housing services per household is stated as a function of the price per unit of the services, permanent income per household, and average family size.[24]

It is very likely that for annual time-series data, a dynamic model is appropriate. In particular, the researcher may specify a stock-adjustment model of Section 2.4.1, which implies that the lagged dependent variable is to be used as an additional regressor. The reason a dynamic model is appropriate is because the observed demand for housing services is very unlikely to be the desired level, and a partial adjustment toward the desired level would be observed for each data point.

2.5.2 A Cross-Section Model

Now consider applying the same model to cross-section data. Assume that the observations are taken for a recent census year and are taken for each sampled household in a particular city. This model should be specified differently from the annual time-series model. The first obvious respecification is changing the dependent variable to Q_i, the market value of the house of the ith household, instead of Q_t/HH_t. Notice that conceptually the "per household" interpretation of the time-series model is kept intact. Also notice that in the cross section it does not matter whether the house value is expressed in nominal or real terms because the value of the price deflator (a time-series concept) would be the same for all observations. Division of a variable by the same number will not alter the essential interpretation of the equation since it would

---

[24] Deflating by the number of households allows the equation to focus more sharply on the behavior of households. If HH_t were included as a regressor to help explain Q_t, there may be dimensional misspecification (see Section 2.2.2), and such a relationship would be more tautological than behavioral (because households are defined in terms of occupying housing units). Also note that it is possible to incorporate dynamic elements, for example, in a stock adjustment framework. For such an approach, Q/HH, lagged one year, may be included as a regressor. This possibility is emphasized below.

only change the scale of the estimated coefficient (see Section 1.3.5(b) on "Units of Measurement"). Family size is, of course, in per-household terms for the cross section, and so is annual income. (It may be appropriate to estimate the permanent income for households from an analysis of their past levels of income.)

The cross-section model corresponding to the time-series model (equation 2.5.1) may be written as:

$$Q_i = f(\overset{-}{P_i}, \overset{+}{Y_i}, \overset{+}{F_i}) \tag{2.5.2}$$

The subscript i referring to households replaces the denoter of time, t.

Assume that both the cross-section and the time-series models are in double-log form, so that the coefficients represent elasticities (see Section 2.2 on "Functional Form"). The point here is that *the respective estimated coefficients in the two models must usually be interpreted differently.*[25] For illustrative purposes, take the coefficient on income, the elasticity of the per household demand for housing services with respect to household permanent income. In the annual model, the lagged dependent variable should be included as a regressor to account for the dynamic nature of the data because the observations showed only the movement toward their equilibrium, desired values. In this case, the estimated income elasticity (the estimated coefficient of the logarithm of Y_t/HH_t) represents the *short-run* and not the long-run elasticity. The long-run estimate comes from dividing this coefficient by one minus the coefficient of the lagged dependent variable [as discussed in Section 2.4.3(c)].

2.5.3 A Decennial Time-Series Model

Contrast this specification and interpretation of the annual model to the case in which the time-series observations come from decennial censuses, say over a 200-year period. In this case, each observation may be thought of as representing (approximately) an equilibrium situation, so it is not appropriate to specify a dynamic model because the movement of the variables from one observation point to another over 10 years represents primarily the movements in desired, equilibrium levels of housing demand. These movements, due to changes in the desired level of demand, are much more important than the differences between the desired and actual levels of the housing stock. Thus, the lagged dependent variable need not be included as a regressor to account for the dynamics, and the estimated coefficient of the income variable represents the *long-run* income elasticity.

Theoretically, the two long-run estimates are comparable in that both have an indefinite time dimension. However, empirically, the long-run estimator from the annual model may be inferior to that from the decennial model. If the annual data covered only a 20-year period, the annual observations could not vary enough from

---

[25] Intriligator states that time-series and cross-section data are different and that estimates using each kind of data "are generally not comparable." See Michael D. Intriligator, *Econometric Models, Techniques, and Applications* (Englewood Cliffs, N.J.: Prentice-Hall, Inc., 1978), p. 63. He further states that "time-series data usually reflect short-run behavior while cross-section data reflect long-run behavior, in particular a greater adjustment to long-run equilibrium" (p. 64 n. 5). These are the notions developed in this section.

observation to observation to produce a reliable estimator of the long-run elasticity. (This is explained in Chapter 4 as a high variance of the estimator.) The data set, in other words, does not display enough alternative long-run situations to be used for predictions of various long-run conditions. (This does not preclude an annual data series of 200 observations from providing a reliable long-run estimate.) The decennial observations, on the other hand, constitute a rich data set because income and housing services consumed are very low and very high and family size shows considerable variation from observation to observation, in contrast with the variations in the annual data set. At the empirical level, the two estimates of the long-run elasticity are likely to differ, and more reliance should be placed on the estimate from the decennial data.

2.5.4 Cross-Section Estimates

The character of the cross-section data set is more like that of the decennial time-series data set than that of the annual time-series data set. That is, although each household is not likely to be in equilibrium at a given point in time, it is likely that various households consume less or more than their equilibrium level of housing services in a random fashion. Thus, comparing one household with the next in the cross-section data set, it is likely that the data will show the long-run equilibrium by individual households. If it can be assumed that various households represent random movements toward their desired levels of housing consumption, with some households consuming less than would be desired economically and others consuming more (because of the "lumpiness" or discrete nature of the home purchase or rental decision and the high transactions costs of moving and financing), then, with many high- and low-income households in the sample and with varying family sizes included, the data would appear to resemble the decennial time-series data. In fact, empirically, there may be more independent variations in the regressors and more movement in the dependent variable than in the decennial data set. Thus, more reliance or confidence can be placed on the estimators (as is discussed in Chapters 4 and 6).

The point is that the estimates from the cross-section data usually represent long-run equilibrium.[26] The over- and undershooting of desired equilibrium levels of each household is essentially random noise, a relatively small part of the variation in the movements of the dependent variable. Since regression analysis attempts to explain the movements in the dependent variable and those movements come primarily from vast differences in income and family size, most cross-section equations should be specified and interpreted as showing the long-run equilibrium behavior of the economic entities.[27]

---

[26] See especially Edwin Kuh, *Capital Stock Growth: A Micro-Econometric Approach* (North-Holland, 1963), pp. 182–88.

[27] In consumption functions for various commodities, Kuh and Meyer say that "while the cross-section would basically measure long-run effects, on the assumption that the majority of the observed families have enjoyed their present relative real income for some time, the same would not be true of income changes observed over time. Specifically, income changes over time would represent temporary shifts, and it would be expected that the recipients or losers from income changes would not adjust immediately to the consumption habits of their new income group." See Edwin Kuh and John R. Meyer, "How Extraneous are Extraneous Estimates?" *Review of Economics and Statistics*, Nov. 1957, pp. 380–93. The quote is from p. 390.

It is useful, if possible, to estimate several cross-section equations, each observed at different points in time. By examining how different the estimated coefficients are from one cross section to another, one could assess whether the particular time period selected was one of radical transition from one equilibrium level to another—in which case the household's deviations from equilibrium could be relatively large and possibly systematically different from a more "normal" period. (Chapter 10 describes statistical tests to determine whether the coefficients are different.)[28]

To summarize, most cross-section models depict long-run, equilibrium behavior whereas annual (or quarterly) time-series models are more likely to have observations continually embroiled in the dynamics of adjustment from one equilibrium level to another, without ever achieving any equilibrium level because of the stream of continual shocks to the participants (e.g., changes in exogenous factors, such as income and prices, as well as random shocks). It would be appropriate to estimate, for example, a stock-adjustment model for the time-series model but to use the long-run, static equilibrium behavioral relationship directly for the cross-section model.

2.5.5   Inappropriateness of Dynamic Cross-Section Models

Researchers have estimated stock adjustment or other dynamic models using cross-section data, but they usually warn the reader that the literal, dynamic interpretation of the equation is likely not valid. For example, Goldfeld estimated demand equations for savings and loan deposits, using state and individual savings and loan data for two sets of estimates (and each of these was estimated for several different years).[29] Deposits were regressed on interest rates and a number of other variables. Using state data, the coefficient of the lagged dependent variable was estimated at greater than unity, which was unsatisfactory since it shows an unstable dynamic process; this was his linear equation. For his double-log (or log-linear) equation, the coefficient on the lagged dependent variable was 0.94, which suggests a speed of adjustment (γ of section 2.4.1) of 0.06 per year. This was also unacceptable because it was obviously too slow.[30] The lagged dependent variable was not representing a dynamic process for his cross-section equation. What is more likely is that it "explained" the current level of deposits in a state simply because the naive predictor, namely, last year's state deposits, is usually the best single "predictor" in a cross

---

[28] Notice that a supply equation was not written for the housing model. In time-series models, if the supply is assumed to be fixed for a short period of time, the supply curve is completely inelastic, and the demand curve becomes "traced" out by period-by-period shifts in the supply curve. Thus, treating the demand curve as a single equation for estimation purposes is appropriate in this instance even though the assumption of the inelastic supply function should be noted in the documentation. For the long-run interpretation of the cross-section demand curve, the assumption of a perfectly elastic supply curve may be used because, in the long-run, all factors of production are mobile. As is discussed in Chapter 9 (dealing with simultaneous equations), focusing on just the demand equation is usually appropriate in this instance as well.

[29] Stephen M. Goldfeld, "Savings and Loan Associations and the Market for Saving : Aspects of Allocational Efficiency," in Irwin Friend, ed., *Study of the Savings and Loan Industry* (Washington, D.C.: Federal Home Loan Bank Board, July 1969), pp. 569–658.

[30] Goldfeld, "Savings and Loan Associations," p. 623.

section. That is, the major variations in the dependent variable from one observation to another (i.e., from one state to another) can be "explained" statistically by last year's variations in the level of state deposits. As a result, the lagged dependent variable does not "explain" anything in a behavioral sense but acts only as a scale factor that can "predict" the relative size or scale of the dependent variable with a high degree of statistical accuracy, relative to the observed interstate variations. The lagged dependent variable thus acts more in a tautological than a behavioral sense. That is why Goldfeld's estimated coefficient on the lagged dependent variable was close to unity in both his linear and log-linear models.

Goldfeld was mindful of the problems of ascribing a dynamic interpretation to models estimated with cross-section data. Using data for individual savings and loan deposits, he first redefined the dependent variable as the deposit growth rate. This accomplishes two objectives. First, it abstracts, at least in part, from the scale problem just cited (which is very similar to the dimensional misspecification cited in Section 2.2.2); second, it avoids the problem of heteroskedasticity, which is defined and discussed in Chapters 4 and 8. However, even when deposits are measured in percentage growth terms, it is a fact that savings and loan associations that were growing fast last year are likely to be growing fast this year, so again the lagged dependent variable may act as a naive predictor or scale factor and hence convey little, if any, behavioral (i.e., dynamic) interpretation. Even though the estimated coefficients showed rapid adjustment, as expected, Goldfeld warns the reader concerning their dynamic interpretation:

> "While these results seem plausible, they are nevertheless to be viewed with caution. The primary reason is that it is a rather tricky proposition to estimate dynamic relationships with cross-section data. More particularly, unless one fully specifies the kinds of variables which characterize interassociation or inter-SMSA differences, the lagged dependent variable may easily reflect some of these factors."[31]

2.5.6 Pooled Cross-Section—Time-Series Models

Given that cross-section data tend to show the long-run, static equilibrium behavior and that time-series data tend to show short-run, dynamic behavior (to the extent that it exists at all), it is not at all clear what "pooled cross-section and time-series" data will represent. Pooled data combine the cross-section and time-series observations, and all the data are used to estimate the equation. In the housing demand example, the cross section consisted of observations on households in a given city at a given point in time. A pooled data set would add a similar set of observations for one or more additional points in time. That is, the observation set would contain both cross-section and time-series elements. In the example, each household would be

---

[31] Goldfeld, "Savings and Loan Associations," p. 627. Goldfeld goes on to cite SMSA (Standard Metropolitan Statistical Area) income as one of the variables omitted from the equation for which the lagged dependent variable may act as a proxy.

observed at more than one point in time, with observations on each household for each of the years.

As above, whether the equation can in this case include dynamic elements depends on an examination of the character of the data set. The researcher should examine the variation in the dependent and independent variables from the time-series component relative to the variation from the cross-section component of the data base. In the example, if ten years of annual data were obtained, the relative cross-section movement of the dependent variable (the movement of housing consumption across households) is still likely to be greater than the average variation for each household over time. Thus, the model probably should not be modeled or interpreted dynamically. However, with thirty years of observations on the cross section of households, the dynamic variations in housing consumption are likely to be much more important, which may require that the dynamics be incorporated into the model. At least in part, however, a lagged dependent variable would be acting as a naive predictor for each of the cross sections; thus, to give it its literal, dynamic interpretation would not be completely correct.

The determination of the specification and interpretation of the dynamic elements is thus a matter of judgment for each application of pooled data. It is noteworthy that Fisher, using pooled data for a model of the supply of natural gas, did not attribute any dynamic interpretation to his lagged dependent variable,[32] similar to the cautious interpretation of Goldfeld cited above, using just cross-section data.

2.5.7 Summary

In summary, the structure of the model may need to be altered by the cross-section nature of a given data base, especially when it comes to models that are inherently dynamic for time-series applications. Also, some variables may require different definitions for cross-section data than they would for time-series data. Further, some variables may not be relevant for time-series models but are relevant for cross-section models, and vice versa. Price variables often do not vary in a given cross section, such as the price of bread for households in a given city. Thus, these variables cannot be included in a cross-section model. The theoretical development of the model very likely requires that the cross-section or time-series nature of the data base be explicitly considered concurrently with the theoretical development.

In general, cross-section models represent long-run, static equilibrium situations, and it is very difficult to give them a timewise interpretation. Like the annual and decennial time-series models, the long-run elasticity from cross-section models has an indefinite time dimension, but, at an applied level, the estimates of the long-run elasticity are likely to differ for each model because the nature of the data sets differs.

Researchers have suggested estimating the income elasticity of demand, for ex-

---

[32] Franklin M. Fisher, *Supply and Costs in the U.S. Petroleum Industry, Two Econometric Studies* (Baltimore: The Johns Hopkins University Press, 1964). In fact, Fisher explicitly *assumed* that in his model the lagged dependent variable was picking up, *in part*, the cross-district effect, and therefore, he assumed that it was not appropriate to use the lagged dependent variable in any price elasticity estimate. In his words, ". . . the dynamics of the process are *hopelessly* obscured by the district-distinguishing roles of the lagged dependent variables" (p. 37, n. 50).

ample, from cross-section data (because income varies more for these data) and then estimating the price elasticity from time-series data (because price varies more for these data than for cross-section data).[33] In the latter estimation, the income elasticity is assumed to be the cross-sectional value instead of the value estimated for the time series. (See Chapter 10 on estimating equations in which some of the coefficient values are not estimated but assumed.) The reason they suggest this approach is that the unrestricted time-series estimates of the income elasticity are usually not of the expected sign or magnitude, generally alleged to be caused by the presence of multicollinearity in the time-series regressors. However, the problem with this approach is that the cross-section estimator of the income elasticity should be interpreted as representing the long-run, static equilibrium response to income changes, and imposing this type of response *period-by-period* in the time-series model likely involves a misspecification of the dynamic properties of the time-series model.[34] The consequence is a type of specification error that may bring into question the appropriate interpretation of the entire estimated equation.

Appendix to Chapter Two: Dominant Variables

This appendix presents a situation that arises relatively infrequently. The reader should be advised of it and may want just to skim the material on the first reading, saving it for future reference.

A dominant variable is a regressor the presence of which is so powerful in statistically "explaining" the dependent variable that the coefficients of the other variables become statistically insignificant or have the wrong sign.[35] As an example of the problem and one way to deal with it, notice that production functions are normally written and estimated in the form of output (Q) as a function of capital (K) and labor (L), such as in the exponential function:

$$Q = AK^\alpha L^\beta e^\epsilon \qquad\qquad (2.A.1)$$

where A, α, β, and e are constants and ϵ is the error term. But output is not possible without raw materials (M), so the function should be:

$$Q = AK^\alpha L^\beta M^\gamma e^\epsilon \qquad\qquad (2.A.2)$$

But this equation, when estimated, yields unbelievable estimates of α and β, such as negative values. The problem is that, while in theory there is substitution between raw materials on the one hand and labor and capital on the other, empirical obser-

---

[33] Most econometrics texts cite this usage of cross-section and time-series data. See, for example, Intriligator, *Econometric Models*, pp. 63–64 and p. 154.

[34] See Kuh and Meyer, "Extraneous Estimates."

[35] The term "dominant variable" was at least popularized (if not coined) by Potluri Rao and Roger LeRoy Miller, *Applied Econometrics* (Belmont: Wadsworth Publishing Co., 1971), pp. 40–43. They show the empirical results of estimating all three equations 2.A.1–2.A.3.

vations reveal little, if any, such substitutions. Since raw materials and output are usually one-for-one, the raw material variable *dominates* the empirical equation; after M, little is left for K and L to explain statistically.

One way to deal with such a dominant variable is to postulate a separate equation for the output-raw material relationship:

$$Q = BM^{\gamma}e^{\epsilon^*} \qquad (2.A.3)$$

This equation, then, is used in conjunction with equation 2.A.1. Given the estimates, the two equations are assumed to hold simultaneously, and zero substitution is assumed between raw materials on the one hand and capital and labor on the other.

For example, an extra page of newspaper can be produced if another unit of newsprint is supplied. Capital and labor are necessary, yet the statistical relationship between newsprint and newspaper is so strong that there is nothing left to explain statistically by capital and labor, which are also required to produce newspapers. Thus, equations 2.A.1 and 2.A.3 can be assumed to hold simultaneously.[36]

Another way to treat a potentially dominant variable is to make it a deflator. In the demand for housing services example in Section 2.5 on "Cross-Section Models," variables in the time series model were deflated by the number of households. The number of households could very easily have been a dominant variable in the demand for housing services, but another important reason for using it as a deflator instead of as a regressor is that important behavioral relationships may become sharper empirically when variables are expressed in per-household terms rather than in aggregate terms. That is, one less key coefficient to estimate allows the data to describe better the housing demand behavior.

The dominant variable problem is essentially one of a high degree of multicollinearity. Both equations 2.A.1 and 2.A.3 may have high degrees of statistical fit when each is estimated (and so does an estimate of equation 2.A.2). The problem is that the L and K variables are highly correlated with Q, and so is M. Thus, M is highly collinear with the L and K variables, and its one-for-one relationship with output dominates the empirical relationship. This procedure is one way to deal with such a high degree of multicollinearity. Other ways are indicated throughout the text, especially in Chapter 6.

---

[36] The author arrived at this approach independently from Rao and Miller, *Applied Econometrics*, in a model of the supply of and demand for newspapers and newsprint. Unfortunately, the report is proprietary: Norman B. Ture, Henry J. Cassidy, and Norman H. Jones, Jr., "The Future of Newsprint," PRC Systems Sciences Company, February 1971.

3 Ordinary Least Squares (OLS), Random Variables, and the Central Limit Theorem

Ordinary Least Squares (OLS, pronounced O-L-S) is the most widely used estimating technique, and the results from most other techniques are often compared to those of OLS because it has become the standard technique. Its popularity is due to two primary factors. First, it ensures that the estimated regression line will fit the data with the least aggregate error in terms of the sum of squared residuals, which most researchers agree is an appropriate goal of the estimation procedure. Second, it is the simplest of the computer-based estimating techniques. Most other estimating techniques are extensions of OLS, involve complicated, nonlinear estimating formulas, or are difficult to computerize for all situations.

The first section presents the rationale for and the mechanics of the OLS estimating technique. Regression users are rarely called upon to apply the analytic approach this method of estimation represents, so the emphasis in this book is on understanding what OLS attempts to do and on some of the statistics generated during the process. Of particular importance is the coefficient of correlation, which indicates the degree to which two variables move in similar or opposite directions.

Up to this point in the text, the error term has played a very inconsequential role. The elements of model building discussed in Chapter 2 focused on the deterministic portion of the regression equation. The deterministic, or ''modeling,'' portion is probably the most important for regression users, and its early emphasis is warranted, but sample data must be drawn to compute the estimates. Drawing the sample and computing the estimates necessarily brings into play the error term, the random component of the regression equation. An understanding of randomness and how it affects the estimates is essential to achieving an understanding of and an ability to interpret the statistics generated in the estimation process.

The notion of randomness is introduced through an illustration of one of the basic theorems of regression analysis, the Central Limit Theorem. This theorem states that the error term can be assumed to have a normal distribution. A normal distribution is explained in this chapter; Chapter 4 then takes the basic notions developed here and applies them to the problem of estimating the regression coefficients, and more advanced notions of randomness are developed there in the context of the regression model. (These are the notions of expected value and variance.) Those readers familiar with these notions may skip over this material; however, most statistics courses teach these notions in a context different from the regression model, and even those who have had a statistics course may find the method of presentation here enlightening and useful.

The notion of randomness is very important in applied regression analysis. Estimates of regression coefficients are only the "best guess" of what the true coefficients are. The element of randomness that is always present in estimation causes the estimated coefficients *always* (or almost always) to be different from their true values (the parameter values). Thus, reliance has to be made on the fact that, *on average,* if the coefficients could be estimated a repeated number of times, the estimates would be near their true values. The exact interpretation of this reliance on central tendencies in the face of randomness is explained in the context of the regression model in this and the subsequent chapter.

The first section is a brief digression on a notational convention that is used whenever possible in the remainder of the text and throughout the econometrics literature. This convention greatly simplifies most analytic expressions.

3.1   The Deviations-from-the-Mean Transformation of the Variables

The major emphasis in regression analysis is on the slope coefficients (β_1, β_2, . . ., β_K), not on the intercept or constant term, β_0. To show this emphasis and especially to make the algebra simpler, the linear equation can be transformed so that the transformed equation does not have an intercept. The intercept term is merely made transparent by this transformation, it is not suppressed (i.e., set to zero).

The transformation is to subtract from each variable its own sample mean. The lower case letters represent the "deviation-from-the-mean" form, the upper case letters stand for the original data, and the "bar" above a variable denotes its sample mean; thus, the transformations are:

$$y_i = Y_i - \overline{Y}$$
$$x_{i1} = X_{i1} - \overline{X}_1$$
$$x_{i2} = X_{i2} - \overline{X}_2$$

.

.

.

$$x_{iK} = X_{iK} - \overline{X}_K$$

Figure 3.1.1 shows such a transformation for the simple linear regression model. In terms of the original variables, the estimated equation is:

$$Y_i = \hat{\beta}_0 + \hat{\beta}_1 X_i + e_i \qquad (3.1.1)$$

But in deviation form, the equation becomes:

$$y_i = \hat{\beta}_1 x_i + e_i \qquad (3.1.2)$$

where $\hat{\beta}_0$ disappears, and $\hat{\beta}_1$ is *exactly* the same as in equation 3.1.1, and so is the residual e_i. The original axes are labeled X and Y, and the new axes are labeled x and y. As may be seen in Figure 3.1.1, the y-intercept (where $x = 0$) is zero with the new axes, and the slope of the line is unchanged by this transformation. As also seen in Figure 3.1.1, the change of axes does nothing to change the relationship between the estimated regression line and the sample data points; thus, the residuals for each observation are totally unaffected by this procedure.

The reason this transformation works is that all the estimating techniques dealt with in this text have the property that the estimated regression line passes through the sample means. That is, the estimates satisfy the equation:

$$\overline{Y} = \hat{\beta}_0 + \hat{\beta}_1 \overline{X}_1 + \hat{\beta}_2 \overline{X}_2 + \cdots + \hat{\beta}_K \overline{X}_K \qquad (3.1.3)$$

Thus, subtracting the mean from each variable leaves the slopes and the residuals unchanged. Given estimates of the slope coefficients $\beta_1, \beta_2, \ldots, \beta_K$, the intercept can be estimated as:

$$\hat{\beta}_0 = \overline{Y} - \hat{\beta}_1 \overline{X}_1 - \hat{\beta}_2 \overline{X}_2 - \cdots - \hat{\beta}_K \overline{X}_K \qquad (3.1.4)$$

This equation lurks in the background whenever the deviation-from-the-mean form is used. It should be emphasized that this form does *not* suppress the constant term.

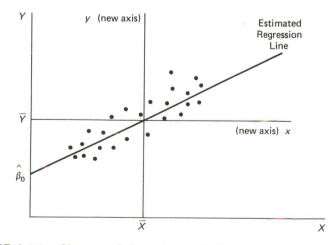

FIGURE 3.1.1 Change of Axes by Deviation-from-the-Mean Transformation on the Variables

Once the slope coefficients are estimated, equation 3.1.4 can always be used to estimate the constant term. In fact, it is usually incorrect to set the constant term to zero or to use estimates of it for inference, as is discussed in Chapter 6.

3.2 Ordinary Least Squares (OLS)

Given a regression equation to estimate, among the many estimating techniques available—and there are many, popular examples of which are presented in Chapters 7–9—the most popular one, at least for a first look at the estimates, is called ordinary least squares, or OLS. This section discusses what OLS accomplishes, presents some of the terminology associated with it, and introduces an important statistic that OLS regression programs usually produce, the coefficient of correlation between two variables.

3.2.1 Minimizing the Sum of Squared Residuals

As was pointed out in Chapter 1, the measures of the overall statistical fit of the estimated equation typically involve the sum of squared residuals, called the error sum of squares (SSE). Most researchers agree that the smaller the SSE relative to the total sum of squares (SST, the sum of the squared deviations of Y_i from its sample mean) or relative to the regression sum of squares (SSR, the "explained" portion of the total sum of squares), the better the estimated regression line appears to fit the data. Thus, given the SST, which no estimating technique can alter, researchers desire an estimating technique that minimizes the SSE. That technique is OLS. That is, *the method of OLS selects those parameter estimates that minimize the SSE*. Recall that the coefficient of determination $R^2 = 1 - (SSE/SST)$, *so the OLS routine also provides the largest possible* R^2, given the linear specification of the equation. However, this procedure does not guarantee that the OLS estimators will always be the best possible estimators because situations often arise in which more is required than just straightforward minimization of the SSE. Those situations are examined in the rest of the text, starting with Chapter 7.

The basic approach of OLS is as follows. Recall the definition of the residual:

$$e_i = Y_i - \hat{Y}_i = y_i - \hat{y}_i$$

The latter equality holds because taking deviations from the mean does not alter the residuals, as discussed in Section 3.1. The procedure of OLS is to select estimates $\hat{\beta}_0, \hat{\beta}_1, \ldots, \hat{\beta}_K$ that minimize the sum of squared residuals, summed over all the sample data points:

$$\sum_{i=1}^{n} e_i^2 = \sum_{i=1}^{n}(Y_i - \hat{Y}_i)^2 = \sum_{i=1}^{n}(y_i - \hat{y}_i)^2$$

For the simple model (in deviation-from-the-mean form), since $\hat{y}_i = \hat{\beta}_1 x_i$, OLS minimizes:

$$\sum_{i=1}^{n}(y_i - \hat{\beta}_1 x_i)^2 \qquad (3.2.1)$$

by selecting $\hat{\beta}_1$ judiciously. For the K-regressor model, OLS minimizes:

$$\sum_{i=1}^{n}(y_i - \hat{\beta}_1 x_{1i} - \hat{\beta}_2 x_{2i} - \cdots - \hat{\beta}_K x_{Ki})^2 \qquad (3.2.2)$$

by selecting $\hat{\beta}_1, \hat{\beta}_2, \ldots,$ and $\hat{\beta}_K$ judiciously. The resulting OLS estimating formula (called an estimator) for the simple model is:

$$\hat{\beta}_1 = \frac{\Sigma x_i y_i}{\Sigma x_i^2} \qquad (3.2.3)$$

The estimating formulas become more complicated for more regressors, because they are obtained by solving the following system of K equations in K unknowns (the estimators), known as the normal equations:

$$m_{1y} = \hat{\beta}_1 m_{11} + \hat{\beta}_2 m_{12} + \cdots + \hat{\beta}_K m_{1K}$$

$$\vdots$$

$$m_{jy} = \hat{\beta}_1 m_{j1} + \hat{\beta}_2 m_{j2} + \cdots + \hat{\beta}_K m_{jK} \qquad (3.2.4)$$

$$\vdots$$

$$m_{Ky} = \hat{\beta}_1 m_{K1} + \hat{\beta}_2 m_{K2} + \cdots + \hat{\beta}_K m_{KK}$$

where

$$m_{jk} = \frac{\sum_i x_{ij} x_{ik}}{n} \qquad (3.2.5)$$

and

$$m_{jy} = \frac{\sum_i x_{ij} y_i}{n} \qquad (3.2.6)$$

The so-called cross-product terms, m_{jk} and m_{jy} for all pairs of variables, can be calculated from the sample data and thus are considered as constants in the normal equations (3.2.4). The computer regression program solves this linear system of K equations for the K unknowns $\hat{\beta}_1, \hat{\beta}_2, \ldots, \hat{\beta}_K$. This set of normal equations is usually obtained by differential calculus, and many methods exist to solve these equations. However, a regression user does not have to know either how the normal equations were derived (which is the job of the theoretical econometrician) or how they are solved (which is the job of the computer). The estimate of the constant term, $\hat{\beta}_0$, is obtained by using equation 3.1.4.

3.2.2   The Coefficient of Correlation

Some of the computer output, however, may include the cross-product terms, such as m_{jk} for variables x_j and x_k, which constitute the coefficients of the system of normal equations. These terms are usually of limited interest, but a variant of these measures is of considerable interest, the correlation coefficient for two variables, say X_k and X_j, called r_{kj}. It shows the degree to which the two variables move together or in opposite directions in the sample. Notationally, the correlation coefficient is:

$$r_{kj} = r_{jk} = \frac{\sum x_{ij} x_{ik}}{(\sum x_{ij}^2 \sum x_{ik}^2)^{1/2}} \qquad (3.2.7)$$

The coefficient of correlation always lies in the interval $-1 \leq r_{kj} \leq 1$. A positive value of r_{kj} indicates that values of X_k above its mean are associated with values of X_j above its mean and that values of X_k below its mean are associated with values of X_j below its mean. A negative value of r_{kj} indicates that values of X_k above its mean are associated with values of X_j *below* its mean. The higher the magnitude of r_{kj} in absolute value is, the stronger is the association of X_k and X_j. A value of unity implies that their movements are perfectly correlated, so, except possibly for scale (i.e., $X_j = a + b X_k$, where a and b are constants), they are the same variable. It is not surprising, then, that, in this case of *perfect collinearity,* the OLS estimating procedure is unable to assign each of them separate and distinct estimated coefficients because, for all practical purposes, they are the same variable. Sometimes, but only because of rounding error, computer programs will provide estimates of all the coefficients when two (or more) regressors are perfectly collinear, but the calculated standard errors of the estimated coefficients will be quite large, which is often the only clue that some regressors are perfectly collinear.

The coefficient of correlation shows the degree of linear relationship between two regressors. If the degree is high (in absolute value), but not perfect, the computer program will provide coefficient estimates, but the reliability of these estimates is questionable, except possibly for the case in which the number of observations is very large (such as 100 or more). The general case of at least some degree of a linear relationship among more than two regressors is called *multicollinearity.* Multicollinearity is examined throughout this text, and especially in Chapters 6 and 10.

Often the computer program will provide the simple coefficients of correlation between the dependent variable and the regressors. (The formula is found by substituting y_i for x_{ik} in equation 3.2.7.) For the case of one regressor, r_{yx}^2 is simply the coefficient of determination for the estimated equation, R^2. For more than one regressor, the usefulness of the $r_{yx_1}, r_{yx_2}, \ldots, r_{yx_K}$ statistics is limited because each of them does not account for (and thus does not hold constant) the other regressors. (There are "partial" correlation coefficients that do account for all the regressors, but they are included in the output of only a few regression programs.) Similarly, the interpretation of the r_{kj}'s is clouded when there are more than two regressors because they do not indicate the degree of *multi*collinearity, which is a statistical association in the sample involving more than two regressors.

3.3 The Normal Distribution of the Error Term

The t-statistic and F-statistic of Chapter 1 are only truly applicable for assessing the statistical significance of the estimated regression coefficients and the estimated regression equation, respectively, when the error term is normally distributed. The connection between the assumption of normality of the error term and the *t*-statistic of an estimated coefficient is developed in Chapter 5. This section describes the normal distribution, explores the notion of randomness, and demonstrates the usual rationale for the assumption of normality for the error term, the Central Limit Theorem.

The error term ϵ_i is called a *random variable* because the value it assumes is determined by chance. This section is a mini-lesson in random variables that leads to a justification of the assumption of normality. The concept of a normal distribution is developed in the process.

3.3.1 The Central Limit Theorem

The error term in a regression model is assumed to be caused by, among other things, the omission of a number of variables from the equation. As was stated in Section 1.2.2, these variables are expected, *a priori*, to have relatively small individual effects on the hypothesized regression relation, and it is not necessary to include them as regressors. Thus, the error term represents the combined, or mean, effects of these omitted variables. It is this component of the error term that usually is cited for the justification of the assumption of normality, although the normal distribution could be and often is cited as an adequate approximation for whatever the distribution of the error term turns out to be.

In general, a random variable that is generated by the combined effects of a number of omitted, individually unimportant variables will be normally distributed according to the *Central Limit Theorem* (also called the Law of Large Numbers), which states: *The mean (or sum) of a number of random variables will generally tend to be approximately normally distributed, regardless of the specific distribution of those random variables, if the number of observations on the random variables is large enough.*

3.3.2 Small and Large Samples from a Random Variable

To illustrate this theorem, first take *n* observations on a random variable. Assume that the random variable is an omitted, relatively unimportant regressor, X_{K+1}. (*K* is the number of regressors in the equation.) Further, assume, for illustrative purposes only, that this omitted variable is distributed as the uniform distribution, which has equally likely outcomes between two numbers, zero and unity. (Actually, X_{K+1} could be distributed according to almost any pattern, and the Central Limit Theorem would typically apply; it is that powerful.) Even though in practice X_{K+1} is observed only once for each observation on the included *X*'s, the dependent variable, *Y*, and the error term, ϵ; more observations on X_{K+1} are required in order to demonstrate its distribution function, assumed here to be the uniform distribution.

The distribution of X_{K+1} can be demonstrated by examining its *n* observations corresponding to the sample observations on the other *X*'s and on *Y*. Figures 3.3.1 through 3.3.7 show the histogram, or relative frequency, of the hypothesized uniformly distributed X_{K+1} for the number of drawings $n = 10, 30, 60, 120, 500, 1000,$ and 2000. For example, in Figure 3.3.1, 10 numbers were picked at random from the

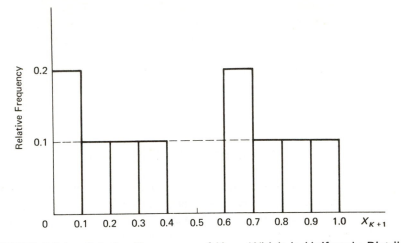

FIGURE 3.3.1 Relative Frequency of X_{K+1}, Which Is Uniformly Distributed, for 10 Observations

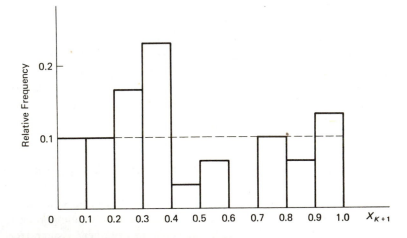

FIGURE 3.3.2 Relative Frequency of X_{K+1}, Which Is Uniformly Distributed, for 30 Observations

zero-one uniform distribution. Dividing the zero-one interval into tenths in order to plot the relative frequency function, two observations were obtained in the first and seventh intervals (0.0–0.1 and 0.6–0.7), one observation was drawn in six of the intervals, and no observations were drawn from the remaining two intervals. The *relative frequency* is the number of observations (or drawings) in each interval divided by the total number of drawings, in this case ten.

These numbers were selected at random by the computer, in much the same manner as selecting them by ten spins of a roulette wheel that had ten equally likely

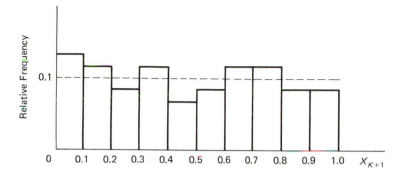

FIGURE 3.3.3 Relative Frequency of X_{K+1}, Which Is Uniformly Distributed, for 60 Observations

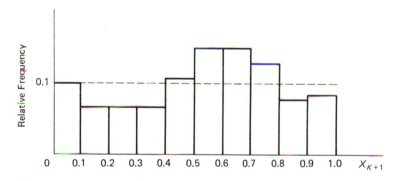

FIGURE 3.3.4 Relative Frequency of X_{K+1}, Which Is Uniformly Distributed, for 120 Observations

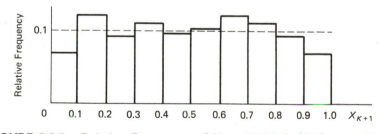

FIGURE 3.3.5 Relative Frequency of X_{K+1}, Which Is Uniformly Distributed, for 500 Observations

outcomes (e.g., ten spaces of equal length marked one through ten). In other words, randomness implies that each of the ten outcomes had a chance of being selected in each drawing of the observations; and in this case with the uniform distribution, each number had an equally likely chance of being selected on each drawing. The dashed line in Figure 3.3.1 shows the 0.1 or 10 percent chance, or *probability*, for each

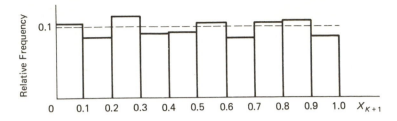

FIGURE 3.3.6 Relative Frequency of X_{K+1}, Which Is Uniformly Distributed, for 1000 Observations

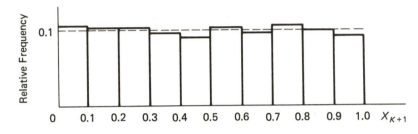

FIGURE 3.3.7 Relative Frequency of X_{K+1}, Which Is Uniformly Distributed, for 2000 Observations

outcome. The entire dashed line represents the *probability distribution* of the outcomes. The difference between the probability distribution and the relative frequency distribution is that the probability distribution is a forward-looking or *ex ante* concept, i.e., before each drawing takes place; it influences the eventual draw. The relative frequency distribution, on the other hand, is an *ex post* concept, describing the draws that have been taken and observed. Since each drawing is taken at random, the relative frequency distribution will likely differ from the underlying probability distribution—this is the essence of randomness for a small number of observations. However, as more observations are drawn, the element of randomness becomes less important in shaping the relative frequency distribution, and the underlying probability distribution becomes more important and evident in the histogram.

The sequence of Figures 3.3.1 through 3.3.7 shows the tendency for the relative frequency function (or distribution) to resemble the probability function (the 10 percent chance per interval) as the number of observations on X_{K+1} increases. In general, an infinite number of drawings reveals the underlying probability distribution. In fact, *the probability distribution can be regarded as the relative frequency distribution if an infinite number of drawings could be taken.*

The probability distribution can serve as a guide for the likelihood of a given outcome (such as the first interval being selected) if the experiment is conducted a repeated number of times. This information can be helpful even if only a few drawings are observed, under the presumption that some information is better than none and with the knowledge that, if a repeated number of drawings are taken, the information can be very useful.

To illustrate and emphasize this very important point, suppose a 10-space roulette wheel was observed for thousands of spins and it was discovered that the wheel was slightly biased, or worn in such a way that the number two came up 15 percent of the time and the number seven came up only 5 percent of the time, while the other numbers came up the expected 10 percent of the time. In placing bets using this roulette wheel, given equal payoffs for each of the numbers, one would be foolish to place money on number seven, even if only a few spins were available. That would be "bucking the odds." Rather, placing bets on number two would be the wise thing to do. Furthermore, since the underlying probability shows through only for a large number of drawings, it would not be wise to put one's entire bankroll on number two for a single spin because the chance (or probability) of losing on that spin is 85 percent (one minus the chance of success, or 100−15). Instead, the bets should be of a more modest value in order to allow a large number of spins of the wheel so that the odds work in favor of winning over the longer run.

3.3.3 Illustration of the Central Limit Theorem

Now to the application of these notions of randomness to illustrate the Central Limit Theorem. Suppose that there are two independent, relatively unimportant variables (X_{K+1} and X_{K+2}) that are omitted from the equation and that each of them is a random variable having the uniform distribution as X_{K+1} above. Suppose further that these two omitted variables are the only cause of the error term in the regression equation (which is unlikely in practice). Thus, the error term ϵ_i is the average value of the two random observations on X_{K+1} and X_{K+2}. In the computation of the relative frequency distribution of the error term, n observations are used. These are the n observations on Y and the X's for a given sample. In other words, all n observations on the error term ϵ_i are used to portray its relative frequency distribution, just as a number of observations on the first extra variable X_{K+1} was required to portray its relative frequency distribution.

In Figure 3.3.8, five observations ($n = 5$) on the average of the two missing variables X_{K+1} and X_{k+2} give rise to the relative frequency function portrayed. There are two observations (or 40 percent) in the third interval, and one each (20 percent) in the fifth, seventh, and eighth intervals. Notice that the observations tend to be near the center instead of scattered all across the zero-one interval as in the previous graphs of X_{K+1}. The averaging of $X_{K+1,i}$ and $X_{K+2,i}$, each of which is distributed according

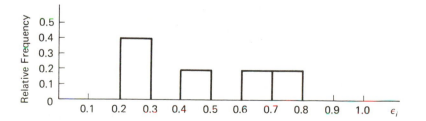

FIGURE 3.3.8 Relative Frequency of the Error Term as an Average of 2 Omitted Variables from the Uniform Distribution: 5 Observations

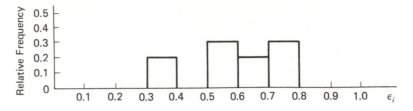

FIGURE 3.3.9 Relative Frequency of the Error Term as an Average of 2 Omitted Variables from the Uniform Distribution: 10 Observations

to the uniform distribution, produces the bunching of the observations on $\epsilon_i = (X_{K+1,i} + X_{K+2,i})/2$ toward the middle.

Figures 3.3.9 and 3.3.10 show the distribution of the average X_{K+1} and X_{K+2} for 10 and 30 observations, respectively. The tendency for these distributions to bunch toward the middle is only somewhat clearer.

Figures 3.3.11–3.3.13 show the relative frequency functions of ϵ_i when 10 variables, each of which is uniformly distributed, compose the error term. The number of sample observations on the ten variables is 5, 10, and 30, respectively, in the three graphs, just as in Figures 3.3.8–3.3.10 in which only 2 variables composed the error term. The extra eight variables have made the tendency of the Central Limit Theorem become evident: the distribution bunches toward the middle, with most of the observations in the middle and the rest tapering off smoothly on either side.

The Central Limit Theorem theoretically is valid only as the number of observations (n) approaches infinity, but, as shown in the illustrations, even a few observations are sufficient to show the tendency toward the bell-shaped distribution that is the normal distribution. The number of omitted variables is important only because, for finite example sizes (as illustrated here), the larger the number is, the more evident is the tendency. Furthermore, normality is an assumption that is a "working hypothesis," i.e., one that is rarely, if ever, questioned. Even in those cases in which it is clear that the error term is not normally distributed, the normal distribution is often assumed as an approximation to the true distribution.[1]

By the way, the relative frequency distributions of drawings on the error term in Figures 3.3.8–3.3.13 were not centered on zero. To achieve a zero mean, the average value of the drawings of the error term are placed (or "dumped") into the constant term (β_0) by the estimation process. Then the mean of the relative frequency of the error term becomes zero for those observations on ϵ found in any given sample (even though the values are unknown in practice). It is always assumed that the normal *probability distribution* of ϵ_i is centered on zero, but there is no reason to expect the average of a sample of n observations on ϵ_i to be zero, for the same reasons that the relative frequency distribution for X_{K+1} for a finite sample deviated from its underlying

---

[1] Also, the omitted variables do not have to be uniformly distributed in order to achieve the normal distribution as an approximation. All that is required is that each of the variables have a finite mean and variance. Furthermore, their inclusion in the error term is scaled by their minute, but probably not zero, coefficients (the β's).

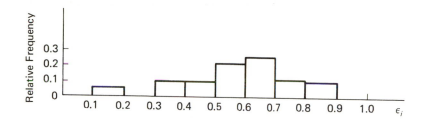

FIGURE 3.3.10   Relative Frequency of the Error Term as an Average of 2 Omitted Variables from the Uniform Distribution: 30 Observations

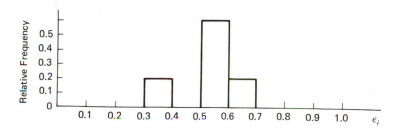

FIGURE 3.3.11   Relative Frequency of the Error Term as an Average of 10 Omitted Variables from the Uniform Distribution: 5 Observations

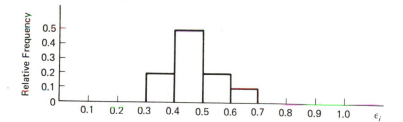

FIGURE 3.3.12   Relative Frequency of the Error Term as an Average of 10 Omitted Variables from the Uniform Distribution: 10 Observations

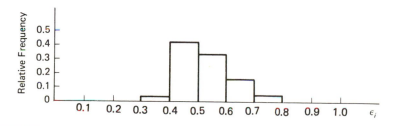

FIGURE 3.3.13   Relative Frequency of the Error Term as an Average of 10 Omitted Variables from the Uniform Distribution: 30 Observations

uniform probability distribution. The constant term absorbs the exact amount to achieve a zero sample mean for the error term, which is one reason not to rely on the estimated magnitude of the constant term for inference, as is emphasized in Section 6.1.

3.3.4 A Description of the Normal Distribution

The tendency for a distribution of the error term ϵ_i to take a particular shape by the omission of a number of variables was just demonstrated. As the sample size goes to infinity, the true, underlying distribution is observed, just as the relative frequency distribution for the omitted variable X_{K+1} approached its underlying probability distribution as the sample size approached infinity. The underlying distribution for the error term is called the normal distribution. With an infinite sample size, the size of the intervals used to measure the relative number of observations can be smaller, and the shape of the distribution will still be shown. If the intervals shrink to an infinitesimal size, as is assumed now, the histogram gives way to a smooth, continuous curve. The resulting normal distribution is a symmetrical, continuous, bell-shaped curve.

Two normal distributions are shown in Figure 3.3.14. The normal distribution for the random variable ϵ_i has two parameters: a measure of central tendency, the mean denoted μ, and a measure of dispersion, the variance denoted σ_ϵ^2. The distribution denoted $f_2(\epsilon_i)$ in Figure 3.3.14 has a smaller variance than the distribution denoted $f_1(\epsilon_i)$ has, meaning that $f_2(\epsilon_i)$ is more compactly distributed about its central tendency. It has a variance of 0.5 compared with a variance of unity for $f_1(\epsilon_i)$. Since the normal distribution is symmetrical about its central tendency, the mean μ is also the median and the mode of the distribution.[2]

As shown in Figure 3.3.14, the entire distribution is shifted if the mean is different. For example, if $f_2(\epsilon_i)$ had a variance $\sigma_\epsilon^2 = 1$ as does $f_1(\epsilon_i)$, then it would look exactly like $f_1(\epsilon_i)$, only centered over $\epsilon_i = 2$.

In Figure 3.3.14, $f_1(\epsilon_i)$ represents the standard normal distribution, which has a mean of zero (the distribution is centered on zero) and a standard deviation of unity. This is the usual distribution given in look-up tables, such as Statistical Table A-7 at the end of the text. (Regression users rarely need the normal look-up table.) In the second distribution, $f_2(\epsilon_i)$, the mean μ and variance σ_ϵ^2 take on values $\mu = 2$ and $\sigma_\epsilon^2 = 0.5$.

3.4   Summary

The notational convention of lower case letters standing for the variables after their sample mean has been subtracted from each observation simplifies the formulas presented in the text. In the deviations-from-the-mean format, the constant term is no

---

[2] The median is the sample point that divides the observations into two groups having the same number of observations. The mode is a point at which the distribution peaks. Some distributions have more than one mode as the distribution peaks more than once. An example of a bimodal distribution is given in Section 6.4.2.

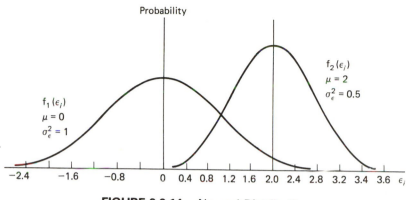

FIGURE 3.3.14 Normal Distributions

longer explicitly shown, but its presence is still assumed and it can be estimated by evaluating the regression line at the sample means, given the estimates of the slope coefficients.

The estimating method of OLS selects coefficients by minimizing the residual sum of squares. For the simple model, the OLS estimator of the slope $\hat{\beta}_1$ is $\Sigma xy/\Sigma x^2$. For the K-regressor model, K normal equations are provided and solved by the computer for the K estimates $\hat{\beta}_1, \hat{\beta}_2, \ldots, \hat{\beta}_K$.

Exact use of the t-statistic and F-statistic requires that the probability distribution of the ϵ_i's is the normal distribution. This distribution is usually justified by the Central Limit Theorem, but in some cases the normal distribution is used simply as an approximation of some other distribution of the error term. Chapter 5 demonstrates the connection between the assumption of normality of the error term and the distribution of the t-statistic.

It is very important that applied regression users understand the notion of randomness. It implies, as is discussed in detail in Chapter 4, that the estimates of the coefficients are unlikely to be exactly equal to their true values. An appreciation of this fact will lead to better use and understanding of the entire regression estimation procedure and a more cautious use of the estimated regression line.

The concepts of probability and relative frequency distributions were developed in this chapter. A probability distribution is the law or "guiding hand" that underlies the generation of sample data points for a random variable, and it is forward looking. The relative frequency distribution, on the other hand, is a plot of the relative frequency of occurrence of the outcomes *after* the sample has been drawn. For small samples, the relative frequency function may not resemble the underlying probability distribution, because of the element of chance, or randomness; however, for very large samples, the element of chance is suppressed, and the relative frequency distribution resembles the underlying probability distribution. Even though in applied situations small samples are all that are available, researchers must rely on the fact that, if the sample was large, the observed relative frequency function would resemble the probability distribution. Since the element of chance negates any possibility of describing what the frequency distribution would look like in small samples, a major portion of regression analysis is based on the description of the probability distribution of the error term, which the relative frequency distributions would represent if the sample size approached infinity. These notions are explored in the context of the simple regression model in Chapters 4 and 5.

4 The Classical Model

One of the basic problems in applied (and theoretical) econometrics is to select the appropriate formula or estimating technique, such as OLS (ordinary least squares, described in the previous chapter) and alternative estimators (described in subsequent chapters). Some estimators are better than others for a particular model and for a given empirical situation. The problem is to discern those situations in which one technique is clearly superior. This is rarely an easy task, but for some situations there are general guidelines to follow. These guidelines are developed in this and subsequent chapters.

Unfortunately, there is no single measure of the degree of "goodness" of an estimator, and the task of selecting the appropriate estimating technique is made more difficult by having to examine more than one attribute, or property, of alternative estimators. One measure (the mean square error, or MSE) is usually relied on more than other measures. It turns out that in most applied situations, it is extremely difficult to be assured that the estimating technique selected is the best available. Thus, applying guidelines and selecting the appropriate estimating technique is truly an art, and, as will be demonstrated in Chapters 6 through 9, using the wrong estimating technique can lead to disastrous results.

This chapter presents the basic set of assumptions—called the classical assumptions—that are required to insure that OLS estimators are the best available. When one or more of the classical assumptions do not hold, other estimation techniques *may* be better although OLS still may have optimal properties under certain circumstances. However, the fundamental procedure in regression analysis is to examine, in the regression application, whether or not the classical assumptions apply. If they do apply, the OLS estimating technique is the best available (in a particular sense). If they do not apply, the pros and cons of alternative techniques must be weighed.

All alternative estimating techniques discussed in the text use the OLS formulas, but in special ways. The alternative techniques use the OLS formulas on modified regression equations. Many computer regression packages contain these alternative estimating techniques; if they do not, the researcher can usually make the appropriate modifications to the equation and use the OLS technique to accomplish the alternative estimating procedure. Many alternative estimating techniques do not use the OLS formulas in any way, but these techniques are beyond the scope of this text.

In the context of the single-regressor (i.e., simple) model, the notions of expected value and variance are developed. These measures are very important because they form the basis for selecting alternative estimating formulas in various circumstances. These notions are developed in this text via Monte Carlo simulations. This technique is explained in detail in connection with the OLS estimator and is used throughout the text in more complicated circumstances, so a thorough understanding of it is essential. Moreover, the Monte Carlo analysis reinforces the notions of randomness that were introduced in Chapter 3, and, in particular, it reinforces how randomness affects the regression estimation procedure.

It is demonstrated (in Section 4.1.1) that the OLS estimator of the slope coefficient, $\hat{\beta}$, has the normal distribution because of the assumption developed in Chapter 3 that the error term, ϵ_i, has the normal distribution. It is also explained in Chapter 5 that the t-statistic is appropriate for purposes of assessing the statistical significance of $\hat{\beta}$, again based on the assumption of the normality of the error term.

In developing all these ideas, a set of traditional notation is introduced. Since the notation may be quite confusing to beginners, it is summarized in Table 4.3.1.

4.1   The Classical Assumptions

The seven basic classical assumptions that underlie the standard approach for applying OLS are needed to insure that the ordinary least squares estimators are the best possible. (The eighth assumption is always assumed to hold.) Subsequent chapters investigate the major violations of these assumptions and introduce alternative estimating techniques that *may* provide better estimates, in the sense developed in this and subsequent chapters.

Because of their importance in applied regression analysis, the classical assumptions are presented three ways: they are listed in the accompanying box for reference purposes, they are explained in words, and their standard notational presentation is shown, after the required statistical notation has been explained in the context of the linear regression model.

I.   The regression model is linear in the parameters and in the error term.   That is, the regression model is as shown in Chapter 1:

$$y_i = \beta_1 x_{i1} + \beta_2 x_{i2} + \cdots + \beta_K x_{iK} + \epsilon_i \quad i = 1, 2, \ldots, n$$

Nonlinear equations such as $y_i = \beta^2 x_i + \epsilon_i$, and others discussed in Section 2.2.8, do not pertain to the classical linear model. The coefficients of these nonlinear equations can be estimated, perhaps even by using OLS in special ways. For example, the

---

The Classical Assumptions

I.   The regression model is linear in the parameters and in the error term.

II. The error term has a zero population mean.

III. All regressors are uncorrelated with the error term.

IV. The error term is not autocorrelated (i.e., the error term for one observation is not systematically related to the error term for another observation).

V.   The error term is homoskedastic (i.e., has a constant variance).

VI. There is no perfect multicollinearity among the regressors.

VII. *The error terms are normally distributed.

(VIII. **There are positive degrees of freedom.)

---

* This assumption is optional but is usually invoked.
** This assumption is usually not stated explicitly but is always understood to apply, or else estimation is impossible.

An error term satisfying Assumptions I-V is called a classical error term, or ''white noise.'' If it also satisfies Assumption VII, it is called a classical normal error term.

---

coefficient in the above example, β^2, could be relabeled β^*, and the model would appear linear in β^*:

$$y_i = \beta^* x_i + \epsilon_i$$

OLS could be applied to this equation, and one would likely take the positive square root of the OLS estimate of β^* as the estimate of β (although the negative square root would also be a possible estimator). However, this is a nonlinear estimate of β because taking the square root is a nonlinear arithmetic operation. The only problem with this *ad hoc* approach is that the properties of such an estimate are not generally known; that is, one usually does not know how ''good'' such an estimate is. Nonetheless, it is suggested in Section 11.4 that using a modified OLS technique, such as the one in this example, to obtain estimates of parameters that are inherently nonlinear may be an acceptable procedure, and one that may be fruitfully applied in such circumstances.

It was stressed in Section 2.2 that nonlinear forms of the *variables* do not impede the application of the OLS technique. The good properties of OLS estimators hold regardless of the functional form of the *variables,* as long as the form of the equation to be estimated is linear in the *coefficients.* For example, the exponential function of Section 2.2.2:

$$y_i = x_i^\beta e^{\epsilon_i}$$

can be transformed as:

$$\log(y_i) = \beta \log(x_i) + \epsilon_i$$

The variables can be relabeled as $y_i^* = \log(y_i)$ and $x_i^* = \log(x_i)$, and the form of the equation for estimation is linear in β:

$$y_i^* = \beta x_i^* + \epsilon_i$$

To this modified equation, the good properties of the OLS estimator of β apply.

II.   The error term ϵ_i has a zero population mean.   The error term is
a random variable: its specific value for each observation is determined by chance. Thus, the mean value of a small number of ϵ_i's would not likely be zero. But this assumption refers to a large number of ϵ_i's, and their mean value would be zero. If all the possible observations on ϵ_i could be drawn and observed, the *population* of ϵ_i is said to be observed. But there are an infinite number of outcomes in the population because ϵ_i can take on any value on the (continuous) number line. However, the relative frequency distribution for a large number of observations on ϵ_i behaves very similarly to that for the entire set of all possible observations, as was demonstrated in Chapter 3. (When the sample size goes to infinity, the relative frequency distribution becomes—and is defined as—the probability distribution.)

Moreover, the mean of ϵ_i for any *sample,* no matter how small, is *forced* to be zero by the inclusion in the equation of the constant term. If the sample mean of ϵ_i is μ, then μ is implicitly subtracted from ϵ_i and added to the constant term, leaving the equation unchanged except that the new error term, $\epsilon_i^* = \epsilon_i - \mu$, has a zero mean for the sample and that the constant term has been changed from β_0 to $\beta_0^* = \beta_0 + \mu$. Since no reliance is to be placed on the estimated magnitude of the constant term (see Section 6.1), this result is quite acceptable, and the eventual error term for the equation, ϵ^*, satisfies this classical assumption, even for each sample. The algebra of these steps is as follows. (1) The original model (not in deviation-from-the-mean form) is:

$$Y_i = \beta_0 + \beta_1 X_i + \epsilon_i$$

(2) If ϵ_i has a sample mean μ, then $\Sigma(\epsilon_i - \mu)$ equals zero (see Appendix to Chapter 1 on summations to work out a proof, if needed). Thus, by adding and subtracting μ to the original equation, it can be written equivalently as:

$$Y_i = (\beta_0 + \mu) + \beta_1 X_i + (\epsilon_i - \mu)$$

(3) By relabeling the constant term and the error term, without loss of generality, the equation is written in a form that has a zero sample mean for the error term:

$$Y_i = \beta_0^* + \beta_1 X_i + \epsilon_i^*$$

This form is always assumed to apply; therefore, this second classical assumption is assured as long as the constant term is included in the equation.

III.   All regressors are uncorrelated with the error term ϵ_i.   It is as-
sumed that the observed values of the x_i's are determined independently of the values of the dependent variable and, hence, independently of the error term. That is, their values are determined outside the set of equations considered to be the relevant model. Their values are *predetermined,* and the x's are said to be *predetermined variables.* When the equation is part of a simultaneous equations system, for example (as was discussed in Section 2.3.2), then one or more of the regressors may not be predetermined. In the supply and demand model, a demand equation may have the quantity

demanded as the dependent variable and price as one of the regressors. Since price and quantity may be jointly determined, price as well as quantity may be correlated with the equation's error term; a random shock (from the error term) affects both price and quantity. Both variables then are "dependent" variables and are called *endogenous* variables. This type of model violates this classical assumption. An alternative estimator for this case, two-stage least squares (TSLS), is discussed and compared with OLS in Chapter 9.

Predetermined regressors are of two kinds: *exogenous,* such as household income in a demand equation, the value of which is determined outside the supply and demand model; and *lagged endogenous,* such as the quantity demanded in the previous time period. Although predetermined regressors are usually assumed to be uncorrelated with the error term, in some cases lagged endogenous variables could be correlated with the error term (as is discussed in Section 9.8)

IV.   The error term for one observation, ϵ_t, is not systematically correlated with the error term for another observation, ϵ_s (t $\neq$ s).   It is customary to discuss this assumption in the context of time-series models, using the subscript t to denote the time period. This assumption says that a random shock in one period—as from an extreme value of an omitted variable—does not show up in, or affect in any way, the error term in subsequent time periods. In other words, the error term ϵ_t could have been a different value if some special random shock had occurred in period $t,$ but the subsequent error terms for time $t+1$, $t+2$, etc. would not be affected in any systematic way. If, over all the observations in the sample, ϵ_{t+1} tended to show some correlation with ϵ_t, then the error terms are said to be *autocorrelated,* or *serially correlated,* and this assumption of *nonautocorrelation* would not hold. Violation of this classical assumption is discussed in Chapter 7, where alternative estimating techniques such as CORC are introduced and compared to OLS.

V.   The degree of dispersion (the variance) of the error term ϵ_i is the same for each observation.   It is customary to discuss this assumption in the context of a cross-section model. (See Section 2.5 for a discussion of cross-section models.) The assumption is called *homoskedasticity,* and the condition (or "malady") in which the variance of the error term σ_ϵ^2 is different for at least one observation is called *heteroskedasticity,* and the error terms are said to be *heteroskedastic.* As an example, in a cross-section analysis of household consumption patterns, the variance (or dispersion) of the consumption of certain goods might be greater the higher the level of income is, because the higher-income households have more discretion about what can be purchased with their incomes than the low-income households do. Thus, the absolute amount of the dispersion would be greater even if the percentage deviation was the same. This violation and an alternative estimating technique (generalized least squares, or GLS type of procedure) are discussed in Chapter 8.

VI.   There are no exact linear combinations among the regressors; that is, there is no perfect multicollinearity.   Perfect collinearity between two regressors implies that they are the same variable except for a scale factor or an addition of a constant to one of the regressors. That is, the movements in one regressor are matched one for one with the movements in the other regressor although the absolute size of the movements could differ between the regressors. (In the notation of Section 3.2.2, for two regressors x and z, the squared coefficient of correlation, r^2_{xz}, is equal to unity.) Thus, the computer regression program is unable to assign the regressors different coefficients that supposedly show their individual relationship with the dependent variable.

Many instances of perfect collinearity (or multicollinearity if more than two variables are involved) are the result of the researcher's not accounting for identities among the regressors, and these cases can be corrected easily. In the example of dummy variables given in Section 2.1.3(a), D_1 was defined as unity if a Bachelor's degree was obtained (and zero otherwise), and D_2 was defined as unity if a Master's degree was obtained (and zero otherwise), where these were assumed to be the only two possibilities for beginning high school teachers. Including both D_1 and D_2 as regressors gives rise to perfect multicollinearity because the "variable" of the y-intercept β_0 is unity and $D_{1i} + D_{2i} = 1$ for all observations. When two variables always sum to a third (in this case unity), in an exact linear relationship among the regressors, it is defined as perfect multicollinearity. The computer program is unable to separate the effects of the constant term on the one hand and of D_1 and D_2 on the other. Thus, it is unable to estimate coefficients for D_1 and D_2 in such a case (except for rounding error): it will either produce an error message or take a very long time to produce what will appear to be "bad" estimates of the coefficients, with high estimated standard deviations. The correction procedure is easy in this case: just delete either D_1 or D_2 as a regressor and interpret the coefficients accordingly.

VII.   The error terms are normally distributed.   Given Assumptions II–V, this assumption implies that each ϵ_i is drawn independently (Assumption IV) from a normal distribution with a zero mean value (Assumption II) and a constant variance (Assumption V). The motivation for this assumption is usually the Central Limit Theorem, as was discussed in Section 3.3. The values of ϵ_i will be centered about zero, with very infrequent extreme observations, depending on the magnitude of the variance of the error term. The error terms are said to be independent (nonautocorrelated), identically distributed (homoskedastic and with the same mean, zero) random variables, or "iid" normal random variables. The normality assumption is not necessary to obtain OLS (or even other) estimators, but its usefulness is in *hypothesis testing*, which uses the calculated regression statistics to accept or reject hypotheses about economic behavior, such as whether the demand curve for a product is elastic.

For future reference, an error term satisfying Assumptions II through VI is called a "classical" or white noise error term; and if Assumption VII is included, the error term is called a classical normal error term. Unless otherwise stated, it is also understood that a classical error term is not correlated with any other random variable in the given model, except the dependent variable (a connection that is explained in Section 4.2).

VIII.   There are positive degrees of freedom.   This assumption is usually not stated explicitly. It says that there must be at least one degree of freedom. In the notation here, n must be greater than $K+1$: the number of observations must be greater than the number of coefficients to be estimated (including the constant term

β_0). This requirement was discussed in Section 1.3.5(a) on "Degrees of Freedom." Unless this requirement is met, computer programs will be unable to estimate the coefficients.

4.2 The Sampling Distribution of the OLS Estimator $\hat{\beta}$

This section introduces the methodology of Monte Carlo simulation and demonstrates how the assumption of normality of the error term implies that the OLS estimator of the slope coefficient in the simple model, $\hat{\beta}$, is also normally distributed. The simple model is sufficient to demonstrate the necessary points:

$$y_i = \beta x_i + \epsilon_i \qquad (4.2.1)$$

The error term is a random variable, and its value for a given observation i could be any number—positive, negative, or zero. In practice, an applied researcher "draws" (but does not actually observe) only one value of ϵ_i from all its possible values for each observation i. (The "drawing" is in effect usually done for the researcher because the data are taken as given, rather than being generated in a controlled experiment.) Given the assumed "true" model (equation 4.2.1), the value of x_i (because x_i is assumed to be exogenous), and that β is a specific numeric value (such as $\beta = 1$), only one value of y_i is observed in practice. However, in theory, many values of y_i would be compatible with the model, given the values of β and x_i. These alternative values of y_i are the result of the random nature of the error term. In theory, ϵ_i could be any value, and through equation 4.2.1, so could y_i.

All of econometric theory is based on this view of the random nature of the error term, and the procedure called *Monte Carlo simulation* uses this approach to compute a number of values of y_i for each value of x_i. Then the OLS (or some other) estimating formula is applied to these sets of values of y_i and x_i to obtain a number of estimates of β even though in practice only one estimate of β is observed. The many estimates of β are constructed in order to discover the chances (or likelihood or probability) that a single selection of $\hat{\beta}$ that is usually obtained in practice will be close to the true value of β. In particular, the relative frequency distribution of the computed $\hat{\beta}$'s generated by a Monte Carlo simulation indicates the degree of reliance that can be placed on a single estimate.

4.2.1 The Monte Carlo Approach

This section gives a detailed presentation of the Monte Carlo approach, applied to the classical, normal, linear regression model. In this text, the Monte Carlo approach is the major pedagogical device to explain the underlying philosophy of regression analysis. Because of its importance in this text and in econometrics in general, the steps of a typical Monte Carlo experiment are listed for reference in the accompanying box.

Steps in Monte Carlo Experiments

1. Assume a true model.

2. Select values for the parameters and the exogenous variables.

3. Select the estimating techniques.

4. Create numerous sets of values of the endogenous variables.

5. Compute the estimates.

6. Evaluate the results.

7. Vary model parameters or exogenous variables, and do it all over again (i.e., conduct sensitivity tests).

The following are the typical and essential steps taken during a Monte Carlo simulation, applied to the estimation of β in the classical normal model. Section 4.2.2 outlines some essential sensitivity tests that should be included in any Monte Carlo experiment, shown as step 7 in the accompanying list. Subsequent chapters use the Monte Carlo approach in all its richness to compare OLS to other estimating techniques, such as CORC (Chapter 7) and TSLS (Chapter 9).

Step 1:   Assume a true model.   In this case, the simple model (equation 4.2.1) is assumed along with all the classical normal assumptions, through Assumption VII.

Step 2:   Select parameter values and values for the exogenous variable x_i.   For this illustration, assume $\beta = 1$ and let the variance of ϵ_i, σ_ϵ^2, be 0.25. (The classical normal assumptions imply that the mean value of ϵ_i is zero and that each ϵ_i is "generated" by the same normal distribution.) Assume that the number of observations, n, is 5 and that the values of x_i are (in deviation-from-the-mean form) $x_1 = 0.0979$, $x_2 = -0.1806$, $x_3 = -0.1937$, $x_4 = -0.0345$, and $x_5 = 0.3110$. These values were taken at random from the uniform $(0,1)$ distribution (as the variable X_{K+1} was in the demonstration of the Central Limit Theorem in Section 3.3) and their mean value was subtracted from each observation.

Step 3:   Select the estimating technique(s).   In this case, only one estimating technique is used, the OLS estimator of Section 3.2.1:

$$\hat{\beta} = \frac{\sum_{i=1}^{n} x_i y_i}{\sum_{i=1}^{n} x_i^2} \tag{4.2.2}$$

Step 4:   Create numerous sets of values of the dependent variable, y.   A large number of sets of n values of y_i must be created because each set, along with the single set of values of x, is used in the OLS formula (equation 4.2.2) to compute a value of $\hat{\beta}$. One such $\hat{\beta}$ is computed for each set of the y_i, using the same x_i. The desired end product of this simulation is an analysis of the relative frequency distribution of these values of $\hat{\beta}$.

To compute values of y_i in this case, one draws a large number of sets (of n values each, the sample size), say $p = 5000$ such sets, of the error term ϵ_i and uses the assumed model to compute the resulting value of y_i (recall that β was assumed to be unity):

$$y_i = x_i + \epsilon_i \tag{4.2.3}$$

The p sets of values of n error terms come from a computer program that generates random observations from the standard normal distribution. Call this variable z_i; it has a mean of zero and variance of unity. The following equation then translates this standard normal variable z_i into values of ϵ_i, which has a variance of 0.25 instead of unity:

$$\epsilon_i = (0.25)^{1/2} z_i \tag{4.2.4}$$

As an illustration, the first four sets of ϵ_i and y_i have been tabulated in Table 4.2.1. All three variables, ϵ_i, x_i, and y_i, are in the deviation-from-the-mean form in order to deemphasize the intercept term β_0 and to make the computations easier. (Actually, the mean of the ϵ_i was not zero in each of the cases shown. As the sample size became larger, the means became closer to zero; just as in Chapter 3, the frequency distributions approximated their true population distribution as the sample size increased.)

TABLE 4.2.1

Monte Carlo Simulations of OLS on
$y_i = \beta x_i + \epsilon_i$: First Four Sets of Data and Statistics
($\beta = 1$, $\sigma_\epsilon^2 = 0.25$, and $n = 5$)

Observation	Data Set 1			Data Set 2			Data Set 3			Data Set 4		
	ϵ_i	x_i	y_i	ϵ_i	x_i	y_i	ϵ_i	x_i	y_i	ϵ_i	x_i	y_i
1	0.29	0.10	0.38	−0.27	0.10	−0.17	−0.12	0.10	−0.02	−0.35	0.10	−0.25
2	0.72	−0.18	0.54	−0.62	−0.18	−0.80	−0.33	−0.18	−0.51	−0.19	−0.18	−0.37
3	−0.35	−0.19	−0.55	0.80	−0.19	0.61	0.65	−0.19	0.45	0.44	−0.19	0.25
4	−0.12	−0.03	−0.16	−0.82	−0.03	−0.86	−0.66	−0.03	−0.70	0.85	−0.03	0.81
5	−0.53	0.31	−0.22	0.91	0.31	1.22	0.47	0.31	0.78	−0.75	0.31	−0.44

Estimates												
$\hat{\beta}$		−0.10			2.37			1.51			−0.97	
$\hat{\sigma}_\epsilon^2$		0.27			0.76			0.39			0.32	
$\hat{\sigma}_{\hat{\beta}}^2$		1.52			4.26			2.17			1.78	
t		−0.07			0.56			0.70			−0.54	
R^2		0.00			0.30			0.26			0.15	

Notes: Data and statistics are rounded off. The true value of $\sigma_{\hat{\beta}}^2$ here is 1.41.

Notice that the x_i's remain the same for the repeated drawings of new sets of the ϵ_i's. That is, the x_i's are "fixed in repeated samples" of the error term, to use the customary terminology. The x_i's are held fixed in order to infer the probability distribution of $\hat{\beta}$ conditional on a given set of x_i's. This is compatible with Assumption III that the regressors are independent of the error term. *If* their values had been given, the value of y_i would be determined through the assumed model, equation 4.2.3, using the random error terms generated through equation 4.2.4. Actually, the x_i's could be random. In that case, as long as they move independently of movements in the error term, this analysis and the ultimate conclusion still apply, but only conditional on a given set of the x_i's being drawn.

It is best to use a large number of sets of values of y_i because then a smooth relative frequency distribution of $\hat{\beta}$ can be constructed. If an infinite number of drawings could be taken and the relative frequency were constructed for very small intervals of values of $\hat{\beta}$, then the resulting histogram would resemble a smooth, continuous function, as was discussed in Section 3.3. It is this function that is the *probability* or *sampling distribution* of the estimator $\hat{\beta}$. The histogram of the 5000 $\hat{\beta}$'s generated attempts to approximate this "true" distribution.

Step 5: Compute the estimates. Also shown in Table 4.2.1 are the first four estimates of $\hat{\beta}$ (and a number of other statistics to be used later) estimated by the OLS formula (equation 4.2.2) applied to the x, y pairs. In actual practice, only one estimate is available. Since it is drawn at random, any one of these four values has the same chance of being the estimate observed in practice.

Figure 4.2.1 shows a plot of the third set of data in Table 4.2.1. Graphed are the estimated regression line and the "true" regression line. In the deviation-from-the-

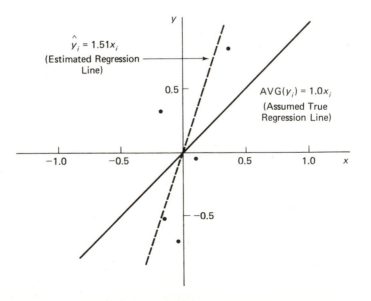

FIGURE 4.2.1 True and Estimated Regression Lines and Observations from the Third Set of the Monte Carlo Data

mean coordinate system (x, y), the estimated regression line passes through the origin. The true regression line is unlikely to pass through the sample means $(\overline{X}, \overline{Y})$ (and thus through the (x, y) origin), but it was drawn as such in Figure 4.2.1 in order to emphasize the slope (β) estimate and to deemphasize the intercept (β_0) estimate. As shown in the figure, the estimated regression line is different from the true regression line. But of the first four data sets generated, the third set provided the best estimate of β, 1.51. In general, some data sets are better than others; which one is observed in practice is a matter of chance. All too often, beginners fail to distinguish between the *estimate* of the parameter β (here, 1.51) and the parameter itself (which is unity). This demonstration may help to avoid that confusion.

Step 6: Evaluate the results.

Figure 4.2.2 shows the relative frequency function of the $\hat{\beta}$'s (shown as a histogram) for the 5000 estimates of β generated by the Monte Carlo simulation. The smooth line in the figure represents the relative frequency function that would be generated if an infinite number of $\hat{\beta}$'s were computed and the intervals along the $\hat{\beta}$ axis were made very small. It was drawn freehand on the basis of the histogram. In most of the subsequent graphs, only this smooth curve is plotted. It represents the true sampling distribution from which inferences are made about the properties, or "goodness," of the estimator.

Note that the sampling distribution of $\hat{\beta}$ is centered on the assumed true value β = 1. In fact, if β had been set at the value 2, the entire distribution, without any change in its shape, would have been shifted over and centered on $\beta = 2$. The property of an estimator the sampling distribution of which is centered on the true value of β is called *unbiasedness*, the formula for computing $\hat{\beta}$ is called an *unbiased estimator*, and the single drawing of $\hat{\beta}$ in practice is called an *unbiased estimate*.[1] Since only

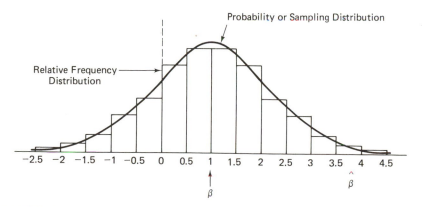

FIGURE 4.2.2 Sampling Distribution on the OLS Estimator $\hat{\beta}$ for $\beta = 1$, $\sigma_\epsilon^2 = 0.25$, and $n = 5$.

---

[1] In this particular example, the sampling distribution is symmetric, so the "center" of the distribution is at its peak, or mode. In Section 4.4.5, a sampling distribution is shown that is not symmetric, so its "center" is not at its mode.

one value of β is obtained in practice, the property of unbiasedness is useful because the single estimate β that is drawn randomly from this sampling distribution is more likely to be near the true value $\beta = 1$ than if the same sampling distribution were centered over $\beta = 2$, even though the true value of β was unity. If the distribution had been centered on two when $\beta = 1$, the OLS estimate would be called a *biased* estimator. Examples of biased estimators are presented in Chapters 6 and 9. In general, when the classical (not necessarily normal) assumptions hold, OLS estimates of the coefficients are unbiased. (This holds as well for the multivariate model. In fact, unbiasedness requires only the classical Assumptions I through III.)

Step 7: *Vary model parameters and do it all over again.* Because of its importance, the last step of the Monte Carlo simulation is presented as the following separate section.

4.2.2 Varying Model Parameters: Sensitivity Analysis

The last step in Monte Carlo analysis is called sensitivity analysis, through which it may be learned whether the conclusions drawn for one particular set of parameters hold for all other feasible values.

In theoretical econometrics, analytic (i.e., mathematical) techniques are used to derive the various properties (or characteristics) of estimators, such as unbiasedness. In most cases, the various properties are *proven* to hold. Monte Carlo simulations could rarely *prove* that a property holds for an estimator because of the infinite number of combinations of values of the parameters (β and σ_ϵ^2) and the alternative values for the x_i's that would have to be examined before a proof would be achieved. Monte Carlo simulations do have their scientific (as opposed to pedagogical) usefulness, however. They can *suggest* whether a property holds when the analytic approach fails to provide a proof. Also, Monte Carlo techniques can be used to provide a counterexample showing that a given property may not hold (so the analyst can stop searching for an analytic proof that does not exist).

The reader is reminded that the Monte Carlo simulations in this text are used as a teaching tool in lieu of analytic proofs. Unless otherwise stated, the simulations merely demonstrate the results of analytic proofs already a part of the econometrics literature.

4.2.2(a) *More Degrees of Freedom Imply More Precise Estimates.*
In the model in Section 4.2.1, a number of elements could be changed, and the β distribution could be computed over again. Previous analytic research has shown that two changes in particular produce interesting and predictable results. One of them is changing the number of observations. As was discussed in Section 1.3.5(a), the greater the degrees of freedom, which, given the model to estimate, implies more observations, the more precise or reliable the estimates. Presented here is a demonstration of that assertion.

In Figure 4.2.3, increasing the number of observations from $n = 5$ to $n = 15$ produces a more peaked sampling distribution. The distribution for $n = 15$ is less widely dispersed than the one produced for $n = 5$. The degree of dispersion is called

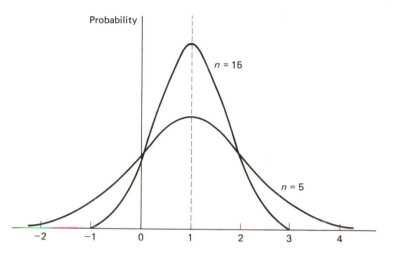

FIGURE 4.2.3 Sampling Distribution of $\hat{\beta}$ for Various Values of the Number of Observations (n)

the *variance,* and its square root is called the *standard deviation.* Thus, the variance decreases as the sample size n increases. A lower variance is a welcome attribute because it enhances the likelihood that a single drawing of $\hat{\beta}$ as observed in practice is closer to the true value $\beta = 1$, given the situation here in which $\hat{\beta}$ is unbiased.

In this simulation for $n = 15$, all the other elements of the experiment were kept the same. Of course, 10 more observations had to be chosen for x_i. In this case, the first 5 observations of x were repeated 2 more times. With this procedure, the magnitude of the additional x_i's is held "constant" in some sense, and the simulation results show more clearly the effects of an increase in the number of sample observations *per se.*

Since the error term is random, however, 15 new observations were drawn for each set of data in the same manner that the 5 were drawn before. (It would be a violation of Assumption IV, the independence of the error terms, if the ϵ's were repeated as the x's were).

The first 10 values of $\hat{\beta}$ are shown in Table 4.2.2, for the cases $n = 5$ and $n = 15$ (the variance $\sigma_\epsilon^2 = 0.25$ for both cases). Although it is not necessarily the case that each value of $\hat{\beta}$ when $n = 15$ will be closer to the true value $\beta = 1$ than each value is when $n = 5$ (because chance can cause any result), it is true for the ten estimates shown, and the general tendency is clear. In econometrics, the general tendencies must be relied on: the element of chance, a random occurrence, is always present in estimating regression coefficients, and the estimate may not be near the true value, no matter how good the estimating procedure is. However, when most of the sampling distribution is centered around the true value, as is the case when $n = 15$ compared with the distribution of $\hat{\beta}$ when $n = 5$ (see Figure 4.2.3), the element of chance is less likely to produce a bad estimate.

The lower variance of $\hat{\beta}$ as shown in Figure 4.2.3 when n increases is the reason that more observations are preferred to fewer. In technical terms, the $\hat{\beta}$ estimator

TABLE 4.2.2

First 10 Monte Carlo Estimates of $\hat{\beta}$ for $n = 5$ and $n = 15$ ($\sigma_\epsilon^2 = 0.25$ throughout)

		Observation Set									
		1	2	3	4	5	6	7	8	9	10
Number of observations (n)	5	−0.10	2.37	1.51	−0.97	2.93	0.26	1.63	0.61	3.42	−0.47
	15	0.88	1.88	0.94	1.04	0.70	0.88	0.51	0.94	1.02	0.87

becomes more *precise* as the number of observations increases. More precision refers to the lowering of the variance of the sampling distribution of the estimator, which means that the possible estimates that can be obtained in practice are more likely to be near the true value of the parameter, for unbiased estimates (i.e., for estimators that have sampling distributions centered over the true value of the parameter). If one of the first 10 possible $\hat{\beta}$'s of Table 4.2.2 had been observed in practice, when $n = 5$, an estimate of 3.42 could have been obtained, but, when $n = 15$, the worst estimate would have been 1.88, much closer to the true value of β of unity. Thus, as the variance gets smaller, for unbiased estimates, the probability increases that the $\hat{\beta}$ *typically* observed just once in practice will be within a specified interval of β.

If the sampling distribution was centered on a different value from the true value of β—that is, if $\hat{\beta}$ was biased—then increased precision would imply that most of the sampling distribution of $\hat{\beta}$ would be concentrated around the wrong value. However, if this value was not very different from the true value of β, the greater precision may still be very valuable. Illustrations of this idea are presented in Section 6.2.

Some students have suggested that, instead of having one estimate of β from 15 observations, split up the observation set into several smaller samples and compute a number of estimates of β. Then a sampling distribution could be observed with these few calcualtions of $\hat{\beta}$, and its central tendency could be observed in practice. Thus, why not compute three $\hat{\beta}$'s of five observations each? The answer to this question is that the sampling distribution thus observed for each of the three samples is for the wide distribution in Figure 4.2.2 for which $n = 5$, not the narrow one for which $n = 15$. Furthermore, the central tendency of these 3 observations must some-how be computed. If the simple arithmetic mean were computed, the resulting estimate would be *less precise* (i.e., its sampling distribution would be more widely dispersed) than the sampling distribution shown in Figure 4.2.3 for $\hat{\beta}$ using all 15 observations. Only a special weighted average of the 3 samples of $\hat{\beta}$ would produce a single estimate as precise as when all 15 observations were used, and the best such weighted average would turn out to be exactly the OLS formula using all 15 observations. Thus, nothing is to be gained by not using all the available observations in computing $\hat{\beta}$ (see also Section 10.4 on "*Ex Post* Forecasting").

4.2.2(b) Higher Error Variance Implies Less Precise Estimates.

Another parameter, the variance of the error term, can be varied, and the resulting sampling distribution of $\hat{\beta}$ can be predicted. If the number of observations is held constant, say at $n = 15$, and the error variance σ_ϵ^2 increases, then the variance of $\hat{\beta}$ increases by the same proportion. Such a sampling distribution is shown in Figure 4.2.4, holding n at 15 and doubling σ_ϵ^2 from 0.25 to 0.5; also shown are the two distributions shown in Figure 4.2.3.

The reason for the increased variance of $\hat{\beta}$ is that, with the larger variance of ϵ_i, some of the more extreme values of ϵ_i are observed with increased frequency, and the error term becomes more important in determining the values of y_i than before, relative to the deterministic portion of the regression equation, βx_i, which was kept the same in this experiment. Thus, the relative portion of the movements of y_i "explained by" the deterministic component βx_i is less, and the larger "unexplained" movements in y_i caused by the stochastic element ϵ_i imply that the empirical inference of the value of β is more tenuous. On average, the R^2 of the equation is lower when σ_ϵ^2 increases, and the accuracy or precision of the OLS estimator $\hat{\beta}$ is less.

Section 4.3 shows that the tendencies discussed here when n or σ_ϵ^2 changes are quite predictable on the basis of formulas for the measures of central tendency and variance of the OLS estimator $\hat{\beta}$.

4.3   Notation Conventions

This section presents the classical assumptions in their standard notational representation. The necessary statistical background for the symbols to be introduced was developed in Section 4.2 with the Monte Carlo experiment. The notation is used to represent the measures of the central tendency and the degree of dispersion of sampling

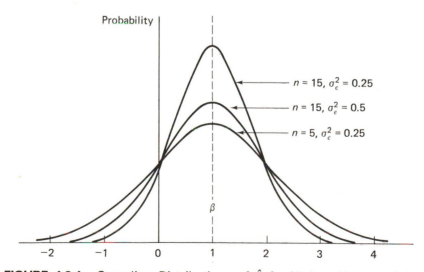
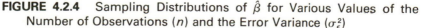

FIGURE 4.2.4 Sampling Distributions of $\hat{\beta}$ for Various Values of the Number of Observations (n) and the Error Variance (σ_ϵ^2)

(and all probability) distributions. In this section, the Monte Carlo experiment is used once more to show that the estimate of the variance of the estimated coefficient also has a sampling distribution, one that is quite different from the normal distribution. Finally, since the notation by this time has become very complex, a table is presented that summarizes the notation conventions.

4.3.1   Expectation Notation

While Section 4.2 portrayed the notions of central tendency and dispersion graphically, this section and the next present their notational representations. This notation is standard in the econometrics literature, so it is necessary to understand it. The measure of the central tendency of the sampling distribution of $\hat{\beta}$, the mean or modal values of its sampling distribution for the cases just examined, is denoted as $E(\hat{\beta})$, read as "the *expected value* of $\hat{\beta}$." The symbol E is called the expectations operator. Rules have been developed for algebraic manipulations using this operator, but these need not be of concern to regression users. Rather, regression users need to understand the expectations concept and to be able to interpret its meaning in the academic articles that they read.

The $AVG(Y_i)$ notation of the first three chapters was actually an expectations operator, representing the average or expected value of Y_i. The concept is exactly the same. If it was understood there, the reader should have no problem understanding it now. From this point on, the expectation notation will be used instead of the AVG notation.

4.3.2   Variance Notation

The variance of $\hat{\beta}$ is the degree of dispersion of its sampling distribution. For the same reasons that were mentioned regarding the expectations operator, the variance operator is merely presented here, without the accompanying rules for mathematical manipulations. The variance operator has several alternative notational representations: $VAR(\hat{\beta})$, $\sigma^2(\hat{\beta})$, or $\sigma_{\hat{\beta}}^2$. Each of these is read as the "variance of $\hat{\beta}$," and each represents the same measure of the degree of dispersion of the sampling distribution of $\hat{\beta}$.

4.3.3   The Classical Assumptions in Notational Form

Most econometrics texts and articles delineate the classical model in terms of expectations and variance operators. For completeness and in order that the student be able to read those texts, the classical assumptions that are usually stated in these terms (Assumptions II through V) are presented here.

II.

$$E(\epsilon_i) = 0 \qquad\qquad i = 1, 2, \ldots, n$$

That is, the error term has a central tendency of zero. In terms of the Monte Carlo simulations, for a "large" number of Monte Carlo drawings, the mean value of ϵ_i tends to zero, for any sample size n.

III.

$$E(x_{ik}\,\epsilon_i) = 0 \quad k = 1, \ldots, K \quad \text{and} \quad i = 1, 2, \ldots, n$$

The lack of correlation of each regressor x_k and the error term, for all observations, is defined in terms of the expected value of their product equalling zero. If x_{ik} and ϵ_i are not independent, then it follows as a mathematical property that the expected value of their product is not zero. This would occur if values of X_k above its mean varied systematically with positive values of ϵ_i, for example. It will be recalled that this assumption of the independence of x_i and ϵ_i is violated in the simultaneous equations model.

IV.

$$E(\epsilon_i\,\epsilon_j) = 0 \qquad\qquad\qquad i \neq j$$

Nonautocorrelation is likewise stated in terms of the expected value of the product of error terms from different observations equalling zero. If one error term were systematically related to another, then the expected value would not be zero.

V.

$$VAR(\epsilon_i) = \sigma_\epsilon^2 \qquad\qquad\qquad i = 1, 2, \ldots, n$$

Homoskedasticity is defined as a constant variance for all observations and heteroskedasticity is stated as the variances being different for at least one observation.

4.3.4 Formulas for the Expected Value and Variance of the OLS Estimator

Since the mathematical derivations are not shown in this text, only the analytic *results* of applying the expectations and variance operators to the OLS estimator (equation 4.2.2) under the classical assumptions in the single-regressor model are presented:

$$E(\hat{\beta}) = \beta \qquad\qquad\qquad (4.3.1)$$

$$VAR(\hat{\beta}) = \frac{\sigma_\epsilon^2}{\Sigma x_i^2} \qquad\qquad\qquad (4.3.2)$$

The expected value formula is the statement of the *unbiasedness* of $\hat{\beta}$, i.e., it says that the central tendency of the sampling distribution of $\hat{\beta}$ is the true value β. This property of unbiasedness holds as well for the K-regressor model, viz.,

$$E(\hat{\beta}_k) = \beta_k$$

Two inferences are evident from the variance formula. First, the variance of $\hat{\beta}$ is proportional to the variance of the error term ϵ_i. This relationship was explained and demonstrated in Section 4.2.2(b) (see Figure 4.2.4); to reiterate, the higher the error variance is, the more difficult it is to obtain an accurate estimate of β because the sampling distribution of $\hat{\beta}$ is more widely dispersed. Second, the larger is the denominator of equation 4.3.2, $\Sigma x_i^2 = \Sigma(X_i - \overline{X})^2$, the smaller is the variance of $\hat{\beta}$. This may be achieved with more observations on X_i different from its mean value, as was discussed in Section 4.2.2(a). But in addition to more degrees of freedom, given the number of observations, it is a desirable attribute to have a regressor that exhibits a considerable amount of variation. Then the expression Σx_i^2 is larger so the variance of $\hat{\beta}$ is smaller, according to the variance formula (equation 4.3.2).

Thus, sample variation in the regressor is a welcome attribute, but in practice usually nothing can be done to achieve it. However, researchers should never exclude data because they contain extreme observations. Rather, the extreme observations should be actively sought and used. The appendix to this chapter provides a heuristic explanation of why a high degree of variation in the regressors produces more precise estimators.

The formulas for the variances of the estimators in the two-regressor model are the same as the variance in the simple model except for one major difference. In the equation:

$$y_i = \beta_1 x_{i1} + \beta_2 x_{i2} + \epsilon_i \qquad (4.3.3)$$

the variances of the OLS estimators $\hat{\beta}_1$ and $\hat{\beta}_2$ are:

$$\sigma_{\hat{\beta}_1}^2 = \frac{\sigma_\epsilon^2}{(1-r_{12}^2)\,\Sigma x_{i1}^2} \qquad (4.3.4)$$

$$\sigma_{\hat{\beta}_2}^2 = \frac{\sigma_\epsilon^2}{(1-r_{12}^2)\Sigma x_{i2}^2} \qquad (4.3.5)$$

where r_{12} is the coefficient of correlation between x_1 and x_2 (defined in Section 3.2.2). The only difference between these formulas and the one for $\sigma_{\hat{\beta}}^2$ in the single-regressor model is the term involving the simple coefficient of correlation between X_1 and X_2:

$$r_{12} = \Sigma x_1 x_2 / (\Sigma x_1^2 \Sigma x_2^2)^{1/2}$$

The factor r_{12}^2 represents the degree of collinearity between X_1 and X_2 (and x_1 and x_2), and the variance of both $\hat{\beta}_1$ and $\hat{\beta}_2$ increases as r_{12}^2 increases (toward unity). In cases of extreme collinearity, in which movements of x_1 cannot be distinguished from movements in x_2 (e.g., the movements in x_1 are twice the movements in x_2), r_{12}^2 approaches unity, and the variances approach infinity. The OLS routine is not capable of assigning separate coefficient estimates to x_1 and x_2 because these variables have not exhibited separate movements in the sample. That is, the computer program, except for rounding error, will not generate coefficient estimates. In a controlled experiment, x_1 would be held constant while x_2 was varied, but social scientists rarely have the luxury of a controlled experiment.

The problem of collinearity is basic. The appropriate theoretical interpretation of β_1 in the two-regressor model is the change in the expected value of y given a unit change in x_1, holding x_2 constant. But when x_2 is not held constant in the sample, the empirical interpretation along the theoretical lines is in jeopardy. In the extreme case of perfect collinearity, when $r_{12}^2 = 1$, no spearate estimates of β_1 are available because x_2 is not held constant even in the slightest degree as x_1 varies.

4.3.5 Estimate of the Variance of $\hat{\beta}$

The variance of the estimated slope coefficient in the single-regressor model, $\hat{\beta}$, indicates the degree of dispersion of the sampling distribution of $\hat{\beta}$, hence the degree to which a single estimate obtained in practice is likely to be close to the true value β (given that $\hat{\beta}$ is unbiased). However, the variance is unobservable in practice, so an estimate of $\sigma_{\hat{\beta}}^2$ would be a useful indication of the degree of reliance to be placed on the single estimate $\hat{\beta}$. An unbiased estimator of $\sigma_{\hat{\beta}}^2$ can be obtained by substituting in the variance formula 4.3.2 an unbiased estimator of the variance of the error term, σ_ϵ^2. In turn, an unbiased estimate of the error variance, for the K-regressor model, is:

$$s^2 = \frac{\Sigma e_i^2}{(n-K-1)} \qquad (4.3.6)$$

The numerator is the sum of squares of the residuals (SSE), and the denominator is the degrees of freedom, the number of observations less the coefficients that are estimated (including the constant term). Often s^2 is denoted $\hat{\sigma}_\epsilon^2$ or $\hat{\sigma}^2$. The (positive) square root of s^2 is called the *standard error of the equation,* or SEE.

Thus, for the single-regressor model, an unbiased estimate of $\sigma_{\hat{\beta}}^2$, also written as $s_{\hat{\beta}}^2$ or $\hat{\sigma}_{\hat{\beta}}^2$, is found by substituting s^2 for σ_ϵ^2 in the variance formula for $\sigma_{\hat{\beta}}^2$:

$$s_{\hat{\beta}}^2 = \frac{s^2}{\Sigma x_i^2} \qquad (4.3.7)$$

In the two-regressor model, the estimates of $VAR(\hat{\beta}_1)$ and $VAR(\hat{\beta}_2)$, found by substituting s^2 for σ_ϵ^2 in equations 4.3.4 and 4.3.5, show the same dependence on the collinearity between x_1 and x_2 as do the true variances themselves. That is, the variances increase as r_{12}^2 increases, and the variances approach infinity (i.e., "explode") as it approaches unity. The formulas for the estimated variances of the estimated coefficients in the K-regressor model are complicated and are not reproduced here. However, they also reflect the multicollinearity among the regressors, with the estimated variances increasing as the degree of multicollinearity increases.

The estimator of $\sigma_{\hat{\beta}}^2$ is stochastic, or random, a fact that is sometimes overlooked. Thus, a single estimate will likely differ from the true value. Table 4.2.1 showed the estimates of σ_ϵ^2 and $\sigma_{\hat{\beta}}^2$ for each of the first four sets of Monte Carlo drawings. Compare these estimates respectively to the true variance of ϵ, assumed to be 0.25, and to the true variance of $\hat{\beta}$, which in this case is 1.41 (applying equation 4.3.2).

Figure 4.3.1 shows the sampling distributions of $\hat{\sigma}_{\hat{\beta}}^2$ (or $s_{\hat{\beta}}^2$) for the number of observations $n = 5$ and $n = 15$ (for $\sigma_\epsilon^2 = 0.25$). Just as for the sampling distribution of β, the sampling distribution of $\hat{\sigma}_{\hat{\beta}}^2$ becomes more concentrated about its central tendency $\sigma_{\hat{\beta}}^2$ (i.e., the distribution has a smaller variance) as the number of observations increases. Also notice that the true variance decreases as n increases. Thus, the measure of central tendency of the unbiased estimator $\hat{\sigma}_{\hat{\beta}}^2$ must also decrease along with the true variance as n increases.

It will also be noticed that the values of $s_{\hat{\beta}}^2$ are only positive and that the distribution is not symmetric but is skewed to the right. The measure of central tendency usually used is still the population mean (i.e., expected value), not the mode or the median. Thus, the estimate is unbiased because the mean of the distribution equals the true value of the parameter, $\sigma_{\hat{\beta}}^2$, however, in this case, the true value decreases as the number of observations (or the degree of dispersion in the values of the regressor x_1, as discussed in Section 4.3.4) increases. For reference purposes, the sampling distribution of $s_{\hat{\beta}}^2$ is called a chi-square distribution.

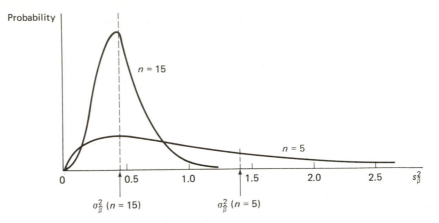

FIGURE 4.3.1 Sampling Distributions of $s_{\hat{\beta}}^2$ for $n = 5$ and $n = 15$ ($\sigma_\epsilon^2 = 0.25$)

4.3.6 Summary of the Notation Conventions

A review of the notation is in order at this point. Table 4.3.1 presents alternative notation used to represent the various population (or "true") parameters and their corresponding estimates. Often, estimated coefficients in a three-regressor model are denoted (in Yule notation) as, for example, $b_{y1.23}$, read as the estimated coefficient for y regressed on x_1, given that x_2 and x_3 are also regressors.

To review Table 4.3.1, the true coefficient β_k is estimated by $\hat{\beta}_k$. The estimator is stochastic, or random, because its value depends on the values of the error term in the true function. Thus $\hat{\beta}$ has a probability or sampling distribution based on the distribution of the ϵ_i's, namely, the normal distribution. The expected value of the estimated coefficient, denoted $E(\hat{\beta})$, is a population concept that does not have an empirical or sample counterpart, unless it equals β.

Two population parameters, the mean and the variance (or the standard deviation), fully describe the $\hat{\beta}$ distribution. The mean, the measure of the central tendency of the sampling distribution, is $E(\hat{\beta}_k)$, which equals β_k if and only if the estimator is unbiased. Its variance is $\sigma_{\hat{\beta}_k}^2$. While the variance describes the degree of dispersion in the sampling distribution of $\hat{\beta}_k$, it too is a population parameter and is not observed in practice. It is estimated as $\hat{\sigma}_{\hat{\beta}_k}^2$, based on an estimator of the variance of ϵ. Note that $\sigma_{\beta_k}^2$ is zero because β_k (as opposed to $\hat{\beta}_k$) is a constant and thus has no dispersion; $\hat{\sigma}_{\beta_k}^2$ correspondingly has no usefulness since its population counterpart is known to be zero. Thus, (1) the *estimated* variance of the *estimated* coefficient is defined and observed, (2) the *estimated* variance of the true regression coefficient is not defined, (3) the variance of the estimated coefficient is defined but unobservable, and (4) the variance of the true regression coefficient (a parameter) is zero. The reader must understand these nuances in order to be comfortable with the notational representation of regression analysis.

It may be asked, since the variance of $\hat{\beta}_k$ refers to the variance of the sampling distribution, which is based on repeated samples of sets of n error terms (ϵ_i), how can

TABLE 4.3.1

Notation Conventions

Population Parameter (True Values, but Unobserved)		Estimate (Observed from Sample)	
Name	Symbols(s)	Name	Symbol(s)
Regression coefficient	β_k	Estimated regression coefficient	$\hat{\beta}_k$ or b_k
Expected value of the estimated coefficient	$E(\hat{\beta}_k)$		
Variance of the error term	σ_ϵ^2, σ^2, or $VAR(\epsilon_i)$	Estimated variance of the error term	s^2, $\hat{\sigma}_\epsilon^2$, or $\hat{\sigma}^2$
Standard deviation of the error term	σ_ϵ or σ	Standard error of the equation	s, $\hat{\sigma}_\epsilon$, $\hat{\sigma}$, or SEE
Variance of the estimated coefficient	$\sigma_{\hat{\beta}_k}^2$, $\sigma^2(\hat{\beta}_k)$, or $VAR(\hat{\beta}_k)$	Estimated variance of the estimated coefficient	$s_{\hat{\beta}_k}^2$, $\hat{\sigma}_{\hat{\beta}_k}^2$, $\hat{\sigma}^2(\hat{\beta}_k)$ or $\widehat{VAR}(\hat{\beta}_k)$
Standard deviation of the estimated coefficient	$\sigma_{\hat{\beta}_k}$ or $\sigma(\hat{\beta}_k)$	Standard error of the estimated coefficient	$s_{\hat{\beta}_k}$, $\hat{\sigma}_{\hat{\beta}_k}$, or $\hat{\sigma}(\hat{\beta}_k)$
Error or disturbance term	ϵ_i	Residual (estimate of error in a loose sense)	e_i

an estimate of the variance of $\hat{\beta}_k$ be obtained from just one sample of n observations as is usually found in practice? The answer is that each ϵ_i, for each of the n observations, as well as for repeated drawings on each observation, is assumed to be distributed exactly the same, namely, according to the classical assumptions. Thus, while repeated drawings for each observation would add to the degrees of freedom of an estimate of $\sigma_{\hat{\beta}_k}^2$, they are not necessary, and the n observations are sufficient to provide an estimate (as long as there are positive degrees of freedom).

4.4   The Gauss-Markov Theorem on Least Squares

The Gauss-Markov Theorem on OLS is proven in all advanced econometrics texts. This theorem states that with Assumptions I through VI—the assumption of normality is not needed for this theorem—the OLS estimate of β is the best, linear, unbiased estimator, or *BLUE*, of β.

The unbiasedness of the slope coefficient in the single regressor model was shown above ($E(\hat{\beta}) = \beta$). Linear here refers to the OLS estimator being linear in the y's.

(Recall that the x's are assumed to be "fixed" and are to be considered the same as coefficients.) Since Assumption I shows that the y's are linear in the β's, the fact that $\hat{\beta}$ is linear in the y's also assures that $\hat{\beta}$ is linear in the β's. (Substitute the simple model (equation 4.2.1) into the OLS formula (equation 4.2.2) for y if this proposition on linearity needs to be proven.)

"Best" means that $\hat{\beta}$ has the smallest variance of all linear, unbiased estimators of β. An unbiased estimator with the smallest variance is called efficient, and the estimator is said to possess the property of efficiency.[2] An example discussed in Section 4.2.2(a) of an alternative unbiased estimator of $\hat{\beta}$ that has a greater variance is one that uses the same OLS formula (equation 4.2.2) but fewer than the n available observations.

The power of the Gauss-Markov theorem is that, if the classical assumptions are satisfied, the OLS estimator has the lowest variance of any linear, unbiased estimator of β. Therefore, *checking whether the classical assumptions hold is the first step in deciding which estimating technique to use.* Both theoretical considerations and empirical evidence are used to check for the classical assumptions, and the major portion of the remainder of this book is devoted to such an analysis. The "Regression Mechanic's Guide" of Section 11.2 is a summary of the type of diagnostic checking usually done and of some of the suggested corrective remedies, if they are necessary. In the rest of the text, the sampling distribution of the OLS estimator $\hat{\beta}$ is compared to the sampling distributions of alternative estimating techniques that attempt to correct for possible deficiencies or "maladies" in the OLS estimator when a classical assumption does not hold. The procedure of comparing OLS estimates with other estimates is standard practice in applied econometrics.

4.5   Map of Subsequent Chapters

The plan of the rest of the book can now be explained. Chapter 5 extends the Monte Carlo analysis of the current chapter to develop the notion of hypothesis testing. The rationale for the t-test of the regression coefficients is explained in detail. Chapter 5 must be inserted at this point in order to understand the material on hypothesis testing contained in all the remaining chapters. Chapter 10 reviews all the hypothesis testing material of Chapter 5 and of all the intervening chapters, and presents standard tests of hypotheses involving more than one coefficient.

Chapters 6 through 9 are based on violations of various assumptions of the classical model. Chapter 6 examines specification errors of the type in which the model used for estimation differs from the true model. In one case, a relevant variable is excluded from the estimating equation. In a second case, an irrelevant variable is included. These two cases present one of the most perplexing problems for applied econometricians: should a variable be included or excluded from the regression equa-

---

[2] For advanced readers, efficiency is sometimes defined in the mean square error sense, so that it would apply to biased estimates as well.

tion? A third case involves the use of the incorrect functional form for estimation purposes. All three of these cases represent a violation of the form of the true model (Assumption I) during the estimation procedure.

Assumption II of a zero mean for the error term is never questioned because it is always assured by including in the estimating equation the constant term β_0. Since a finite number of n observations on ϵ_i would be unlikely to yield a sample mean of the ϵ_i's of exactly zero (although the probability of being close to zero is greater with more observations), the inclusion of β_0 is strongly recommended, as is stressed in Section 6.1.

Chapter 9 deals with violations of Assumption III that the regressors are uncorrelated with the error term. The simultaneous equations model forms the primary basis for this investigation.

Autocorrelation and heteroskedasticity, violations of Assumptions IV and V, are studied separately, in Chapters 7 and 8, respectively.

Assumption VI, the absence of perfect multicollinearity, is not studied as a separate topic although repeated references are made to it throughout the text, especially in Chapter 6, and testing for its presence and seriousness is discussed in Chapter 10.

In this text, the normality of the error term, Assumption VII, is assumed to hold because of the Central Limit Theorem, as was discussed in Chapter 3. However, for constrained dependent variables, such as those that take on only values of zero or one, normality no longer holds. In these cases, preliminary estimation is usually carried out assuming normality, and advanced techniques may be used. These techniques are beyond the scope of this text.

4.6   Summary

This Chapter discussed two possible properties of an estimator, unbiasedness and efficiency. Unbiasedness holds when the mean of the sampling distribution of the estimator equals the true value of the parameter, and efficiency implies the lowest possible variance (for the class of linear, unbiased estimators).

Under the classical assumptions, OLS (ordinary least squares) is BLUE, the most efficient, unbiased, linear estimator of the regression coefficients (i.e., best, linear, unbiased estimator). When one or more of the classical properties do not hold, OLS is no longer BLUE, but it may still provide better estimates in some cases than alternative techniques that are discussed in subsequent chapters.

In this book, Monte Carlo simulations play the role of a teaching tool, and the Monte Carlo approach was explained in the context of OLS applied to the simple regression model. It revealed the probability underpinnings of regression analysis, emphasizing the notion that the single estimate of a regression coefficient encountered in practice is only one of a whole spectrum of values that could have been obtained if a different set of random disturbances (ϵ_i's) had been observed. The approach of econometrics is to recognize this random process and to attempt to use estimators (such as OLS) that have sampling distributions that indicate they will provide estimates that can be relied on most of the time.

The sampling distribution of the OLS estimator $\hat{\beta}$, being BLUE, has desirable properties. Moreover, the variance, or degree of dispersion of the sampling distribution of $\hat{\beta}$, decreases as the number of observations or the degree of dispersion of the regressor increases. The only element over which we have at least some control is the number of observations, and the rule here is simple: if the cost of additional observations is within reason, obtain and use them for estimation.

This chapter introduced and demonstrated the standard notation for the expected value and variance of an estimator. Table 4.3.1 presented a rather complex set of notational conventions in regression analysis. This table should be reviewed periodically as a refresher, because this notation is used throughout this text and throughout the econometrics and economics literature.

Appendix to Chapter Four: Illustration that More Variation in Regressors Produces More Precise Estimators

The material of this appendix is presented here in order to avoid disturbing the flow of material in this chapter. Yet it covers a very important point that was made in Section 4.3.3: more variation in the regressors leads to more precise estimators, i.e., estimators that have a lower variance. For the two-regressor model, more variation in the regressors implies that Σx_1^2 and Σx_2^2 are larger, so the variances of the estimated coefficients are lower, as shown by the equations 4.3.4 and 4.3.5. Also, more variation in the regressors *may* imply that the sample correlation of the regressors is smaller. It is possible, but not necessarily a result, that greater sample variation provides more nearly the type of observations in which one regressor is held constant while the other one varies, and vice versa. Thus, according to equations 4.3.4 and 4.3.5, the variances are smaller with the lower sample correlation among the regressors.

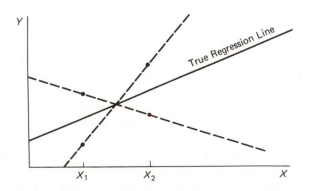

FIGURE 4.A.1 Extreme Regression Lines with Values of X Close to Each Other

In the single-regressor model, equation 4.3.2 shows that the variance of the estimated slope coefficient is smaller when there is more sample variation in the regressor. A heuristic explanation of this result is illustrated by Figures 4.A.1 and 4.A.2. In both graphs, the true regression line and the variance of the error term are the same. In Figure 4.A.1, the values of the single regressor X are closer together than they are in Figure 4.A.2. Given extreme values of the error term ϵ that produce extreme values of Y, two possible extreme estimated regression lines are shown in the two graphs as the dashed lines. (For illustrative purposes, only two points are shown for each estimated regression line.) As portrayed in the two graphs, the extreme estimated regression lines that could be observed in practice diverge more from the true regression line if the X-values are close together, as in Figure 4.A.1, than if the X-values are widely dispersed, as in Figure 4.A.2.

Even though estimated regression lines require more than two observations, the idea is that, if the values of X are far apart, given the same absolute level of the variance of the error term, OLS will be more likely to produce an estimated regression line that is closer to the true regression line than if the values of X are close together.

In fact, a variable X that does not vary much in the sample creates the problem of collinearity. Such a variable is almost a constant and thus is collinear with the "variable" of the y-intercept (β_0), which is unity for every observation.

Furthermore, again on a heuristic level, the regression coefficient is supposed to indicate the change in the expected value of Y given a unit change in X. But if X has not changed much in the sample, the estimated coefficient is not likely to be able to show this relationship with much accuracy.

As was mentioned in Section 4.3.3, the applied researcher is usually unable to alter the degree of variability in the regressors. However, the author has read papers in which it was claimed that some observations were deleted because they represented extreme observations. This is not a valid reason for throwing them out, but just the

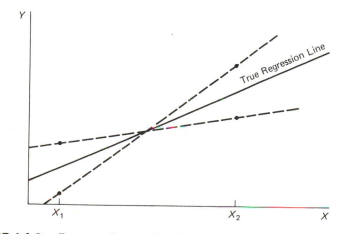

FIGURE 4.A.2   Extreme Regression Lines with Widely Dispersed Values of X

opposite: it is a valid reason for including them. The researchers probably threw these observations out because their model was not constructed properly (such as having the correct functional form) so it could ''explain'' these observations. Thus, these observations, when included, likely produced what seemed to be strange and unwanted coefficient estimates.

5 Hypothesis Testing and the *t*-Test

Up to this point, the text has stressed statistical inference: from a set of data on x and y, a "point" (or single) estimate of one or more slope coefficients, such as β, is calculated. It was also emphasized, however, that a single estimate of β would be only one of many such possible estimates because any estimator of β has a probability or sampling distribution, and the single estimate observed in practice must necessarily be drawn from one of many possible outcomes, as governed over the long run by this probability distribution. This was demonstrated in Chapter 4 and is reinforced here.

This chapter presents a step-by-step development of and the rationale for the *t*-test. It demonstrates the connection between the assumption of normality of the error term and the use of the *t*-statistic. Readers with sufficient background in statistics and hypothesis testing can skip this chapter and proceed directly to Chapter 6. However, the development here is in terms of the regression model, which may be instructive even to those with some familiarity with statistics. Chapter 10 completes the lessons on hypothesis testing, but an understanding of the standard approach, as illustrated in this chapter with the *t*-statistic, is necessary for all the intervening chapters, because in those chapters special tests are discussed on how to discern whether or not several of the classical assumptions are valid for a given model.

5.1 Type I and Type II Errors

One of the most commonly used procedures in regression analysis is to decide whether a slope coefficient β is different from zero. For this case, there are two distinct possibilities. The first is that $\beta = 0$. When $\beta = 0$, unbiased estimates of β will be distributed about zero, yet any given estimate is very unlikely to equal zero. Thus,

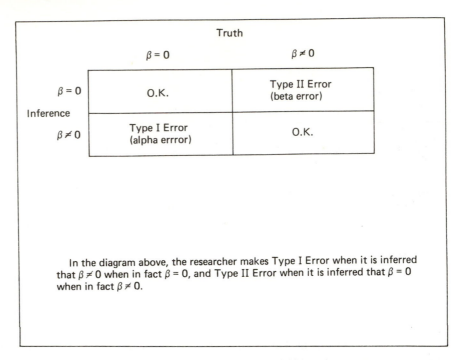

	Truth	
	$\beta = 0$	$\beta \neq 0$
Inference $\beta = 0$	O.K.	Type II Error (beta error)
$\beta \neq 0$	Type I Error (alpha errror)	O.K.

In the diagram above, the researcher makes Type I Error when it is inferred that $\beta \neq 0$ when in fact $\beta = 0$, and Type II Error when it is inferred that $\beta = 0$ when in fact $\beta \neq 0$.

even if the true parameter $\beta = 0$, the single drawing from its sampling distribution obtained by the researcher (i.e., the estimate in practice) may be sufficiently different from zero to lead to the conclusion that $\beta \neq 0$. The error that is made when the true parameter $\beta = 0$ but the inference from the estimate is that $\beta \neq 0$ is called *Type I Error* (or alpha error).

The second possibility is that $\beta \neq 0$. Depending on the specific value of β (and on other factors), it is possible to obtain an estimate of β that is close to zero for all practical purposes, because the sampling distribution usually has some positive probability around the value $\beta = 0$. The error that is made when $\beta \neq 0$ but the inference from the estimate is that $\beta = 0$ is called *Type II Error* (or beta error). The diagram above illustrates these concepts.

5.2 Development of a Decision Rule: Example of Two Possible Values for β

In general, the purpose of hypothesis testing is to accept or reject hypotheses about the values of the parameters of an assumed model. Hypotheses are accepted or rejected according to a *decision rule* that is based solely on the results of estimates obtained through the regression procedure. For most testing of hypotheses, a single statistic is computed from the regression results, and the hypothesis is accepted or rejected depending on the magnitude of that statistic compared to a "critical" value found in tables such as those at the end of this text.

5.2.1 Null and Alternative Hypotheses

To illustrate these basic notions, suppose that there are only two alternatives for the slope coefficient β, zero and unity, in the simple classical model, $y_i = \beta x_i + \epsilon_i$. The researcher must select, according to the regression results, which one is more likely the true one (only one of them can be true at any given time). Thus, the two hypotheses, involving just the unknown parameter β, are either $\beta = 0$ or $\beta = 1$. One of these is called the *null* hypothesis, and the other is called the *alternative* hypothesis. For reasons that will become clear shortly, suppose that the null hypothesis, denoted H_0, is $\beta = 0$ and that the alternative hypothesis, H_A, is $\beta = 1$. This is written formally as:

$$H_0: \beta = 0$$
$$H_A: \beta = 1$$

$$(5.2.1)$$

5.2.2 Reliance on the Sampling Distribution of $\hat{\beta}$

In order to formulate a decision rule to determine which hypothesis is more likely to be correct, we can construct the sampling distributions of the OLS estimator $\hat{\beta}$ assuming alternatively that $\beta = 0$ and $\beta = 1$. This formulation of a decision rule is done before regression estimates are obtained. Recall from Section 4.2.1 that the sampling distribution of $\hat{\beta}$ is normal because the error term is normally distributed. Figure 5.2.1 shows the sampling distributions of β when it is assumed that $\beta = 0$ or, alternatively, that $\beta = 1$. The notation for these distributions is $f(\hat{\beta}: \beta = 0)$ and $f(\hat{\beta}: \beta = 1)$, where the colon indicates that the statement following it is assumed to be true. These are also called the conditional distributions of $\hat{\beta}$ because they are constructed conditional on $\beta = 0$ and $\beta = 1$, respectively. These sampling distributions were generated by Monte Carlo simulations in which it was alternatively assumed that $\beta = 0$ for $f(\hat{\beta}: \beta = 0)$ and $\beta = 1$ for $f(\hat{\beta}: \beta = 1)$, for the number of observations $n = 25$ and the variance of the error term $\sigma_\epsilon^2 = 0.25$. The error term is of the classical, normal

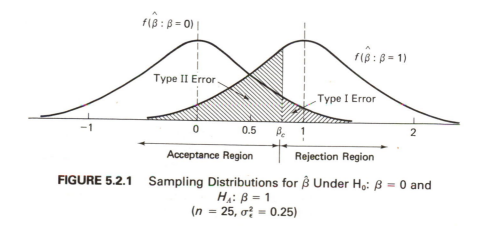

FIGURE 5.2.1   Sampling Distributions for $\hat{\beta}$ Under $H_0: \beta = 0$ and $H_A: \beta = 1$ $(n = 25, \sigma_\epsilon^2 = 0.25)$

variety. Notice that the shapes of the distributions are identical. Only the location differs between $\beta = 0$ and $\beta = 1$. Both distributions show that the OLS estimator is, of course, unbiased, since the respective distributions are centered on their true values.

5.2.3 Acceptance and Rejection Regions: Selecting the Critical Value

There are several approaches to establishing a test for whether H_0 or H_A appears to be correct. The classical approach is the one taken in this text; more advanced texts also present an alternative approach called Bayesian. In Figure 5.2.1, the horizontal axis is divided into two regions, an *acceptance region* and a *rejection region*. (How these regions are formulated will be made clear in Section 5.3.) That is, a critical value of β is selected, β_c, in such a manner that, if the single estimate $\hat{\beta}$ is less than β_c, it will be inferred that H_0: $\beta = 0$ is correct—i.e., the null hypothesis is not rejected—and if $\hat{\beta}$ is greater than β_c, it will be inferred that H_A: $\beta = 1$ is correct, and the null hypothesis is rejected. Notationally, the decision rule is:

$$\text{Do not reject } H_0 \text{ if } \hat{\beta} \leq \beta_c$$
$$\text{Reject } H_0 \text{ (and accept } H_A) \text{ if } \hat{\beta} > \beta_c \tag{5.2.2}$$

To make this rule operational, we need to select the critical value β_c. In Figure 5.2.1, a value of β_c has been selected at 0.8, for the moment in an arbitrary manner. But given this value of β_c, the two types of error can be assessed. If the observed $\hat{\beta}$ is greater than β_c but $\beta = 0$, we would reject H_0 when in fact it is true, thus making a Type I Error. The amount of the error is denoted by the area under the conditional distribution f($\hat{\beta}$: $\beta = 0$) to the right of β_c. Recall that a sampling distribution is just a relative frequency distribution with a "very large" number of drawings and very small intervals along the horizontal axis. Just as the area under any relative frequency curve (or histogram) must sum to unity (or 100 percent), so must the area under the sampling or probability distribution. For the value of β_c selected, 10 percent of the area under the curve f($\hat{\beta}$: $\beta = 0$) lies to the right of β_c, the rejection region. This indicates that, if in truth $\beta = 0$, then the decision rule would reject H_0 10 percent of the time because 10 percent of the time the estimate $\hat{\beta}$ would be greater than β_c. The 10 percent refers to a repeated number of drawings, as if we were conducting a Monte Carlo simulation to determine the rejection rate, given our decision rule. Of course, in practice we take only one drawing, but we must rely on the longer-run percentages. (Why bet against the odds? See Section 3.3 for a review of the notion of randomness.)

We can never eliminate Type I Error because to do so would increase Type II Error. Type II Error results when the alternative hypothesis is falsely rejected, in this case when H_A is rejected when in fact $\beta = 1$. The amount of Type II Error is shown by the area under the sampling distribution f($\hat{\beta}$: $\beta = 1$) to the left of β_c. In this case, when the critical value β_c is set at 0.8, the amount of Type II Error is about 40 percent. That is, these values of $\hat{\beta}$ are possible about 40 percent of the time when $\beta = 1$ according to the area shown as Type II Error in Figure 5.2.1. As may be seen in the figure, if β_c was increased in an effort to reduce or eliminate Type I Error, the amount of Type II Error would increase. And lowering β_c makes the amount of Type

II Error smaller at the expense of an increased amount of Type I Error. Thus, there appears to be a dilemma in selecting the appropriate cut-off point β_c.

In this present situation with only two possible outcomes, $\beta = 0$ or $\beta = 1$, if the loss or penalty inflicted on the researcher were the same for each type of error, the decision rule would likely be constructed by selecting $\beta_c = 0.5$. (This approach, in fact, is Bayesian.) With this value, the amounts of Type I and II Errors would be identical, about 25 percent each. However, the case typically encountered in practice is unlike the one here in which only two outcomes are possible. In practice, any outcome on the number line is a possible value for β; thus, the approach to hypothesis testing must account for this reality, as is now discussed.

5.3 One-Sided Tests on β

In practice, we are usually interested in whether the regression results would indicate that β is of a particular sign. Suppose we suspect on the basis of theory that β is positive and would like the statistical results to verify that hypothesis. In order to control the amount of error we would make, on average if done a very large number of times, if this hypothesis is accepted, we set up the alternative hypothesis as H_A: $\beta > 0$, the one in which we are interested, and relegate to the null hypothesis the one in which we have little interest, H_0: $\beta < 0$. We set up the hypotheses in this particular way in order to be able to say that, if the data and statistical results have rejected H_0 and accepted H_A, this result would ensue only 10 percent of the time if in fact the null hypothesis H_0 were true. Thus, we have limited Type I Error to 10 percent by this formulation. If the sign of β is expected to be positive, most researchers do not want a relationship between x and y unless the data show convincingly that the sign of β is positive. Thus, researchers are willing to accept an unknown amount of Type II Error in exchange for assurances from the test that β is in fact positive. They are usually willing to have no relation at all if they cannot have a 90 percent (or so) assurance that their *a priori* notion is correct.

5.3.1 Limiting the Maximum Amount of Type I Error

Figure 5.3.1. explains these ideas a bit further. The two sampling distributions for $\hat{\beta}$ from Figure 5.2.1 are reproduced, and two new ones are added, for illustrative purposes, for assumed values of β of -1 and 2. Under the null hypothesis, β can be at most zero. Thus, the maximum amount of Type I Error occurs for the limiting case in which $\beta = 0$. When β is less than zero, the amount of Type I Error, given the value of β_c, is always smaller. At $\beta = -1$, for example, the amount of Type I Error is virtually zero since virtually none of the area under the curve f $(\hat{\beta}: \beta = -1)$ is to the right of β_c. Thus, selecting β_c by making the amount of Type I Error equal to 10 percent under the ''border hypothesis'' $\beta = 0$ has the effect of limiting the *maximum* amount of Type I Error to 10 percent for all possibilities under the null hypothesis, $\beta \leq 0$.

Whereas the amount of Type II Error is 40 percent when $\beta = 1$, it could be very small, such as 3 percent as shown in Figure 5.3.1 when $\beta = 2$. It could also be almost 90 percent, when $\beta = 0.001$, for example, and the sampling distributions under $\beta = 0$ and $\beta = 0.001$ are virtually indistinguishable. If $\beta = 0.001$, we would no doubt be perfectly satisfied with accepting H_0: $\beta \leq 0$, because 0.001 may not be different enough from zero to matter. The larger the true value of β is, the smaller is the amount of Type II Error, just as we would like it since we only want to accept H_A: $\beta > 0$ if in fact the true value of β is "significantly positive."

5.3.2 Level of Significance and Level of Confidence

The words "significantly positive" usually carry the statistical interpretation that H_0 ($\beta \leq 0$) was rejected in favor of H_A ($\beta > 0$) according to the preestablished decision rule, which was set up with, in this case, a *10-percent level of significance*, which is also stated as a *90-percent level of confidence*. Thus, if H_0 is rejected in favor of H_A, we say that β has been shown to be "statistically significantly positive," or just "statistically significant" or "statistically different from zero," at the 10-percent level of significance or the 90-percent level of confidence.

It is arbitrary whether Type I Error, the level of significance, is set at 10-percent, 5-percent, 1-percent, or some other level. Researchers are supposed to specify, before the estimate $\hat{\beta}$ is computed, how confident they want to be in the event H_0 is rejected. Unfortunately, there is usually very little to guide this decision other than the vague notion that the error rate when H_0 is rejected should be "small."

If β_c in this example is set at 1.0 instead of at 0.8 (see Figure 5.2.1), the level of significance falls to about 5 percent from the previous level of 10 percent, and the level of confidence correspondingly increases from 90 to 95 percent. Selection of β_c, in other words, is the mechanism by which the researcher controls the level of confidence. But recall that the greater the level of confidence is, the larger is the amount of Type II Error, so the researcher cannot make the level of confidence too large. When β_c is increased from 0.8 to 1.0, the amount of Type II Error increases from 0.4 to 0.5, or from 40 to 50 percent, as can be seen by examining Figure 5.2.1.

5.3.3 *H₀* as the "Strawman"

A mistake often—sometimes unavoidably—made by researchers is to establish the null hypothesis as the one in which they are interested. Once the null hypothesis

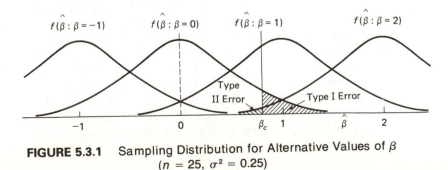

FIGURE 5.3.1 Sampling Distribution for Alternative Values of β
($n = 25$, $\sigma^2 = 0.25$)

is accepted, there is no way to determine how much error (of Type II) is made. The classical approach to hypothesis testing requires that the null hypothesis be the "straw-man," the hypothesis opposite to the one in which the researcher is interested in accepting, but accepting only if the maximum amount of error is some predesignated, arbitrarily small level, such as 10 percent. Then, when the null hypothesis is rejected, the researcher can have 90 percent confidence in the result. If the null hypothesis is accepted, the researcher abides by that result and implicitly is willing to accept the unknown amount of Type II Error that is possible. With this approach, it is not very comforting to have to accept the null hypothesis, but there is considerable satisfaction in rejecting it, in which case the error rate is some known, arbitrarily small amount. In fact, instead of "accepting" the null hypothesis, it is standard terminology to say that the researchers "cannot reject H_0" when they are left with the null hypothesis, because of the unknown amount of error when H_A is rejected.

5.4   Two-Sided Tests

Often, the expected sign of a coefficient is not known *a priori*. But, as before, researchers normally do not want to include a variable x and to make inferences from its estimated coefficient unless they can be assured that the variable belongs in the relation, i.e., that its estimated coefficient is "statistically different from zero." To investigate the appropriate testing procedure, consider the following hypotheses, which involve three alternative values of the true parameter:

$$H_0: \beta = 0$$
$$H_A: \beta = 1 \text{ or } \beta = -1$$

(5.4.1)

In this case, the decision rule must be a bit more complicated than for the one-sided test. The usual approach taken is to select two critical values, β_L (a lower critical value) and β_U (an upper critical value), and to use the following decision rule, a two-sided or two-tailed test:

$$\text{Reject } H_0 \text{ if } \hat{\beta} < \beta_L \text{ or } \hat{\beta} > \beta_U$$
$$\text{Do not reject } H_0 \text{ if } \beta_L \leq \hat{\beta} \leq \beta_U$$

(5.4.2)

Again, the critical values are selected to limit the amount of Type I Error to some specified, arbitrarily small level.

Figure 5.4.1 illustrates the construction of such a decision rule. The acceptance region (for accepting H_0) lies between β_L and β_U, the two critical values of β. The amount of Type I Error is now the area under the sampling distribution when $\beta = 0$ at both ends outside the interval (β_L, β_U). It is customary (and makes for a better test) to select β_L and β_U symmetrically about the null hypothesis value $\beta = 0$. For example, β_U is set at 0.8, and β_L is set at -0.8, both of which are a distance of 0.8 from $\beta = 0$. For these values of β_U, β_L, and β, the amount of Type I Error (and the level of significance) is 20 percent, which consists of 10 percent from each tail of the sampling distribution. Accordingly, the one-sided or two-sided tests are often called one-tailed or two-tailed tests, referring to the "tails" of the distribution.

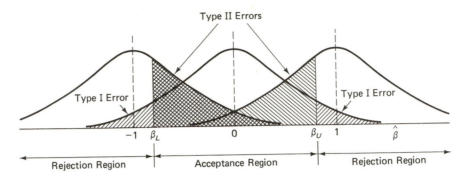

FIGURE 5.4.1   Decision Rule for Two-Sided Alternatives $\beta = -1$ and $\beta = 1$, versus $H_0: \beta = 0$

Even though β_U is the same as β_c in the one-sided case, the level of significance has doubled because the left tail of the sampling distribution must now also be included. If $\hat{\beta}$ turns out to be greater than β_U, for example, it would appear that the possible amount of Type I Error is only the amount indicated by the right tail, 10 percent. But the amount of Type I Error remains at 20 percent simply because the hypotheses were originally established as two sided and not one sided as previously, and $\hat{\beta}$ could just as easily have been negative before the estimate was observed.

There is an obvious gain in using the *a priori* information to construct the hypotheses and to perform one-sided instead of two-sided tests because, for the same level of β_c and β_U, the amount of Type I Error is halved for the one-sided approach. In order to achieve the same level of significance for the two-sided test as before in the one-sided test, 10 percent, β_U would have to be raised to 1.0, and β_L would have to be lowered to -1.0. Then the area in both tails would amount to 10 percent, the same as the area in the right-hand tail when the one-sided critical value $\beta_c = 0.8$.

Thus, the acceptance region must be *widened* in order to achieve the same level of significance with a two-sided test as can be achieved with a one-sided test. The consequence of a wider acceptance region is that the amount of Type II Error is larger. In Figure 5.4.1, the amount of Type II Error when $\beta_U = 0.8$ and $\beta_L = -0.8$ is shown as either the same area as for the one-sided test to the left of $\beta_U = 0.8$ under the sampling distribution when $\beta = 1$, or the area to the right of $\beta_L = -0.8$ under the sampling distribution when $\beta = -1$. Since β can only be either 1 or -1, only one of these areas applies. Thus, for $\beta_c = 0.8$ in the one-sided test and for $\beta_U = 0.8$ and $\beta_L = -0.8$ in the two-sided test, the amount of Type II Error remains the same, about 40 percent. But to maintain the same level of significance, 10 percent, in the two-sided test by raising β_U to 1.0 and lowering β_L to -1.0, the amount of Type II Error increases to 50 percent. Thus, one-sided tests are *always* preferred to two-sided tests because, for the same level of significance, the amount of Type II Error is less. One-sided tests should be used whenever the researcher's priors permit.

Just as with the one-sided test, there are usually an infinite number of possibilities for the alternative hypothesis, not just the two selected for illustration, $\beta = -1$ or $\beta = 1$. Thus, in general, the two-sided hypotheses can be stated as:

$$H_0: \beta = 0$$

$$H_A: \beta \neq 0$$

$(5.4.3)$

Researchers establish $\beta = 0$ as the null hypothesis because they want to include the variable x only if its coefficient is not zero. Selection of β_U and β_L is based on the sampling distribution under the null hypothesis $\beta = 0$ to insure the researchers that, if they reject the null hypothesis, they do so with a specified level of confidence. For $\beta_U = 0.8$ and $\beta_L = -0.8$, researchers have 80-percent confidence when H_0 is rejected. For $\beta_U = 1.0$ and $\beta_L = -1.0$, they have 90-percent confidence. It turns out that the same decision rule (or test) (equation 5.4.2) used for the simple alternatives $\beta = -1$ and $\beta = 1$ is used for the compound alternative hypothesis $\beta \neq 0$, involving an infinite number of outcomes. In both cases, the critical values are determined on the basis of the same sampling distribution, that under the null hypothesis.

To recapitulate, the null hypothesis is selected as the strawman, and the acceptance and rejection regions of the test are established on the basis of the sampling distribution under that null hypothesis (or at the border between the two hypotheses) so that the error rate when H_0 is rejected (i.e., Type I Error) is held to some arbitrarily small level, called the level of significance. One minus that error rate is called the level of confidence.

5.5 Violation of the Strawman Approach

The following illustration represents, unfortunately, an occurrence that is not uncommon. Suppose the researcher strongly suspects that the coefficient $\beta = -1$ and wants a test to verify this suspicion. The coefficient β could be the price elasticity of demand in an equation linear in the logarithms: $\log(q) = \beta \log(p) + \epsilon$ where q is quantity and p is price, and the (transformed) variables $\log(q)$ and $\log(p)$ are in deviation-from-the-mean form. From Section 2.2.2, β is interpreted as an elasticity for such an equation. (Assume that the supply of q is either perfectly elastic or inelastic in order to avoid the problem of simultaneous equations.) Thus, the researcher's priors indicate that the price elasticity is (negative) unity. If the hypotheses were to be set up as:

$$H_0: \beta \neq -1$$

$$H_A: \beta = -1$$

then H_0 is indeed the strawman. However, the critical values of β for the decision rule could only be established, according to the classical approach, for the sampling distribution when $\beta = -1$. That is, the border hypothesis, the value that divides H_0 from H_A, is $\beta = -1$, and a classical test can only be established on the basis of this border hypothesis (to control the maximum amount of Type I Error). Thus, these hypotheses can just as easily be stated as:

$$H_0: \beta = -1$$

$$H_A: \beta \neq -1$$

and the same decision rule would apply because the border hypothesis on which the rule is based is the same, $\beta = -1$. In this case, the null hypothesis is not the strawman; thus, there is no way to control the amount of error of Type II when the null hypothesis is accepted. But $\beta = -1$ is the result in which the researcher is interested, in this case, so Type II Error should form the level of significance, not Type I Error as is customary. One possible way to avoid a large amount of Type II Error is to narrow the acceptance region, thus increasing Type I Error. For example, the researcher could select a level of significance of 50 to 80 percent instead of 5 or 10 percent, but even then the amount of Type II Error when H_0 is accepted is still unknown. This procedure is hardly, if ever, followed in practice because of the arbitrariness involved.

This situation is unfortunate, but what should be remembered when the null hypothesis is no longer the strawman—or whenever the null hypothesis is accepted—is that the classical approach of limiting Type I Error to some arbitrarily small level does not necessarily limit to some small amount the error that can possibly be made (of Type II) when the null hypothesis is accepted.

The choice of a one-sided or a two-sided test depends on theory. If the theory postulates a negative coefficient for β, then the strawman or null hypothesis is the opposite one, $H_0: \beta \geqslant 0$, and the alternative hypothesis is the one suggested by theory, $H_A: \beta < 0$. The test should be set up so that the null hypothesis will be rejected only at most, say, 10 percent of the time when it is true. This gives researchers the right to claim that they are 90 percent confident that the true coefficient is, in fact, negative whenever the null hypothesis is rejected.

5.6 Review of the Steps

Note the essential steps in setting up null and alternative hypotheses. The alternative hypothesis is the one in which the researcher is interested, but only if the level of Type I Error is controlled. When the null hypothesis is accepted, there is usually an unknown amount of Type II Error possible since the alternative hypothesis is usually a composite one (e.g., $\beta < 0$). Notice also that the hypotheses are stated strictly in terms of the population parameters (the β's) and do not involve statistics of any kind. The decision rule is stated strictly in terms of statistics (in our example, $\hat{\beta}$) and numbers, called critical values (β_c, β_L, and β_U), that are derived prior to obtaining any statistics (or estimates). A general procedure for obtaining these numbers is described in Section 5.7. The population parameters are absent from the decision rule. In other words, the statistics (the parameter estimates) yield information that, when used in the decision rule, allows the researcher to infer something as stated in the hypotheses about the population parameters.

5.7 The *t*-Test

The tests developed in this chapter apply to each coefficient in a multiple regression equation. Notions were developed on how to construct one-sided and two-sided tests, and these apply to each coefficient separately. The alternative hypothesis is the one that the researcher wishes to accept only with a known and preset level of confidence, usually 90, 95, or 99 percent. The risk of increasing the level of confidence, say to 99 percent, is the increased probability of making a Type II Error. Thus, 90 or 95 percent levels of confidence are ordinarily used. Furthermore, it is best to use a one-sided test instead of a two-sided test whenever possible.

5.7.1 Problem of Standardization

The decision rule entails a preselection of one or two critical values of β, called β_c, or β_L and β_U. The problem with establishing such a rule for each coefficient for all regression equations estimated is that the β's are measured in units of the x's and y. In other words, in the two-regressor model

$$y_i = \beta_1 x_{i1} + \beta_2 x_{i2} + \epsilon_i \qquad (5.7.1)$$

β_1 is measured in units of y divided by units of x_1. That is, β_1 must perform the role of translating values of x_1 into values of y. For example, in a supply equation, if y is measured as units of output, say bushels per year, and x_1 is measured as its price, or dollars per bushel, then β_1 is necessarily measured as the converting factor, the number of bushels per year times the number of bushels per dollar. Then, an increase in the price by one *dollar per bushel* increases the quantity supplied by β_1 *bushels per year*, other things held constant. Similarly, if x_2 is rainfall, in inches per year, β_2 is measured in terms of bushels per year per inches of rainfall per year. Thus, if there is one more *inch of rainfall per year,* the quantity supplied increases by β_2 *bushels per year,* other things held constant. Quite obviously, the development of critical values (such as β_c) on the basis of the absolute measurement of the β's would require a separate analysis for each coefficient, and a standard set of tables of the critical values of the β's would be difficult to develop.

Also, each $\hat{\beta}_k$ has a different variance, or standard deviation, and the selection of β_c depends on the variance. In the single-regressor illustrations of Sections 5.2 and 5.3, the variance of $\hat{\beta}$ is $\sigma_\epsilon^2/\Sigma x_i^2$. Given the x_i, if the variance of the error term, σ_ϵ^2 is increased from 0.25 to 0.50, as in the example, then under the null hypothesis the sampling distribution of $\hat{\beta}$ widens out (or flattens out) as shown in Figure 5.7.1. For

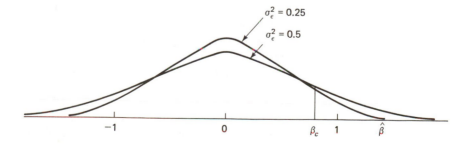

FIGURE 5.7.1 Sampling Distributions Under H_0: $\beta = 0$ For $\hat{\beta}$, For $\sigma_\epsilon^2 =$ 0.25 and 0.50 ($n = 25$)

the case in which $\sigma_\epsilon^2 = 0.25$, a value of β_c of 0.8 produces a one-sided level of significance of 10 percent. When σ_ϵ^2 increases to 0.50, the sampling distribution of $\hat{\beta}$ under H_0: $\beta = 0$ flattens out, and in order to construct a one-sided test with a 10 percent level of significance, the value of β_c would have to increase to approximately 1.0.

5.7.2   Solution: The *t*-Statistic

The solution to these two problems is achieved through the t-statistic, because (1) the estimated standard error of the estimated coefficient is also measured in the same units as β_k, so the ratio of $\hat{\beta}_k$ to $s_{\hat{\beta}_k}$ is free from the measurement problem, and (2) the ratio also accounts for differences in the standard deviations of the estimated coefficients. Thus, the measure used for testing for the kth regression coefficient is the t-statistic, which was introduced in Section 1.2.4:

$$t_k = \frac{\hat{\beta}_k}{s_{\hat{\beta}_k}} \qquad k = 1, 2, \ldots, K. \qquad (5.7.2)$$

These test statistics are used for the one-sided hypotheses:

$$H_0: \beta_k \leq 0 \qquad (5.7.3)$$
$$H_A: \beta_k > 0$$

or

$$H_0: \beta_k \geq 0 \qquad (5.7.4)$$
$$H_A: \beta_k < 0$$

and for the two-sided hypotheses:

$$H_0: \beta_k = 0 \qquad (5.7.5)$$
$$H_A: \beta_k \neq 0$$

The decision rule is the same in all three cases:

$$\text{Reject } H_0 \text{ if } |t_k| > t_c \text{ and} \qquad (5.7.6)$$
$$\text{if } \hat{\beta}_k \text{ is of the expected sign under } H_A$$

where $|t_k|$ is the absolute value of t_k as computed by equation 5.7.2, and t_c is the critical value of t_k found in the t-table at the end of the text, A-1. Otherwise, accept (or do not reject) H_0. For the same t_c, however, the level of significance for a two-sided test is twice that for a one-sided test, and the level of confidence is reduced. The t-Table A-1 distinguishes between one-sided and two-sided levels of significance.

These decision rules are based on the fact that, since both $\hat{\beta}_k$ and $s_{\hat{\beta}_k}$ have known sampling distributions, so does their ratio, the t-statistic. The sampling distributions for $\hat{\beta}_k$ and $s_{\hat{\beta}_k}$ were shown in Chapter 4, and they are based on the assumption of the normality of the error term, ϵ_i. Consequently, the sampling distribution of the t-statistic is based on the same assumption of the normality of the error term. Figure 5.7.2 shows the sampling distributions of the t-ratio for the problem in Section 5.7.1 under the null hypothesis $\beta = 0$ for the number of observations $n = 5$ and $n = 30$.

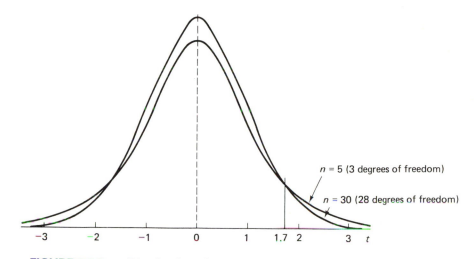

FIGURE 5.7.2 *t*-Distributions for $n = 5$ and $n = 30$ (for 3 and 28 degrees of freedom, respectively)

The same distributions are obtained regardless of the value of the error variance σ_ϵ^2 or the measurement of y or x_k. In this sense, the *t*-distribution is standardized.

These *t*-distributions are considered just as the $\hat{\beta}$ sampling distributions for determining critical values. Thus, as shown in Figure 5.7.2, a given level of t_c of 1.7 produces a one-sided level of significance of about 5 percent for $n = 30$ and about 10 percent for $n = 5$. To obtain a 5-percent level of significance for $n = 5$, a value of t_c of about 2.3 would be required. Thus, the critical value of t_c, which is compared to the *t*-statistic computed in equation 5.7.2, depends on the number of observations or, more appropriately, on the degrees of freedom, and on the level of significance chosen. Also, it depends on whether the test is one sided or two sided.

Figure 5.7.3 illustrates the dependence of the critical value of t_c on these factors. For the simple regression model with 30 observations and two coefficients to estimate (the slope and the intercept), there are 28 degrees of freedom. The acceptance and rejection regions are stated in terms of the decision rule (equation 5.7.6) for several different levels of significance and for one-sided ($H_A: \beta > 0$) and two-sided ($H_A: \beta \neq 0$) alternatives.

Statistical Table A-1 contains the critical values t_c for various degrees of freedom and levels of confidence. The column headings indicate the level of significance, according to whether the test is one sided or two sided, and the rows denote the degrees of freedom. The relationship between the one-sided and two-sided tests is illustrated in Figure 5.7.3. The critical value $t_c = 1.701$ is for a one-sided, *5-percent* level of significance. Since the left-hand tail of the *t*-distribution must be included in the level of significance for two-sided tests, this level of $t_c = 1.701$ represents a *10-percent* two-tailed level of significance. (As can be seen in the graph, the *t*-distribution is symmetrical about its central value, as is the sampling distribution for $\hat{\beta}$. However, the magnitude of the central value of the *t*-distribution is of no direct concern.)

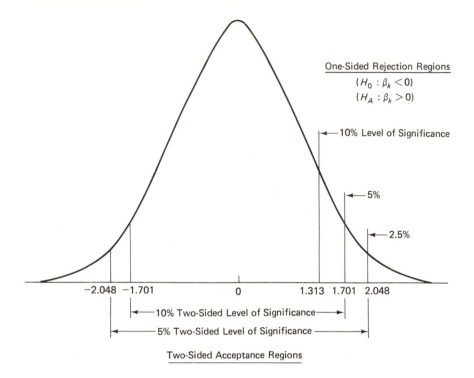

One-Sided Rejection Regions
$(H_0 : \beta_k < 0)$
$(H_A : \beta_k > 0)$

10% Level of Significance

5%

2.5%

−2.048 −1.701   0   1.313 1.701 2.048

10% Two-Sided Level of Significance

5% Two-Sided Level of Significance

Two-Sided Acceptance Regions

FIGURE 5.7.3   One-Sided and Two-Sided *t*-Tests for Various Levels of Significance, for 28 Degrees of Freedom

Many economists use as a rule of thumb a value of two for the critical value of the *t*-statistic. A value of t_c of 2 provides approximately a two-sided level of significance of 5 percent for 10 or more degrees of freedom. But the one-sided level of significance varies. For example, with 10 degrees of freedom, a value of t_c of 2 produces a level of Type I Error between 2.5 and 5 percent for a one-sided test; for 20 degrees of freedom, it produces a level of about 2.5 percent. Although the choice of the permissible level of Type I Error (the level of significance) is arbitrary and consequently the choice of t_c is essentially arbitrary, beginners are advised to use the more "scientific" approach outlined here and not the rule of thumb $t_c = 2$, especially since one-sided tests are preferred whenever possible.

5.7.3 Illustration

As an example of the applied use of the *t*-test, consider the following estimated equation:

$$Y_t = 1.30 + 4.91X_{t1} + 0.00123X_{t2} - 7.14X_{t3} + e_t \qquad (5.7.7)$$
$$\quad\quad\quad (2.1) \quad\quad (5.4) \quad\quad (-0.01)$$

where the *t*-statistics are in parentheses below the estimated coefficients. Assume that the hypothesized model is:

$$Y_t = f(\overset{+}{X_1}, \overset{-}{X_2}, \overset{-}{X_3}) \qquad\qquad (5.7.8)$$

Thus, β_1 is expected to be positive, and β_2 and β_3 are expected to be negative. Although theoretically a single test for all three slope coefficients should be applied here, nearly every practitioner examines each coefficient separately by the *t*-test, as follows. Notice that H_0 is always the strawman and that one-sided tests are used because of the existence of the priors. From equation 5.7.8, the one-sided hypotheses are set up as:

1. H_0: $\beta_1 \leqslant 0$

H_A: $\beta_1 > 0$

2. H_0: $\beta_2 \geqslant 0$

H_A: $\beta_2 < 0$

3. H_0: $\beta_3 \geqslant 0$

H_A: $\beta_3 < 0$

If there were 10 observation, the degrees of freedom is $10 - 4 = 6$ (three slope coefficients and a constant term are estimated). At a 95-percent level of confidence (or a 5-percent level of significance), the critical value of t_c is, from Statistical Table A-1, 1.943. For $\hat{\beta}_1$, the computed *t*-statistic is 2.1, and the null hypothesis that $\beta_1 \leqslant 0$ can be rejected with a 95-percent confidence level since $2.1 > 1.943$.

For $\hat{\beta}_2$, the *t*-statistic, while large in absolute value, 5.4, is of the incorrect sign—it has the same sign as $\hat{\beta}_2$—as is indicated by the theory. Thus, the null hypothesis cannot be rejected, and we are left with an unknown amount of Type II Error. Notice that the absolute magnitude of $\hat{\beta}_2$, 0.00123, is of no particular importance because a change in the units of measurement of x_2 can alter $\hat{\beta}_2$ by an exactly compensating amount [see Section 1.3.5(b)]. However, the *t*-statistic is not altered by a change in the units of measurement of x.

The coefficient $\hat{\beta}_3$ is not statistically different from zero since $|-0.01| = 0.01 < 1.943$, the latter being the critical value t_c, and the null hypothesis $\beta_3 \geqslant 0$ cannot be rejected.

Notice that if β_2 had been tested according to a two-sided test H_0: $\beta_2 = 0$ and H_A: $\beta_2 \neq 0$, the null hypothesis would have been rejected with a 95-percent level of confidence because 5.4 is greater than the critical value of 2.447 (read from Table A-1 for 6 degrees of freedom and a 5-percent, two-sided level of significance). But one's priors should be exercised whenever possible. It usually is not acceptable to use a formula such as equation 5.7.7, e.g., for prediction, if one of the signs of the coefficients is incorrect, because then an assessment of what the prediction would be if x_2 were larger, holding x_1 and x_3 constant, would produce perverse (and embarrassing) results. For example, if the price (x_2) increases, the quantity demanded (y) increases! For most goods, this would be a surprising result.

Students are urged to be able to analyze the results of tests on the estimated coefficients of equation 5.7.7 assuming a different number of observations and different levels of significance. For example, for 10 observations and a 99-percent, one-tailed level of confidence, the null hypothesis of $\beta_1 \leq 0$ cannot be rejected since the critical value t_c is 3.143 instead of 1.943 as under the 95-percent level of confidence. Thus, β_1 is inferred to be positive (H_0 is rejected) at a 95-percent confidence level, but not at a 99-percent confidence level. Sometimes researchers note in their results the maximum level of confidence achieved by an estimated coefficient. Since the level of confidence is arbitrary, such an approach allows readers to form their own assessments about the acceptance or rejection of hypotheses. It also conveys the information that the null hypothesis can be rejected with more confidence for some estimated coefficients than for others.

Notice that a *t*-statistic or a standard error was not reported for the estimated constant term in equation 5.7.7. Such a procedure is consistent with the idea explained in Chapter 6 that estimates of the constant term are not reliable, especially for testing hypotheses. Thus, reporting such statistics is not necessary, even though most computer regression packages do compute them. Also, it is unnecessary and inappropriate to suppress the constant term if a *t*-test on it indicates that it equals zero (statistically speaking).

5.7.4 General Form of the *t*-Test

In general, the same approach may be used to test whether a coefficient β_k is equal to a specific value, say β_k^*, which may or may not be zero (as was assumed for the *t*-statistic of equation 5.7.2), by constructing the following *t*-statistic:

$$t_k = \frac{\hat{\beta}_k - \beta_k^*}{s_{\hat{\beta}_k}} \tag{5.7.9}$$

The degrees of freedom do not change. For example, when the equation is in double-log form and the coefficients can be interpreted as elasticities, other values of β_k^* may be appropriate, such as 1 and -1. But then the problem arises that the null hypothesis $H_0: \beta_k = \beta_k^*$ is no longer the strawman, and, if it is accepted, the amount of possible Type II Error is not known.

5.8   Summary

This section is summarized in the summary of Chapter 10 (Section 10.5), after additional, related elements of hypothesis testing are introduced in subsequent chapters and after additional hypothesis testing procedures are introduced in Chapter 10.

What is important to note at this point is the general approach for hypothesis testing:

1. Establish as the alternative hypothesis the one of interest.

2. Construct a decision rule prior to estimation.

3. Use statistics generated during estimation to accept or reject the alternative hypothesis, using the decision rule.

An understanding of these basic steps is required for all of the subsequent chapters.

At this point, the reader should be warned about the limitations of the t-test, which are discussed in subsequent chapters. A very common misuse of the t-test is to apply the test to one coefficient after a decision has been made concerning the inclusion of another regressor, which is in turn based on a t-test on its estimated coefficient. In this case of sequential testing, the t-statistic no longer has the t-distribution, thus the critical values found in Table A-1 are no longer valid. This procedure is a "stepwise" one, and it is discussed in Section 6.4.2.

Furthermore, when one or more of the classical assumptions do not hold, the t-statistic is misleading because its numerator (the estimated coefficient), its denominator (its estimated standard error), or both are biased. Some Monte Carlo simulations in Section 7.2.6 demonstrate an additional point: comparisons of the t-statistics for coefficients estimated with different estimators is a fruitless endeavor and can lead to no particular conclusion.

In Chapter 9, however, it is stressed that the t-test serves as a useful approximation to the theoretically correct test in the case of simultaneous equations, as long as a simultaneous equations estimating technique is used.

All these points are reinforced in Section 10.5, on extensions of the notions of hypothesis testing to more complicated situations.

6 Basic Specification Errors

This chapter investigates three basic specification errors: omitting a relevant regressor, adding an irrelevant regressor, and using an incorrect functional form. These errors are called specification errors because they involve specifying the regression model (Assumption I) incorrectly. Incorrectly specifying the error term, ϵ_i, to have a particular property that may or may not be included in the set of classical assumptions is also called a specification error; however, in this chapter this type of error is not covered. Subsequent chapters deal with misspecifications of the error term, although they are not singled out explicitly as specification errors.

Each of the three specification errors of this chapter is important empirically. The first two, combined, relate to the question, "Do I put an additional regressor in the equation?" The first consideration is theoretical: is the regressor essential to the equation on the basis of theory? If the answer is yes, there is no question that the regressor should be included; however, if theory is ambivalent, a dilemma arises. Leaving out a relevant variable will likely bias the remaining estimates although their variances will be lower. Including an irrelevant variable leads to higher variances of the remaining estimated coefficients, but no bias is introduced. In practice, it is difficult to tell whether a variable is relevant or not, so the dilemma often remains unsolved.

Included in this discussion is an analysis of the stepwise regression procedure, which is part of many computer regression packages. This procedure introduces regressors into the estimating equation from a candidate list specified by the researcher. It injects them one at a time on the basis of the relative improvement in the overall statistical fit of the equation. The reader is warned against using this approach for four basic reasons. First, it ignores the theoretical aspects of estimation, in terms of which variables are more important theoretically and what the signs of the coefficients should be. Second, testing of hypotheses becomes more tenuous using the stepwise procedure. Third, the "final" equation is arbitrary in the sense that which variables are included may depend on the order in which each candidate regressor was included or deleted. Fourth, the estimates are likely biased.

Another section, on incorrect functional form, assesses the consequences of using an incorrect functional form. The conclusions are that in some cases it is serious while in others it is not, and that little practical guidance is available to applied researchers to discern which case is which. For both this problem and the one concerning the selection of regressors, *a priori* or theoretical considerations usually play the most important role in deciding on a course of action. (For a review of the procedure to select the appropriate functional form, see Section 2.2.)

This chapter also develops the concept of the mean square error, or MSE. Mathematically, the mean square error is the squared bias of an estimator plus its variance, two properties of estimators discussed in Chapter 4. Operationally, it combines into one measure these two properties. It is a widely (but not universally) accepted criterion for selecting one estimator over another when at least one of the estimators is biased. (If neither is biased, the best estimator is the one with the least variance.)

The first section discusses a very important concept: the use and misuse of the constant or intercept term. Since it is usually a specification error to suppress or leave out the constant term, this discussion is included in this chapter. Two major points are made: it is usually incorrect to suppress the constant term, and the researcher should not rely on estimates of it. These two points are so closely related that they are both presented here, and in the first section because of their importance.

6.1   Use and Misuse of the Intercept or Constant Term, β_0

In the linear regression model, β_0 is the intercept or constant term. It is the value of Y when all the explanatory variables (and the error term) are set equal to zero. At times, the constant term is of direct importance. Consider, for example, the cost equation:

$$C_i = \beta_0 + \beta_1 Q_i + \epsilon_i$$

where C_i is the total operating cost of a production process and Q_i is the corresponding level of output. The term $\beta_1 Q_i$ represents the *variable* cost associated with output level Q_i, and β_0 represents the fixed costs, the cost when output $Q_i = 0$. Thus, a regression equation would appear to be useful to determine the relative magnitudes of the two types of costs.

Alternatively, it may be supposed that fixed costs are virtually zero, such as providing services that require little capital equipment. In this case, one might want to set the constant term to zero, because to do so would conform to the *a priori* notions and would conserve a degree of freedom (which would presumably make the estimate of β_1 more precise).

However, neither suppressing the constant term nor relying on it for inference is advisable even when *a priori* reasoning can be brought to bear on such decisions. The reasons are summarized here and then expanded in Sections 6.1.1 and 6.1.2.

The constant term should not be suppressed because:

1. It does not permit the expected (or mean) value of the error term to be zero, in violation of Assumption II. If it is suppressed, the mean effects of all omitted variables must affect the estimated slope coefficients.

2. It biases the estimates of the slope coefficients and may artificially inflate their t-statistics.

The constant term should not be relied on for inference because:

1. It absorbs the mean effects of all omitted variables, acting as a garbage term.

2. It absorbs any nonzero mean of the sample values of the error term, an additional garbage collector role.

3. It usually lies outside the relevant range of observations on the regressors, making inferences tenuous.

4. There may be nonlinearities in the true function in the range in which the regressors equal zero.

6.1.1 Do Not Suppress the Constant Term

Chapter 3 explained that one of the rationales of the assumption of the normality of the error term is that the error term absorbs the effects of a number of variables, each of which is not significant enough to be included as a regressor in the equation. Chapter 4 stressed that Assumption II (the error term has an expected value of zero) requires that the constant term absorb the mean effect of all these variables. Thus, suppressing the constant term violates this classical assumption. The only time that this assumption would not unambiguously be violated is when the error term is virtually zero for all observations, a rare case indeed. Furthermore, no matter how thorough the researcher is in specifying the model, some effects are bound to be left out because the researcher is not omniscient and, as a practical matter, the inclusion of too many relatively unimportant regressors makes estimation tenuous. (As discussed in Section 6.2.2 and in Chapter 4, the variances of the estimators increase as new regressors are added.)

The consequence of violating Assumption II is that the slope coefficient estimates are likely to be biased and their t-statistics inflated. This is demonstrated in Figure 6.1.1. Given the scatter of the X, Y observations, estimating a regression equation with a constant term would likely produce an estimated regression line very similar to the true regression line, which has a constant term, β_0, quite different from zero. The slope of this estimated line is very low, and the t-statistic of the estimated slope coefficient may be very close to zero, implying that the slope coefficient is statistically insignificant, i.e., it does not differ much from zero.

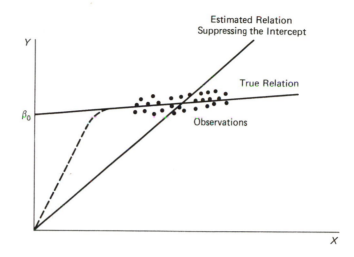

FIGURE 6.1.1   Effect of Suppressing the Y-Intercept or Constant Term

These results should be accepted by the researcher, because in this case the true relationship has this appearance. However, if the researcher were to suppress the constant term, which implies that the estimated regression line must pass through the origin, then the estimated regression line as shown in the figure would result, given the positive values of X and Y. The slope coefficient is now large, i.e., it is biased upward compared with the true slope coefficient, and the t-statistic may very well be much larger, large enough to show the estimated slope coefficient to be statistically significantly positive. Such a conclusion is incorrect, and the methodology of suppressing the constant essentially represents a method by which to lie with statistics.

It is possible that the true relationship is nonlinear and passes through the origin. In Figure 6.1.1, such a relation is shown by the appended dashed line that deviates from the straight portion of the true line and passes through the origin. If this nonlinear relationship was to be approximated by a linear regression line, it would be important *not* to suppress the constant term. Over the "relevant" range of the observations, i.e., the sample range, the estimated regression line with the constant suppressed does not provide an adequate approximation of the true regression line, compared with an estimated regression equation that includes the constant term. It is a legitimate exercise in applied econometrics to use linear approximations of nonlinear functional forms; suppressing the constant term does not permit an accurate approximation over the sample range of observations.

Thus, even though some regression packages allow the constant term to be suppressed (set to zero), the general rule is: *do not*.

6.1.2   Do Not Rely on Estimates of the Constant Term

The four reasons given in Section 6.1 for not relying on estimates of the constant term are now explained. They relate closely to the reasons not to suppress it.

First, since the error term is generated, in part, by the omission of a number of unimportant variables, the mean effect of these variables is placed in the constant term. The constant term, then, acts as a "garbage collector," with an unknown amount of this mean effect being "dumped into" it. Thus, the constant term may be larger or smaller than it would be without performing this task, which is done for the sake of the equation as a whole.

The second reason is closely related to the first. The arithmetic mean of the n observations on the error term may not be zero even though the mean would be zero if n were allowed to go to infinity. This result is due to the random nature of the error term. Hence, the constant term also acts as a garbage collector for the nonzero mean of the finite sample of the error terms, and inferences concerning the magnitude of the constant term become more tenuous.

Third, the constant term is actually the value of the dependent variable when all the regressors and the error term are zero. The values of most variables used for economic analysis are positive. Thus, the origin lies outside the range of sample observations. Since the constant term is an estimate of the dependent variable when the regressors are zero and this is outside the range of the sample observations, it is shown in Section 10.3 that estimates of it are tenuous. Estimating the constant term is like forecasting beyond the range of the sample data, a procedure that inherently contains more margin for error than within-sample forecasts.

Finally, there may be a nonlinearity in the true relation in the neighborhood of the origin. Using the cost function in Section 6.1, Figure 6.1.2 portrays this situation. If the estimated regression line is to be an approximation over the relevant range of observations, then the estimated constant term is very unlikely to be near the true Y-intercept, which in this illustration is zero.

The lesson here is very simple: do not suppress the constant term, but also, do not rely on estimates of it for inference.

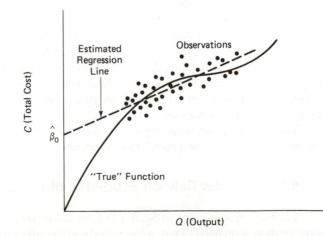

FIGURE 6.1.2   Linear Cost Function *Vs.* the "True" Function

6.2   The Missing Relevant Variable Model

When an important regressor is omitted from the regression equation, such as the price of the product in a demand equation, the interpretation and use of the estimated equation become suspect. Leaving out a "relevant" variable, such as price, usually produces a bias in the estimators of the remaining coefficients. However, the variances of these estimators are generally lower than they otherwise would be, possibly by enough to offset the bias. These considerations are investigated in this section.

In a multivariate regression model, the interpretation of a regression coefficient changes depending on which other variables are included as regressors. The coefficient β_k represents the change in the expected value of the dependent variable y given a unit change in x_k, *holding the other regressors constant*. If a variable is not included as a regressor, then it is not being held constant for the interpretation of β_k. Thus, leaving out a relevant regressor is usually taken as *prima facie* evidence that the entire estimated equation is suspect, even though it may be satisfactory. Even if the coefficient of determination of the estimated equation, the R^2, is high, which may seem to indicate that all the relevant variables are included, the same conclusion can be drawn because a high R^2 can be caused by common time trends, e.g., in each of the dependent and independent variables. (This type of high R^2 is usually referred to as spurious correlation because it does not explain economic behavior.)

However, in the sample, when the omitted variable is not correlated with the set of included regressors, the coefficient estimates will be exactly the same as when the variable was included. Thus, there is no bias, and the entire equation is just as good with or without the variable, except for some possible loss of explanatory power without the variable. But perfectly uncorrelated variables are a rarity in practice, which is why the usual accusation is made that the entire equation is suspect when a relevant variable is excluded.

The discussion in Section 1.3.3 stressed that it is a matter of judgment as to which variables are relevant and which are not, and that researchers have to impose their priors in order to select only the primary determinants of the dependent variable. In this section and Section 6.3 (on "Irrelevant Variables"), it is stressed that, although theoretical rules have been developed to determine the relevancy of a regressor, in practice no single guideline is available, and a number of considerations have to be brought to bear in the analysis. Section 6.4.1 summarizes these considerations, and the introduction to Section 6.4 summarizes the missing relevant regressor and the included irrelevant regressor cases.

6.2.1   The Model and the Maladies

The missing relevant variable problem can be portrayed notationally as follows. Suppose that the true model (in deviation-from-the-mean form) is:

$$y_i = \beta_1 x_{i1} + \beta_2 x_{i2} + \epsilon_i \qquad (6.2.1)$$

where ϵ is a classical error term. Further, suppose that the researcher estimates instead a model of the form:

$$y_i = \beta_1 x_{i1} + \epsilon_i^* \qquad (6.2.2)$$

In this misspecified model, the error term may be stated as:

$$\epsilon_i^* = \beta_2 x_{i2} + \epsilon_i \tag{6.2.3}$$

This type of error term poses three possible violations of the classical assumptions, and all three violations cause serious problems at the applied level. The violations are (assuming $\beta_2 \neq 0$):

1. Lack of independence of a regressor, x_1, and the error term, ϵ^*, a violation of Assumption III if x_1 and x_2 are correlated (because then x_1 and ϵ^* are correlated).

2. Autocorrelation, a violation of Assumption IV if x_2 (and thus ϵ^* to some degree) is autocorrelated.

3. Heteroskedasticity, a violation of Assumption V if x_2 (and thus ϵ^* to some degree) is heteroskedastic.

The second and third maladies are discussed in Chapters 7 and 8, respectively; only the first violation is discussed here.[1]

Whenever there is a violation of one of the classical assumptions, the Gauss-Markov Theorem on least squares (Section 4.4) no longer applies, and the OLS estimates are no longer BLUE. Econometricians then investigate which of the properties is violated. Given linear estimators, they examine whether the estimator is biased or inefficient (that is, has a higher variance than another unbiased, linear estimator), or both. They usually attempt to suggest an alternative estimating technique that will, in some sense (discussed in Section 6.2.2), be better than OLS.

There are two conditions under which the OLS estimator of β_1 in this misspecified model will still be BLUE: (a) $\beta_2 = 0$, that is, x_2 is not a relevant variable in the true model (equation 6.2.1), and (b) the simple correlation between x_1 and x_2 (r_{12} of Section 3.2.2) is zero. The technical aspects of each of these conditions is examined in turn.

(a) If $\beta_2 = 0$, then none of the three maladies obviously applies, but what about the "in-between" situation in which β_2 is not very large? The concept of β_2 being "near zero" has been quantified in terms of the population parameters as a kind of t-statistic, labeled instead τ (tau):

$$\tau = \frac{\beta_2}{\sigma_{\hat{\beta}_2^+}} \tag{6.2.4}$$

where $\sigma_{\hat{\beta}_2^+}$ is the true (not estimated) standard deviation of $\hat{\beta}_2$, the estimate of β_2 in the regression of y on x_1 and x_2 (i.e., OLS is applied to the true model, equation 6.2.1). It has been shown[2] that, when $\tau^2 < 1$, the OLS estimate of β_1 is "better"

---

[1] Note that reordering the observations does not alter the correlation between x_1 and x_2 because both x_{i1} and x_{i2} are moved together to a new location in any reordering. Thus, reordering the observations does not alleviate this problem. Reordering the observations does alleviate the symptoms of the autocorrelation and heteroskedasticity problems, and this possibility is discussed in Chapters 7 and 8.

[2] T. D. Wallace, "Efficiencies for Stepwise Regressions," *Journal of the American Statistical Association*, Vol. 59, 1964, pp. 1179–82.

when x_2 is left out of the equation than when it is included. ("Better" here is defined in terms of mean square error, a concept developed in Section 6.2.2.) Unfortunately, τ is not observable, being composed of population parameters, so its practical applicability is nil. However, this concept is used extensively below and in subsequent chapters in the Monte Carlo simulations because, in the simulations, the true parameter values are known by the person conducting them.

(b) If the correlation between x_1 and x_2 is zero ($r_{12} = 0$), then the error term ϵ^* is no longer correlated with x_1, and the estimate of β_1 when x_2 is not included as a regressor is BLUE. In fact, the estimate itself will be *exactly* the same as when x_2 is included. To show this, the OLS estimator of β_1 when x_1 and x_2 are included as regressors may be written as:

$$\hat{\beta}_1^+ = \frac{\Sigma x_1 y}{\Sigma x_1^2} \left[\frac{1 - r_{12} r_{2y}/r_{1y}}{1 - r_{12}^2} \right] \qquad (6.2.5)$$

where r_{12} is the simple coefficient of correlation between x_1 and x_2, and r_{1y} and r_{2y} are similar simple coefficients of correlation between x_1 and y, and x_2 and y, respectively. Thus, when $r_{12} = 0$, the term in brackets becomes unity, so the estimator $\hat{\beta}_1^+$ (in which x_2 is included as a regressor) becomes exactly the same as the estimator $\hat{\beta}_1$ when x_2 is omitted (namely, $\Sigma x_1 y/\Sigma x_1^2$).

In summary, the OLS estimate of β_1 in the regression of y on x_1 is BLUE if either $\beta_2 = 0$ or $r_{12} = 0$.

6.2.2 Bias, Variance, and Mean Square Error (MSE)

This section covers two of the primary properties of estimators with which econometricians concern themselves, bias and variance, as they relate to the missing regressor model. (The reader may want to review these notions in Section 4.2.)

It can be shown that, in general, the bias of $\hat{\beta}_1$ when x_2 is excluded from the estimating equation is:

$$\text{BIAS}(\hat{\beta}_1) = \beta_2 r_{12} \frac{\Sigma x_2^2}{\Sigma x_1^2} \qquad (6.2.6)$$

It also can be shown that there is no bias when x_2 is included. Thus, excluding a regressor produces a biased estimate, and the amount of the bias is given by equation 6.2.6.

But biasedness is not the only concern. When x_2 is included as a regressor, the variance of the OLS estimate of β_1 is *increased*, as long as $r_{12} \neq 0$. This is shown as follows. In the two-regressor model of y on x_1 and x_2, the variance of the OLS estimator of β_1 is:

$$\text{VAR}(\hat{\beta}_1^+) = \frac{\sigma_\epsilon^2}{\Sigma x_1^2(1 - r_{12}^2)} \qquad (6.2.7)$$

But when $r_{12} = 0$ or in the single-regressor model:

$$\text{VAR}(\hat{\beta}_1^+) = \text{VAR}(\hat{\beta}_1) = \frac{\sigma_\epsilon^2}{\Sigma x_1^2} \qquad (6.2.8)$$

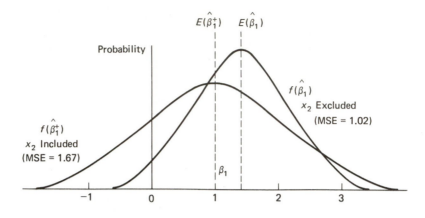

FIGURE 6.2.1   Sampling Distributions for Estimates of β_1 for the Missing Relevant Variable Case

$$(\beta_1 = 1, \beta_2 = 1, \sigma_\epsilon^2 = 1, n = 20, r_{12}^2 = 0.5)$$

Thus, even though $\hat{\beta}_1^+$ is BLUE in the correctly specified model of y regressed on x_1 and x_2, it may not be the preferred estimator because it has a higher variance than when x_2 is excluded. This notion is illustrated by the sampling distributions for $\hat{\beta}_1^+$ and $\hat{\beta}_1$ (in which x_2 is and is not included, respectively), shown in Figure 6.2.1. These distributions were generated by Monte Carlo simulations, given values for x_1 and x_2 and for the parameters.[3] Even though $\hat{\beta}_1$ is biased—its sampling distribution is not centered on the true value of β_1—its lower variance in this instance implies that it would be more likely to provide an estimate closer to the true value β_1 than the unbiased estimator $\hat{\beta}_1^+$ would. In other words, the possible estimates obtained from OLS with y regressed on x_1 alone are more heavily concentrated near the true value β_1 than the estimates of β_1 from y on x_1 and x_2 are, because the smaller variance of $\hat{\beta}_1$ more than compensates for its bias, *in this instance*.

If $\hat{\beta}_1^+$ is BLUE, how can another estimator be better? The answer is that $\hat{\beta}_1^+$ has the least variance of all linear, *unbiased* estimators; it does not preclude a biased estimator from having a smaller variance and, in some sense, providing a better estimate. The example here was specifically selected to demonstrate this point.

A measure that allows one to determine which is better, $\hat{\beta}_1^+$ or $\hat{\beta}_1$, is called the *mean square error* (MSE or, equivalently, its positive square root, the root mean square error, RMSE). The MSE measures the degree of dispersion of possible estimated values about the *true* parameter value, in this case β_1. It differs from the variance in that the variance measures the degree of dispersion of possible estimated values about the *expected value of the estimator,* instead of around β_1 itself. The two measures differ if the expected value of $\hat{\beta}_1$ differs from the true value, i.e., if the estimator is biased.

---

[3] Given x_1, the values of x_2 were computed as $x_{i2} = r_{12}x_{i1} + (1-r_{12})u_i$, where u_i was drawn from a uniform distribution, as were the original values of x_1. Repeated drawings were made on u_i and thus on x_{i2} until the computed r_{12}^2 was within a tolerance level (0.015) of the specified correlation r_{12}^2.

Notationally, the MSE of $\hat{\beta}_1$ (or of any estimator) is defined as the expected value of the squared difference of the true value β_1 and the estimator, $\hat{\beta}_1$:

$$MSE(\hat{\beta}_1) = E(\hat{\beta}_1 - \beta_1)^2 \qquad (6.2.9)$$

This formula is not very useful for regression users, but the following equation is useful for an understanding of the concept. It turns out that the MSE for any estimator is equal to the bias squared plus the variance:

$$MSE(\hat{\beta}_1) = [BIAS(\hat{\beta}_1)]^2 + VAR(\hat{\beta}_1) \qquad (6.2.10)$$

Thus, the MSE combines the bias and variance concepts into one measure, constituting a weighting of the two. Since some researchers place more emphasis on bias than on variance, Monte Carlo studies usually present all three measures so that readers can draw their own inferences.

For Monte Carlo experiments, a number of values of $\hat{\beta}_1$ are computed and the bias, variance, and MSE are calculated, as follows. First, the mean value of the 2000 or so Monte Carlo estimates is computed as:

$$\bar{\beta}_1 = \sum_{j=1}^{p} \hat{\beta}_{1j}/p \qquad (6.2.11)$$

where $\hat{\beta}_{1j}$ is the jth Monte Carlo estimate of β_1, and the index j scans the $p = 2000$ (or so) Monte Carlo estimates. The Monte Carlo measures are computed as:

$$BIAS(\hat{\beta}_1) = \bar{\beta}_1 - \beta_1 \qquad (6.2.12)$$

$$VAR(\hat{\beta}_1) = \sum_{j=1}^{p} (\hat{\beta}_{1j} - \bar{\beta}_1)^2/p \qquad (6.2.13)$$

$$MSE(\hat{\beta}_1) = \sum_{j=1}^{p} (\hat{\beta}_{1j} - \beta_1)^2/p \qquad (6.2.14)$$

(Alternatively, equation 6.2.10 could be used to compute the MSE.)

For sampling distributions shown in Figure 6.2.1, the bias of $\hat{\beta}_1^+$ (in which x_2 is included as a regressor) is zero, and the bias of $\hat{\beta}_1$ (which excludes x_2) is 0.41. However, though biased, the variance of $\hat{\beta}_1$ is only 0.85, whereas that for $\hat{\beta}_1^+$ is 1.67. Thus, the MSE for $\hat{\beta}_1$ is less than that for $\hat{\beta}_1^+$, 1.02 compared with 1.67. (It is only the relative values of the MSE's that matter, not their absolute values.) But, as mentioned previously, this example was contrived to demonstrate that a biased estimator *can* be better than an unbiased one, but it need not always be so.

6.2.3 A Digression on Extreme Multicollinearity

To extend the conclusions of Section 6.2.2 to the multivariate model, missing relevant variables produce biased estimates of all the remaining coefficient estimates, as long as the excluded variables are correlated with one or more of the included regressors. While this is true, for "high" degrees of multicollinearity, the high variance of the OLS estimators when all relevant regressors are included outweighs the biasedness of the estimators in the misspecified model, in terms of the MSE (mean square error).

In the two-regressor model in Section 6.2.2, it was stressed that, depending on the specific values of the parameters and exogenous variables ($\sigma_\epsilon^2, \Sigma x_1^2, \Sigma x_2^2, n$, and β_2^2), it may be better to exclude x_2 in cases of high correlation between x_1 and x_2. In the extreme case of *perfect collinearity* between x_1 and x_2 when $r_{12}^2 = 1$, the variance of $\hat{\beta}_1^+$ goes to infinity, as can be seen by examining equation 6.2.7. The practical result is that the computer regression program will be unable to assign a value to the coefficients of the separate regressors x_1 and x_2, except for rounding error. A representation of perfect collinearity is:

$$x_2 = bx_1$$

where b is a nonzero constant. (A term d could also be added, as in $x_2 = bx_1 + d$. The additive term d only changes the constant term and is thus unimportant.) In this case, the true equation becomes:

$$y_i = \beta_1 x_{i1} + \beta_2 x_{i2} + \epsilon_i = \beta_1 x_{i1} + \beta_2(bx_{i1}) + \epsilon_i = (\beta_1 + \beta_2 b)x_{i1} + \epsilon_i \quad (6.2.15)$$

Thus, estimating y on just x_1 would be appropriate, but the expected value of the OLS-estimated cofficient (as shown by the true slope coefficient in equation 6.2.15) would be $\beta_1 + \beta_2 b$ instead of β_1, as may have been thought by an unsuspecting researcher who has no knowledge of the true model. Thus, the estimate is biased, with the amount of the bias being $\beta_2 b$, which is positive or negative depending on the values of β_2 and b. But the MSE is less than that for $\hat{\beta}_1^+$, which approaches infinity because its variance approaches infinity.

The effects of extreme multicollinearity, then, are quite severe, and the moderate degrees of multicollinearity usually found in practice cause researchers to be concerned over the inclusion of regressors.

After one more aspect of excluding a relevant regressor is examined (the biasing of the estimate of the variance) and the irrelevant variable problem is discussed, some practical guidelines are discussed.

6.2.4 Biased Estimator of the Variance

When x_1 and x_2 are perfectly correlated, as in the example of Section 6.2.3, the movements in x_1 convey all the information of the movements of both x_1 and x_2. Thus, regressing y on x_1 insures that the residual variance is a minimum . However, at the opposite extreme, when x_1 and x_2 have a zero sample correlation, even though the estimate of β_1 is unbiased and exactly the same as when x_2 is excluded, part of the residual variance is left unexplained, the part that the variable x_2 explains. Thus, it turns out that the usual estimate of the variance of the error term (and, hence, of the estimated coefficient) is biased when r_{12}^2 is less than unity.

In general, the estimator of the error variance is:

$$s^2 = \frac{\Sigma e_i^2}{(n - K - 1)} \quad (6.2.16)$$

When y is regressed on x_1 and x_2, s^2 is an unbiased estimator of σ_ϵ^2, and the denominator is $n-3$ in this case. But when y is regressed on x_1 alone, given the true model with both x_1 and x_2 as regressors, two things happen. First, as long as x_1 and x_2 are not perfectly correlated (and $\beta_2 \neq 0$), the sum of squares of the residuals, the numerator, is larger. Second, when x_1 is the only regressor, the denominator is larger, $n-2$ instead of $n-3$. However, for moderate and large numbers of observations (n), this second consideration is not very important.

When both these considerations are taken into account, it turns out that s^2 is biased and that the bias is positive and equal to $\sigma_\epsilon^2 \tau^2/(n-2)$.[4] Thus, the bias increases the more "relevant" x_2 is, as indicated by a high value of τ^2. However, from this expression, it is seen that the bias may or may not disappear as the number of observations increases because τ^2 increases in an unknown way with the number of observations. But the bias disappears as r_{12}^2 approaches unity (because then $\tau^2 = 0$).

Without the regressor x_2, the estimated value of the variance of the estimated coefficient ($s_{\hat\beta}^2$) may be larger or smaller than the estimated variance when x_2 is included because, while s^2 is biased upward, exclusion of the factor $(1-r_{12}^2)$ in the denominator makes it smaller, unless $r_{12}^2 = 0$. (Recall the definitions of the respective estimators of the variance, equations 6.2.7 and 6.2.8.)

For the t-ratio in the omitted regressor model, $t = \hat\beta_1/s_{\hat\beta_1}$, the numerator is biased when $r_{12} \neq 0$, and the denominator is biased when $r_{12}^2 \neq 1$. Thus, at least one element, the numerator or the denominator, is biased for all values of r_{12}^2. In general, then, the t-statistic could be larger or smaller when x_2 is not included as a regressor.

6.2.5 Another Review of the Notation and a Monte Carlo Illustration

As in Chapter 4, the notation may be confusing. Readers accustomed to the notation and not needing the reinforcement of the points made in Section 6.2 up to this point via a Monte Carlo experiment should skip to Section 6.3.

Table 6.2.1 summarizes the notation for the various parameters and supplies the average statistics from a Monte Carlo experiment. The superscript "+" denotes an estimate when x_2 is included as a regressor, and the absence of this superscript means that x_2 is excluded. For all but the true variance of $\hat\beta_1^+$ (which, from equation 6.2.7 varies with r_{12}^2), the parameters have a single value for all values of r_{12}^2. In this particular experiment, $\Sigma x_1^2 = 1.148$, and the true variance of $\hat\beta_1^+$ is computed as a function of r_{12}^2, it is not simulated by the computer. The number of observations (n) is 20.

For the Monte Carlo simulations, the true model was assumed to be:

$$y_i = 1x_{i1} + 1x_{i2} + \epsilon_i$$

and ϵ_i was assumed to be a classical normal error term with mean zero and variance

---

[4] This form for the bias may be inferred from an expression of Kmenta, after correcting for an interaction term that he forgot and after adjusting for the fact that he was examining the estimated variance of an estimated coefficient. See Jan Kmenta, *Elements of Econometrics* (New York: Macmillan, 1971), pp. 392–95, esp. p. 394.

TABLE 6.2.1

Notation and Monte Carlo Results for the Missing Relevant Variable Model

x_2	Parameter Notation	Parameter True Value	Estimator	Estimates (Average of Monte Carlo Simulation Value) for r_{12}^2 of 0	0.5	0.8	0.9	1.0
	Coefficient of X_1							
Included	β_1	1	$\hat{\beta}_1^+$	1.0	1.0	1.0	1.0	NA
Excluded	β_1	1	$\hat{\beta}_1$	1.0	1.4	1.6	1.8	2.0
	Variance of the Error Term							
Included	σ_ϵ^2	1	$s^{+2} = \dfrac{\Sigma e^{+2}}{n-3}$	1.0	1.0	1.0	1.0	NA
Excluded	σ_ϵ^2	1	$s^2 = \dfrac{\Sigma e^2}{n-2}$	1.1	1.0	1.0	1.0	1.0
	Variance of the estimated coefficient			0.87*	1.74*	4.36*	8.71*	$\pm\infty$
Included	$\sigma_{\beta_1^+}^2 = \dfrac{\sigma_\epsilon^2}{\Sigma x_1^2(1-r_{12}^2)}$		$s_{\hat{\beta}_1^+}^2 = \dfrac{s^{+2}}{\Sigma x_1^2(1-r_{12}^2)}$	0.87	1.78	4.41	8.82	$\pm\infty$
Excluded	$\sigma_{\hat{\beta}_1}^2 = \dfrac{\sigma_\epsilon^2}{\Sigma x_1^2}$	0.87	$s_{\hat{\beta}_1}^2 = \dfrac{s^2}{\Sigma x_1^2}$	0.97	0.87	0.88	0.88	0.88
Included	---	---	$t_1^+ = \hat{\beta}_1^+/s_{\hat{\beta}_1^+}$	1.3	0.7	0.3	0.13	NA
Excluded	---	---	$t_1 = \hat{\beta}_1/s_{\hat{\beta}_1}$	1.2	1.8	2.0	2.3	2.5
	$\tau^2 = \beta_2^2/\sigma_{\hat{\beta}_2}^2$		---	2.33	0.16	0.09	0.08	0

Notes: NA = Not Available. True model is $y_i = 1x_{i1} + 1x_{i2} + \epsilon_i$. It was assumed that $n = 20$, $\Sigma x_1^2 = 1.148$, and $\sigma_\epsilon^2 = 1$

* True value.

$\sigma_\epsilon^2 = 1$. The first row of Table 6.2.1 demonstrates that $\hat{\beta}_1^+$ (the estimated coefficient of β_1 for the true model of y regressed on x_1 and x_2) is unbiased regardless of the value of r_{12}^2: the average value of the (2000) Monte Carlo simulations equals unity. When x_1 and x_2 are perfectly correlated, the variance of $\hat{\beta}_1^+$ becomes infinite, and an estimate of β_1 cannot be computed. When x_2 is excluded, as shown in the second row, the bias in $\hat{\beta}_1$ becomes more pronounced the larger the r_{12}^2 becomes, reaching the value of 2 as r_{12}^2 approaches unity, in which case it is assumed that $x_1 = x_2$.

The estimates of the variance of the error term are shown in the next two rows. The estimator of the variance of the error term with x_2 excluded is biased only when $r_{12}^2 = 0$. Even the 20 observations, usually considered a small number by most researchers, are sufficient to eliminate the bias in this case, given the value of τ^2, the MSE measure of the relevance of x_2, as shown in the last row. (Of course, higher values of τ^2 and σ_ϵ^2 would lead to more bias in s^2.)

The mean values of the estimates of the variance of the estimated coefficients, as shown next in the table, are nearly equal to their true values.[5] The true value of the variance of $\hat{\beta}_1^+$ depends on the magnitude of r_{12}^2, whereas that for $\hat{\beta}_1$ does not. There is a small amount of upward bias in $s_{\hat{\beta}_1}^2$ in this case when $r_{12}^2 = 0$.

The two-sided critical values of the t-statistic, at the 5-percent level of significance for $n-3 = 20-3 = 17$ degrees of freedom, are 2.11 when x_1 and x_2 are both regressors and 2.10 when x_1 is the only regressor. Thus, when $r_{12}^2 = 0$, the variable x_1 would be rejected by the t-test as having, on average, a statistically insignificant coefficient because the average t-statistic is 1.3. Incidentally, the τ^2 for x_1 in this case is 1.2 (the value of τ^2 in the table refers to x_2), which is greater than unity, implying according to this theoretical rule that x_1 is a relevant variable. Thus, the inference from the t-test does not necessarily agree with the inference from the theoretical τ^2 rule: the t-test would exclude x_1, whereas the τ^2 rule would include it.

The t-statistic for $\hat{\beta}_1^+$ decreases as r_{12}^2 increases, and the t-statistic for $\hat{\beta}_1$ increases as r_{12}^2 increases, becoming greater than 2.0 when r_{12}^2 is above 0.8. When $r_{12}^2 = 1$ and all the movements in x_2 are shown by the movements in x_1, the t-statistic for $\hat{\beta}_1$ becomes 2.5. This indicates that the entire expression is statistically significant (as would be shown by an F-test for the entire equation). As r_{12}^2 increases, the variable x_2 contributes less in the explanation of y, given x_1 is included as a regressor, as shown by the declining value of τ^2 across the last row of the table.

One of the lessons of this experiment is that a given variable may become statistically significant according to the t-statistic if another correlated variable is excluded from the equation. But if that other variable is also important theoretically, perhaps the researcher would be better off including both x_1 and x_2, even though neither has a high t-statistic. (But note that two t-tests on the two coefficients is not equivalent to a single F-test on the whole equation. Chapter 10 discusses testing both coefficients simultaneously.)

After the irrelevant regressor model is discussed, all the notions developed in Section 6.2 are reviewed in Section 6.4.

6.3   Irrelevant Variables

The irrelevant variable model is the mirror image of the missing relevant variable model, and it can be analyzed by using the model developed in Section 6.2. Whereas the missing relevant variable model has two regressors in the true model but only one

---

[5] The mean values of the estimates would be equal to their respective true values except for an error tolerance in selecting values of x_2 and except for an allowance for randomness.

of them in the estimating equation, the irrelevant variable model has only one regressor in the true model but an extra regressor in the estimating equation. In the notation of the missing relevant variable model, the true model is:

$$y_i = \beta_1 x_{i1} + \beta_2 x_{i2} + \epsilon_i \qquad (6.3.1)$$

where ϵ is a classical normal error term, and $\beta_2 = 0$. In other words, the researcher estimates equation 6.3.1 with two regressors, whereas the true model has $\beta_2 = 0$, so only x_1 is a relevant variable. The OLS estimate of β_1 using equation 6.3.1 as the form of the estimating equation yields the estimate $\hat{\beta}_1^+$. This estimate, just as in the missing relevant variable case, is compared to $\hat{\beta}_1$, the estimate of y regressed on x_1 alone, which in this case is the "true" model (equation 6.3.1) with $\beta_2 = 0$.

Thus, the analysis of the previous section applies fully. Whereas $\hat{\beta}_1$ (excluding x_2) was biased when $\beta_2 \neq 0$, it is unbiased when $\beta_2 = 0$. Furthermore, $\hat{\beta}_1^+$ (including x_2) is still unbiased because the true value of β_2 is zero. Since both $\hat{\beta}_1$ and $\hat{\beta}_1^+$ are unbiased, the MSE's are equal to the variances of the estimators. From equations 6.2.7 and 6.2.8 with $\beta_2 = 0$, the variance (and thus the MSE) of $\hat{\beta}_1^+$ is *always greater* than that of $\hat{\beta}_1$ as long as $r_{12} \neq 0$. Since in practice two variables rarely have a zero correlation, the general conclusion is that the inclusion of an irrelevant variable, because it increases the variance of the estimated coefficient of the other regressor by a factor of $1/(1-r_{12}^2)$, leads to a higher MSE and is costly to the accuracy of a given estimate. Furthermore, the t-statistic of the estimated coefficient of x_1 is usually lowered upon the inclusion of the irrelevant variable x_2, as long as the correlation between x_1 and x_2 is nonzero.

In summary, including an irrelevant variable does not bias the other estimated coefficients, but it usually increases their variances.

These conclusions, and the ones developed in Section 6.2 on the estimated variances and the t-statistic, are summarized in Table 6.4.1, which is introduced in Section 6.4.

6.4   Summary of the Two Cases and an Illustration of the Misuse of the *t*-Test

This section first summarizes the conclusions of the missing relevant variable case and the included irrelevant variable case. Then, some practical guidelines are discussed, and, finally, the misuse of the t-test is demonstrated in a very commonly applied situation: when the t-test is applied to one coefficient before it is applied to another. This procedure is generically called stepwise regression, and should be avoided by most researchers, for the reasons stated in Section 6.4.2.

A summary of the cases is presented in Table 6.4.1. Excluding a relevant regressor biases the remaining coefficient estimates, as long as the excluded variable is correlated with the included regressor. However, excluding the relevant variable lowers the variance of the estimated coefficient of the included regressor, and this may or may not offset the bias.

The conclusions can be generalized to a multivariate model. If an excluded rel-

TABLE 6.4.1

Summary of Consequences of Missing Relevant Regressor and Included Irrelevant Regressor

Effect on Remaining Coefficient Estimate	*Omitted Relevant Regressor*	*Included Irrelevant Regressor*
Bias?	Yes (unless $r_{12}^2 = 0$)	No
Increases or Decreases Variance?	Decreases (unless $r_{12}^2 = 0$)	Increases (unless $r_{12}^2 = 0$)
Increases or Decreases Estimated Variance of Error Term?	Increases (unless $r_{12}^2 = 1$)	Uncertain
Increases or Decreases Estimated Variance of Included Coefficient and its *t*-Statistic?	Uncertain	Uncertain

Note: r_{12}^2 = the simple squared correlation coefficient between x_1 and x_2

evant variable is correlated with one or more of the included regressors, *all* the estimated coefficients are usually biased but have a lower variance. (A general measure of the degree of correlation is presented in Section 10.2.)

It is interesting to note that the τ^2 rule ($\tau^2 > 1$ for the inclusion of x_2 to lower the MSE of the estimated coefficient of x_1) also applies to estimated or fitted values of the dependent variable. That is, $\hat{Y}_i$ has a lower MSE with x_2 excluded when $\tau^2 < 1$ and has a lower MSE with x_2 included when $\tau^2 > 1$. Thus, the concern with whether x_2 should be included applies to predicting values of Y as well as to obtaining the lowest MSE estimator of β_1.

6.4.1 Practical Application

In practice, the question is whether to include a regressor or to exclude it. Formally, one may include the variable and test whether its coefficient is different from zero. But as pointed out above in the Monte Carlo experiment, deleting a regressor on the basis of a *t*-test may increase the MSE of the remaining coefficient estimator. Also, many other considerations are usually important, the most important of which is whether the variable in question is clearly required on the basis of theory, as was discussed in Section 1.3.3.

The second thing to examine is whether the inclusion of the suspect variable alters the other estimated coefficients "sufficiently." If its inclusion does alter the other coefficients, then there are no clear-cut guidelines on whether to include the variable because, with collinearity, the researcher is never certain of the importance of the variable. Unfortunately, how much change in the coefficients is ''sufficient'' is a matter of judgment and is not quantifiable.

Given that a variable is theoretically suspect and that its inclusion does not alter the other estimated coefficients significantly, then and only then can the inclusion of the variable become strictly a statistical matter. The admittedly *ad hoc* procedure, which uses the $\bar{R}^2$, usually applied in practice is as follows. (Recall from Chapter 1 that the $\bar{R}^2$ is the R^2 adjusted for the fact that the additional regressor uses up an additional degree of freedom.) If the inclusion of the theoretically suspect variable does not alter the other estimated coefficients ''sufficiently,'' the variable may be excluded if the $\bar{R}^2$ decreases upon its inclusion. When this occurs, the variable is termed *superfluous* and is dropped from the equation.[6] Since one never knows the true model—namely, whether β_2 is zero or not—one can never be sure that the variable is irrelevant. The final consideration in this *ad hoc* procedure is that, if the $\bar{R}^2$ increases and the other coefficients do not change much, then the variable may be included, since it appears to be ''explaining'' in a statistical sense some of the residual variance. However, if the other coefficients do change appreciably, use judgment to determine whether it should be included even if the $\bar{R}^2$ increases.

If the sign of an estimated coefficient is incorrect, it will not change by deleting a variable that has a lower *t*-statistic (in absolute value) than the *t*-statistic of the coefficient estimate that has the incorrect sign. Furthermore, the sign in general will likely not change even if the variable to be deleted has a larger *t*-statistic.[7] Thus, one should not attempt to search for a correct sign by adding or deleting variables since this procedure will usually be a waste of time. Furthermore, Section 6.4.2 demonstrates the dangers of adding and deleting variables in a regression equation.

In the irrelevant variable model, the estimate of β_2^+ (the estimated coefficient of x_2, where x_2 is the irrelevant regressor) in general will not be zero because of sampling error, even though it has an expectation of zero. Also, its variance is similarly affected by the correlation of x_1 and x_2. Thus, estimated values different from zero may be expected. However, 95 percent of the time the *t*-test will indicate that the true coefficient is zero, for a 95-percent level of confidence. The problem with relying on the *t*-statistic alone is that many other maladies, such as the exclusion of another regressor that is relevant and autocorrelation (discussed in Chapter 7), may be present, biasing the *t*-statistic and possibly leading to erroneous conclusions. The *t*-statistic is like the theoretical τ of Section 6.2.1, but estimates of β_2 and $\sigma_{\hat{\beta}_2^+}$ replace their true values:

$$t_2 = \frac{\hat{\beta}_2^+}{\hat{\sigma}_{\hat{\beta}_2^+}} \qquad (6.4.1)$$

It is very rare that the estimating equation has as its theoretical counterpart an equation that satisfies all the classical properties. Thus, either the numerator or the denominator of the *t*-statistic, or both, will likely be biased (as shown in Section 6.2.4 and in Chapters 7 and 8), to some degree, and thus strict, mechanical reliance on the *t*-statistic is not suggested.

---

[6] This term is used by Rao and Miller, *Applied Econometrics*, pp. 35–40.

[7] See Ignazio Visco, ''On Obtaining the Right Sign of a Coefficient Estimate by Omitting a Variable from the Regression,'' *Journal of Econometrics*, February 1978, pp. 115–17.

Most researchers are embarrassed to report as their "final" equation one that has any of the *t*-statistics less than the critical value. When such an equation seems appropriate, for theoretical reasons or from an examination of all the statistics in an alternative regression equation in which the suspect regressor is excluded, the variable should be included along with a brief explanation of why it is included. Often, multicollinearity is cited as the reason for the low *t*-statistic. While this may be true, its citation is usually used as a ruse not to discuss the important reasons for its inclusion, such as the effect on other coefficient values when it is removed. Furthermore, collinearity and multicollinearity are a matter of degree, and there are no completely adequate tests for them. (But see Section 10.2 for an approach that has been used.) Thus, the researcher is advised not to cite multicollinearity as an excuse for low *t*-statistics unless the evidence is very clear, such as in the "classic" case in which there is a high degree of overall statistical fit for the entire equation (as shown by the R^2 and *F*-statistic) but none of the coefficient estimates have a *t*-statistic greater than the critical value (because their denominators, the estimated standard deviations, are very large).

If a variable is deleted because of high collinearity with another regressor, the researcher should understand that the estimated coefficient of the included variable will necessarily include the combined effects of both variables; the researcher should be more careful the higher the degree of collinearity is. The reader might want to review Table 6.2.1 for the illustration of how the expected value of the coefficient $\hat{\beta}_1$ (excluding x_2) goes from 1 to 2 ($2 = \beta_1 + \beta_2$) when the sample correlation coefficient between x_1 and x_2 is increased from zero to unity.

6.4.2 Stepwise Procedures

This section presents an analysis of an all too commonly applied approach to regression analysis: "fiddling" with the equation or using a stepwise regression procedure, in which variables from a "shopping list" are included or excluded as regressors depending on their contribution to the R^2. A measure of the supposed contribution of each regressor is the "R^2 delete" or the "R^2 change," the increase in the R^2 as the regressor is added. Unfortunately, multicollinearity causes this procedure to be deficient. In the presence of multicollinearity, it is impossible to determine unambiguously the individual contribution of each variable in order to say which one is more important and thus should be included first. (Based on equation 6.2.5, the simple coefficient of correlation is an integral part of the formula for each regression coefficient estimate, and attempts to untangle its effect have generally been thwarted. But see the discussion of ridge regression in Section 11.5.) Some regression programs compute beta coefficients, which are the estimated coefficients for an equation in which all variables are in a deviation-from-the-mean form and all variables have been divided by their own standard deviations. The higher the beta of a regressor is in absolute value, the more important it is thought to be in explaining the movements in the dependent variable. But, like the R^2 delete, the beta coefficients are deficient in the presence of multicollinearity. So are the partial coefficients of correlation, which are like simple coefficients of correlation between a regressor and the dependent variable but with all the other regressors "held constant."

Thus, because of multicollinearity, most practitioners should avoid stepwise procedures. The major pitfalls with such a procedure are (1) the signs of the estimated coefficients at intermediate or final stages of the routine may be incorrect; (2) such procedures may result in the exclusion of a relevant variable, which was excluded just because of the rather arbitrary order in which the selection takes place (according to the contribution to the R^2); and (3) the coefficients may be biased, and the t-statistics no longer have the t-distribution, so the t-table (A-1 at the end of the text) is not appropriate for the critical values of the resulting t-statistics.

Using a stepwise procedure is an admission of ignorance concerning which variables should be entered. Only in rare circumstances is such ignorance justified. For example, for a particular cross-sectional model, the list of possible regressors may be very large. If the number of observations is large (such as several thousand), then multicollinearity may not be a serious problem. However, for such instances, sets of certain regressors, such as regional or locational dummy variables, should be included as a set, regardless of the magnitude of the t-statistic for one or several of them. (See Chapter 10 for a procedure to test for the significance of the coefficients of a set of dummies as a group.) As always, the researcher should assess the reasonableness of the final estimated regression equation and examine closely which variables were included and excluded.

The remainder of this section illustrates the problems of possible bias in the estimated coefficients and the effect of a stepwise procedure on the t-statistic caused by a stepwise procedure. Readers satisfied with the conclusions just presented may skip to Section 6.4.3.

A particular type of stepwise procedure is specified, based on the values of the t-statistics as opposed to the R^2, but the same type of results can occur for any stepwise approach. In fact, this particular exercise is illustrative of the actual, applied approach used by numerous researchers, an approach called "mining the data" or going on a "fishing expedition."

Suppose, in a regression of y on x_1 and x_2, that the researcher wanted first to test whether x_2 should be included as a regressor because theory was not clear concerning its inclusion. Suppose the researcher includes or excludes x_2 according to whether its t-statistic is above or below the critical value. Then the researcher applies a t-test to the estimated coefficient of x_1. This second test is "conditional" on the outcome of the first test because, after the first test, x_2 may or may not be included as a regressor. Thus, the following two-step procedure is postulated:

Step 1:

$$\text{Exclude } x_2 \text{ if } |t_{\hat{\beta}_2}| < t_c. \tag{6.4.2}$$

Include it otherwise.

Step 2:

$$\text{Test } H_0: \beta_1 = 0$$
$$H_A: \beta_1 \neq 0 \tag{6.4.3}$$

The second step is carried out by a second t-test, this time on the coefficient of x_1.

TABLE 6.4.2

Mean Simulation Values of $\hat{\beta}_1$ After the Decision on the Inclusion of x_2

$$(n = 30, \sigma_\epsilon^2 = 1, \beta_1 = 1)$$

		r_{12}^2			
		0	0.4	0.8	0.95
	0	1.0	1.0	1.0	1.0
	0.1	1.0	1.0	1.1	1.2
β_2	0.2	1.0	1.1	1.2	1.4
	0.25	1.0	1.1	1.1	1.4
	0.5	1.0	1.0	1.1	1.2

$\tau_2^2 > 1$ and MSE ($\hat{\beta}_1$) Increases or Stays the Same After the Conditional Test on $\hat{\beta}_2$

MSE (y on x_1) Greater than Both the Conditional and Unconditional MSE

For this illustration, $\beta_1 = 1$, $\sigma_\epsilon^2 = 1$, and $n = 30$.[8] The Monte Carlo simulation assesses this two-step procedure for various values of β_2 and r_{12}^2. (The data used here are the same as used in Chapter 7 with, in the notation of Chapter 7, $\rho = 0$).

Table 6.4.2 highlights some of the results of this simulation. The columns show the various values of r_{12}^2 and the rows show selected values of β_2. To show the varied results, β_2 needs to go only from 0 to 0.5. The results in this table demonstrate the general conclusion that the conditional stepwise procedure may or may not be better than the regression of either y on x_1 or y on x_1 and x_2. They also demonstrate that there is no reliable way to determine which procedure is best on a practical level.

The figures in the body of Table 6.4.2 are the mean simulation values of $\hat{\beta}_1$ conditional on the *t*-test of β_2 and the subsequent decision about the inclusion of x_2. (Before the test on β_2, the mean values of $\hat{\beta}_1$ are 1.0, the true value of β_1, because $\hat{\beta}_1$ is then unbiased.) These figures show that, for high values of β_2 and r_{12}^2, the resulting estimate of β_1 is biased.[9] Since $\hat{\beta}_2^+$ is statistically insignificant when $|t_{\hat{\beta}_2}| < t_c$, at least for that sample, one might have suspected that the exclusion of x_2 under those circumstances would not lead to any bias in the conditional $\hat{\beta}_1$; but it does.

Furthermore, as shown in Table 6.4.2, for high values of r_{12}^2 and β_2 below the solid line, the stepwise procedure causes the mean square error (MSE) of the conditional $\hat{\beta}_1$ to increase compared with the unrestricted regression of y on x_1 and x_2. (The

---

[8] The notation refers to the coefficient of x_1, the variance of the error term, and the number of observations, respectively.

[9] However, this bias is less than the bias that would take place had y been regressed unconditionally on x_1 alone. Conceptually, the bias in the conditional case is the result of a weighted average of an unbiased estimate (from y on x_1 and x_2 when x_2 is included) and a biased one (from y on x_1 alone when x_2 is excluded).

MSE is the same for an r_{12}^2 of zero.) This area includes all the cases (of those shown) for which x_2 has a value of τ_2^2 greater than unity.

For low values of β_2 for which τ_2^2 is less than unity, the MSE of $\hat{\beta}_1$ of the conditional, stepwise procedure is less than that from the unconditional regression of y on x_1 and x_2. But for these cases, the unconditional regression of y on just x_1 produces the lowest MSE. When $\beta_2 = 0.2$ and τ_2^2 is greater than unity, the unconditional regression of y on x_1 and x_2 produces the lowest MSE, followed by the unconditional regression of y on just x_1, and then the conditional, stepwise regression procedure, in that order. The box at the bottom shows those cases in which the unconditional regression of y on x_1 and x_2 produces the lowest MSE, followed by the conditional, stepwise procedure, and then the unconditional regression of y on just x_1, in that order.

Because of these differing results and our inability to discern the various cases in practice, little practical guidance is available for using a stepwise approach. This text thus stresses the reliance on theory to determine whether x_2 should be included as a regressor *and* an examination of the magnitude of $\hat{\beta}_1$ with, *versus* without, the inclusion of x_2 before a decision is made on the inclusion of x_2. Even if the theory is unclear, if $\hat{\beta}_1$ shifts "sufficiently" upon the inclusion on x_2, then it may be appropriate empirically to include—or to exclude—x_2, even if the t-statistic for $\hat{\beta}_2$ is low.

As mentioned above, another problem caused by the stepwise procedure is that the t-statistic of $\hat{\beta}_1$ no longer has the t-distribution, so the table of critical values in Statistical Table A-1 is not appropriate anymore. As a demonstration of this result, let $\beta_1 = 1$, $\beta_2 = 0.2$, $r_{12}^2 = 0.8$, $\sigma_\epsilon^2 = 1$, and $n = 30$. The Monte Carlo experiments showed that the null hypothesis $\beta_1 = 0$ was accepted (according to the t-test) 31 percent of the time when x_1 and x_2 are the regressors, but only 18 percent of the time for the conditional, stepwise procedure. In this instance, the average t-statistic for $\hat{\beta}_1$ increased from 2.2 to 5.6. As shown in Figure 6.4.1, the sampling distribution of the t-statistic of $\hat{\beta}_1$ when x_1 and x_2 are included as regressors (the unconditional distribution) has the usual shape of a t-distribution and is centered on a value of 2.2. (This value 2.2 is of no particular importance since the t-statistic usually is not compared to a population parameter, such as τ.) However, the distribution of the t-statistic from the conditional, stepwise procedure is bimodal, having two peaks, because part of the distribution has x_2 included (like the unconditional distribution) about 25 percent of the time and part has x_2 excluded about 75 percent of the time (in this instance, given the above parameter values). The distribution is actually a combination (with weights 25 and 75 percent, respectively) of the distributions for $t_{\hat{\beta}_1}$ with x_2 included and for the t-statistic for the misspecified model when x_2 is excluded. Notice in Figure 6.4.1 that 31 percent of the unconditional distribution is less than t_c, whereas only 18 percent of the conditional distribution is below (a slightly different value of) t_c, showing that H_0: $\beta_1 = 0$ would be rejected *fewer* times under the conditional, stepwise approach than is appropriate under the unconditional testing procedure.

Only the first, unconditional t-distribution (before any decisions were made on x_2) is appropriate, because making the decision on x_2 prior to an examination of $\hat{\beta}_1$ implies that the critical value should be higher than that found in the t-table. Procedures for dealing with sequential testing have been developed, but they are beyond the scope of this text and not widely used. The reader is warned to avoid stepwise procedures.

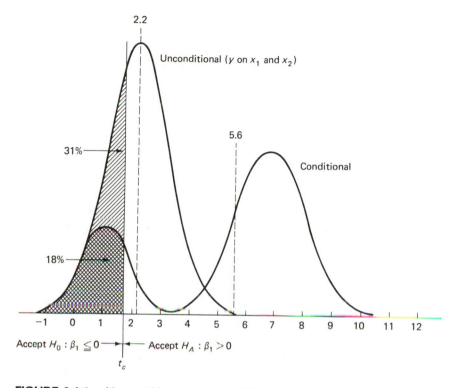

FIGURE 6.4.1   Unconditional and Conditional Sampling Distributions of the *t*-Statistics of Estimates of β_1, Conditional Upon the Inclusion of x_2 According to a *t*-Test on $\hat{\beta}_2$ ($n = 30$, $\beta_1 = 1$, $\beta_2 = 0.2$, $r^2_{12} = 0.8$, $\sigma^2_\epsilon = 1$)

6.4.3   Torturing the Data

Many practitioners estimate a number of alternative formulations of combinations of regressors and select among the best of them, without accounting for the fact that they have examined prior specifications before settling on the one selected. Thus, their reported *t*-statistics overstate the degree of statistical significance of the estimated coefficients. On the other hand, most practitioners are not expected to be familiar with the appropriate sequential testing procedures. Thus, faced with a situation of perhaps knowing that a few variables are relevant (on the basis of theory) but not knowing whether other, additional variables are relevant, recourse to the usual *t*-tests for all variables, both before and after selection or exclusion of some regressors, appears to be the common, generally accepted practice. But the reader should be aware of the consequences of such procedures.

Furthermore, "data mining" and "fishing expeditions" to obtain desired statistics for the "final" regression equation are ultimately dishonest methods of empirical research. These procedures include not only using alternative combinations of regressors, but also alternative functional forms, lag structures, and what are offered as "sophisticated" or "advanced" estimating techniques. A saying goes, "If you just torture the data long enough, they will confess."[10] In other words, if enough alternatives are tried, the chances of obtaining the results desired by the researcher are increased tremendously. And the final result is essentially worthless because the data were so tortured. Consequently, the researcher has not found any scientific evidence to support the original hypothesis.

6.5 Problems of Incorrect Functional Forms

In this section, only one of the relatively large number of possible misspecifications (in the estimating equation) of the true form of the regression model will be investigated. The method of analysis presented here is perhaps more important, given the large number of alternative functional forms possible, than are the conclusions drawn from the specific case investigated. The conclusions are that in some cases an incorrect functional form does little damage, whereas in others it does considerable damage, and that which case is which is hardly discernible in practice. Readers may want to skip this section, keeping the conclusions in mind, and use it for reference when the problem of selecting a correct functional form arises.

Recall the discussion in Chapter 2 stressing that the functional form should make sense theoretically and should be able to be usefully interpreted and applied. These theoretical considerations are to precede any empirical analysis of alternative functional forms.

However, one situation in which the R^2 can help select the functional form is the following. Suppose theory is not clear about the precise functional form of a regressor and that both X_k and $\log(X_k)$, for example, provide theoretically appealing interpretations of the form of the regressor (in terms of the change in Y with respect to a unit change in X_k) for the same formulation of the dependent variable. Then the form of the regressor that produces the highest R^2 (or, equivalently, the lowest SSE) can be selected.[11] But be clear that on theoretical grounds one form is just as appealing as another.

This simple empirical approach clearly applies only in rare instances, and it does not apply when the dependent variable changes functional form (because then the total sum of squares changes and the R^2's and SSE's are not comparable).

The model dealt with here investigates the very real problem of attempting to use a linear approximation to a nonlinear model. In many instances, such an application is appropriate as long as the equation is used within the range of observations on X and Y.

For the case investigated here, assume that the true model is the exponential or double-log form of Section 2.2.2:

---

[10] Thomas Mayer, "Economics as a Hard Science: Realistic Goal or Wishful Thinking?" *Economic Inquiry*, April 1980, p. 175.
[11] This empirical approach is suggested by Rao and Miller, *Applied Econometrics*, pp. 18–20 and p. 107.

$$\ln Y_i = \beta_0 + \beta_1 \ln X_i + \epsilon_i \qquad (6.5.1)$$

where the variables are stated in their levels not deviations-from-the-sample-mean form. Assume that the researcher is unaware of this functional form and estimates instead the linear relationship:

$$Y_i = \beta_0^L + \beta_1^L X_i + \epsilon_i^L \qquad (6.5.2)$$

where the superscript L denotes the linear form.

To examine the properties of the OLS estimate of β_1^L, it is necessary to compare it to the OLS estimates of β_1 in which the true functional form (equation 6.5.1) is assumed, call it $\hat{\beta}_1$. However, the alternative estimates of β_1 cannot be compared directly because the interpretation of β_1 from equation 6.5.1 is an elasticity (the percentage change in Y for a unit percentage change in X), whereas the interpretation of β_1^L is a slope (the change in Y for a unit change in X). Several methods of comparison, fortunately, are possible.

The first is to examine how well each equation can predict the value of Y_i. An appropriate measure is SSE $= \Sigma_i(Y_i - \hat{Y}_i)^2$. For the true model form, the anti-logs of the predicted values of $\log(Y_i)$ need to be computed before the SSE is calculated.

Another comparison is to compute from the linear model an estimate of the elasticity. The usual estimate of an elasticity in a linear model is $\hat{\beta}_1^L$ $(\overline{X}/\overline{Y})$, that is, the elasticity is computed at the sample means. (A corresponding estimate of the implied slope coefficients is not appropriate because the true model does not have a "slope" coefficient.)

For illustrative purposes, assume for the true model (equation 6.5.1) that $\beta_0 = 1$, $\beta_1 = 1$, and $\sigma_\epsilon^2 = 1$. Table 6.5.1 shows the mean values of the SSE's and elasticities estimated (via Monte Carlo simulations) from the two estimating models (equations 6.5.1 and 6.5.2), along with the MSE, VAR, and BIAS (mean square error, variance, and bias) of the elasticity estimates, for various values of n.

From the table (allowing for slight round-off and sampling errors in the Monte Carlo simulations, run 2000 times), the elasticity estimates from the double-log (and correct) form of the equation are unbiased, whereas the elasticity estimates $\hat{\beta}_1^L$ $(\overline{X}/\overline{Y})$ derived from the linear model have a slight downward bias, which becomes smaller as the sample size increases. The variance and hence the mean square error of the elasticity estimate is lower for the true log form than for the linear form; however, for the particular experiment here, the difference is fairly small, especially for large sample sizes.

The biggest difference between the logarithmic and the linear forms of the equations is in their abilities to predict Y_i on the basis of the sample values of X_i and the estimated coefficients. The linear form appears to be quite inferior. However, further experiments are reported in Table 6.5.2. This table uses data for X generated for Section 7.3.2, from a normal distribution, instead of from the rectangular distribution used for the experiment reported in Table 6.5.1. In Table 6.5.2, the ratios of the SSE's for Y_i of the linear to the logarithmic forms of the estimating equation are reported for various values of β_1, the number of observations n, and σ_ϵ^2 (with $\beta_0 = 0$). In this instance, there are a number of cases in which the linear form does better than the logarithmic form, shown by ratios less than unity. However, it does not appear that a general guideline concerning which one is better can be discerned.

TABLE 6.5.1

Monte Carlo Simulation Results for Incorrect Functional Form

| | Number of Observations | Elasticity | | | | SSE of $\hat{Y}$ (Mean Values) |
		Mean Value	Variance	Bias	MSE	
True (log) Form	10	0.99	0.18	−0.01	0.19	87
Linear Form		0.91	0.22	−0.09	0.23	6,321
True (log) Form	30	1.01	0.06	0.01	0.06	310
Linear Form		0.97	0.09	−0.03	0.09	21,130
True (log) Form	50	1.00	0.04	0.00	0.04	554
Linear Form		0.98	0.06	−0.02	0.06	37,360

NOTE: True Model is $\ln(Y_i) = \beta_0 + \beta_1 \ln(X_i) + \epsilon_i$, where ϵ_i is distributed normally with zero mean and variance of unity. The X_i are numbers between zero and 10 generated from the rectangular distribution. For this exercise, $\beta_0 = \beta_1 = 1$. The linear model is $Y_i = \beta_0^L + \beta_1^L X_i + \epsilon_i^L$. The number of observations n is 10, 30, and 50.

TABLE 6.5.2

Ratio of SSE (Linear) to SSE (Log), for Various Values of β_1, n, and σ_ϵ^2.

		Number of Observations (n)								
		$n = 10$			$n = 30$			$n = 50$		
		σ_ϵ^2			σ_ϵ^2			σ_ϵ^2		
		0.5	1.5	2.5	0.5	1.5	2.5	0.5	1.5	2.5
β_1	1	1.4	1.4	1.5	0.57	0.58	0.61	0.90	0.95	1.07
	3	3.0	3.9	3.2	0.29	0.25	0.29	1.21	0.89	1.04
	5	6.3	6.1	8.2	0.16	0.10	0.16	1.54	0.90	0.82

Linear is better here.

Note: See Section 7.3.1. for a description of the data. These results accompany the experiments reported in Table 7.3.2 (before correction for autocorrelation).

In summary, a linear approximation may or may not give rise to estimation problems. However, if theory is not clear about the functional form of the equation, econometricians generally prefer the simple, linear form. Only in the case in which the functional form of a regressor can logically take on a different form can the estimated equations help to decide which form is best: usually that form that produces the highest R^2 is best. However, when the dependent variable changes form, the R^2's are no longer comparable. One can compute an R^2 based on the level of Y_i by transforming the predicted values of a nonlinear dependent variable to their levels form. This provides a heuristic measure of the suitability of one form over another. In the Monte Carlo examples here, only the comparable sum of squares of the residuals were computed, but, for a given sample size and number of regressors, this is equivalent to comparing R^2's.

7 Time-Series Analysis: Autocorrelation

A violation of the classical assumptions that is typically ascribed to time-series analysis is autocorrelation. Since time-series analysis occupies so much of many applied researchers' time, it is important to understand the malady, to understand its consequences for OLS estimators, and to know how to detect and correct for it. This chapter is directed toward this end.

The first section distinguishes between "pure" and "impure" autocorrelation. Pure autocorrelation is the type typically assumed by most applied researchers. Impure autocorrelation, discussed in detail in the third section, is autocorrelation in the residuals that is caused by missing regressors or by incorrect functional form. With impure autocorrelation, the corrective procedures normally applied typically produce far inferior estimators than direct procedures, such as supplying the missing regressor or using the correct functional form. Thus, the standard corrective procedures should be used only when these direct methods are not feasible. The standard corrective procedures may or may not do better than OLS when both types of estimators are applied to the incorrectly specified equation.

The second section presents the standard procedures that are typically used by applied researchers. It is concluded that applying OLS (ordinary least squares) to an equation that has an autocorrelated error term produces unbiased estimates, but ones that do not have the minimum variance. The corrective procedures suggested (generalized least squares or GLS types of approaches) achieve (asymptotically) the minimum variance.

The special problems of forecasting and documenting autocorrelation-corrected equations are discussed in the fourth section. These are usually two necessary considerations when regression equations are so corrected.

The fifth section presents the rudiments of procedures that are becoming increasingly popular, called ARIMA or Box-Jenkins methods. These methods are used for time-series forecasting. The major characteristic of these methods is simultaneously their major advantage and disadvantage: they are non-theoretical. Such a technique may be useful for forecasting, yet it is often difficult to understand why the forecast values are what they are. Univariate ARIMA, discussed first, uses only information embodied in the past behavior of a variable to forecast its future values. Multivariate ARIMA, discussed next, uses information in other data series as well and is often used to examine whether a regressor is exogenous or endogenous. Beginners are warned against using these techniques, but, because of their current popularity, a certain amount of familiarity with them is required in order to be able to read some of the literature.

The final section summarizes the major elements that should be learned from this chapter.

7.1   Pure *vs.* Impure Autocorrelation

Autocorrelation is usually suspected in all time-series models. Section 7.2 sets out the usual procedures for detecting autocorrelation and correcting for it. This section discusses the nature and causes of the autocorrelation.

Assume in the simple model:

$$y_t = \beta x_t + \epsilon_t$$

that the error (or disturbance) term, ϵ_t, is positively autocorrelated. This means that, if an error term were by chance to take on a large value, subsequent error terms would tend to take on large values. In other words, in time-series models, a large random shock in one period may linger over to several other periods. Pure autocorrelation is due to shocks that cause the error term to tend to be positive for a number of observations, then negative for several more, and then back again. An example of such an error term is shown in Figure 7.1.1. For autocorrelation to exist, the pattern does not have to be perfectly smooth, only the tendency has to exist for the level of one error term to affect the level of (one or more) subsequent error terms.

The error terms were plotted in Figure 7.1.1 according to the *order* of the observations. For time-series models, the order of the observations is usually assumed to be according to the calendar date, with the first observation being the first point in time that the data are available and with subsequent observations being placed according to the calendar sequence. Then the "lingering over" of random events not accounted for by the regressors make logical sense.

However, for any set of data, including time-series data, the order of the observations could be (but should not be) changed to produce any specified pattern of the error term, such as that in Figure 7.1.1. Most researchers do not alter the usual sequence of observations for time-series data, but the sequence is usually arbitrary for cross-section data. Given that the sequence is arbitrary, researchers generally do not suspect or look for autocorrelation in cross-section models. However, it should be noted that the "lingering over" theory of autocorrelation can apply to cross-section data if some logical ordering of the data is found and applied. For example, suppose

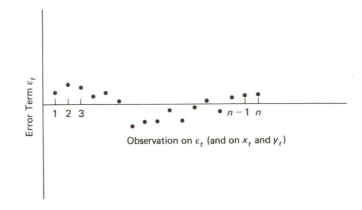

FIGURE 7.1.1   Example of an Autocorrelated Error Term

that observations of firm profits as regressed on investment and advertising were ordered according to the size of the firm (as perhaps measured by assets or volume of sales). Then random shocks that primarily affect small firms may perhaps have a diminished impact on larger firms, and a pattern of the error terms when the data are ordered by the size of the firm could resemble that of Figure 7.1.1. But some logic should be brought to bear in the sequencing of observations before autocorrelation is to be expected and its presence investigated. The data should *not* be ordered to achieve some particular pattern in the residuals.

Some students ask why the paired *x, y* observations should not be "scrambled," or placed in a random order; then the error terms would appear to be purely random and not autocorrelated, and the coefficient estimates would be the same. The answer is that scrambling the data discards useful information, namely, the possibility of autocorrelation. Actions can and should be taken if autocorrelation is detected.

In practice, of course, the error terms are unobservable. However, just as with the error terms of Figure 7.1.1, the pattern of observed residuals from OLS estimation is usually examined in order to detect the presence of autocorrelation in the error term. In Section 7.2.7, statistical tests for autocorrelation are discussed. Remember that a logical ordering of the observations is required before examining the pattern of the residuals for its presence, because the residuals can be made to conform to any given pattern if the observations are sequenced solely to achieve it. Also note that OLS produces residuals that sum to zero. Thus, there always have to be both positive and negative residuals, and positive autocorrelation, the kind usually suspected, is detected by checking for positive and negative "runs" of residuals, as with the error terms of Figure 7.1.1.

One of the primary reasons to test for autocorrelation is to attempt to determine whether relevant variables have been excluded from the estimated equation or whether the functional form is correct. In Section 6.2, it was shown that an error term in an estimating equation that omits a regressor is:

$$\epsilon_t^* = \beta_2 x_{2t} + \epsilon_t \qquad \textit{(Repeat of Eq. 6.2.3)}$$

If x_{2t} is autocorrelated with itself—that is, the x_{2t} data series can be represented by an equation:

$$x_{2t} = r_x x_{2,t-1} + v_t$$

where r_x is a specified coefficient of autocorrelation in x_2 (similar in form to ρ of equation 7.2.1) and v_t is a classical error term—then, even if ϵ_t is nonautocorrelated, the error term ϵ_t^* will appear to be autocorrelated to a degree that depends on the relative magnitudes of the parameters σ_ϵ^2, σ_v^2, r_x, and β_2.

Thus, when autocorrelation is detected in the residuals, one of the primary ways to eliminate this apparent malady is to find and include the appropriate regressor(s), or at least a good proxy. Indeed, an autocorrelated missing regressor is hardly a malady of the true error term, which in this case is ϵ_t: the values of x_2 are assumed to be fixed in repeated drawings of ϵ_t. Thus, the autocorrelation of ϵ_t^* is merely the result of the peculiar sample observations on x_2 and is not due to some systematic way the error terms are generated.

Another possibility when autocorrelation is detected is that it is caused by an incorrect functional form. Figure 7.1.2 shows such a possibility. In Figure 7.1.2(a),

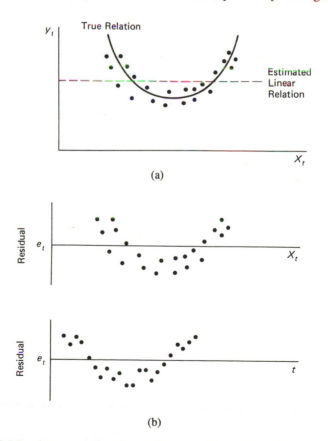

(a)

(b)

FIGURE 7.1.2 Incorrect Functional Form, with Residuals Plotted According to X_t and t (time)

a straight line is fitted to data that are generated from a nonlinear functional form. The residuals, when plotted against the level of X_t, show an autocorrelated pattern, being generally positive, then negative, and positive again. (The pattern would be inverted if the true relationship was inverted.) Also, if the residuals are sequenced according to time, as in Figure 7.1.2(b), the autocorrelation pattern of the residual may or may not be intensified. In this example, the autocorrelation pattern is intensified because X_t was strongly autocorrelated. However, one of the conclusions of the Monte Carlo experiments of Section 7.3.2 is that, for most time-series analyses, a finding of autocorrelation in the residuals is usually *not* caused by an incorrect functional form.

But because the correct form of the equation usually produces far superior results than the techniques examined in this chapter on misspecified models, the basic remedy when serious autocorrelation is detected in these cases that I call "impure autocorrelation" is to find missing relevant variables or the correct functional form. What the detected autocorrelation in the residuals may be indicating is that either of these maladies applies. These considerations are taken up in Section 7.3.

In Section 7.2, it is assumed that pure autocorrelation is at work. That is, the equation is correctly specified in terms of the inclusion of relevant variables and functional form, and the only cause of the autocorrelation is the lingering over of shocks from one observation to the next. Presumably, this type of autocorrelation should be lessened if the frequency is lengthened, for example from quarterly to annual, but switching from quarterly to annual observations may be a very inefficient remedy since it eliminates observations and hence information that may be of importance in estimating the relationship. Discussion along these lines is pursued in Section 7.3.3.

7.2   Pure Autocorrelation

This section presents relatively standard material on autocorrelated error terms. Presented are the standard model of autocorrelation, its implications for OLS, several correctional procedures, a Monte Carlo comparison of one of these procedures (CORC) with OLS, and methods to test for autocorrelation (primarily by using the Durbin-Watson statistic).

7.2.1   The Model

The traditional notational representation of (pure) autocorrelation is $E(\epsilon_t \epsilon_s) \neq 0$ for two distinct observations t and s. That is, if error terms are not correlated (non-autocorrelation), then the expected value of their product is zero. The simplest form of autocorrelation is that the current error term ϵ_t is a fraction of the error term of the preceding period, ϵ_{t-1}, plus a classical error or disturbance term. This is called *first-order autocorrelation* (or a first-order Markov scheme) and is written notationally as:

$$\epsilon_t = \rho \epsilon_{t-1} + v_t \qquad (7.2.1)$$

where ρ is the coefficient of autocorrelation, $-1 < \rho < 1$, and v_t is the classical error term (usually assumed to be normally distributed), assumed to be uncorrelated with ϵ_{t-1} and x_t.[1]

The degree of autocorrelation is indicated by the magnitude of ρ. If $\rho = 0$, then the error term ϵ_t becomes v_t, the classical error term, and there is no autocorrelation. If ρ approaches unity, the value of the previous error term becomes much more important in determining the current value of ϵ_t, and a high degree of autocorrelation results.

A negative value of ρ implies that the error term has a tendency to switch signs from negative to positive and back again in subsequent observations. This is counter to the intuitive explanation of the pure autoregressive process in which random shocks last (or linger) for more than one observation, implying positive autocorrelation ($\rho > 0$). However, impure sources of autocorrelation, such as a missing relevant variable or incorrect functional form, can cause apparent negative autocorrelation. In these cases of impure autocorrelation, whether positive or negative, representing the auto-correlation by equation 7.2.1 and acting on that representation as shown in Section 7.2.5 may be misleading and inappropriate, as is discussed in Section 7.3.

The form of equation 7.2.1 resembles a simple regression equation, with ϵ_t being the dependent variable and ϵ_{t-1} the single regressor with coefficient ρ. In fact, one of the methods used to estimate ρ applies this analogy, using residuals in place of the unobservable error terms.

7.2.2   The Consequences of Autocorrelation

Simply put (without proof), applying OLS to an equation that satisfies the classical assumptions except for the autocorrelation equation 7.2.1: (1) still provides unbiased estimates of the regression coefficients if there are no lagged dependent variables (in which case see Section 9.8), but (2) is no longer "best" in the sense of having the minimum variance. The value of having a low variance was discussed in Chapter 4; suffice it to say here that it is very important to select an estimator that has the lowest possible variance.

7.2.3   The Generalized Least-Squares Correction

If the autocorrelation can be adequately represented by equation 7.2.1, an alternative estimator, called *generalized least squares* (GLS) or the *Aitken* estimator (after the person who first suggested it), produces the minimum variance. The idea of the GLS approach to this problem of autocorrelation, as well as applied to the problem of heteroskedasticity of Chapter 8, is to transform an entire equation, the error term

---

[1] It is also assumed that the initial error term prior to the first sample observation, ϵ_0, on which the first term ϵ_1 is based, according to equation 7.2.1, is a classical error term unrelated to v_t. The equation is assumed to hold for *all* t through the nth observation, i.e., for $t = \ldots, -1, 0, 1, \ldots, n$. Second-order autocorrelation is expressed as $\epsilon_t = \rho_1\epsilon_{t-1} + \rho_2\epsilon_{t-2} + v_t$. Higher-order expressions are similarly formed. The justifications for assuming these higher-order forms is usually much weaker than the justification for the first-order form, which in most cases is itself not very strong.

of which does not satisfy the classical assumptions, into an equation with a resulting error term that does satisfy them. Since in equation 7.2.1 the error term v_t is assumed to satisfy the classical assumptions, the initial regression equation is transformed to result in having v_t as the error term. Then OLS is applied to this transformed equation, appropriately now, because its error term (v_t) satisfies the classical properties.

For (true) first-order autocorrelation, the following transformation achieves the desired result. It is simple enough and widely used enough that it shoud be learned even by beginners. It is assumed for now that the value of the autocorrelation (or autoregression) coefficient, ρ, is known and does not have to be estimated. From the assumed basic model:

$$y_t = \beta x_t + \epsilon_t \tag{7.2.2}$$

multiply both sides of the equation by ρ and lag once:

$$\rho y_{t-1} = \beta \rho x_{t-1} + \rho \epsilon_{t-1} \tag{7.2.3}$$

and take the difference between the two equations:

$$y_t - \rho y_{t-1} = \beta(x_t - \rho x_{t-1}) + (\epsilon_t - \rho \epsilon_{t-1}) \tag{7.2.4}$$

then substitute equation 7.2.1:

$$(y_t - \rho y_{t-1}) = \beta(x_t - \rho x_{t-1}) + v_t \tag{7.2.5}$$

Since ρ is assumed to be known, new variables can be formed:

$$y_t^* = y_t - \rho y_{t-1} \tag{7.2.6}$$

$$x_t^* = x_t - \rho x_{t-1} \tag{7.2.7}$$

The first observations on the transformed variables can be obtained by multiplying $(1-\rho^2)^{\frac{1}{2}}$ times the first observation of the original variables (although many computer programs drop the first observation). These new variables are called the rho-differences, quasi-first differences, or generalized differences of the original variables. First-differences assume a value of ρ of unity, which is usually an unlikely assumption. If there are more regressors, their generalized differences are similarly computed.

Thus, the transformed equation can be written as:

$$y_t^* = \beta x_t^* + v_t \tag{7.2.8}$$

This equation has the classical error term and GLS is achieved by applying OLS to this equation. The variance of the GLS estimator of β is as small as possible. It can be shown that the variance of the GLS estimator is smaller the larger the absolute value of ρ is, both absolutely (usually) and relative to the OLS estimator of β on the original, untransformed data (which is GLS with an assumed value of ρ of zero).

Notice that the coefficient β of the transformed equation (7.2.8) is identical to the β of the original equation (7.2.2). Thus, no manipulation is necessary after the estimation in order to use the equation. (Although it is usually unnecessary, to obtain the estimate of the constant term in the untransformed model, the estimate of the constant term in the transformed model is divided by $1-\rho$.) It might be asked, since β is the same in both the OLS and the GLS approaches, will the OLS and GLS estimates differ? The answer is yes, because the variances are different. If the two estimates would always be identical, then there would be no reason to undertake the GLS transformation and estimation procedure. Which estimator is more appropriate depends primarily on the amount of faith that the researcher has in the autoregressive model (equation 7.2.1) as an adequate representation of the underlying malady.

7.2.4 Alternative Estimation Approaches

In practice, ρ has to be estimated along with β. However, the transformed equation is nonlinear in the two parameters β and ρ. To show this clearly, the transformed model (equation 7.2.5) can be written as:

$$y_t = \beta x_t - \beta \rho x_{t-1} + \rho y_{t-1} + v_t \qquad (7.2.9)$$

OLS can be applied to this equation. However, the coefficient of x_{t-1} is identically (-1) times the product of the coefficients of x_t and y_{t-1}, and OLS would not account for this identity; only a nonlinear estimating routine would. However, a procedure called Durbin's method suggests that OLS be applied to equation 7.2.9 solely to obtain an estimate of ρ as the estimated coefficient of y_{t-1}. Then the GLS transformation and estimation procedure shown in Section 7.2.3 is followed with this estimated value of ρ instead of the (assumed) true value of ρ. Also, OLS is often applied to equation 7.2.9 in order to assess whether the model is autoregressive or dynamic. For the former, the estimated coefficient of x_{t-1} would approximately equal (-1) times the product of the estimated coefficients of x_t and y_{t-1}; for the latter, this relationship would not hold. Section 7.2.7 explains how to test for autocorrelation when there are lagged dependent variables as regressors.

Another procedure, called the search procedure, or sometimes called the Hildreth-Lu or Dhrymes procedure, estimates transformed equations by OLS for various assumed values of ρ in the interval $-1 < \rho < 1$, for example by letting ρ be -0.9, $-0.8, \ldots, 0.8, 0.9$. That equation is selected that exhibits the minimum residual sum of squares (SSE).[2] For example, if the minimum SSE were found at $\rho = 0.5$, then the estimate of ρ is 0.5, and the estimate of β is the GLS estimate with $\rho = 0.5$.

However, the most popular technique for estimating the (first-order) autoregressive model appears to be the Cochrane-Orcutt (CORC) iterative method.

7.2.5 The CORC Estimating Procedure

Like the other methods, CORC (pronounced "cork") uses an estimate for ρ in place of the true value of ρ in the GLS transformation that attempts to account for

---

[2] A more general search procedure, assuming that the error terms are normally distributed, calls for finding the minimum of $T/2 \ln(\text{SSE}) - \frac{1}{2} \ln(1-\rho^2)$. This is a "maximum likelihood estimator." See Phoebus J. Dhrymes, *Distributed Lags* (San Francisco: Holden-Day, 1971), pp. 64–70.

first-order autocorrelation. Actually, a series of estimates may be used. The steps are as follows:

Step 1.   Obtain OLS estimates of the original regression equation 7.2.2 and compute the residuals $e_t = y_t - \hat{\beta} x_t$. Then estimate ρ as e_t regressed on e_{t-1}, as if the residuals had come from a regression equation $e_t = \rho e_{t-1} + w_t$, where w_t is a classical error term. This regression equation may be thought of as the empirical counterpart of the autoregressive equation 7.2.1, where the observed residuals replace the unobserved error terms.

Step 2.   With this estimate of ρ, apply OLS on the transformed equation. That is, compute the $\hat{\rho}$ differences of the variables and apply OLS (and include a constant term). If one stops with these estimates of β and ρ, the resulting estimates are two-stage CORC estimates. However, most computer programs recompute the residuals again (on the original untransformed values of the variables), then estimate ρ again, and obtain another estimate of β by OLS on the newly transformed variables. This iterative procedure stops when the latest estimate of ρ is within some given tolerance level (say 0.01) of the previous estimate of ρ, that is, the procedure stops when the iterative routine converges on a value of $\hat{\rho}$.

Usually, convergence is achieved within a few iterations, but sometimes the estimated value of ρ will tend to be outside the acceptable range (less than unity in absolute value), and convergence will not be achieved if the acceptable range is adhered to.

7.2.6 Monte Carlo Comparison of CORC and OLS

Recall the caveats that the coefficient estimates are not biased because pure autocorrelation is assumed (for now) rather than that the autocorrelated residuals are caused by an omitted relevant variable or an incorrect functional form. If the true autoregressive model (equation 7.2.1) is operating, then both OLS and CORC give unbiased estimates of β, and a comparison of the two methods should center on precision or its inverse, variance.[3]

Table 7.2.1 presents some of the results of a Monte Carlo experiment. It was assumed that, for the simple model 7.2.2, the error terms were generated by the autoregressive process of equation 7.2.1. It was assumed that the variance of the classical error term v_t was unity and that that of ϵ_0 was $1/(1-\rho^2)$.[4] The assumed value of β was unity. Also, analytic work has shown that it makes a difference whether x_t is autocorrelated as well as the error term ϵ_t and that for time-series data for which

---

[3] Actually, it has not been proven analytically that CORC yields unbiased estimates of β, but, for the Monte Carlo experiments shown here, no bias was detected (allowing for a small tolerance of 0.02 for randomness). When there is a lagged dependent variable in the model, however, both OLS and CORC are biased and inconsistent estimators. See Section 9.8.

[4] This is the usual assumption made concerning the variance of ϵ_0. This assumption is in turn based on the assumption that equation 7.2.1 holds for all t less than or equal to n, even approaching negative infinity.

TABLE 7.2.1

Monte Carlo Results for CORC and OLS Estimates of β from $y_t = \beta x_t + \epsilon_t$; $\epsilon_t = \rho\epsilon_{t-1} + v_t$; Number of Observations $= 30$; $r_x =$ regression coefficient of x_t regressed on x_{t-1}

True Value of ρ (1)	Average CORC Estimate of ρ $(r_x = 0)$ (2)	Variance of Estimates of β $(r_x = 0)^*$		Average Ratio of the CORC to the OLS Estimates of the Variances of the Estimated Coefficients			
		CORC (3)	OLS (4)	$r_x = 0$ (5)	$r_x = 0.6$ (6)	$r_x = 0.8$ (7)	$r_x = 0.9$ (8)
0	−0.03	48	44	0.97	0.96	0.95	0.95
0.2	0.14	38	39	0.95	1.13	1.20	1.28
0.4	0.33	41	53	0.89	1.37	1.47	1.77
0.6	0.52	31	65	0.80	1.51	1.85	2.27
0.8	0.68	26	72	0.70	1.63	2.23	3.27
0.9	0.75	21	80	0.65	1.71	2.48	3.93
0.95	0.80	21	93	0.63	1.79	2.68	4.21

* Divide figures by 1000 for the actual results.

CORC is usually applied, such autocorrelation in x_t may be expected because of the often trend-dominated nature of time-series data.[5]

The first column shows the true value of ρ. It was alternatively assumed that ρ was 0, 0.2, . . ., 0.8, 0.9, and 0.95. A closer look at the upper end of the spectrum is called for because the major differences between OLS and CORC show up there.

The second column shows the resulting average estimates of ρ by the CORC iterative procedure. Comparing the estimates to the true values, it is seen that there is a downward bias in the CORC estimates of ρ and that the amount of the bias increases as ρ increases toward unity. (For negative values of ρ, the bias is toward zero as well.) It has been shown that the estimator of ρ is consistent, a term that is developed in Chapter 9. For purposes here, consistency implies that the bias disappears as the sample size (n) approaches infinity.

The variances of the estimated coefficient for the CORC and OLS methods are shown in the next two columns. The variances are nearly equal up to a value of ρ of 0.4; however, for values greater than 0.4, the variance of the OLS estimate rises

---

[5] The x_t series was computed by randomly drawing values from a classical normal error term u_t and applying:

$$x_t = r_x x_{t-1} + u_t$$

where r_x, the autocorrelation coefficient for x_t, is specified as having various alternative values. When an OLS regression of x_t on x_{t-1} produced an estimated value of r_x within some tolerance limit (here 0.012) of the specified value of r_x, that series on x_t was selected for these Monte Carlo experiments.

It was assumed in constructing Table 7.2.1 that the number of observations (T) was 30. (The number of Monte Carlo drawings for the set of 30 observations was 500.)

considerably above that of the CORC estimate. Thus, when the first-order autoregressive model is truly operating and the value of ρ is high (in absolute value), the CORC estimates are substantially more precise than the OLS estimates are. This is the primary reason why CORC (or some other corrective method) is so popular. The variance of the CORC estimator actually falls as ρ increases, whereas that of the OLS estimator increases substantially.

The first several columns were computed for a variable x_t with no autocorrelation, because the CORC estimate of ρ and the relative magnitudes of the variances do not change much with r_x, the coefficient of autocorrelation in x_t. However, the relative *estimated* variances of the CORC and OLS estimates do change as r_x changes. For r_x near zero, the estimated variance of the CORC estimator is less than that of the OLS estimator, as shown in the fifth column of Table 7.2.1 (the average ratio of the two estimated variances is less than unity). That is, the OLS estimates *appear* to be less precise than they should be (if CORC were used), and the t-statistic is thus lower than it should be.

Just the opposite conclusion emerges for values of r_x above 0.4. As shown in the last few columns of Table 7.2.1, the CORC-estimated variance can be two and three times the size of the OLS-estimated variance. That is, the OLS estimates of the coefficients *appear* to be more precise than they should be, and thus their t-statistics are unduly inflated.

One lesson to be observed from this experiment is that inferences about which estimating procedure provides the more precise estimates of the coefficients *cannot* be discerned by comparing the estimated variances of the estimated coefficients from the OLS and CORC routines. As is shown in the third and fourth columns of Table 7.2.1 and was emphasized above, CORC provides the lowest variance and is by definition more precise for nonzero values of ρ.

Another concern with autocorrelated errors is the possibility of selecting the incorrect value for ρ for the GLS transformation. As is shown in Table 7.2.1, the CORC estimates of ρ are biased; more accurate estimates would lead to greater efficiency (i.e., lower variance). However, the CORC method is usually thought to be accurate enough so that the researcher need not be concerned about its loss of efficiency. A procedure that is not recommended, however, is taking first differences of the variables to eliminate autocorrelation, that is, letting ρ equal unity, with the new transformed variables being:

$$y_t^* = y_t - y_{t-1}$$

and

$$x_t^* = x_t - x_{t-1}$$

It can be shown that, depending on the true values of ρ and r_x, this approach can lead to a considerable loss of efficiency. Some researchers take first differences of all the variables in order to reduce multicollinearity, since first differencing usually eliminates the correlation among variables even though the original variables are highly correlated. This practice is discouraged because it automatically introduces at least some degree of negative autocorrelation into the error term and usually lessens (by as much as 70 percent) the efficiency of the estimates, possibly offsetting the gain in efficiency produced by the decrease in multicollinearity. In fact, the whole procedure involves guesswork about the outcome to such an extent that its practice should be viewed as curve fitting and should be avoided.

7.2.7 Testing for Autocorrelation

Autocorrelation is defined as a correlation between error terms for different observations. The most common model is that of first-order autocorrelation (equation 7.2.1), which is repeated here:

$$\epsilon_t = \rho\epsilon_{t-1} + v_t \qquad (7.2.1)$$

where ρ is the first-order autocorrelation coefficient and v_t is the pure white noise or classical error term (not having autocorrelation or heteroskedasticity).

The most widely used test for autocorrelation is the Durbin-Watson test. The Durbin-Watson (DW) statistic is computed by most regression programs. The formula is:

$$DW = \frac{\sum\limits_{t=2}^{T}(e_t - e_{t-1})^2}{\sum\limits_{t=1}^{T} e_t^2} \qquad (7.2.10)$$

where e_t is the OLS residual.

The DW statistic is approximately equal to:

$$DW \cong 2\left[1 - \frac{\sum\limits_{2}^{T} e_t e_{t-1}}{\sum e_t^2}\right] \qquad (7.2.11)$$

In this expression, the term $\sum e_t e_{t-1}/\sum e_t^2$ is a correlation coefficient between e_t and e_{t-1}, call it r_e. Thus, equation 7.2.11 may be written as:

$$DW \cong 2(1-r_e)$$

If e_t is not correlated with e_{t-1}, presumably because the error term ϵ_t is not correlated with ϵ_{t-1}, then $r_e = 0$ and DW = 2. If $r_e > 0$, as would likely occur with positive autocorrelation, then DW < 2. At most, $r_e = 1$, so the minimum value of DW is 0. If $r_e < 0$, as would likely occur with negative autocorrelation, then DW > 2; at most, DW = 4 because, at the least, $r_e = -1$. Thus, a DW between 0 and 2 may indicate *positive* autocorrelation of the error terms; a DW "around" 2 may indicate no autocorrelation; and a DW between 2 and 4 may indicate negative autocorrelation. The actual test is shown in Section 7.2.7(a), and 7.2.7(b) points out that the DW statistic is biased toward 2 if there are lagged dependent variables.

It is difficult to envision what negative autocorrelation is; its existence probably identifies some kind of specification error. Pure positive autocorrelation, however, is more easily understood: a random shock in one period holds over to the next period (in a time-sequence model), at least in part. But positive autocorrelation can also be caused by specification error, such as a missing relevant variable or an incorrect functional form, so the GLS remedy outlined in Section 7.2.3 is not necessarily the appropriate one, as is discussed in Section 7.3.

7.2.7(a)   Using the Durbin-Watson Test.

The DW test is not always conclusive; that is, there are three possible outcomes in applying the test: accept, reject, or inconclusive. Most researchers interpret the inconclusive outcome as an acceptance of the null hypothesis of no autocorrelation, because it is usually interpreted as not calling for any further action on the part of the researcher. On the contrary, it is probably appropriate in most of these cases to suspect the existence of autocorrelation.

A one-sided Durbin-Watson test should be used to test for the existence of positive autocorrelation:

$$H_0: \rho \leq 0$$
$$H_A: \rho > 0$$

(7.2.12)

A pure first-order autocorrelation scheme is likely to have a positive coefficient if the scheme exists at all. According to the methodology developed in Chapter 5, this hypothesis is stated as the alternative one.

The decision rules involve two critical statistics, d_L and d_U, as follows:

$$\text{Reject } H_0 \text{ if DW} < d_L$$
$$\text{Accept } H_0 \text{ if DW} > d_U$$
$$\text{Inconclusive if } d_L \leq \text{DW} \leq d_U$$

(7.2.13)

The values of d_L and d_U are found in the Statistical Tables A-4, A-5, and A-6 at the end of the text. There is a different pair of such numbers for a different number of regressors K (excluding the constant term, as has been the notation in this text), for different degrees of freedom, and for different levels of significance. Only a limited set of critical values of d_L and d_U have been constructed; at least 15 observations are required, and the values have not been constructed for more than 5 regressors. As an example of its use, for a 95-percent one-sided level of confidence, look at the 5-percent significance table (A-4). For three regressors and 25 observations, for example, $d_L = 1.12$ and $d_U = 1.66$. Thus, if the computed DW is less than 1.12, H_A is accepted (positive autocorrelation exists); if it is between 1.12 and 1.66 (inclusive), the test is inconclusive; and if the DW is greater than 1.66, H_0 is not rejected, and the conclusion is that there is no positive autocorrelation. If the regressors are "smooth" in some sense, the inconclusive region may be grouped with the *rejection*

---

[6] The reason for the inconclusive outcome of the test is that the residual, and hence the DW statistic, depends on the values of X. A test that eliminates the inconclusive region has been constructed, but it depends on the values of the X's. See H. Theil and A. L. Nagar, "Testing the Independence of Regression Disturbances," *Journal of the American Statistical Society*, December 1961, pp. 793–806.

region (a finding of positive autocorrelation), contrary to the casual practice noted above.

For a two-sided test:

$$H_0: \rho = 0$$
$$H_A: \rho \neq 0 \qquad (7.2.14)$$

the decision rule is:

Reject H_0 if DW $< d_L$ or DW $> 4 - d_L$

Accept H_0 if $4 - d_U >$ DW $> d_U \qquad (7.2.15)$

Otherwise, test is inconclusive.

In this case, however, the critical values from the 5-percent table give a 10-percent level of significance, or a 90-percent level of confidence. As with all hypothesis testing, as stressed in Chapter 5, a one-sided test should be used whenever possible.

7.2.7(b)   Other Tests.

Another test is similar to the Durbin-Watson test, but it does not contain an inconclusive region. It is based on the von Neumann ratio and is called, appropriately enough, the modified von Neumann ratio. Some computer programs compute this statistic. Critical values for one-sided tests are presented in Henri Theil, *Principles of Econometrics* (New York: John Wiley and Sons, 1971), pp. 726–29.[7] A value of the ratio greater than the tabled critical value rejects the null hypothesis of no autocorrelation.

There is a special problem in applying all these tests when there is a lagged dependent variable as a regressor: the Durbin-Watson statistic is biased toward two (and the von Neumann ratio test is also biased). Since the value two represents no autocorrelation, simple application of the test is more likely to show no autocorrelation. Durbin has suggested the following approach.[8] Consider the equation estimated by OLS:

$$y_t = \hat{\beta}_1 y_{t-1} + \hat{\beta}_2 y_{t-2} + \cdots + \hat{\beta}_J y_{t-J} + \hat{\beta}_{J+1} x_{1t} + \cdots + \hat{\beta}_{J+K} x_{Kt} + e_t \quad (7.2.16)$$

The suggested test statistic is:

$$h = (1 - 0.5 DW) \frac{n}{1 - n s_{\hat{\beta}_1}^2} \qquad (7.2.17)$$

where DW is the Durbin-Watson statistic, n is the number of observations, and $s_{\hat{\beta}_1}^2$ is the estimated variance of the estimated coefficient $\hat{\beta}_1$, the coefficient of the first lagged term. The statistic h is asymptotically distributed as a standard normal variable. Thus, select a value of the level of significance α for a one-sided test and find the critical value of Z in the standard normal table (A-7) at the end of the text. For a 2.5-percent

---

[7] They were originally reported in S. J. Press and R. B. Brooks, "Testing for Serial Correlation in Regression," Report No. 6911, Center for Mathematical Studies in Business and Economics, University of Chicago, 1969.

[8] J. Durbin, "Testing for Serial Correlation in Least-Squares Regression When Some of the Regressors are Lagged Dependent Variables," *Econometrica*, May 1970, pp. 410–21.

level of significance, for example, the critical value of Z is 1.96. If $h > Z_c$, reject the null hypothesis that the errors are independent and accept H_A that they are positively autocorrelated; otherwise, do not reject this null hypothesis. (Two-tailed tests can also be conducted.) This test may not apply for only a few observations; and if $ns_{\hat{\beta}_1}^2$ is greater than or equal to unity, the test is not defined.

7.3   Impure Autocorrelation

Section 7.2 discussed pure autocorrelation, autocorrelation in the error term that can be characterized by an autoregressive scheme. This section discusses impure autocorrelation, which is caused by missing relevant regressors or by an incorrect functional form. The entire section consists of results of Monte Carlo experiments. Most readers can simply read this introduction, which presents the findings of the experiments, and leave the details for future reference.

For missing relevant regressors and a true error term that is not autocorrelated, autocorrelation in the residuals is detected, on average, (beyond the set level of significance of the test) only to the extent that the missing regressor is itself autocorrelated. Recall that, for the missing relevant regressor model, OLS usually produces a biased estimator of the coefficient of the included regressor. The Monte Carlo results shown in Section 7.3.1 suggest that an autocorrelation correction routine (in particular, CORC) applied only when autocorrelated residuals are detected sometimes compares favorably, and sometimes unfavorably, to OLS applied to the missing regressor model. The CORC routine produces a higher variance of the estimated coefficients when the missing regressor is not correlated with the included one. For a high degree of correlation of the regressors, the OLS and CORC estimates achieve about the same results. But the CORC routine reduces the bias and the MSE for moderate values of the sample correlation between the included and excluded variables. In a sense, the CORC routine is acting as a proxy for the autocorrelated portion of the missing regressor. However, those cases in which the CORC procedure produces less bias and a lower MSE usually compare very unfavorably to the results when the missing regressor is included in the equation and OLS is applied.

Thus, when autocorrelation in the residuals is detected, it may indicate a missing regressor. The best corrective procedure is, in this case, to find and include the regressor. In lieu of that, application of the CORC procedure can lead to improvement in the bias and MSE in those cases in which there is a moderate degree of correlation between the (unknown) missing regressor and the included regressor(s).

From the Monte Carlo results in Section 7.3.2, incorrect functional form can only be systematically detected in the residuals by the Durbin-Watson test when there is high autocorrelation in the regressor or, to achieve the same end, when the observations are ordered according to the magnitude of the regressor or the dependent variable. The Monte Carlo simulations show that CORC, applied when autocorrelation is detected, is inferior to OLS for estimation and prediction.

Therefore, indiscriminate application of CORC or some other fix-up technique when autocorrelated residuals are detected is cautioned against. It is much better to find and correct the source of the impure autocorrelation than to apply CORC. It may or may not be better to apply OLS than CORC to the incorrectly specified model.

Section 7.3.3 shows that, if data are timewise aggregated, for example from quarterly to annual, and the true (pure) autocorrelation mechanism is quarterly, the autocorrelation is detected empirically far fewer times with the aggregated annual data than with the quarterly data. Since autocorrelation may be expected more for short time intervals, the inference is that detected autocorrelation with annual data or cross-section data (arranged in some logical order) in at least some cases indicates impure rather than pure sources of autocorrelation. Thus, these caveats about the indiscriminate use of CORC will usually apply.

Again, readers that are uninterested in the details of the Monte Carlo experiments now presented may proceed directly to Section 7.4.

7.3.1 Missing Relevant Variables

Section 6.2 showed that, when a relevant regressor is omitted from the estimating equation, it becomes part of the error term of the estimating model. This model is repeated here; namely, let the true model be:

$$y_t = \beta_1 x_{1t} + \beta_2 x_{2t} + \epsilon_t \qquad (7.3.1)$$

and the estimating model be:

$$y_t = \beta_1 x_{1t} + \epsilon_t^* \qquad (7.3.2)$$

So the error term of the estimating model is:

$$\epsilon_t^* = \beta_2 x_{2t} + \epsilon_t \qquad (7.3.3)$$

Thus, even though the true error term, ϵ_t, has all the classical properties—and, in particular, it is not autocorrelated—the error term for the estimating model will be autocorrelated if the missing regressor, x_2, is autocorrelated. The extent of the auto-correlation of ϵ_t^* depends on the degree of autocorrelation of x_2 *and* on the relative magnitudes of the movements (or variances) of $\beta_2 x_{2t}$, on the one hand, and ϵ_t, on the other. The latter condition determines the extent to which the autocorrelation in x_2 shows up in ϵ_t^*, which depends on how important the component $\beta_2 x_{2t}$ is relative to ϵ_t.

The following Monte Carlo experiment assesses whether one of the most widely used correction procedures for detected autocorrelation, CORC, would result in better or worse estimates than simple OLS; both procedures are applied to the missing regressor model (equation 7.3.2). However, the CORC procedure is not applied if the Durbin-Watson test does not detect autocorrelation. (A value of the DW statistic below the "upper" critical value is taken to indicate positive autocorrelation.) Thus, the conditional CORC estimate of β_1 is taken to be the OLS estimate when the DW statistic is above (or equal to) the critical value and to be the CORC estimate using the iterative procedure when the DW is below the critical value. (Only positive autocorrelation is examined.)

For this experiment, values of x_2 are drawn randomly from the standard normal distribution. Varying degrees of autocorrelation are incorporated into several series of

x_2 in the manner described for the x_1 of Section 7.2.6. Then candidate values of x_1 are drawn at random from the standard normal distribution until they exhibit varying degrees of correlation with x_2. As was shown in Section 6.2, the degree of correlation between x_1 and x_2 is very important in determining the properties of $\hat{\beta}_1$ from the misspecified model. Thus, the sample correlation (or its square, r_{12}^2) also plays an important role in this analysis.

As might be expected, the conditional CORC procedure (conditional on the outcome of the DW test) produces different estimates than does the OLS procedure only if the autocorrelation in the missing regressor x_2 differs from zero. Otherwise, ϵ_t^* is nonautocorrelated since ϵ_t is nonautocorrelated, and the DW test detects positive autocorrelation only about 5 percent of the time, the chosen level of significance (thus, the CORC procedure is applied only 5 percent of the time). To illustrate the results, a high value of the autocorrelation in x_2, 0.8, is used.

Table 7.3.1 presents the results of one set of simulations, which is sufficient to tell the following general story. For low values of r_{12}^2, the conditional CORC procedure produces a higher MSE than the OLS procedure does. (The slight bias in the OLS and CORC estimates when $r_{12}^2 = 0.01$ is due to the nonzero correlation.) The CORC procedure has a higher variance, which shows up for all values of r_{12}^2. However, for moderate values of r_{12}^2, the case in which the missing relevant variable produces a biased OLS estimator, CORC reduces that bias and has a lower MSE than OLS does. Finally, for high values of r_{12}^2, both CORC and OLS tend to produce the same estimator of β_1 with the same MSE and BIAS.

In cases in which there is bias but not perfect collinearity between x_1 and x_2, the CORC procedure seems to be able to act as the missing variable to the extent that this variable is autocorrelated. This reduction in bias eventually reaches a point to offset its higher variance, as r_{12}^2 increases from zero.

Another phenomenon that tends to make the two approaches identical as the r_{12}^2 increases toward unity also shows itself. For an r_{12}^2 of zero, CORC was applied, in this case, 97 percent of the time (the number of times is determined by the results of the DW test). When r_{12}^2 increased to 0.4, it was applied only 50 percent of the time; at $r_{12}^2 = 0.8$, it was applied only 4 percent of the time. The reduction in the percentage of applications of CORC is because x_2 becomes less of a relevant variable as r_{12}^2 increases, as indicated by the lower value of τ_2^2 (see Section 6.2). That is, as r_{12}^2

TABLE 7.3.1

Monte Carlo Results of OLS vs. "Conditional" CORC on Missing Regressor Model ($\beta_1 = \beta_2 = \sigma_\epsilon^2 = 1$ and the autocorrelation coefficient of $x_2 = 0.8$. 30 observations)

Sample Correlation between x_1 and x_2	MSE OLS	MSE CORC	Mean Value of $\hat{\beta}_1$ OLS	Mean Value of $\hat{\beta}_1$ CORC	Variance of $\hat{\beta}_1$ OLS	Variance of $\hat{\beta}_1$ CORC	Mean τ_2^2	Mean t-statistic OLS	Mean t-statistic CORC	Percent CORC Applied	Mean Estimate of ρ
$r_{x_1 x_2}^2$ 0.01	0.049	0.051	1.13	0.92	0.031	0.044	58.7	3.61	2.90	97%	0.54
0.40	0.45	0.30	1.66	1.49	0.019	0.055	35.5	8.37	7.43	50%	0.25
0.80	0.40	0.40	1.63	1.62	0.008	0.009	11.9	15.3	15.2	4%	0.02

increases, by definition the movements in x_1 and x_2 resemble each other more closely. Thus, the residuals show less of a pattern of autocorrelation because x_1 acts like x_2 enough not to let the autocorrelation in x_2 show up in the residuals: the movements in x_2 are already explained by the movements in the included regressor x_1.

These tendencies are magnified (reduced) for higher (lower) values of the autocorrelation in x_2 and for higher (lower) values of β_2. Of course, when β_2 is low enough so that x_2 is an irrelevant variable (with a τ_2^2 less than unity), CORC is applied less frequently, and the OLS and conditional CORC procedures essentially become the same, the OLS procedure.

There are few practical guidelines available because the conditional CORC procedure may lead to a higher or a lower MSE, compared with OLS, on the missing regressor model. The degree of autocorrelation in the missing regressor is usually not observable (or else why is the regressor excluded?), and the degree of correlation between the excluded and included variables is likewise not observable.

However, if one is especially interested in reducing bias, with less emphasis on variance and the MSE, the use of CORC (or some other autocorrelation correction procedure) would be appropriate. To the extent that the bias does exist (because of a nonzero correlation between the excluded and included regressors) *and* to the extent that the excluded regressor is itself autocorrelated, the conditional CORC procedure tends to act as a proxy for at least the autocorrelation component of the missing regressor, and thus reduces the bias (and possibly the MSE).

In time-series analyses, many regressors are thought to contain at least some degree of autocorrelation. For moderate levels of collinearity, using the conditional CORC procedure may produce higher or lower MSE's, although the bias will be reduced. In many cases, the autocorrelation may be high in both included and excluded regressors, which may lead to a high degree of (multi-)collinearity between the variables. In this case, the conditional CORC cannot hurt and could possibly improve the bias and MSE.

For cross-section analyses, unless the observations are given some logical order, the DW test and CORC should not be applied. But given some logical ordering, the same conclusions apply to cross-section as well as to time-series analyses, with one major exception: regressors usually exhibit a much lower degree of collinearity than in time-series analyses. Thus, the MSE is more likely to be increased than decreased by the conditional CORC procedure, compared with the time-series applications.

For both types of analyses, the detection of autocorrelation in the residuals (by the DW test) may imply that a regressor has been omitted from the equation. If x_2 is a relevant regressor (with a $\tau^2 > 1$), it is *always* better to find and include that variable than to apply the conditional CORC procedure. For the simulations reported in Table 7.3.1, for example, the MSE is 0.03 when x_1 and x_2 are included in the estimating equation compared with an MSE of 0.30 for the conditional CORC procedure, for an r_{12}^2 of 0.4. Of course, including x_2 completely eliminates the biasedness of $\hat{\beta}_1$, and considerable bias remains for the conditional CORC procedure (a bias of 0.49, compared with a bias of 0.66 for the OLS estimator when y was regressed unconditionally on x_1 alone). When x_2 is not very relevant in the sense of its τ^2 being less than unity (see Section 6.2), the conditional CORC procedure can lead to both lower bias and lower MSE than the regression either of y on x_1 and x_2 or of y on x_1 (and, as discussed in Section 6.2, the latter yields a lower MSE for $\hat{\beta}_1$ than the regression of y on x_1 and x_2),[9] but then autocorrelation is rarely detected.

7.3.2 Incorrect Functional Form

Another possible source of autocorrelation in the *residuals* (as opposed to the true error term) is incorrect functional form. This was shown diagrammatically in Figure 7.1.2. In this section, the results of a set of Monte Carlo simulations demonstrate the consequences of correcting for autocorrelation (by CORC) if the estimating model is a linear approximation of a nonlinear model. In particular, the true model is the same as that of Section 6.5, namely, exponential, or linear in the logarithms of the variables:

$$\ln Y_i = \beta_0 + \beta_1 \ln X_i + \epsilon_i \qquad (7.3.4)$$

where ϵ_i is a classical error term, without autocorrelation. The estimating model is linear:

$$Y_i = \beta_0^L + \beta_1^L X_i + \epsilon_i^L \qquad (7.3.5)$$

where the superscript L denotes the linear-form counterparts.

The OLS residuals e_i^L will be autocorrelated only to the extent that the observations are appropriately ordered. If the observations are "scrambled" as they usually are (initially at least) for most cross-section data, then autocorrelation will not be detected in the residuals (except 5 percent of the time, if that is the chosen level of statistical significance). Only when the observations have a logical ordering can the autocorrelation show up in the residuals.

One such logical ordering is to arrange the observations according to the magnitude of the regressor X. (The logarithm of X also has the same order.) This would apply to cross-section data, for example, if firm operating costs (Y) were being regressed on firm output (X). Ordering the observations according to the size of the firm (as measured by output) allows the legitimate investigation of autocorrelation in the residuals. (The OLS coefficient estimates are not altered by rearranging the observations.) That is, more information is obtained by applying this reordering procedure. The information obtained may indicate incorrect functional form (as well as possibly indicating pure autocorrelation or a missing regressor).

For time-series models, the regressor X may be positively autocorrelated, which tends to coincide at least partially with the order of magnitude of X. The results of some simulations with autocorrelated regressors are also discussed in this section.

The data on X are the same as were used in Section 7.3.1, except that, for this experiment, negative values of X are changed to positive values, so that their logarithm can be taken. Variations in the degree of autocorrelation in X, then, are not observable for this set of experiments. The degree of autocorrelation in X, with the ordering according to its magnitude, is near unity (being slightly below unity for 10 observations and slightly above unity for 30 and 50 observations).

---

[9] These results and others are presented in Arthur J. Bruckheim and Henry J. Cassidy, "On the Application of the Cochrane-Orcutt Technique to an Omitted Relevant Variable Model," *forthcoming*.

In order for there to be any significant difference in the OLS and CORC procedures, the CORC procedure has to be applied a number of times during the simulation. CORC is applied, as in Section 7.3.1, when the DW test shows positive autocorrelation at the 5-percent level of significance. Table 7.3.2 shows the percentage of times CORC was applied for various levels of the parameters. For this experiment, β_0 was set to zero, and three alternative values were assigned to β_1, σ_ϵ^2 and n. In general, the more the deterministic portion of the true equation 7.3.4 shows up relative to the error term, the more the autocorrelation in the residuals will be detected by the DW test. Increased detection occurs (as can be seen from Table 7.3.2) (1) the lower the level of the error variance σ_ϵ^2 is, (2) the higher the level of β_1 is, and (3) the higher the number of observations n is.

Two cases of Table 7.3.2 are explored via Table 7.3.3, for $n = 50, \sigma_\epsilon^2 = 0.5$, and $\beta_1 = 1$ and, alternatively, $\beta_1 = 5$. When $\beta_1 = 1$, CORC is applied only 11 percent of the time (out of 2000 drawings). Thus, the conditional CORC estimate has approximately the same mean estimate of the elasticity, β_1. (The elasticities for the misspecified models are computed at the sample means.) However, its variance is higher than that for the OLS estimate, so its MSE is higher. Since CORC applies only 11 percent of the time, the estimate of Y, as measured by the SSE (sum of squared residuals) of Y, is nearly the same as that from the linear estimate.

However, when $\beta_1 = 5$, the CORC procedure applies 92 percent of the time, and the conditional CORC estimator of β_1 (which is 5) has more bias (but of the opposite sign in this case) than the bias of the OLS estimate. It also has a much larger MSE, 25.5, compared with 2.22 for OLS. Further, the SSE of Y is 2.75 times as large for the conditional CORC estimate as for the OLS estimate. These particular results are only suggestive because they depend on the particular variables and parameters selected for these Monte Carlo experiments.

These same general results hold for all the cases in Table 7.3.2. The conditional CORC procedure is clearly inferior to the OLS procedure in the experiments here, with the magnitude of the differences in the results of the two estimating procedures being magnified the more CORC is applied (when autocorrelation in the residuals is detected).

TABLE 7.3.2

The Percentage of Times the CORC Procedure is Applied:
X Ordered Lowest to Highest
(for various n, β_1, and σ_ϵ^2. $\beta_0 = 0$)

		\multicolumn{9}{c}{Number of Observations (n)}
		10			30			50		
		\multicolumn{3}{c}{σ_ϵ^2}	\multicolumn{3}{c}{σ_ϵ^2}	\multicolumn{3}{c}{σ_ϵ^2}
		0.5	1.5	2.5	0.5	1.5	2.5	0.5	1.5	2.5
	1	6	6	4	9	6	7	11	11	8
β_1	3	13	10	9	49	25	22	73	36	27
	5	24	14	11	83	50	39	92	70	53

TABLE 7.3.3

**Summary Measures for Selected Applications of the Conditional
CORC Procedure on the Incorrect Functional Form:
X Ordered Lowest to Highest
($n = 50$, $\sigma_\epsilon^2 = 0.5$)**

	Mean Elasticity	MSE of Elasticity	SSE
$\beta_1 = 1$			
Double Log Form	1.00	0.0096	179
Linear Form	0.99	0.0574	161
Linear Form with Conditional CORC (applied 11%)	0.99	0.0655	162
$\beta_1 = 5$			
Double Log Form	5.00	0.0091	11,380,000
Linear Form	3.54	2.22	17,520,000
Linear Form with Conditional CORC (applied 92%)	8.05	25.2	48,200,000

Some experiments were conducted using just autocorrelated regressors instead of perfectly autocorrelated regressors that almost always resulted when the observations are arranged according to their magnitude. It turns out that the percentage of times that autocorrelated residuals are detected falls off very rapidly for less than perfect autocorrelation in the regressor. Consequently, the OLS and conditional CORC procedures yield nearly identical results.

For example, with 50 observations (and $\sigma_\epsilon^2 = 0.5$), when X had a 0.72 coefficient of autocorrelation, CORC was applied only 18 percent of the time. The MSE of the conditional CORC estimate of the elasticity was 7.12, whereas that of the OLS estimate was 7.06; and the mean SSE for the conditional CORC estimate was identical to within three significant digits to that for the OLS estimate. (Here, $\beta_1 = 5$.)

Thus, in time-series analyses, where the regressors are not rearranged according to magnitude, (1) the Durbin-Watson test does not often detect autocorrelation in the residuals caused by incorrect functional form, and (2) correcting for autocorrelation, even if the cause is incorrect functional form, does not produce results much worse than OLS. These conclusions are of course contingent on the particular type of functional form selected here, on the range of parameter values examined, and on the particular type of regressors selected. However, when the researcher logically reorders the observations (such as according to the magnitude of the dependent variable), the particular results found here would seem to have more general applicability, namely, correcting for autocorrelation produces worse results than OLS.

One of the guidelines that can be derived from this analysis is that, when positive autocorrelation is detected, one possible source of that autocorrelation is incorrect functional form. This source is relatively unlikely, however, if the observations are not ordered according to the magnitude of one of the regressors. If this is suspected to be the source of the autocorrelation and the correct functional form cannot be found (primarily on the basis of theory, not statistics), it is better to use OLS and not an autocorrelation correction routine such as CORC.

7.3.3   Timewise Aggregation

Quite often in applied regression analysis, the Durbin-Watson statistic will indicate positive autocorrelation for annual observations or for cross-sectional data (arranged in a logical order). In many of these instances, the positive autocorrelation may indicate an incorrect functional form or a missing relevant variable rather than the pure type of autocorrelation. In general, we should expect this pure autocorrelation more for weekly, monthly, or quarterly data than for annual or cross-section data. For weekly data, for example, there is usually a large amount of noise, so the deterministic portion of the equation hardly shows up relative to the error term (as shown by low R^2's). Pure autocorrelation, then, is more likely to occur just because of the high—and possibly persistent over several observations—level of noise.

Moreover, the decision interval, or the interval of adjustment in dynamic models, is more likely to be encompassed the longer the observational time interval is. Often, theory is not clear about the precise length of the decision interval. Even if it is, different participants under the scrutiny of the model may not have decision time periods of the same length. Thus, theory is often not able to dictate which time interval is appropriate for the analysis.

To illustrate these notions, the following hypothetical scenario is postulated. Suppose that the error term is generated by the pure autocorrelation equation 7.2.1 on a quarterly basis. The purpose here is to compare the application of OLS on a quarterly versus an annual basis. For the annual model, suppose that the observations on y and x are simply the sums of the four quarters (or, equivalently, their average over the four quarters). As shown in Table 7.3.4, the DW test detects the pure autocorrelation, when it exists, many fewer times for the annual data than it does for the quarterly data (when there is positive autocorrelation in the error term). And the annual data show less of a tendency toward exhibiting autocorrelation as the degree of autocorrelation in x increases, whereas the quarterly data are rather insensitive to r_x in this respect. (The data used here for x are the same as used in Sections 7.3.1 and 7.3.2.)

These results show that, when regressions are estimated over several levels of timewise aggregation (e.g., quarterly and annual) and the Durbin-Watson statistic shows *more* of a likelihood of positive autocorrelation as the time interval is lengthened, the researcher can be fairly assured that the source of the autocorrelation is *not* of the pure type. It could be because of a missing relevant variable or an incorrect functional form. It is a rather complex question as to which level of timewise aggregation should be used. Generally, a more dynamic model may be needed (accounting

TABLE 7.3.4

**Percentage of Times Positive Autocorrelation is Detected by the DW Test:
Comparison of Annual Aggregates to Quarterly Data**
$(\beta = 1, \sigma_\epsilon^2 = 1)$

Autocorrelation in the Quarterly Error Term (ρ_ϵ)	Quarterly Observations (40 observations)	Quarterly: Annual:	Annual Observations (10 observations)			
			Autocorrelation in x (r_x)			
			0 −0.01	0.4 −0.03	0.8 0.67	0.98 0.97
0	5%		7%	12%	6%	4%
0.4	75		9	23	9	9
0.8	100		29	57	37	29
0.95	100		48	83	58	55

Note: Based on 500 Monte Carlo Drawings

for longer lags) with shorter time intervals, and a more static (or equilibrium) model should be used for the longer time intervals. However, in principle, either time interval may be appropriate for a given estimation problem as long as the dynamics are appropriately handled.[10]

One observation made in Chapter 2 is worth repeating. While short time intervals give the appearance of increased degrees of freedom, is the amount of information truly better? If there is only one major change in a policy parameter, such as the legislated minimum wage, over the period of observation and the focus is to assess its effect on wages and employment by industry, perhaps a time-series analysis by industry would not capture the effects of the change nearly as well as would a collapsed timewise analysis pooled across industries. That is, only two observations are used per industry, one before and the other one after the change, with the observations from each industry pooled for a single regression equation. This approach recognizes that there are basically two degrees of freedom for each industry—before and after the change in the minimum wage—whereas a time-series analysis industry by industry attempts to model the employment and wage effects annually, and perhaps the effects of the minimum wage will not be discernible (via, e.g., a dummy variable).

7.4 Forecasting and Documentation

When an autoregressive correction is made, such as CORC of Section 7.2, the transformation involved is used in forecasting and may or may not be apparent in the

---

[10] It is interesting to note that, in practice, estimates of the length of a distributed lag relationship often increase as the data are timewise aggregated. I suspect that this is caused by problems of multicollinearity for short time intervals or by incorrect specification of the relationship (e.g., missing relevant regressors).

documentation. These topics, which are of considerable importance to applied researchers, are discussed in this section.

7.4.1 Forecasting

With OLS, the usual procedure to forecast values of the dependent variable Y is to forecast values of the regressors and then to use the estimated equation to forecast values of Y. (For regressors that are lagged values of the dependent variable, the forecasting is done in steps, in a recursive manner, using the current forecast for Y as next period's value of the lagged dependent variable.) With an autoregressive transformation, the procedure is slightly more complicated.

Recall that the generalized differences in the GLS correction for autocorrelation in the simple model, given an estimate of the first-order autocorrelation coefficient ρ, are:

$$X_t^* = X_t - \hat{\rho}X_{t-1} \tag{7.4.1}$$

$$Y_t^* = Y_t - \hat{\rho}Y_{t-1} \tag{7.4.2}$$

Let the last sample point be $t = n$. Usually, the researcher projects the regressor X; call these projects $\hat{X}_{n+1}, \hat{X}_{n+2}, \ldots$ Then the generalized first differences for these variables are computed according to equation 7.4.1, where the last bit of sample information on X, X_n, is used for the first projection of X^*:

$$\hat{X}_{n+1}^* = \hat{X}_{n+1} - \hat{\rho}X_n$$

$$\hat{X}_{n+2}^* = \hat{X}_{n+2} - \hat{\rho}\hat{X}_{n+1}$$

and so on.

Since the estimated coefficients from the CORC estimating routine to correct for autocorrelation use the generalized difference form of the variables, the projected generalized differences, X^*, are used in the estimated equation to forecast values of Y^*:

$$\hat{Y}_{n+1}^* = \hat{\beta}_0 + \hat{\beta}_1\hat{X}_{n+1}^*$$

$$\hat{Y}_{n+2}^* = \hat{\beta}_0 + \hat{\beta}_1\hat{X}_{n+2}^* \tag{7.4.3}$$

$$\cdot$$
$$\cdot$$
$$\cdot$$

Finally, the transformation equation 7.4.2 is used to compute the forecast value of Y itself from these forecasted generalized differences:

$$\hat{Y}_{n+1} = \hat{Y}_{n+1}^* + \hat{\rho}Y_n$$

$$\hat{Y}_{n+2} = \hat{Y}_{n+2}^* + \hat{\rho}\hat{Y}_{n+1} \tag{7.4.4}$$

$$\cdot$$
$$\cdot$$
$$\cdot$$

As with the projection of X, the last sample value of Y, Y_n, is used in forecasting the first extra-sample value of Y.

7.4.2 Documentation

Suspecting autocorrelation in all time-series models is the rule instead of the exception. Thus, for any application of OLS to time-series data, the Durbin-Watson statistic should be reported, as was shown in Section 1.3.8. Unless the data have been given a logical ordering, the DW statistic should not be reported for cross-sectional data because it has no interpretation.

For first-order autocorrelation and for any of the autocorrelation correction techniques, the value of the estimated first-order autocorrelation coefficient is reported in place of the DW statistic. Usually, the estimated model is shown in its transformed state, *without* the asterisks on the variables to denote generalized differences, even though the variables are in their generalized difference form. The reason for this convention is that the emphasis is usually on the slope coefficients, and these estimates do not change in making the transformation back to the levels form of the variables.

An example of the usual method of documentation is:

$$\hat{Y}_t = 3.02 + 0.59\,X_t \qquad\qquad (7.4.5)$$

$$(4.2)$$

$$\bar{R}^2 = 0.95 \qquad SEE = 79.1 \qquad \bar{Y} = 4231.$$

$$\hat{\rho} = 0.49 \qquad \text{Quarterly} \qquad \text{Period: 1964:I} - 1981:\text{II}$$

$$(0.09)$$

Notice that $\hat{\rho}$ has replaced the Durbin-Watson statistic in the documentation of the OLS estimates (refer to equation 1.3.13). It is no longer necessary to report the DW statistic for this equation since first-order autocorrelation, for which the DW statistic tests, has been taken into account. (The DW statistic given by many computer routines upon correction for first-order autocorrelation indicates, conditional upon $\hat{\rho}$ being the correct first-order autocorrelation coefficient—which it is unlikely to be—the potential existence of *second*-degree autocorrelation.) The 0.09 in parentheses below the CORC estimate of ρ of 0.49 is the estimated standard error of $\hat{\rho}$ provided by many CORC computer routines. It gives a heuristic indication of the reliability of the CORC estimate of ρ. Often, the standard error of $\hat{\rho}$ is omitted in the documentation. (The documentation accompanying the equation should also indicate which autocorrelation correction procedure was used.)

It is often difficult to use documented results like equation 7.4.5 because the documentation usually does not indicate whether the variables are in their generalized differences or levels form. An alternative method of documenting the empirical results is to give them in their levels form and to indicate so in the written documentation. Then the only change that is required in the documentation is that the estimate of the constant term is divided by one minus the estimate of ρ. In the example above, the constant term should be $3.02/(1-0.49) = 5.92$. Usually, the $\bar{R}^2$, SEE, and $\bar{Y}$ will be different in the levels form, and a good practice is to recompute these measures as well if the levels form is shown. (They can be computed, with the estimated coefficients, using the formulas of Section 1.2.4.) Most researchers do not bother with these extra computations and opt instead to present the results when the variables are in their transformed state.

7.5 ARIMA, or Box-Jenkins Methods

A very popular econometric technique is time-series analysis, using the Box-Jenkins methods. Another name for it is ARIMA, or *autoregressive (AR) integrated (I) moving average (MA) analysis*. It is a method of analysis that most beginners should avoid, but it is presented here because of its growing popularity. The basic technique is used for forecasting the values of a single variable based only on its current and previous values, although its extension to multivariate analysis has also become very popular, as is discussed in Section 7.5.2. In its univariate application, a rather complex model is applied to a given data series in order to extrapolate (or forecast) that series into the future. The objective of this section is to acquaint the reader with this technique and to point out its pitfalls and benefits.

Its primary pitfall is that ARIMA is a non-theoretical procedure; it is strictly an empirical, highly refined, curve-fitting device. Its primary advantage is that it may provide better forecasts than the most theoretically sophisticated model.

7.5.1 Univariate ARIMA

ARIMA involves estimating a number of parameters that relate the current value of a variable Z to its previous values. Two different functional forms are combined into one to produce the single equation explaining (in a statistical sense) the current value of Z. The first is an autoregressive process for the variable Z itself (instead of for the error term as in Section 7.2):

$$Z_t = \phi_1 Z_{t-1} + \phi_2 Z_{t-2} + \cdots + \phi_p Z_{t-p} + v_t \qquad (7.5.1)$$

where v_t is a classical error term and the ϕ's are parameters to be estimated.[11] (In all these procedures, the variables are assumed to be in deviation-from-the-mean form, or a constant term is included.) The order of the autoregressive process is p, which is selected by the researcher. For a first-order scheme ($p = 1$), the equation reduces to:

$$Z_t = \phi_1 Z_{t-1} + v_t$$

which is similar in form to the first-order autoregressive process examined in Section 7.2, except that the error term ϵ replaced the variable Z.

---

[11] In purely autoregressive models like equation 7.5.1, the residual v_t is commonly referred to as the "innovation" in Z, since it represents the component of Z_t that is not predictable from its own past history.

The second functional form is a moving average of the current and previous error terms:

$$Z_t = v_t - \theta_1 v_{t-1} - \theta_2 v_{t-2} - \cdots - \theta_q v_{t-q} \qquad (7.5.2)$$

The order of the moving-average process is q, again selected by the researcher. The term moving average has been used because the equation resembles the mechanics of this process. For example, for a first-order scheme ($q = 1$), with $\theta_1 = 0.5$, successive values of Z are forecast (given values of v) as:

$$\hat{Z}_{t+1} = v_{t+1} - 0.5 v_t$$
$$\hat{Z}_{t+2} = v_{t+2} - 0.5\, v_{t+1}$$
$$\hat{Z}_{t+3} = v_{t+3} - 0.5\, v_{t+2}$$

Thus, as new values of v are used, the old values are discarded, as in a moving-average formulation.

The ARMA model (the "I" will be discussed below) is essentially a mixture of these two processes, the autoregressive and the moving-average processes, the former on the variable Z itself and the latter on the error term v:

$$Z_t = \phi_1 Z_{t-1} + \phi_2 Z_{t-2} + \cdots + \phi_p Z_{t-p}$$
$$+ v_t - \theta_1 v_{t-1} - \theta_2 v_{t-2} - \cdots - \theta_q v_{t-q} \qquad (7.5.3)$$

The ARMA technique provides estimates for these parameters. The technique is not simple because the error terms, v_t, v_{t-1}, etc., are not observable, but computer programs have been constructed to produce the estimates.

Before the data on Z can be fed into the ARMA estimating routine, they have to be transformed into a stationary series. (That is, the mean of Z must be constant over different portions of the observations. Also, the variances and covariances must be constant over the observations in order for the series to be stationary.) For most economic time series, this means that there can be no trend in the data. The trend is normally removed by taking first differences of the variable, such as:

$$\Delta Z_t = Z_t - Z_{t-1}$$

Sometimes this is not sufficient to produce stationarity, and the ΔZ series has to be first differenced, which amounts to the second difference of the original series Z:[12]

$$\Delta^2 Z_t = \Delta Z_t - \Delta Z_{t-1}$$

In general, d such differences may have to be taken:

$$\Delta^d Z_t = \Delta^{d-1} Z_t - \Delta^{d-1} Z_{t-1} \qquad (7.5.4)$$

The researcher must specify how many differences of Z are to be taken. Although formal statistical tests exist that are useful in this context, a description of them is beyond the introductory nature of this text. In practice, a number of heuristic devices are available to help determine whether a time series Z, or $\Delta^d Z$, is stationary. For

---

[12] As an example, a time series of real GNP will not be stationary since its mean is increasing over time. Its first difference, $GNP_t - GNP_{t-1}$, is likely to have the same property. However, the second difference, which is approximately the rate of growth in GNP, will usually be a stationary series.

example, a plot of the series itself is often helpful as a first step in checking for a constant mean and variance.

A useful tool for this stage of the investigation is the correlogram of the series. A correlogram for the original series Z is computed as follows:

$$\hat{\rho}_1 = \frac{\Sigma Z_t Z_{t-1}}{\Sigma Z_t^2}$$

$$\hat{\rho}_2 = \frac{\Sigma Z_t Z_{t-2}}{\Sigma Z_t^2}$$

and so on. The elements of the correlogram, $\hat{\rho}_1$, $\hat{\rho}_2$, . . ., are called the autocorrelation coefficients of the time series Z; they measure the strength of the relationship between observations of Z that are various distances (in time) apart. For example, if Z is a quarterly series, the autocorrelation coefficient $\hat{\rho}_4$ measures the relationship among Z's spaced one year apart. The definition of stationarity can be interpreted loosely as meaning that the behavior of the time series should display a kind of "persistence" over time. Consequently, observations of a stationary series Z that are located in the distant past should be less important than more recent observations in explaining current Z's. With respect to the correlogram of Z, this means that the elements $\hat{\rho}_1$, $\hat{\rho}_2$, . . . should display an appearance of overall decline (in absolute value). Since this pattern of decline may not be apparent immediately, one should compute as many of the autocorrelation coefficients as are reasonable, given the number of observations on Z that are available. A useful rule of thumb is to compute approximately $n/4$ such coefficients, where n is the size of the sample. By then, the decline of the correlogram to zero should be apparent, or else the series is probably not stationary. Also, if the correlogram is flat and near zero, the series is stationary.[13]

If inspection of the correlogram and the plot of the series lead to rejecting the hypothesis that Z is stationary, the procedure should be repeated using ΔZ, $\Delta^2 Z$, . . ., etc. until a stationary series is found. Experience has shown that, for most economic time series, the value of d will be less than four. In addition, other transformations, such as a logarithmic one, can produce a stationary series and can be analyzed in the manner described previously in this section.

The term *integrated* of ARIMA is derived from the fact that, after, say, the first difference of Z (instead of Z itself) is fit to the ARMA model (equation 7.5.3), the forecast values of ΔZ, called $\hat{\Delta Z}$, that come out of that process need to be translated into forecast values for the original Z series, according to the definitional formula:

$$\hat{Z}_{n+1} = Z_n + \hat{\Delta Z}_{n+1} \qquad (7.5.5)$$

where n is the last available data point on the Z series.[14] Notice that the actual data point, Z_n, is used, along with the forecast value of the change in Z from period n to

---

[13] Actually, a declining correlogram, which may be shown graphically by plotting $\hat{\rho}_1$, $\hat{\rho}_2$, etc., against the length of the lag in Z, is the result of a Z series that has first-order autocorrelation. A flat correlogram near zero shows no autocorrelation in Z. By the way, a correlogram of the *residuals* of any regression equation is often computed to examine for autocorrelation schemes higher than the first degree.

[14] In the time-series literature, the process of transforming a nonstationary series into one that is stationary is often referred to as prewhitening the data. The reverse process, as in equation 7.5.5, is then called recoloring the data.

$n+1$, to forecast Z_{n+1}. Then, to forecast Z_{n+2}, the forecast for Z of period $n+1$ from equation 7.5.5 is applied as:

$$\hat{Z}_{n+2} = \hat{Z}_{n+1} + \hat{\Delta} Z_{n+2} \qquad (7.5.6)$$

And so on. The term *integrated* comes from the fact that this discrete operation resembles the integration operation of calculus. (It does not come from the fact that the ARMA procedure integrates the autoregressive and moving-average concepts into one operation.)

To continue with the example, suppose that first differencing ($d=1$) did produce a stationary series, ΔZ, and that this data series was fed into the ARMA computer estimating routine. Assume that $p = 2$ and $q = 2$ were selected by the researcher. The forecast values of ΔZ are then obtained as follows. For the first forecast data point beyond the sample, $n+1$:

$$\hat{\Delta} Z_{n+1} = \hat{\phi}_1 \Delta Z_n + \hat{\phi}_2 \Delta Z_{n-1} - \hat{\theta}_1 \hat{v}_n - \hat{\theta}_2 \hat{v}_{n-1} \qquad (7.5.7)$$

where the hats represent estimates and the $\hat{v}$'s are the residuals of the data series, e.g., $\hat{v}_n = \Delta Z_n - \hat{\Delta} Z_n$. To obtain subsequent forecasts:

$$\hat{\Delta} Z_{n+2} = \hat{\phi}_1 \hat{\Delta} Z_{n+1} + \hat{\phi}_2 \Delta Z_n - \hat{\theta}_2 \hat{v}_n \qquad (7.5.8)$$

$$\hat{\Delta} Z_{n+3} = \hat{\phi}_1 \hat{\Delta} Z_{n+2} + \hat{\phi}_2 \hat{\Delta} Z_{n+1} \qquad (7.5.9)$$

and so on. Notice that in this procedure, the sample values of the residuals and the ΔZ series are used until they drop out of the formulation. Forecasts of Z itself are then utilized as demonstrated in equations 7.5.5 and 7.5.6.

Diagnostic checking refers to evaluating whether the estimated ARIMA process is adequate. A χ^2-test can be used to do this, but the usual procedure is to let p and/or q increase by one (increasing the length of the AR and MA processes) and to compare the resulting statistical fits over the base period. A Q-statistic and a standard error are usually computed, and a heuristic comparison of the new measures with the old determines the "adequacy" of the ARIMA process estimated. The Q-statistic is a measure of whether the correlogram for a selected first set of observations is near zero. A rule of thumb is that the series is accepted as stationary if the Q-statistic is less than the degrees of freedom (the number of observations n less the parameters estimated $p + q + 1$).

The limitations of this approach should be obvious: there is considerable arbitrariness about the entire procedure, and the forecasts are very mechanical (although one's judgment can be applied to modify the forecasts). The researcher must select the values of p, d, and q. Also, there are a number of techniques that are used to obtain stationary series; some of these remove seasonal components; others involve partial differences, such as creating a new series $Z_t^* = Z_t - 0.75 Z_{t-1}$ or even a second transformation based on this transformed series, $Z_t^{**} = Z_t^* - 0.75 Z_{t-1}^*$. These operations are sometimes called filters, and their application, along with the somewhat arbitrary selection of p and q, make the entire procedure an art instead of a science. Ultimately, it may be viewed as a highly refined, non-theoretical form of curve fitting.

7.5.2 Multivariate ARIMA, Granger-Causality, and Exogeneity

The ARIMA concepts have been extended to more than a single variable, and some of the concepts for a multivariate application are shown here with just two variables, y and z. Each of these variables must be (and are assumed here to have been) transformed into stationary series by the methods discussed in Section 7.5.1.

Suppose that the regression the researcher is interested in estimating is:

$$y_t = a_1 y_{t-1} + a_2 y_{t-2} + b_0 z_t + b_1 z_{t-1} + v_t \qquad (7.5.10)$$

If v_t is assumed to take on a moving-average form, researchers often apply the multivariate ARIMA estimating procedure directly to this equation.

A more important application using this formulation of the equation is to assess whether the regressor z is endogenous or exogenous. If z is endogenous, a simultaneous equations estimator may be desired, as is discussed in Chapter 9. But if z is exogenous, single equation techniques such as OLS may be appropriately applied to equation 7.5.10. (For this aspect of the discussion, the error term v_t is assumed to satisfy the classical properties, with the possible exception of being correlated with elements of z; in particular, a moving-average process is usually not assumed for v_t for this procedure.)

A necessary (but not sufficient) condition for z_t to be exogenous is that "y_t does not Granger-cause z_t." Thus, if y_t is found to Granger-cause z_t, then z_t must be considered endogenous. The variable y_t is found to Granger-cause z_t if, in the regression:

$$z_t = a'_1 z_{t-1} + a'_2 z_{t-2} + b'_1 y_{t-1} + b'_2 y_{t-2} + v_t \qquad (7.5.11)$$

the coefficients on the lagged values of y, here b'_1 and b'_2, are statistically significant. (Chapter 10 presents a method to test whether two or more coefficients, taken as a group, are statistically significant.) Thus, if b'_1 and b'_2 are found to be statistically insignificant, it is possible—but not necessarily true—that z is exogenous in the equation of interest, equation 7.5.10. An alternative, equivalent way to conduct this test is to add the regressors z_{t+1}, z_{t+2}, etc. to the original equation 7.5.10 and to test for their coefficients' being zero. If they are zero, z_t may be exogenous; if they are not zero, z_t is determined to be endogenous.

There are more conclusive tests of whether z_t is, in fact, exogenous, but they are beyond the scope of this text.[15] However, if Granger-causality is at least examined,

---

[15] For some of the burgeoning literature on this subject, see C.A. Sims, "Money, Income, and Causality," *American Economic Review*, September 1972, pp. 540–52; T.J. Sargent, *Macroeconomic Theory* (New York: Academic Press, 1979); and Marc Nerlove, David M. Grether, and Jose L. Carvalho, *Analysis of Economic Time Series* (New York: Academic Press, 1979). For two sources that are authored by people whose names are now part of the terminology, see C.W.J. Granger and Paul Newbold, *Forecasting Economic Time Series* (New York: Academic Press, 1977), and G.E.P. Box and G. Jenkins, *Time-Series Analysis, Forecasting, and Control*, rev. ed. (San Francisco: Holden-Day, 1977). For a readable exposition of univariate ARIMA, see Charles Nelson, *Applied Time Series Analysis for Managerial Forecasting* (San Francisco: Holden-Day, 1973).

then the researcher will have proceeded beyond what has previously been the normal practice, namely, not to test for exogeneity at all.

In these applications, the lag structures are, in theory, infinite, so again the researcher must select the cut-off point on the order of the lag. In equation 7.5.10, the lag on z was only one period, and in equation 7.5.11 the lag on y was only two periods, but both these lags could have been longer. Selecting the length of the lag is one of the pitfalls in applying these methods. Other problems arise in using this approach for a number of other situations, such as the existence of measurement error in the variables, the problem of omitted variables, and the application of the check for exogeneity to variables subject to policy control. Also, the inclusion of the lagged values of y in equation 7.5.10 may produce the complication that these terms are not independent of the error term, as required by the classical assumptions in order to show that OLS is BLUE (see Chapter 4). Section 9.8 explains the problem that lagged values of the dependent variable may cause.

In summary, these time-series techniques related to ARIMA have sufficient pitfalls so that the novice researcher should avoid them. However, readers of econometric studies are very likely to encounter them, perhaps with increasing frequency; therefore, some familiarity with the concepts and some appreciation for the arbitrariness of the results should be acquired.

7.6   Summary and Concluding Remarks

The usual test for autocorrelation is the one based on the Durbin-Watson statistic, and one of the more commonly applied correction procedures is CORC. OLS estimates are unbiased under the presence of pure autocorrelation, as are the CORC estimates, but the CORC estimates have a lower variance (and mean square error). The estimates of the variances by CORC, however, may be larger or smaller than those estimated by OLS; thus, the t-statistics may be larger or smaller.

The usual assumption when testing and correcting for autocorrelation is that the first-order autocorrelation model (equation 7.2.1) is applicable and that a missing relevant variable that is autocorrelated or (possibly) an incorrect functional form is not involved. The latter may be the sources of suspected autocorrelation, and treating them as the autocorrelation model and applying a GLS (generalized least squares) fix-up procedure, such as CORC, can lead to high mean square errors of the estimates and incorrect conclusions about the degree of statistical significance of the estimated coefficients. However, under some circumstances, it can lead to a lower MSE and reduce the bias in a missing regressor model, compared with OLS on the misspecified model.

Moreover, applying a GLS-type correction routine such as CORC tends toward curve fitting. A fad currently growing in popularity is the application of the ARIMA (autoregressive integrated moving average) model to the error term, as contrasted to its at least partial application to variables, as discussed in Section 7.5. These extra refinements are usually not justified on the basis of any theory of how the error term is generated. Rather, they usually represent attempts to "curve fit the residuals."

Such practices, just as curve fitting the x, y observations, should be avoided unless reasons to the contrary are obvious.

Most often, the GLS-transformed equation is documented as if no transformation had taken place. That is, the usual statistics are reported from the CORC (or other) estimating procedures as they are reported for OLS, except that an estimate of the first-order autoregressive coefficient replaces the now meaningless value of the Durbin-Watson statistic.

In forecasting with equations estimated by CORC, use is made of the autoregressive transformation, called generalized differences.

The ARIMA models have become very popular as non-theoretical methods to forecast variables and to examine whether or not a regressor is exogenous. These procedures are as yet rather arbitrarily applied in that the researcher must select, in the simplest of the ARIMA models, the degree of first differencing as a way to filter the variable and the lengths of the moving-average and autoregressive processes. Thus, these procedures should be avoided by beginners.

In the discussion of the GLS correction procedure, a point was made parenthetically on page 178 that should by made explicit here. Section 7.4.1 demonstrated how to forecast beyond the sample period, but the generalized differences form of the variables was used. If the researcher wanted to predict the value of Y in its original, levels form from a single value of each of the regressors in their original, levels form, the following procedure is recommended. Assume CORC was used to estimate the equation. This estimated equation of course holds for the variables in their generalized differences form. To use the original variables, the only change that needs to be made is to the CORC estimate of the constant term. Just divide that estimate by $1 - \hat{\rho}$, where $\hat{\rho}$ is the CORC estimate of ρ. The slope coefficients remain as estimated by CORC, and a prediction of Y can be obtained by multiplying the values of the regressors (in their original, levels form) by their respective slope coefficients, and then adding the modified constant term.

8 Cross-Section Analysis: Heteroskedasticity

While Chapter 7 discussed the autocorrelation problem particularly endemic to time-series models, this chapter discusses the problem of heteroskedasticity, or nonconstant variance of the error term, which is particularly endemic to cross-section models.

Heteroskedasticity and pure autocorrelation are violations of the Classical Assumptions V and IV, respectively. They both result in the same consequences for the OLS (Ordinary Least Squares) estimates; namely, the estimates are unbiased but inefficient, not having the least variance of all unbiased estimators. Furthermore, the same general technique is usually offered to correct for these two maladies, that technique being GLS (generalized least squares) or an approximation of it. Most of the corrective procedures for autocorrelation have a name, such as CORC, and the standard corrective procedure for heteroskedasticity is called weighted least squares. It is a GLS-type of correction for heteroskedasticity. Like the autoregressive GLS fix-up procedure, the heteroskedastic correction provides a transformed equation the error term of which satisfies the classical assumptions, upon which OLS is applied.

In this text, this corrective procedure for heteroskedasticity is not recommended, especially for beginners, and the reason is different from the reason that the corrective procedures for autocorrelation are not highly recommended. (The reason the CORC procedure, for example, is not recommended is because discovering autocorrelated residuals may imply that a relevant regressor is missing or that the functional form of the equation is incorrect, while the latter is less likely than the former. It is better to correct for the underlying problem than to "massage" the equation via CORC.) The reason that the standard GLS-type fix-up procedure for heteroskedasticity is not recommended is the extreme difficulty of empirically discovering the exact GLS-type of transformation to use. Furthermore, often a redefinition of some of the variables will mitigate the problem of heteroskedasticity; this more direct corrective procedure is recommended.

This chapter is much shorter than the previous chapter on autocorrelation, befitting their relative importance at the practical level. The first three sections present the standard textbook depiction of (1) the analytic model of heteroskedasticity, (2) the GLS corrective procedure, and (3) the popular Goldfeld-Quandt test for heteroskedasticity. Section 8.4 describes the direct corrective approach of redefining the variables.

Section 8.5 introduces the notion of impure heteroskedasticity. Like impure autocorrelation (see Section 7.1), the detection of heteroskedasticity in the OLS residuals may signal a missing relevant regressor. As in the impure autocorrelation case, usually the best corrective procedure is to find and include this variable as a regressor in the estimated equation. Application of the standard GLS-type fix-up procedure for heteroskedasticity may or may not do better than OLS on the incorrectly specified model, in terms of MSE (mean square error), but it usually provides an estimate that is less biased than the OLS estimate.

The final section presents some concluding remarks.

8.1   The Model

Heteroskedasticity is a nonconstant variance of the error term over the observations; that is, $E\epsilon_i^2 \neq \sigma^2$, a violation of Classical Assumption V. For this malady, it will be necessary to express the variables in their levels (as opposed to their deviations-from-the-mean) form:

$$Y_i = \beta_0 + \beta_1 X_i + \epsilon_i \qquad (8.1.1)$$

It is assumed that X_i is exogenous. One of the most common models of heteroskedasticity (and there are many diverse models) is that the error variance is proportional to the square (or the level) of an exogenous variable Z_i:

$$E\epsilon_i^2 = \sigma_i^2 = Z_i^2 \sigma_v^2 \qquad (8.1.2)$$

where σ_v^2 is the variance of a classical error term v_i. It is classical especially in that it has a constant variance (and the error terms are independent from observation to observation). The specification of ϵ_i that gives rise to equation 8.1.2 is that the error term in the equation is proportional to a classical error term, with the proportionality factor being the exogenous variable:

$$\epsilon_i = Z_i v_i \qquad (8.1.3)$$

Heteroskedasticity may arise more often with cross-section data than with time-series data. For example, expenditures by low-income households are not likely to be as variable as expenditures from high-income budgets, because the proportion of the low-income budget spent on necessities is much higher. When households are aggregated and viewed in a time-series context, this phenomenon of heteroskedasticity is not likely to arise. In the cross-section model, Y_i might be household expenditures, X_i household income, and the proportionality variable $Z_i = X_i$. In general, it is not necessary that Z_i be equal to X_i.

Figure 8.1.1 illustrates a plot of residuals from an OLS estimation of equation 8.1.1 against X. The heteroskedasticity is reflected in the wider scatter (variance) of the residuals for higher values of X. The dashed lines show the general tendency for the variance to become larger as X increases.[1]

The major problems with treating heteroskedasticity are in identifying the variable Z_i and in determining whether some form of heteroskedasticity other than equation 8.1.2 is appropriate. These problems are why beginning and even intermediate researchers are advised not to correct for heteroskedasticity unless it is clear what Z_i is and what the functional form of equation 8.1.2 is. Given the uncertainty, the usual treatment for heteroskedasticity is an arbitrary operation, which leads to arbitrary estimates. The researcher is never sure whether the resulting estimator is better or worse than the OLS estimator.

With this caveat, presented here is an outline of how to correct for the heteroskedastistic model (equation 8.1.2) and what this treatment does for the estimates; detection of this malady is discussed in Section 8.3.

8.2 Generalized Least Squares

As with autocorrelation, a common corrective procedure for this malady is generalized least squares, or GLS. The general approach of GLS is to transform the equation into an equivalent one in which the error term is no longer heteroskedastic. Equation 8.1.3 is used to write equation 8.1.1 as:

$$Y_i = \beta_0 + \beta_1 X_i + Z_i v_i \qquad . \qquad (8.2.1)$$

It is easily seen that dividing both sides of the equation by Z_i will alleviate the heteroskedasticity since v_i is assumed to be a classical error term, with constant variance:

$$\frac{Y_i}{Z_i} = \frac{\beta_0}{Z_i} + \beta_1 \frac{X_i}{Z_i} + v_i \qquad (8.2.2)$$

The suggested procedure is to estimate equation 8.2.2 by OLS. That is, regress $Y_i^* = Y_i/Z_i$ on $X_{i1}^* = X_i/Z_i$ and $X_{i2}^* = 1/Z_i$. This is sometimes called weighted least squares. In transformations of this kind, the estimate of β_1 from OLS on equation 8.2.2 will differ from the OLS estimate of β_1 on equation 8.1.1 even though the model indicates that it is the same β_1 in both equations. If a different estimate were not likely, then there would be absolutely no reason to make the transformation, so a different value of the estimated coefficients should be expected.

---

[1] The dashed lines in Figure 8.1.1 are called the envelope of the scatter of points. In an equation without heteroskedasticity, the envelope (for the residuals plotted against a regressor) has a natural tendency to widen and then to narrow in a symmetric fashion, as: ⊂⊃ . Thus, some widening should be expected, and the lack of narrowing of the envelope for high values of X may be due to chance. The Goldfeld-Quandt test, discussed in Section 8.3, tests whether the residual variance over the lower range of X is statistically significantly less than the variance over the higher range.

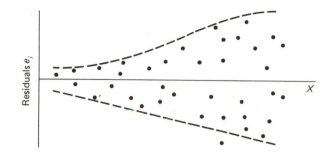

FIGURE 8.1.1   Illustration of Heteroskedastic Residuals

Note that, if the variance was proportional to the level of Z_i in equation 8.1.2 instead of to its square, the variables would be divided by the square root of Z_i, and that the inverse of the square root of Z_i would be another regressor. This assumption is often made instead of the assumption of equation 8.1.2.

It is suggested that, when Y_i^* is regressed on X_{i1}^* and X_{i2}^*, a constant term be added:

$$Y_i^* = \beta_0^* + \beta_1 X_{i1}^* + \beta_2 X_{i2}^* + v_i \qquad (8.2.3)$$

The need for a ''garbage'' term, β_0^*, is not obviated by this fancy transformation.[2]

On presentation and documentation of the estimated equation, researchers normally leave the equation in its transformed state (equation 8.2.3) and do not make the transformation back to the original form (equation 8.1.1), since the emphasis is normally on the estimate of β_1. (With the addition of the constant term, in the transformation back to the original form, Z_i would enter as another variable in equation 8.1.1.) The equation is often used, for example, for prediction or interpretation, in its transformed state (equation 8.2.3).

If Z_i were to equal X_i, the transformed equation would be:

$$\frac{Y_i}{X_i} = \frac{\beta_0}{X_i} + \beta_1 + v_i \qquad (8.2.4)$$

Thus, $Y_i^* = Y_i/X_i$ is regressed on $X_i^* = 1/X_i$. Notice that, when the $Z_i = X_i$, the intercept term of 8.2.4 is implicitly the slope coefficient of X_i in the original equation 8.1.1. The problem is that the estimate $\hat{\beta}_1$ in equation 8.2.4 still acts as the garbage term, collecting the mean values of all omitted variables, and it should not be relied on for inferences about the original slope coefficient. If the interest is in β_1, some other approach, such as the direct approach of Section 8.4, should be used.

If it is suspected that the error variance varies with the expected value of Y_i or Y_i^2, then $Z_i = E(Y_i^{1/2})$ or $Z_i = E(Y_i)$, respectively. A suggested procedure in such a case is to compute the estimated values $\hat{Y}_i$ from an OLS estimation of the original

---

[2] Adding a constant term was suggested by Rao and Miller, *Applied Econometrics*, p. 121. See Section 6.1 for the reasons to include a constant term.

equation 8.1.1 and then to let $Z_i = \hat{Y}_i^{1/2}$ or $Z_i = \hat{Y}_i$ to perform the usual transformation, and then to apply OLS to the transformed equation.

8.3 Testing for Heteroskedasticity

Even more so than autocorrelation, detection of heteroskedasticity is facilitated by reordering the observations. For cross-sectional models, this means ordering the observations according to the magnitude of one of the regressors, the dependent variable predicted by the OLS equation, a scale factor, or some other variable. The attempt is to find the variable Z as one of these possibilities. Plots of the OLS residuals (using the original equation 8.1.1) against these variables are often examined in a heuristic manner to see whether a pattern develops, such as an expanding (or contracting) scatter of residuals as the magnitude of the variable increases, as in Figure 8.1.1. This would indicate a larger (or smaller) variance according to the particular ordering selected. It should be noted that the residual scatter should ordinarily increase and then decrease according to the magnitude of each regressor, because the residual is not independent of each regressor even though the error term is assumed to be.

These heuristic tests are sometimes used to justify a GLS approach to correct for heteroskedasticity. However, before making any GLS transformations, one should conduct a statistical test for the null hypothesis of homoskedasticity versus the alternative hypothesis of heteroskedasticity. Setting the hypotheses up in this manner provides a known level of confidence, such as 90 percent, when the alternative hypothesis of heteroskedasticity is accepted.

There are several tests that may be applied to check for heteroskedasticity; in this text, only one such test is discussed, the one suggested by S. M. Goldfeld and R. E. Quandt, "Some Tests for Homoskedasticity," *Journal of the American Statistical Association,* September 1965, pp. 539–47.

To perform this test, order the observations as suggested by the suspected cause of the heteroskedasticity, for example as suggested by the heuristic tests (residual plots). Partition the observations into three groups, an initial group of m ($< n/2$) observations and a final group of m observations, with $n-2m$ observations in the middle, as a "buffer" group. The test examines whether the variance for the first group of m observations is significantly greater than that for the last m observations. (Needless to say, the order of the observations can be reversed or the ratio below inverted if the latter group is suspected of having a larger variance.) The omitted (buffer) observations heighten the possibility of observing a clear difference in the residual variances. The ratio used is:

$$F = \frac{SSE_1}{SSE_2} \tag{8.4.1}$$

It is the ratio of the residual sum of squares for the first m observations to that of the last m observations. These numbers are obtained by computing separate regression estimates for the first m and for the last m observations. This F-statistic has an F-distribution with $m-K$ numerator and $m-K$ denominator degrees of freedom. (See

Chapter 1 or 10 to review how to use the F-table.) If the computed F is greater than the critical value of F from the F-table, then the alternative hypothesis, that the error variance is larger in the first set of observations than in the second, is accepted. If heteroskedasticity is accepted, then one can use the GLS approach suggested in Section 8.2 or redefine variables as suggested in Section 8.4 to estimate the regression equation.

The selection of the omitted middle (buffer) observations is guided by two opposing forces: the more observations that are omitted, the greater will be the observed differences in residual variances but the greater will be the amount of Type II Error. As a guideline in practice, approximately one-quarter of the observations may be omitted. An illustration of the application of this test is presented in Section 8.5.

8.4   The Direct Approach: Redefining the Variables

Section 2.5 stressed the appropriate interpretation of estimates obtained from cross-sectional data. It also pointed out that very often a redefinition of the variables is required in order to have the estimated equation focus more on the behavioral aspects of the relationship rather than be influenced by spurious correlations that relate to the size or the scale of the variables. The following is an illustration of this type of spurious correlation and a suggested redefinition of the variables in order to avoid it.

In a cross-section analysis explaining expenditures by cities for various services, most of the observations may come from medium- or small-sized cities, with only a few observations from large cities. Suppose that expenditures were explained by income. Such a relationship is shown in Figure 8.4.1. In this case, it is obvious and not very enlightening that the larger cities have larger expenditures in absolute magnitude.

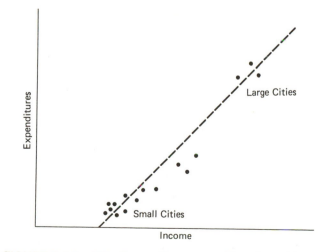

FIGURE 8.4.1   City Expenditures as a Function of Income

And of course the larger cities also have the larger levels of incomes by their inhabitants. Such a relationship hardly explains behavior and is nearly a tautology. Fitting a regression line to such data (see Figure 8.4.1) gives undue weight to the large cities because they would otherwise give rise to large squared residuals. Recall that the technique of OLS minimizes, over all observations, the sum of the squared residuals, so a few large residuals for the large cities, when squared, would not be compatible with that minimization; thus, the large cities are given a relatively large weight in the fitting of the regression line. The problem is not the large cities, but the way in which the model was formulated. As it was formulated, this is simply an example of a bad model.

The answer is not to throw out the extreme observations, but rather to express the relationship in terms that will discount the scale factor (the size of the cities) and emphasize the underlying behavior. Usually, *per capita* expenditures is made the dependent variable and per capita income the regressor, as in Figure 8.4.2. This form of the variables places Chicago and New York on the same scale as Peoria, and thus ascribes to them the same weight in estimation.

Such a transformation avoids the spurious correlation of the scale factor (the size of the cities) and emphasizes the behavioral content. In terms of the problem of heteroskedasticity, this transformation may be thought of as a bastardized method of treating the original relationship for suspected heteroskedasticity, even though it was done for a more fundamental reason. A full-fledged transformation for heteroskedasticity would also include the reciprocal of city population as another regressor, according to the GLS-type of transformation described in Section 8.2. Thus, putting the variables on a per capita basis appears to account for heteroskedasticity in a bastardized way, but such a transformation of the variables really attempts to solve the problem of spurious correlation caused by the scale factor. Any assistance that it provides in mitigating the problem of heteroskedasticity is merely incidental, and heteroskedasticity should not be cited as the primary reason for making the transformation.

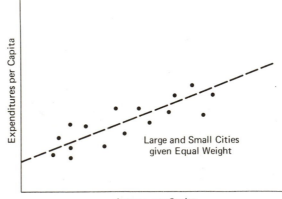

FIGURE 8.4.2 City Expenditures as a Function of Income, per Capita Terms

However, heteroskedasticity could still be suspected in the per capita form of the model. The error variance could be larger for the observations having the larger per capita values of income and expenditures. Thus, it may be legitimate to suspect and test for heteroskedasticity even in this transformed model. However, if detected or even suspected, a transformation different from a GLS-type of transformation may be appropriately applied. One possibility is to measure the variables as percentage changes. Then, the percentage change in per capita expenditures by each city is regressed against the percentage change in per capita income, where the percentage changes are measured, for example, over a five- or ten-year period. Such a transformation may be motivated by theoretical considerations that suggest a focus on the relationship of changes in the variables, but the result is usually that both the scale problem of the original model and any heteroskedasticity problem of the per capita model are alleviated. The GLS-type transformation, then, is not required for this model, and the heteroskedasticity problem would hardly be suspected.

Thus, a thoughtful transformation of the variables, to correct for heteroskedasticity in a bastardized way or to avoid spurious correlation, may be the best approach to solving these problems. In this example, both city expenditures and income were subject to the scale factor (size) and were thus put on a per capita basis. If the cost per unit of the services was another regressor in the original model, it would not be affected by scale and thus would not be transformed in the per capita model. In the percentage change model, however, logic would indicate that the unit cost of the services also be transformed. With some thought, each variable in a cross-section model should be examined for possible transformations that would facilitate a proper interpretation of the entire regression equation.

8.5 Impure Heteroskedasticity

Just as with autocorrelation, it is possible that residuals from an OLS regression could suggest the existence of heteroskedasticity when in fact the true cause of the suspected heteroskedasticity is the omitted variable problem. A case such as this I call impure heteroskedasticity. The conclusions here are the same as those for impure autocorrelation. Although the GLS procedure on the incorrectly specified equation usually does lower the bias and mean square error of the coefficient of the included regressor, it is quite inferior to an estimate of that coefficient using the correctly specified equation. This section presents an impure heteroskedasticity model and the results of a Monte Carlo experiment. This section also illustrates an application of the Goldfeld-Quandt test for heteroskedasticity.

Assume that the true model is:

$$Y = \beta_0 + \beta_1 X_1 + \beta_2 X_2 + \epsilon \qquad (8.5.1)$$

where ϵ is a classical normal error term. Assume that the estimated model omits X_2:

$$Y = \beta_0 + \beta_1 X_1 + \epsilon^* \qquad (8.5.2)$$

The detection of heteroskedasticity depends on the proper ordering of the residuals. Indeed, heteroskedasticity could be the conclusion 100 percent of the time if the observations with the largest residuals are made the first m observations and those with the smallest residuals are made the last m observations, and the Goldfeld-Quandt test of Section 8.3 is applied. But this ordering would not constitute a legitimate test for heteroskedasticity. Rather, the researcher should have some *a priori* notions about the mechanism by which the suspected heteroskedasticity is generated. This step is the most difficult one, and is usually not given enough care by researchers who test and correct for heteroskedasticity.

For illustration, assume that the researcher suspected that the error variance in a regression of Y on X_1 varies in some systematic way with the exogenous variable X_2. The true model is assumed to be equation 8.5.1. Figure 8.5.1 is a plot of the OLS residuals for the first of 500 Monte Carlo drawings from the experiment reported here, ordered according to the magnitude of X_2. (The total number of observations (n) is 50.) The pattern of the residuals is from generally large negative numbers to large positive numbers, going from left to right on the x_2 scale. It was assumed that $\beta_2 = 1$ (and $\beta_1 = 1$ and $\sigma^2 = 1$), so the error term from the misspecified estimating equation ($\epsilon^* = \beta_2 x_2 + \epsilon$) varies with x_2, and the pattern obtained could have been expected. (It is always required when estimating OLS with a y-intercept term that the errors sum to zero, so the residual pattern shown in the figure would be the same whether x_2 was measured, as it is here, in deviations-from-the-mean form or in levels form.)

Of course, when the residuals are plotted according to the magnitude of the missing regressor, positive autocorrelation is evident. This phenomenon was discussed

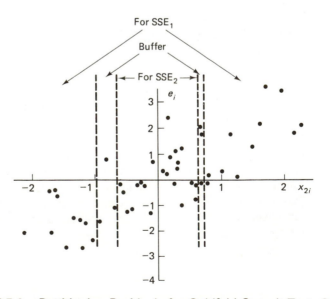

FIGURE 8.5.1 Partitioning Residuals for Goldfeld-Quandt Test: Case of Impure Heteroskedasticity

in Chapter 7. Assume here that the data are cross sectional and that heteroskedasticity is being investigated. But do not lose sight of the fact that ordering residuals according to a variable not included in the equation (and then checking for autocorrelation) is still a valid means of attempting, in an *ad hoc* way, to discover whether that variable (x_2 here) is a relevant variable, even for cross-sectional data. (A more direct way would be to include x_2 as a regressor, even though this is still *ad hoc* because it smacks of the stepwise procedures discussed in Section 6.4.2.)

To test for heteroskedasticity with the Goldfeld-Quandt test, the observations have to be partitioned into three groups: (1) those associated with a high suspected error variance, for the computation of SSE_1; (2) those with a low suspected error variance, for the computation of SSE_2; and (3) a middle group to act as a buffer between the first two.

The procedure used here for the Monte Carlo application is only meant to be suggestive, of both the procedure and the type of results that may be expected for this impure heteroskedasticity case. It was decided to let groups 1 and 2 consist of 22 observations each and to let group 3 consist of 6 observations. Since a high variance comes from the largest deviations of the error term from zero, the first group is composed of the first and last 11 observations ordered according to the magnitude of x_2. (Both y and x_1, as well as x_2, are reordered according to the magnitude of x_2. This does not change the correlation between x_1 and x_2.) The second group, which gives rise to the smallest estimated variance and, from inference, the smallest variance of the error term, consists of the middle 22 observations. The buffer group of 6 observations is split into groups of 3 each. (The usual guideline is to have about one-fourth of the observations in the buffer group, or about 12 observations.)

The Monte Carlo procedure estimated β_1 three ways: (1) from the true specification of y on x_1 and x_2; (2) from y on x_1; and (3) from y on x_1 using the standard GLS correction for heteroskedasticity if the Goldfeld-Quandt test indicates heteroskedaticity, and from y on x_1 if the test indicates homoskedasticity. The third estimating procedure, then, is conditional on the outcome of the Goldfeld-Quandt test.

For the observations that gave rise to the residuals plotted in Figure 8.5.1, the value of the Goldfeld-Quandt F-statistic was 5.49. With this particular set-up, the critical value of the F-statistic is found in the F-table (A-2) at the end of the text, in the column and row for 20 numerator and 20 denominator degrees of freedom. The critical value is 2.12 for a 95-percent level of confidence, so the test indicates heteroskedasticity for the observations shown in Figure 8.5.1. (The test statistic was computed as the ratio of the SSE's from two OLS regressions of y on x_1 for each of the two groups of 22 observations.)

If heteroskedasticity is detected, as it was in this illustration, a GLS fix-up procedure is applied. As a practical matter, it is very difficult (a) to determine the functional form of the heteroskedasticity—for example, does the error variance vary with x_2 or x_2^2?—and (b) to discover with which variable the error variance varies—is it x_2 or another variable, such as x_3? For illustration, it appears from Figure 8.5.1 that the error variance increases with the square of x_2; that is, as x_2, measured in the deviations-from-the-mean form, becomes large in absolute value, the residuals appear to become larger. It is the *spread* of the residuals that indicates a larger *variance* of the error term. Thus, the suggested GLS procedure is to estimate $y^* = y/x_2$ on $x_1^* = x_1/x_2$ and $x_2^* =$

$1/x_2$. As suggested in Section 8.2, a constant term is included for this estimation. The estimate of β_1 is that associated with the transformed regressor x_1^*.

The general results are similar to those obtained for the autocorrelation case, and for similar reasons. Table 8.5.1 presents the results of the Monte Carlo experiments. When x_1 and x_2 are not correlated, the Goldfeld-Quandt test applies most often. (It would apply more if β_2 was larger or if σ_ϵ^2 was smaller, other things held constant.) When x_1 and x_2 are uncorrelated, the GLS procedure produces a higher MSE than estimating either the true model or the misspecified model, and it remains higher for low values of the squared correlation of x_1 and x_2, r_{12}^2. However, for moderate values of r_{12}^2—above 0.2 up through 0.8—the GLS-type procedure reduces the bias and the MSE compared with the simple regression of y on x_1. Just as with the GLS-type correction for autocorrelation in the similar set-up of Chapter 7, the GLS-type procedure here uses information about x_2 that is not used in the simple misspecified equation; thus, the procedure seems to be a proxy for the missing relevant regressor, x_2. However, for high values of r_{12}^2, the movements of x_1 and x_2 are similar, so x_2 provides no new information to assist in the estimation of β_1, unless it is included as another regressor, in which case the true generating model would be estimated. When r_{12}^2 reaches 0.95, the Goldfeld-Quandt test indicates heteroskedasticity in 5 percent of the cases, which is to be expected since a 5-percent level of significance was employed. This 5-percent application implies that x_2 has no further value for a GLS fix-up procedure because it does not yield enough new information.

As was the case for impure autocorrelation, the MSE is by far the lowest (for nonzero r_{12}^2) when the correctly specified equation is estimated. This is the result whenever x_2 is a theoretically relevant regressor, as measured by its τ^2 value, described in Section 6.2. When the value of τ^2 is less than unity, then the test indicates heter-

---

TABLE 8.5.1

Monte Carlo Results for Impure Heteroskedasticity

Squared Correlation between X_1 and X_2 (r_{12}^2)	Percent of Times Goldfeld-Quandt Test Indicates Heteroskedasticity	Mean Square Error of Estimators of β_1			Bias of Estimators of β_1	
		For Y on X_1 and X_2	For Y on X_1	For Y on X_1, with Conditional Correction	For Y on X_1	For Y on X_1 with Conditional Correction
0	82%	0.023	0.023	0.142	0	−0.01
0.2	66	0.019	0.209	0.235	0.44	0.15
0.4	44	0.031	0.431	0.285	0.64	0.36
0.8	10	0.017	0.162	0.160	0.40	0.37
0.95	5	0.013	0.048	0.048	0.22	0.21

Notes: The true model is $y = \beta_1 x_1 + \beta_2 x_2 + \epsilon$, where ϵ is a classical normal error term. The values assumed were $\beta_1 = \beta_2 = \sigma_\epsilon^2 = 1$, and the number of observations $n = 50$. The conditional correction is applied when the Goldfeld-Quandt F-statistic is greater than the critical value at a 5-percent level of significance. It is a regression of $y^* = y/x_2$ on $x_1^* = x_1/x_2$ and $x_2^* = 1/x_2$. The number of Monte Carlo drawings was 500.

oskedasticity a minimal number of times, such as the five percent of the time in this illustration when the r_{12}^2 approached unity and the τ^2 value fell below unity.

Thus, although the MSE and bias can be improved over the misspecified equation of y on x_1 for intermediate values of r_{12}^2, as long as x_2 has been discovered and used in the GLS-type fix-up procedure, it should be included as a regressor instead of applying the standard heteroskedastic correction procedure, providing, as in the case here, the detected heteroskedasticity is caused by a missing relevant regressor. In fact, the case is stronger here than with the standard autocorrelation fix-up technique because the variable x_2 has been discovered. In the autocorrelation fix-up procedure, only the autocorrelated portion of the usually unknown missing regressor is used in possibly improving the properties of estimators of the remaining coefficients; for the heteroskedastic fix-up procedure, the variable itself must be identified and quantified, so the researcher is not excused from using that variable as a regressor.

8.6   Concluding Remarks

Besides the standard GLS transformation and estimation, heteroskedasticity can be avoided by measuring the variables differently. For example, instead of having the level of output of a firm as the dependent variable, the percentage change in output could be substituted, with appropriate modifications of the regressors. Attention should be focused on whether this different model is acceptable theoretically.

As with pure autocorrelation, OLS estimates under the presence of pure heteroskedasticity are unbiased but are not as precise as the GLS estimates. However, Monte Carlo simulations on pure heteroskedasticity showing the gain in precision were not reported here because one must first assume how the heteroskedasticity is generated. This means that the exogenous variable with which the error variance varies must be identified *and* that the functional form of that relationship (such as the square of the variable) must be determined. In practice, it is very difficult to be affirmative about the mechanism that generates the heteroskedasticity. None of the tests to detect this malady, such as the Goldfeld-Quandt test, provide any assurances that the transformation assumed is the appropriate one, because those that attempt to do so have to assume a specific functional form and variable(s) as composing the generating mechanism. Furthermore, if the detected heteroskedasticity is caused by an omitted relevant variable, although the GLS transformation may make some marginal improvement in the properties of the estimators, it usually does not make nearly as significant a contribution as finding the missing variable and including it in the equation. The beginner is thus warned to avoid correcting for heteroskedasticity by a GLS transformation and estimation procedure.

9 The Simultaneous Equations Model

Classical Assumption III stated that all regressors were uncorrelated with the error term. One model that violates this assumption is the simultaneous equations model. This chapter demonstrates the violation, shows the consequences for OLS (ordinary least squares) estimates, and investigates the properties of an alternative estimator for the simultaneous equations model. There are some advanced statistical tests to detect the presence of simultaneity, but they are beyond the scope of this text. Usually, simultaneity is suspected on theoretical grounds.

When OLS is applied to one equation of a simultaneous equations system, the estimator is called direct least squares (DLS). Such an estimator is shown in this chapter to be biased, and the bias does not disappear as the sample size goes to infinity, so DLS is called asymptotically biased. An alternative estimator, two-stage least squares (TSLS), is asymptotically unbiased although it is biased for small samples. There currently is no estimator for the simultaneous equations model that produces unbiased estimates for small samples, so researchers generally rely on the asymptotic (i.e., large sample) characteristic or property of the TSLS estimator, its asymptotic unbiasedness (and consistency, which usually implies that the variance and biasedness of the estimator go to zero as the sample size approaches infinity). This chapter presents a Monte Carlo comparison between DLS and TSLS and shows the tendencies of the sampling distributions of the respective estimators as the sample size gets larger. One inference is that, for small samples (and possibly for other situations), the DLS estimator may be preferred to TSLS.

This chapter also demonstrates that the t-test of individual coefficients is approximately correct for TSLS. Another subject area that is explored is identification, which involves an examination of the estimating equation before TSLS is applied, in order to assess whether TSLS or other simultaneous equations estimating techniques can be applied. If the simultaneous equation of interest is underidentified, then TSLS cannot be applied, that is, the computer program will not be able to produce the TSLS estimates of the equation (except for rounding error). (A capital-intensive approach to determine whether an equation is identified is simply to try to apply TSLS, a technique that many computer regression packages include. If the computer is unable to provide estimates, the equation is probably underidentified.)

This chapter introduces an alternative estimating technique for any equation, including a simultaneous equation, called IVE (instrumental variables estimator). The errors-in-the-variables model is shown to present the same violation of Assumption III as the simultaneity case does. The distributed lag model, if it has an autocorrelated error term, also violates Assumption III. Finally, the chapter introduces the notions of recursive models, seemingly unrelated regressions, and another estimating technique called three-stage least squares (3SLS). The main points of the entire chapter are then summarized.

9.1   Structural and Reduced-Form Equations

A general supply and demand model is used to show the violation of Classical Assumption III. It is assumed that the focus of the researcher's quantification efforts are on one of the equations, say the demand equation of a supply and demand equation system. The entire analysis is done equation-by-equation, so in practice the analysis should be carried out m times in a simultaneous equations system that is composed of m equations. Let the supply and demand model consist of the following equations:[1]

$$q_t^D = \beta_1 p_t + \beta_2 x_t + \epsilon_{Dt} \qquad \text{(Demand)} \qquad (9.1.1)$$
$$q_t^S = \delta_1 p_t + \delta_2 z_t + \epsilon_{St} \qquad \text{(Supply)} \qquad (9.1.2)$$

and the equilibrium condition:

$$q_t^D = q_t^S = q_t \qquad (9.1.3)$$

where q^D and q^S are the quantities demanded and supplied, respectively, p is its price, x is household income, and z is the input price of the major factor of production. The β's and δ's are structural coefficients, referring to their ready interpretation as reflecting the behavior of suppliers or demanders. To avoid the indeterminancy of the time dimension with cross-section data, it is assumed that this is a time-series model, with the subscript t to denote time. However, simultaneity is not precluded just because the data are cross sectional. For example, if the cross-section model represents long-run behavior, then supply and demand forces are probably at work, and some simultaneity can be expected. The equilibrium condition is used to write the model as:

$$q_t = \beta_1 p_t + \beta_2 x_t + \epsilon_{Dt} \qquad \text{(Demand)} \qquad (9.1.4)$$
$$q_t = \delta_1 p_t + \delta_2 z_t + \epsilon_{St} \qquad \text{(Supply)} \qquad (9.1.5)$$

---

[1] Note that the variables are written as deviations from their mean values. In their levels form, the constant terms would appear in equations 9.1.1 and 9.1.2. In the graphs in this chapter, the variables are in the customary levels form, so the supply and demand curves lie in the first quadrant of the graph.

In this equation set, there are two *endogenous* variables, quantity (q) and price (p), the values of which are mutually determined by these two equations. In the demand equation, the equation of interest, both of these variables appear. One is selected as the dependent variable; in this case q is chosen, that is, the equation is *normalized* on q. (Its "coefficient" is unity, whereas the coefficient of p is β_1.) The other endogenous variable is put on the right-hand side as a regressor, along with the household income variable, x. Of course, it is arbitrary in this instance which variable, p or q, is put on the left-hand side of the equation. In all equations with an additive error term, the left-hand variable, which for single-equation models is called the dependent variable, is directly correlated with the error term. Since either p or q could have been put on the left-hand side and both of them are mutually dependent, or endogenous, variables, the error term is correlated with both p and q. Thus, placing one of them on the right-hand side as a regressor violates the assumption of no correlation between each of the regressors and the error term.

To show the correlation more explicitly and for use momentarily, the *reduced-form* equations are derived. The equations 9.1.1 − 9.1.3 and 9.1.4 − 9.1.5 are called *structural* equations because they represent the behavior of identifiable economic entities: households' consumption behavior is depicted in the demand equation, and entrepreneurs' production behavior is depicted in the supply equation.

If the coefficients were known, the two equations 9.1.4 and 9.1.5 could be used to predict the expected values of the p's and q's for period t. That is, the structural equations can be *solved* for the two endogenous variables p and q. To solve for them, set the right-hand sides of both equations equal to each other since they both equal q (the subscript t is deleted for simplicity of notation):

$$\beta_1 p + \beta_2 x + \epsilon_D = \delta_1 p + \delta_2 z + \epsilon_S \qquad (9.1.6)$$

Rearrange:

$$\beta_1 p - \delta_1 p = -\beta_2 x + \delta_2 z + \epsilon_S - \epsilon_D \qquad (9.1.7)$$

and solve for p:

$$p = \left[\frac{-\beta_2}{(\beta_1 - \delta_1)}\right] x + \left[\frac{\delta_2}{(\beta_1 - \delta_1)}\right] z + \frac{(\epsilon_S - \epsilon_D)}{(\beta_1 - \delta_1)} \qquad (9.1.8)$$

A solution for q is found by substituting the solved expression for p of equation 9.1.8 into either equation 9.1.4 or 9.1.5. The solution is:

$$q = \left[\frac{-\beta_2 \delta_1}{(\beta_1 - \delta_1)}\right] x + \left[\frac{\beta_1 \delta_2}{(\beta_1 - \delta_1)}\right] z + \frac{(\beta_1 \epsilon_S - \delta_1 \epsilon_D)}{(\beta_1 - \delta_1)} \qquad (9.1.9)$$

The terms in brackets in these equations are strictly functions of the structural coefficients, the β's and δ's. Thus, they can be relabeled to indicate that they are merely single-valued coefficients. These coefficients have traditionally been denoted as π's, and the two equations for p and q are written as:

$$q_t = \pi_{11} x_t + \pi_{12} z_t + v_{1t} \qquad (9.1.10)$$

$$p_t = \pi_{21} x_t + \pi_{22} z_t + v_{2t} \qquad (9.1.11)$$

These equations are known as *reduced-form equations*. Notice that each equation includes only one endogenous variable, as the dependent variable, and that each equation has exactly the same set of regressors. In general, for linear structural equations, *all* the *predetermined* variables in the entire system of equations will be included as regressors in *each* reduced-form equation. A predetermined variable is either an exogenous variable the value of which is determined outside of the system of equations, or a lagged endogenous variable. In this equation system, x and z are exogenous, hence predetermined, variables. Consider the lagged value of q, for example, as an additional regressor in either (or both) the demand or supply equation. Its value would be determined before time period t. The simultaneity occurs only for a given time period; even though q must be determined simultaneously with p during this period, in the next time period, this period's solved value of q is fixed, unchanged by the ensuing events. Thus, the lagged value of q, q_{t-1}, is treated like an exogenous variable with respect to the problem of estimating the coefficients of the structural model (which will be discussed in Section 9.3).

In terms of *using* a simultaneous equations model the coefficients of which have already been estimated, for example in predicting future values of p and q, there is a distinct difference between exogenous and lagged endogenous variables. In predicting values of p and q for several time periods in the future (outside the sample observations), the lagged endogenous variables can only take on their previously solved-for values. Such a procedure is called a *dynamic solution*. If the predicted values of p and q are generated over the sample observations, the actual values of p and q can also be used for the lagged endogenous variables. Such a procedure is called a *static solution*.

A dynamic solution can also be generated over the sample observation, but this, in general, will provide limited useful information, for the following reasons. Comparing the dynamically solved-for values of the endogenous variables with the actual sample values turns out to be another test of the estimated coefficients, but they are tested in a more formal and appropriate fashion using standard tests of significance.[2] Moreover, if the model is nonlinear in the variables, a dynamic solution over the sample observations is *expected* to generate different observations from those in the sample.[3] Nonlinearity can be introduced rather easily in a simultaneous equations model. For example, a logarithmic transformation of variables can be considered a nonlinearity, if both the logarithms and the levels of variables are included in the model. Even identities can introduce nonlinearities; for example, defining sales as quantity (q) times price (p) introduces a nonlinearity. Thus, a dynamic solution over the sample observations is only an *ad hoc* but not necessarily an informative procedure. Usually, measures such as the RMSE of the endogenous variables are computed, but note that they do not constitute a formal test of the model. However, the dynamic

---

[2] These tests are beyond the scope of this text. See C. F. Christ, *Econometric Models and Methods* (New York: John Wiley and Sons, 1966), Chapter 10.

[3] See E. Philip Howrey and H. H. Kelejian, "Simulation Versus Analytic Solution: The Case of Econometric Models," in Thomas H. Naylor, ed., *Computer Simulation Experiments with Models of Economic Systems* (New York: John Wiley and Sons, 1971), pp. 299–319.

solution itself, not compared with the sample data, may provide insight into the dynamic properties of the model.[4]

Given a set of simultaneous structural equations that are linear in the coefficients, the reduced-form set of equations may be written directly without solving for it as was done above. Each reduced-form equation has one of the endogenous variables as its left-hand variable and *all* the predetermined variables in the entire structural system for its regressors. There is one such equation for each of the endogenous variables.

These reduced-form equations show the net effects on the endogenous variables of the determinants of demand and supply, in this case x and z. The variable x comes from the demand equation and the variable z comes from the supply equation. Thus, the reduced-form equations no longer represent the individual effects of the separate economic entities, households and entrepreneurs, which were represented by the (behavioral) structural equations. However, the expected signs of the reduced-form coefficients, π_{11}, π_{12}, π_{21}, and π_{22}, can sometimes be determined by examining the signs and magnitudes of the structural coefficients. For example, π_{11} from equation 9.1.10 equals, from equation 9.1.9, $-(\beta_2\delta_1)/(\beta_1-\delta_1)$. Since $\beta_1 < 0$ and $\delta_1 > 0$ (being the slopes of the demand and supply curves, respectively), the denominator is negative. Also, it is hypothesized that β_2 is positive, so $-(\beta_2\delta_1)$ is negative. Thus, π_{11} is expected to be positive. This type of analysis is of considerable importance because often researchers desire to estimate and use just the reduced-form equations and not the structural equations, for example for forecasting purposes. Consequently, determining the expected signs of the reduced-form coefficients is, in this case, of considerable importance, for example in setting up one-sided t-tests (see Chapter 5).

But now to return to the main line of reasoning relating to a demonstration of the violation of Classical Assumption III. It is easily shown that the regressor p in the demand equation is correlated with the error term ϵ_D in the demand equation. From the reduced-form equation for p (equation 9.1.11), it is known that p is correlated with the reduced-form error term, v_2. From the derived form of the reduced-form equation 9.1.8, it is seen that $v_2 = (\epsilon_S-\epsilon_D)/(\beta_1-\delta_1)$. Thus, v_2 is a linear function of ϵ_D (with coefficient $-1/[\beta_1-\delta_1]$), as well as a linear function of ϵ_S, but the point is that it is correlated with ϵ_D. Since p is correlated with v_2 and v_2 depends on ϵ_D, it follows (in this case[5]) that p is correlated with ϵ_D. Thus, in the demand equation, Assumption III is violated: one of the regressors is correlated with the error term.

9.2   The Bias of Direct Least Squares (DLS)

All the classical assumptions are required in order to insure that OLS estimates are BLUE. Thus, when one does not hold, the question is, which of the B-L-U properties is violated? It turns out that applying OLS to a structural equation, called DLS,

---

[4] Howrey and Kelejian, "Simulation Versus Solution." See especially the conclusions, pp. 317–18, which were written by Naylor.

[5] In general, just because p is correlated with v_2 and v_2 is correlated with ϵ_D, it is not always the case that p is correlated with ϵ_D. But it is in this case.

produces biased estimates of the coefficients, and such bias has been termed *simultaneous equations bias*.

Monte Carlo simulations can show this bias. Given the values of the coefficients and the values of the variances of the error terms of the structural equations (given that the error terms are normally distributed), the reduced-form equations 9.1.8 and 9.1.9 may be used to compute values of the endogenous variables p_t and q_t, given the values of x and z. Then OLS can be applied to the demand equation 9.1.4, to produce the DLS estimates of β_1 and β_2. To illustrate, assume in the true model that the structural coefficients are $\beta_1 = -1$, $\beta_2 = 1$, $\delta_1 = 1$, and $\delta_2 = 1$. It is also assumed that $\sigma_D^2 = 2$ and $\sigma_S^2 = 3$. It is possible that ϵ_D and ϵ_S may be correlated; this is a likely possibility in a supply and demand context in which price expectations are not quantified as a variable (as perhaps proxied by one or more lagged values of price). Thus, when market expectations about price change, they affect both demanders and suppliers. Thus, the error terms in each equation have a tendency to shift together. In technical terms, the error terms are said to have a nonzero covariance, denoted $\sigma_{DS} \neq 0$. In this particular Monte Carlo experiment, however, it is assumed that the covariance between ϵ_D and ϵ_S is zero. In Section 9.3.1, the effects of nonzero covariances are discussed.

Another parameter that is important, as is shown in Section 9.3, is the degree of correlation between x and z, the two predetermined variables. (The same set of x's and z's used in the missing relevant variable model—x_1 and x_2 in the notation of Section 6.2—are used here. They are drawn from the uniform distribution in such a way to have the specified degree of sample correlation within a tolerance level of 0.015. See footnote 3 of Chapter 6. The value of z was multiplied by 10, for computational reasons.)

The resulting sampling distribution for sample size $T = 20$ for the DLS estimates $\hat{\beta}_1$ and $\hat{\beta}_2$ are shown in Figure 9.2.1. They are the curves labeled $f(\hat{\beta}_1)$ and $f(\hat{\beta}_2)$. The DLS sampling distribution for $\hat{\beta}_1$ is centered on -0.37 instead of on -1.0, which is

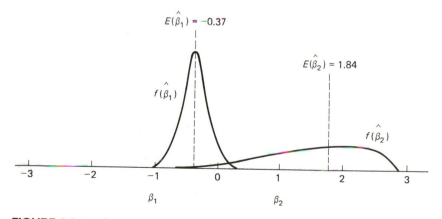

FIGURE 9.2.1 Sampling Distributions for DLS Estimators: $T = 20$, $\sigma_D^2 = 2$, $\sigma_S^2 = 3$, $\sigma_{SD} = 0$, $r_{12}^2 = 0.4$

the true value of β_1. (Notationally, $E(\hat{\beta}_1) = -0.37$.) Thus, the DLS estimator of β_1 is *positively biased*—its expected value is greater than the true value of $\beta_1 = -1.0$. The DLS estimate of β_2 also has a positive bias; its sampling distribution is centered on 1.84 instead of on $\beta_2 = 1.0$.

We shall return to the DLS estimates after investigating an alternative estimation procedure.

9.3 Two-Stage Least Squares (TSLS)

Since DLS gives biased estimates, one way to "purge" p of its correlation with ϵ_D, and thus to *attempt* to eliminate the bias, is the following two-step procedure called two-stage least squares (TSLS).

Stage 1.   Apply OLS to the reduced-form equation for p. Since x and z are fixed in repeated samples (which is one way to make them exogenous variables), they are not correlated with the reduced-form error term, v_2; thus, the OLS estimators of π_{21} and π_{22} are unbiased. Use these unbiased estimates to obtain a "purged" data series for p, found by substituting the observed sample values of x and z in the estimated equation:

$$\hat{p}_t = \hat{\pi}_{21}x_t + \hat{\pi}_{22}z_t \tag{9.3.1}$$

The attempt is to purge the fitted variable $\hat{p}$ of its correlation with v_2 and hence with ϵ_D, because v_2 is not used in the computation of $\hat{p}$. However, the OLS estimates $\hat{\pi}_{21}$ and $\hat{\pi}_{22}$ are not uncorrelated with v_2,[6] so $\hat{p}$ is not completely purged of its correlation with v_2 and hence with ϵ_D, but it is purged "enough."

Stage 2.   Regress q_t on $\hat{p}_t$ and z_t using OLS. The method of TSLS can be generalized to m simultaneous equations. There are then m reduced-form equations, one for each of the m endogenous variables. Each reduced-form equation has as regressors each and every predetermined variable in the entire system of equations. The OLS estimates of the reduced-form equations are used to compute the resulting estimated regression-line values (or adjusted or fitted values) of all the endogenous variables that appear as regressors in the m structural equations. After substituting these fitted values for the values of the endogenous regressors, OLS is applied to each equation (or as many as desired) in the set of structural equations.

---

[6] The regression of p on x and z satisfies all the classical normal properties for single equations. Thus, to see that the OLS coefficient estimators in equation 9.3.1 are correlated with the error term of the reduced-form equation, v_2, recall the discussion in Chapter 4, which showed that the sampling distributions of the estimated coefficients in the classical model are derived from the probability distribution of the error term of the equation. Thus, the estimated coefficients depend on and are correlated with the error term.

9.3.1 Comparisons of the Bias of DLS and TSLS

Because some correlation remains between $\hat{p}_t$ and ϵ_{Dt}, the resulting TSLS estimates of β_1 and β_2, labeled $\tilde{\beta}_1$ and $\tilde{\beta}_2$, are still biased. This is shown in Figure 9.3.1, which also shows the DLS sampling distributions. The sampling distributions for the TSLS estimators are denoted as $f(\tilde{\beta}_1)$ and $f(\tilde{\beta}_2)$. The expected value of $\tilde{\beta}_1$ is -1.25, so the bias is negative, opposite that of the DLS estimator $\hat{\beta}_1$. And $\tilde{\beta}_2$ has the opposite bias compared with $\hat{\beta}_2$. For both $\tilde{\beta}_1$ and $\tilde{\beta}_2$, the amount of the bias in this case is less than the bias of the corresponding DLS estimator, although it need not necessarily be less.

The biases in the opposite direction—the negative bias of the TSLS estimators and the positive bias of DLS estimators—are well known results in the econometrics literature.[7] Notationally, the relationship is expressed in terms of expected values:

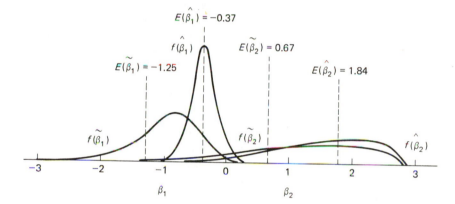

FIGURE 9.3.1 DLS ($\hat{\beta}_1$ and $\hat{\beta}_2$) and TSLS ($\tilde{\beta}_1$ and $\tilde{\beta}_2$) Sampling Distributions: $T = 20$, $\sigma_D^2 = 2$, $\sigma_S^2 = 3$, $\sigma_{SD} = 0$, $r_{12}^2 = 0.4$

---

[7] This footnote is necessary for the more advanced reader. Johnston shows that for a consumption function, the DLS estimator yields a positive bias for the marginal propensity to consume, whereas the TSLS estimator yields a downward bias. See J. Johnston, *Econometric Methods*, 2nd ed. (New York: McGraw-Hill, 1972), pp. 341–346. However, given that the extreme values of the error terms can be observed with some positive probability—as is assumed under the normal distribution, wherein the normal random variable can take on any value on the real number line—Dhrymes has shown that the expected value of the TSLS estimator does not exist and that that of the DLS estimator may not exist. See Phoebus J. Dhrymes, *Econometrics* (New York: Harper & Row, 1970), pp. 176–183. Thus, we really cannot write $E(\tilde{\beta}_1)$ or $E(\hat{\beta}_1)$ because they may not exist. The text uses this notation, however, to develop intuitively the ultimate motivation for TSLS, its consistency, and also to stress once again the difference between the expected value of an estimator and a given estimate.

In the Monte Carlo simulations, there was no problem in forming the mean value of the DLS estimator, but there was in most cases for the TSLS estimator. For many Monte Carlo drawings, the correlation between $\hat{p}$ and x was so close to unity that it caused the computer to be unable to compute the TSLS estimate, during the second stage. This occurred for most levels of the sample correlation between x and z, although the occurrence became more frequent as the degree of correlation between them increased. The correlation occurs just by the chance selection of particular sets of error terms. This inability to compute the estimate during the simulations is the manifestation of Dhrymes's conjecture concerning the lack of existence of an expected value for the TSLS estimator. The implication for practical applications is that the

TABLE 9.3.1

First 10 Estimates of β_1: $T = 20$ (Accompanying Figure 9.3.1)

	Monte Carlo Drawing									
	1	2	3	4	5	6	7	8	9	10
$\hat{\beta}_1$(DLS)	−0.46	−0.70	−0.70	−0.09	−0.76	−0.60	−0.59	−0.61	−0.25	−0.55
$\tilde{\beta}_1$(TSLS)	−0.62	−4.44	−1.02	−2.26	−0.92	−1.49	−1.73	−1.16	−0.58	−0.05

$E(\tilde{\beta}_1) < \beta_1 < E(\hat{\beta}_1)$, which corresponds to this analysis (but see footnote 7). Does this inequality imply that $\tilde{\beta}_1$ is always less than β_1 and that $\hat{\beta}_1$ is always greater than β_1? The answer is no. The relationship involving expectations implies that *on average* such a relationship will hold. As shown in Figure 9.3.1, many TSLS estimates are possible above −1.0, although in this case very few DLS estimates are below −1.0.

Is it also true that $\tilde{\beta}_1 < \hat{\beta}_1$? That is, for a given set of data, will the TSLS estimate always be below the DLS estimate? The answer is no. Table 9.3.1 shows the first 10 Monte Carlo drawings on which the sampling distributions of Figure 9.3.1 were constructed. There is a clear tendency for the TSLS estimate of β_1 to be less than the DLS estimate, but the tenth Monte Carlo drawing shows that that TSLS estimate is −0.05 while, for the same set of data, the DLS estimate is −0.55, less than the TSLS estimate.

Therefore, only on average is it appropriate to estimate the demand equation by DLS and by TSLS and to assume that the true value of β_1 lies between the two estimates. This is not a recommended procedure.

Furthermore, the result that $E(\tilde{\beta}_1) < \beta_1 < E(\hat{\beta}_1)$ is contingent on the assumption that the covariance between ϵ_D and ϵ_S is small. A positive covariance between the two error terms could be the result of a (relatively minor) variable that was omitted from both the demand and supply equations, with its coefficients having the same sign in both equations. Thus, when this variable increases, both ϵ_D and ϵ_S show positive movements together. In the Monte Carlo experiment, it was assumed that $\sigma_D^2 = 2$ and $\sigma_S^2 = 3$. It can be shown that the covariance of ϵ_D and ϵ_S can be at most the square root of their product. For the model investigated here, if the covariance is

---

TSLS estimator may not always be applied to simultaneous equation models, such as equations 9.1.4 and 9.1.5. But the researcher will know when this occurs because the computer will reject the attempt to so estimate one of the equations by giving indications such as (1) error messages, such as "division by zero;" (2) an extremely low value for the determinant (shown in some computer programs); or (3) extremely high values of the estimated standard errors of the estimated coefficients and nearly zero values for the t-statistics. Dhrymes's conjecture will be exhibited in practice perhaps once in a thousand times, or even less frequently.

For purposes of the Monte Carlo simulations, only those TSLS estimates were kept and averaged (in computing the mean) for which the squared correlation coefficient between $\hat{p}$ and x was less than 0.999. Those cases in which the correlation was 0.999 or greater correspond to those in practice for which the computer will not produce the TSLS estimates. Thus, the computation of the mean here is conditional on being able to obtain a TSLS estimate for a given Monte Carlo sample, just as it would be in practice.

However, it should be noted that the expected value of the TSLS estimator $\tilde{\beta}_1$ does not exist. To say that it does not exist means that its variance is infinite. For those cases in which the estimate cannot be computed, one possible value that it could take is (either plus or minus) infinity. Thus, just one of these situations arising in the Monte Carlo simulations is sufficient to indicate that the variance is infinite and that the mean value of the estimator, therefore, does not exist.

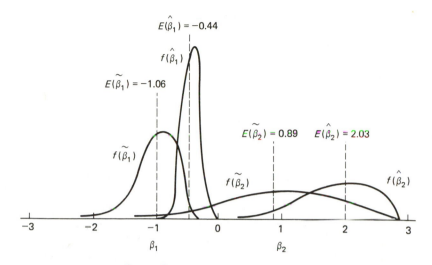

FIGURE 9.3.2 DLS ($\hat{\beta}_1$ and $\hat{\beta}_2$) and TSLS ($\tilde{\beta}_1$ and $\tilde{\beta}_2$) Sampling Distributions: $T = 50$, $\sigma_D^2 = 2$, $\sigma_S^2 = 3$, $\sigma_{SD} = 0$, $r_{12}^2 = 0.4$

less than 2, then the relationship above that $E(\tilde{\beta}_1) < \beta_1 < E(\hat{\beta}_1)$ holds.[8] If the covariance equals 2, then the DLS and TSLS estimates are identical, their sampling distributions are identical, and there is no bias (for either estimate). But if the covariance of ϵ_D and ϵ_S is greater than 2, then the relationship is reversed: $E(\hat{\beta}_1) < \beta_1 < E(\tilde{\beta}_1)$. Unfortunately, this has been a little-explored area in the econometrics literature.

9.3.2 Consistency of TSLS

Thus, the generally cited advantage of TSLS compared with DLS is its lower amount of bias, opposite in sign to that of DLS estimates, for a low value of the covariance of ϵ_D and ϵ_S. The best argument in favor of TSLS is that as the sample size becomes large, the bias of the TSLS estimator disappears entirely, whereas the bias of the DLS estimator remains. Figure 9.3.1 was constructed for a sample size T (or n) of 20 observations. Figure 9.3.2 shows the same distributions for a sample size of 50 observations. Notice that the bias of the TSLS estimator $\tilde{\beta}_1$ is virtually zero, whereas the bias of the DLS estimator $\hat{\beta}_1$ remains approximately the same. The same tendency is shown for the TSLS estimator $\tilde{\beta}_2$, but the sample size is not large enough for the bias of the TSLS estimator to disappear, and the biasedness of the DLS estimator $\hat{\beta}_2$ has increased slightly in this instance.

Notice also that, as the sample size increases from 20 to 50, all the sampling distributions show a lower variance. Also notice that, regardless of the sample size,

---

[8] See Henry J. Cassidy and T. Crawford Honeycutt, "Direct Least Squares Versus Two-Stage Least Squares with Nonzero Covariance of Error Terms," *forthcoming*.

the variances of the DLS estimators are less than the variances of the corresponding TSLS estimators. It is the lower variance of the DLS estimators that is its single redeeming virtue, and this one virtue may, in some circumstances, overcome its biasedness. However, as the sample size increases, both the DLS and TSLS estimators have smaller variances. In the limit, with a ''very large'' sample size, both variances are virtually zero. Thus, for large sample sizes, the superiority of the TSLS estimator is clear. For an infinite sample size, TSLS estimates are unbiased, called *asymptotic unbiasedness,* and have zero variance, a property that when coupled with asymptotic unbiasedness is called *consistency*, whereas the DLS estimates are still biased, although their variance is zero. Thus, in the limiting case, DLS estimates are very precise estimates but of the wrong number, where the TSLS estimates are very precise estimates of the correct number.

As alluded to in Footnote 7, it is actually incorrect to speak of the TSLS estimator as having bias, or even of its being asymptotically unbiased. These terms were used here only to explain the meaning of the term *asymptotic unbiasedness,* and to develop the notion of consistency. In actuality, TSLS has only the property of *consistency*. To explain the distinction is complex and beyond the scope of this text. Also, since the expected value of the DLS estimator may not exist, technically it is *inconsistent* as opposed to biased and asymptotically biased.

9.3.3 Monte Carlo Comparisons

Given these caveats, the Monte Carlo results are now reviewed. Table 9.3.2 shows the summary statistics for the DLS and TSLS estimates for sample size 20, and Table 9.3.3 shows them for a sample size of 50. Focusing on the estimates of β_1, when $T = 20$, the mean value of the DLS estimator $\hat{\beta}_1$ is -0.37 and for the TSLS estimator $\tilde{\beta}_1$ it is -1.25, as was discussed in reference to Figure 9.3.1. Thus, DLS has a greater amount of bias in this case. But notice that the variance of the DLS estimator is only 0.051 compared with 10.46 for the TSLS estimator. Thus, in this case, the MSE of the DLS estimator is less than that of the TSLS estimator. By using the MSE criterion, the DLS estimator is better than the TSLS estimator in this instance because its lower variance has more than offset its larger bias.

TABLE 9.3.2

Summary Statistics from Monte Carlo Simulation to Accompany Figure 9.2.1: $T = 20$

Parameter Value	Estimator	Mean Value	Bias	Variance	Mean Square Error
$\beta_1 = -1$	$\hat{\beta}_1$(DLS)	-0.37	0.63	0.051	0.45
	$\hat{\beta}_1$(TSLS)	-1.25	-0.25	10.46	10.52
$\beta_2 = 1$	$\hat{\beta}_2$(DLS)	1.84	0.84	1.19	1.90
	$\hat{\beta}_2$(TSLS)	0.67	-0.33	14.37	14.48

TABLE 9.3.3

Summary Statistics From Monte Carlo Simulations to Accompany Figure 9.3.2: $T = 50$

Parameter Value	Estimator	Mean Value	Bias	Variance	Mean Square Error
$\beta_1 = -1$	$\hat{\beta}_1$(DLS)	−0.44	0.56	0.016	0.33
	$\hat{\beta}_1$(TSLS)	−1.06	−0.06	0.11	0.12
$\beta_2 = 1$	$\hat{\beta}_2$(DLS)	2.03	1.03	0.50	1.56
	$\hat{\beta}_2$(TSLS)	0.89	0.11	1.18	1.20

However, for a sample size of 50, as shown in Table 9.3.3, the variance of the TSLS estimator is small enough, compared with that of the DLS estimator (0.11 versus 0.016), so that the biasedness of the DLS estimator is overriding, causing its MSE to be greater than that of the TSLS estimator. For completeness, the first 10 estimates when $n = 50$ are shown in Table 9.3.4. It is clear even from this small drawing that, for 50 observations, the TSLS estimator provides estimates usually closer to the true parameter value $\beta_1 = -1$ than does the DLS estimator applied to the same sets of data.

The relative accuracy of the DLS and TSLS estimators depends on a number of factors other than the number of observations. Another important factor is the degree of correlation between the exogenous variable in the demand equation (x) and the exogenous variable in the supply equation (z), as denoted by the squared coefficient of correlation r_{xz}^2. The primary reason that the r_{xz}^2 is important is that, for high values of r_{xz}^2, the variance of the TSLS estimates increases markedly. This is because, if x and z are highly correlated, then the adjusted value $\hat{p}$, which is a linear combination of x and z according to equation 9.3.1 in the first stage of the TSLS procedure, is essentially a function of just one of them, x or z, since their movements closely resemble each other. Thus, during the second stage when q is regressed on $\hat{p}$ and x, the variance of $\tilde{\beta}_1$ is very high since the squared correlation coefficient between $\hat{p}$ and x, $r_{\hat{p}x}^2$, is very high. This may be seen from the familiar formula

$$\mathrm{VAR}(\tilde{\beta}_1) = \sigma_{\hat{D}}^2 / (\Sigma \hat{p}^2 (1 - r_{\hat{p}x}^2))$$

TABLE 9.3.4

First 10 Estimates of β_1: $T = 50$
(Accompanying Figure 9.3.2 and Table 9.3.3)

	Monte Carlo Drawing									
	1	2	3	4	5	6	7	8	9	10
$\hat{\beta}_1$(DLS)	−0.66	−0.45	−0.40	−0.53	−0.51	−0.37	−0.44	−0.51	−0.50	−0.51
$\tilde{\beta}_1$(TSLS)	−1.39	−1.18	−1.02	−1.13	−1.13	−0.77	−0.80	−0.75	−0.97	−1.28

In fact, r_{pz}^2 may be so high that the variance is nearly infinite. In the Monte Carlo simulations reported here, when $r_{xz}^2 = 0.4$ and $T = 20$, 19 of the 5000 random drawings had an r_{px}^2 greater than or equal to 0.999, and 4 had an r_{pz}^2 of 1.0. These drawings were excluded for the purpose of constructing the sampling distributions. The variance of the TSLS estimator is so high in such cases that no reliance can be placed on the result. This indicates, however, that this could occur in practice. The incidence of high r_{px}^2 is greater the higher the r_{xz}^2 and the lower the number of observations.

The effect of various levels of r_{xz}^2 on the estimators is shown schematically in Figure 9.3.3. The horizontal axis represents the degree of correlation between x and z. The lower part of the figure shows that the DLS estimator $\hat{\beta}_1$ underestimates β_1 in absolute value (i.e., the estimates are closer to zero), whereas the TSLS estimator $\tilde{\beta}_1$ usually overestimates β_1, but not by much. The expected value of $\tilde{\beta}_1$ becomes less than -1.0 for a high degree of correlation, most likely because the incidence of perfect collinearity between $\hat{p}$ and x is much greater the higher the r_{xz}^2 is, and these drawings were deleted. (For 20 observations and an $r_{xz}^2 = 0.95$, 309 out of 5000 drawings had an r_{px}^2 greater than or equal to 0.999 and were thus deleted.)

The variance of the DLS estimator $\hat{\beta}_1$, as shown in the top panel of Figure 9.3.3,

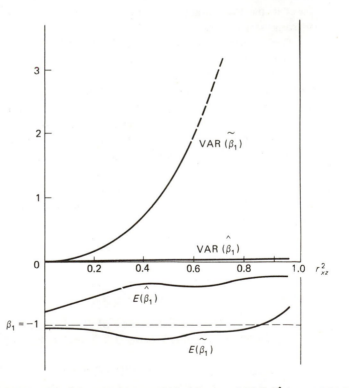

FIGURE 9.3.3   Expected Values and Variances of DLS ($\hat{\beta}_1$) and TSLS ($\tilde{\beta}_1$) Estimators of β_1 from Monte Carlo Simulations as a Function of r_{xz}^2 (Number of Observations $T = 20$)

does not vary as r_{xz}^2 varies, but the variance of the TSLS estimator $\tilde{\beta}_1$ increases markedly with an increase in r_{xz}^2. In fact, the line denoting the VAR($\tilde{\beta}_1$) is dashed instead of solid because, for replications of the Monte Carlo experiment, the resulting estimates of the variance differed significantly and the "true" curve was not observed. (This is because its expected value does not exist; its variance approaches infinity.)

For 20 observations, the MSE of the DLS estimator for r_{xz}^2 of 0.4 was less than that for the TSLS estimator of β_1, as was shown in Table 9.3.2. In general, DLS is better, in terms of a lower MSE, than TSLS the higher the r_{xz}^2 and the lower the number of observations. For the particular sets of data on x and z and for the values of all the various parameters selected (namely, $\beta_1 = -1$, $\beta_2 = 1$, $\delta_1 = \delta_2 = 1$, $\sigma_D^2 = 2$, $\sigma_S^2 = 3$, and $\sigma_{DS} = 0$, the last one being the covariance between ϵ_D and ϵ_S), the general relationship showing which is better, DLS or TSLS, is portrayed schematically in Figure 9.3.4. For 10 observations, DLS is always better, but TSLS is better for more observations, depending on the level of r_{xz}^2. (Note that TSLS is *not* better in a given application if the TSLS estimates cannot be computed. Figure 9.3.4 is drawn conditional on the ability to compute the TSLS estimates.) The shape and position of this iso-MSE curve changes as various model parameters change and as the model configuration changes; thus, this curve is only representative of the guidelines that have been developed here concerning when to select TSLS over DLS. (If there were more exogenous variables in the demand and supply equations, then another measure of the general linear correlation between the set of exogenous variables in each equation would have to be used.)

9.4   Use of the *t*-Tests

The comparisons of TSLS and DLS estimators in Section 9.3 were on the basis of bias, variance, and mean square error. It was shown that, in some instances, DLS estimators were better than TSLS estimators such as when the number of observations

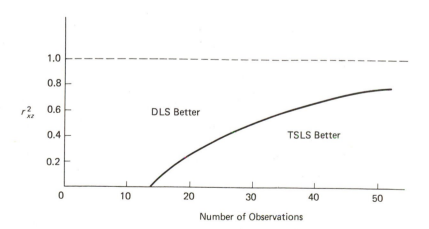

FIGURE 9.3.4   Regions in Which DLS and TSLS Provide the Lower MSE

T is small or when the correlation of the exogenous variables x in the demand equation and z in the supply equation is high. However, the comparisons are quite different when it comes to hypothesis testing. As was pointed out in previous chapters, biased estimates of either the regression coefficient or its estimated standard error produce biased estimates of the t-statistic that is used for hypothesis testing.

In general, the bias of the DLS estimator makes this approach not very satisfactory for testing hypotheses concerning the magnitudes of the regression coefficients, and the relative unbiasedness of the TSLS estimator makes it more suitable for such hypothesis testing, using the t-statistic.

To illustrate these points, the following t-statistics were computed in the Monte Carlo simulations reported in Section 9.3:

$$t_{\hat{\beta}_1} = \frac{\hat{\beta}_1 - \beta_1}{s_{\hat{\beta}_1}} \qquad (9.4.1)$$

$$t_{\tilde{\beta}_1} = \frac{\tilde{\beta}_1 - \beta_1}{s_{\tilde{\beta}_1}} \qquad (9.4.2)$$

These t-statistics, one for DLS and the other for TSLS, may be used to test H_0: $\beta_1 = -1$ instead of the usual hypothesis $H_0 : \beta_1 = 0$ (in which case β_1 would be set to zero in equations 9.4.1 and 9.4.2). These t-statistics, if they are appropriate, will have the t-distribution centered on zero and have the appropriate shape. Then one can use the critical values of the t-statistic as found in Statistical Table A-1.

For illustrative purposes, the case used in Section 9.3 is presented here: the number of observations $T = 20$ and $r^2_{xz} = 0.4$. The parameter values of the assumed model (equations 9.1.4 and 9.1.5) are still $\beta_1 = -1$, $\beta_2 = \delta_1 = \delta_2 = 1$, and $\sigma^2_D = 2$, $\sigma^2_S = 3$, and $\sigma_{SD} = 0$. The resulting t-distributions (equations 9.4.1 and 9.4.2) are graphed in Figure 9.4.1. Because of the relatively little bias of the TSLS estimator, the $t_{\tilde{\beta}_1}$ distribution is centered on zero, whereas the $t_{\hat{\beta}_1}$ (DLS) distribution is centered on 2.97.

The consequences for testing $\beta_1 = -1$ are quite enlightening. The shaded area in the tails of the $t_{\tilde{\beta}_1}$ (TSLS) distribution should be 10 percent if this was truly a t-distribution, according to the (two-tailed) critical value of $t_c = 1.740$ found in Statistical Table A-1. The percentage computed in the Monte Carlo simulation in the two tails of the $t_{\tilde{\beta}_1}$ distribution in the rejection region of H_0: $\beta_1 = -1$ is 19 percent, which is greater that the 10 percent figure. Thus, while the TSLS estimators do not produce t-statistics with exactly the t-distribution appropriate for hypothesis testing, they are usually considered to be approximately appropriate, and the approximation becomes more accurate as the number of observations increases. However, even at 50 observations, 19 percent of t-statistic showed up again in the rejection region, so the required number of observations is not clear. Thus, most researchers use the usual t-statistics computed from the TSLS estimates with the knowledge that they are usually approximately correct (even though actually a different test is sometimes suggested.[9]

The situation is not the same for DLS estimators. Even though the DLS estimator

---

[9] In distribution theory, it has been proven that, as the sampling size goes to infinity, the t-statistic for the TSLS estimator tends toward the standard normal distribution. Thus, some econometricians argue

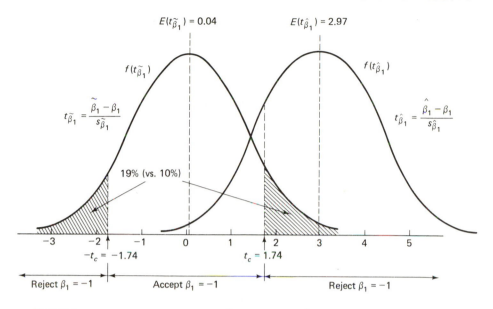

FIGURE 9.4.1 *t*-Distributions for $\tilde{\beta}_1$ (TSLS) and $\hat{\beta}_1$ (DLS) (Differences from $\beta_1 = -1$; $T = 20$, $\beta_1 = -1$, $\beta_2 = \delta_1 = \delta_2 = 1$, $r_{xz}^2 = 0.4$, $\sigma_{\tilde{D}}^2 = 2$, $\sigma_{\tilde{S}}^2 = 3$, $\sigma_{DS} = 0$)

of β_1 had a lower MSE than the TSLS estimator, 0.46 to 8.27, its biasedness renders its *t*-statistic inappropriate for hypothesis testing. In Figure 9.4.1, the *t*-statistic (equation 9.4.1) is centered on 2.97 instead of on zero. Thus, in testing H_0: $\beta_1 = -1$, H_0 would be rejected about 84 percent of the time (84 percent of the $t_{\hat{\beta}_1}$ distribution is in the rejection region.)

The usual use of the *t*-statistic is, in this case, to test H_0: $\beta_1 > 0$ versus H_A: $\beta_1 < 0$. Of course, this test depends on, among other things, the true value of β_1, which is -1 here. This *t*-statistic is defined as the estimated coefficient divided by its estimated standard error (i.e., set $\beta_1 = 0$ in equations 9.4.1 and 9.4.2). For this illustration, for $T = 20$, the null hypothesis $\beta_1 > 0$ is rejected about 60 percent of the time with the TSLS estimator, but only 48 percent of the time under DLS (at the 10-percent level of significance). For $T = 50$, TSLS rejects H_0: $\beta > 0$, 99.8 percent of the time, and DLS would do so 95 percent of the time. Thus, the result of this standard *t*-test would be correct for the TSLS estimator more times than for the DLS estimator, although the distinction may or may not disappear as the number of observations increases. (It did in this illustration, but in general this is not the case.)

---

that the *t*-table should never be used and that the standard normal table should be used instead in order to obtain the critical value. This assumes, in essence, that an infinite-sized sample is used. For the illustration here, from the normal table (A-7), the critical value based on this notion is 1.645 for a 10-percent, two-sided level of confidence, which is less than the critical value from the *t*-table (A-1) for 17 degrees of freedom, 1.74. Thus, the actual amount of Type I Error is, in this instance, *increased* by resorting to the standard normal table for the critical value, whereas it was already too large using the *t*-table.

Thus, on the basis of hypothesis testing, the TSLS estimator is superior to the DLS estimator, even though the same conclusion may not ensue under the MSE criterion. However, these results were predicated on estimating the true models. More than likely, other empirical problems, such as missing relevant variables, irrelevant variables, or incorrect functional form, in combination with the simultaneous equations model, can turn these conclusions completely around. Explorations along these lines are left as an exercise for the interested student.

9.5   Identification

Two-stage least squares has a distinct disadvantage, compared with DLS: it cannot always be applied to every simultaneous equation in such models (not even considering those times in the above Monte Carlo simulations when the TSLS procedure could not be applied due to near perfect collinearity). For purposes of this text, the coefficients of an equation are said to be *identified* when TSLS can be applied to a structural equation, and the coefficients are said to be *underidentified* when TSLS cannot be applied.[10] The term *identification* is a term of art in econometrics, and it refers to the *ability* to apply TSLS (or most other simultaneous equations estimating techniques) to a structural equation. It does *not* indicate whether the resulting estimates, if the equation is identified, are "good" (e.g., in the MSE sense).

There are several ways a structural equation can be identified, but the way most often used is via predetermined variables that are excluded from the equation of interest. For the rest of this chapter the equations are shown with variables in their deviations-from-the-mean form but the graphs are drawn in the levels form. Thus, the constant terms are omitted from the analytics but not from the graphs. Assume first that the structural equations are as follows (omitting the equilibrium condition):

$$q = \beta_1 p + \epsilon_D \tag{9.5.1}$$

$$q = \delta_1 p + \delta_2 z + \epsilon_S \tag{9.5.2}$$

In particular, the single predetermined variable of this system, z, is omitted from the demand equation. Figure 9.5.1 demonstrates the effect of such an omission. For this approach to identification, it is assumed that the variances of the error terms are small enough to render the error terms inconsequential. Thus, the demand curve remains essentially the same while the supply curve shifts as the predetermined variable z shifts from period to period. The sample observations are represented by points 1, 2, 3, and 4 as the supply curve shifts because z changes values. Thus the observations trace out the demand curve.

---

[10] Technically, the parameters of a structural equation are said to be identified when estimates of them can be derived from (consistent) estimates of the reduced-form coefficients. This text avoids the complication of embroiling indentification in the analytics of so deriving estimates from reduced-form estimates. For practitioners, examining for identification is done just to discover whether any simultaneous equations estimating technique can be used on a given structural model.

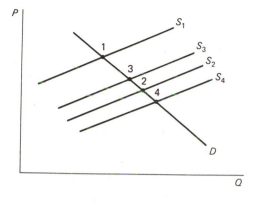

FIGURE 9.5.1 Shifting Supply Curve Identifying the Demand Curve

Figure 9.5.2 demonstrates the possible scatter of the four points if the demand curve also included z, such as in:

$$q = \beta_1 p + \beta_2 z + \epsilon_D \qquad (9.5.3)$$

The shifts in the supply curve are the same as before, but now the demand curve also shifts with z. In this case, it is not possible to identify either the demand curve or the supply curve without prior knowledge of the relative magnitudes of β_2 and δ_2, the coefficients of z in the two equations.

To summarize up to this point in the illustrations, when z is excluded from the demand equation but included in the supply equation, the demand equation is identified. Of course, the supply equation is not identified (i.e., it is *underidentified*), and when z is also included in the demand equation, both equations are underidentified.

By similar reasoning, if a variable x was included in the demand equation but not in the supply equation, given that z was not included in either, the supply equation would thereby be identified and the demand equation would be underidentified.

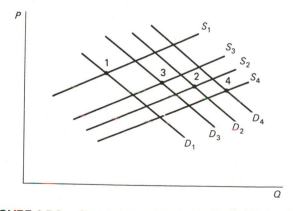

FIGURE 9.5.2 Both Demand and Supply Shifting with z

It might be inferred that, if x was included in the demand equation and excluded from the supply equation, thereby identifying the supply equation, and z was included in the supply equation and excluded from the demand equation, thereby identifying the demand equation, both the supply and demand equations would be identified. This is true, although it is difficult to demonstrate graphically. However, if x and z are perfectly correlated in the data sample so that $x = z$ except for a scale factor and their movments are one-for-one, the situation depicted in Figure 9.5.2 would result, and neither supply nor demand would be identified.

At the other extreme, suppose that the variables x and z had a sample correlation of zero. This could occur in a *controlled experiment* in which the researcher varied one variable, household income x via a subsidy plan, while holding the other variable constant, the input price z via a price support plan. After several observations of this sort, which would be used to identify the supply curve, the researcher would vary z and hold x constant, thereby identifying the demand curve.

In practice, such controlled experiments are very expensive and are rarely done. Thus, even though the supply and demand equations are formulated as in equations 9.1.4 and 9.1.5 to achieve identification of both equations, the covariation of x and z in the sample may interfere with the true identification of demand and supply. However, except for the extreme case in which x is perfectly correlated with z, econometricians refer to the inclusion and exclusion of predetermined variables in such a fashion as *prima facie* evidence of identification, even though in some instances identification may not be achieved.[11]

Identification is a precondition for the application of TSLS (and of most other simultaneous equations estimating techniques). Thus, the inclusion and exclusion of predetermined variables is evidence that TSLS can be applied to a structural equation. This does not insure that the resulting TSLS estimates will be good ones or that TSLS can be applied (because of, by chance, a high correlation between $\hat{p}$ and x), as was shown in Section 9.4.

Two other remarks are appropriate concerning identification. The first concerns the situation in which, instead of equation 9.4.1, the supply equation is:

$$q_t = \delta_1 p_t + \delta_2 z_t + \delta_3 w_t + \epsilon_{St} \qquad (9.5.4)$$

where w_t is another predetermined variable in the supply equation, and the demand equation is either equation 9.5.1 or 9.4.1, which contain neither z nor w as a regressor. In this case, the shifts in the supply curve that trace out and hence identify the demand curve come from two sources, z and w, instead of just one source, z, as before. In such a situation, the demand curve is *overidentified* since more than the sufficient amount of information is contained in the supply equation to achieve identification. Such a situation is of no concern to users of TSLS because the critical thing is whether identification has been achieved, and overidentification is just a form of identification.

The second remark concerns a rule used by econometricians to examine equations of a structural system of equations one at a time for identifiability. This rule is called the *order* condition. It is necessary that an equation satisfy the order condition before

---

[11] That is, examining for the inclusion and exclusion of predetermined variables is not a "sufficient" condition for identification.

it is identified. If it is satisfied, the researcher may attempt to use TSLS on the equation, but in some instances, the equation may turn out to be underidentified, as discovered by the extreme values of the estimated coefficients and their standard errors when TSLS is attempted (or the inability of the computer to produce the TSLS estimates). However, if the order condition is not satisfied, there is no reason to attempt TSLS because the equation is underidentified.

In the order condition, the researcher counts the number of predetermined variables in the entire system of equations to see whether that number is greater than or equal to the number of coefficients in the equation of interest, excluding the constant term. If it is, the equation is (possibly) identified; and if it is not, the equation is (definitely) underidentified. For clarity, the order condition is stated as follows:

ORDER CONDITION: An equation is (possibly) identified if the number of predetermined variables in the entire system of equations is greater than or equal to the number of slope coefficients in the equation of interest (K). The equation is underidentified if the order condition is not met.

Examples of the application of this order condition are now presented. In the model given by equations 9.1.4 and 9.1.5, there are two predetermined variables in the system, x and z. In the demand equation, there are two slope coefficients, β_1 and β_2, so the order condition is satisfied, and the demand equation is (possibly) identified. In the supply equation, there are also two slope coefficients, δ_1 and δ_2, so the order condition is satisfied, and that equation is (possibly) identified. The tentative conclusion is that TSLS can be used on either equation.

In the model given by equations 9.5.1 and 9.5.2, the order condition is satisfied for the demand equation since there is one predetermined variable in the system, z, and one slope coefficient to estimate, β_1; however, there are two slope coefficients to estimate in the supply equation, δ_1 and δ_2, so the supply equation is underidentified. Thus, TSLS may (possibly) be used on the demand equation but not on the supply equation.

(The reader should verify that: (1) if equations 9.5.3 and 9.5.2 constitute the model, neither is identified; (2) if the equations are 9.5.1 and 9.5.4, the demand equation is identified but the supply equation is not; and (3) if the equations are 9.5.3 and 9.5.4, the same conclusion holds as with (2).)

The order condition can be made to depend on whether the constant term (e.g., β_0) is or is not included in an equation (by counting the constant term as a "variable" and including the constant term in the number of parameters to be estimated). However, just as with the single equation model, the constant term should never be suppressed (see Section 6.1).

9.6   Instrumental Variables Estimation

One of the many approaches to providing consistent estimators in cases in which a regressor is correlated with the error term is by using instrumental variables estimation (IVE). This approach has more pedagogical than applied value. It is discussed here because it represents a general class of consistent estimators of which TSLS is one, and the general technique is easily explained. This section may be skipped by those just interested in the application of TSLS.

For the simple regression model, $y = \beta x + \epsilon$, in which x and ϵ are correlated, an instrumental variable z is selected that (1) is not correlated with the error term and (2) is correlated with x. Then a special estimating formula is used. Instead of the OLS estimator:

$$\hat{\beta} = \frac{\Sigma xy}{\Sigma x^2} \qquad (9.6.1)$$

the following formula is used:

$$\hat{\beta}^+ = \frac{\Sigma zy}{\Sigma zx} \qquad (9.6.2)$$

Thus, the instrument z replaces an x in the numerator and in the denominator.

Since x and ϵ are correlated, this estimator is still biased for small samples (if the expected value of the estimator is assumed to exist). But as the sample size approaches infinity, the correlation of z and x and the lack of correlation of z with ϵ yield a consistent estimator. That is, for very large samples, the sampling distribution of $\hat{\beta}^+$ collapses on the true value of β.

For the multivariate model, the same general technique applies, but the formula is not presented here. A separate instrumental variable having the two properties is usually selected for each regressor, and the appropriate formula applies. The TSLS technique is an IVE: the fitted values from the estimated reduced-form equation are the instruments for the endogenous regressors, whereas the predetermined regressors have themselves as their instruments.

9.7   Errors in the Variables Models

The simultaneous equations problem of the correlation between a regressor and the error term can also arise if there is a measurement error in the regressor. Assume that the variable used for estimation, x, is measured with error. This could occur, for example, because the measurement is based on a sample, as are almost all national aggregate statistics, or because the data are reported incorrectly. In a very loose sense, it can also be because the measured variable is aggregated and a weighting system is used in its computation. For example, the price of wheat for a given year has to be aggregated over the various trading days and over the different varieties of wheat. There are several ways to weight each observation, for example by the relative amount of wheat sold. But any weighting scheme produces some amount of bias in terms of what theoretically should be the "correct" measurement of the variable (if we knew what the correct measurement is, which often we do not).

For all these cases, the measured variable x may be stated as the "true" measure, x^*, plus an error term, v:

$$x_i = x_i^* + v_i \qquad (9.7.1)$$

where v has the classical properties of an error term. The important point is that since x is a linear function of v, it is correlated with v.

The regression model is correctly specified as:

$$y_i = \beta x_i^* + \epsilon_i \qquad (9.7.2)$$

But since $x_i^* = x_i - v_i$, the model can be expressed as:

$$y_i = \beta(x_i - v_i) + \epsilon_i \qquad (9.7.3)$$

or

$$y_i = \beta x_i + \epsilon_i^* \qquad (9.7.4)$$

where

$$\epsilon_i^* = \epsilon_i - \beta v_i \qquad (9.7.5)$$

Thus, y is regressed on the measured x_i; however, since the measured x_i is correlated with v_i, and ϵ_i^* is a linear function of v_i, x_i is correlated with ϵ_i^* in the estimating equation. Thus, the errors-in-the-regressor model has the same type of correlation that characterizes the simultaneous equations problem, and the bias (and inconsistency) produced by using OLS to estimate the equation prevails here as well. If any of a set of regressors has measurement error, all the coefficient estimates are biased. Techniques have been developed to estimate this model, but they are rarely used by the beginner. One method used is that of instrumental variables estimation, introduced in Section 9.6.

If the measurement error occurs in the dependent variable, no bias is introduced with OLS. To see this, let the measured value be y_i, the correct value be y_i^*, and the measurement error be w_i:

$$y = y_i^* + w_i \qquad (9.7.6)$$

The regression model is:

$$y_i^* = \beta x_i + \epsilon_i \qquad (9.7.7)$$

In its application, it becomes:

$$y_i - w_i = \beta x_i + \epsilon_i \qquad (9.7.8)$$

or

$$y_i = \beta x_i + (\epsilon_i + w_i) \qquad (9.7.9)$$

But since the dependent variable is always correlated with the error term, nothing has changed. In particular, the regressor is not correlated with the error term, $\epsilon_i + w_i$, and no bias is introduced. However, it is likely that the degree of the overall statistical fit of the equation is less with the measurement error than without it.

Sometimes, when theory is not clear about which is the dependent variable, the variable with the greatest amount of measurement error can be selected as the dependent variable in order to avoid the effects of the "simultaneous equations bias" when the regressor is correlated with the error term. For example, in an equation to describe the size distribution of income, the income classes may be thought of as nonrandom, and the relative frequency of households in each class may be thought of as containing measurement error. Thus, the relative frequency is selected as the dependent variable, and the income classifications are formulated as a regressor.[12]

9.8 The Distributed Lag Model

In Chapter 2 it was shown that several forms of the single-equation distributed lag model with appropriate assumptions, such as the Koyck lag, can be written as:

$$y_t = \beta_1 x_t + \beta_2 y_{t-1} + \epsilon_t \qquad (9.8.1)$$

Given a dynamic model such as this one, with one or more lagged dependent variables, regardless of how it was obtained, if the error term ϵ_t is autocorrelated, then the simultaneous equations bias arises upon applying OLS.

This can be explained as follows. Let the error term follow a pure autoregressive scheme:

$$\epsilon_t = \rho \epsilon_{t-1} + v_t \qquad (9.8.2)$$

where ρ is the first-order autocorrelation coefficient and v_t is a classical error term. Since ϵ_t is correlated with y_t, the lagged dependent variable, y_{t-1}, is correlated with ϵ_{t-1}. Since the error term in equation 9.8.1 can be written as $\rho \epsilon_{t-1} + v_t$, the regressor y_{t-1} is seen to be correlated with the error term (the ϵ_{t-1} part) in violation of Classical Assumption III. Thus, OLS on equation 9.8.1 produces biased estimates of the same nature as simultaneous equations bias, even though there is only a single equation to estimate.

Most researchers use OLS on this type of equation under the assumption that either the error term is not autocorrelated or that OLS, while biased, has the redeeming feature of a low variance. Some researchers use the CORC estimating procedure (see Section 7.2.5), which is a biased but consistent estimator. A number of other techniques have been proposed that are beyond the scope of this text.

9.9 Recursive Models, Seemingly Unrelated Regressions, and Three-Stage Least Squares

The simultaneous equations model, equations 9.1.4 and 9.1.5, had two endogenous variables (in the example, price and quantity) determined simultaneously by two structural (supply and demand) equations. Consider the case in which the quantity supplied

---

[12] For such an approach, see the author's "The Rate of Change in the Size Distribution of Wages as a Vector," *Review of Income and Wealth,* Series 15, No. 4, December 1969, pp. 349–368.

is a fuction not of the current price but of last period's price. This is the well-known "cobweb" model. The model may be written as:

$$q_t^D = \beta_1 p_t + \beta_2 x_t + \epsilon_{Dt} \quad \text{(Demand)} \qquad (9.9.1)$$

$$q_t^S = \delta_1 p_{t-1} + \delta_2 z_t + \epsilon_{St} \quad \text{(Supply)} \qquad (9.9.2)$$

$$q_t^D = q_t^S = q_t \qquad \text{(Equilibrium Condition)} \qquad (9.9.3)$$

Using the equilibrium condition and deleting the subscript t, the model is usually written as:

$$q = \beta_1 p + \beta_2 x + \epsilon_D \quad \text{(Demand)} \qquad (9.9.4)$$

$$q = \delta_1 p_{-1} + \delta_2 z + \epsilon_S \quad \text{(Supply)} \qquad (9.9.5)$$

where the subscript (-1) implies a lag of one period (usually a growing season for animals or crops).

Assuming that the coefficients are known or have been estimated, the *solution* of these equations, in terms of finding the values of the endogenous variables p and q, is *recursive*. If the initial base-period price is given and the error terms in the solution for p and q are ignored, the quantity for the first period is determined from the supply equation. The demand equation is then used to solve for price. Given this first-period solution for price, the process is repeated for the subsequent periods until the values of p and q are determined for all the periods.

It would appear that, since the equations are no longer simultaneous, OLS could be used on each equation without any problem. However, in order for OLS to be the most efficient estimating technique (recall that efficiency concerns the smallest variance), another condition has to be met: the error terms in the supply and demand equations, if normally distributed as usually is assumed, have to be independent. This is usually stated as:

$$E(\epsilon_{Dt}\, \epsilon_{St}) = 0. \qquad (9.9.6)$$

Then the equations can be called recursive for the purpose of estimation (as well as for solution). One may suspect some correlation between error terms if some common disturbance affects both equations, as discussed in Section 9.2.

A more efficient estimating technique (than OLS) under these general circumstances when there is no simultaneity, but the error terms are correlated across equations, is Zellner's seemingly unrelated regressions estimating technique (or the two-stage Aitken estimator). At the heart of this two-stage estimating procedure is the estimating technique discussed previously by the name generalized least squares (GLS), also known as Aitken estimation. The corrections in Chapters 7 and 8 for heteroskedasticity and autocorrelation are GLS approaches, since they transform an equation the error term of which does not satisfy the classical properties into an equation (to be estimated) that does. The seemingly unrelated regression model of two equations may be written in "stacked" form as a single equation, which motivates the use of the GLS technique. (GLS is a single-equation technique.)

The two-stage Aitken procedure is as follows:

Stage 1.   Use OLS on each equation, but only to estimate σ_D^2, σ_S^2, and σ_{DS}, the last one being the covariance of the error terms in the two equations.

Stage 2. Substitute these estimates into a special "stacked" regression equation and estimate at once the Aitken estimates of all the β's and δ's. Some canned programs exist for this purpose, but the explanation of the form of the stacked regression and how the coefficients are estimated is beyond the scope of this text.

The two-stage Aitken estimator is often applied to other situations, e.g., to a series of demand equations for various commodities, where there is no simultaneity but the error terms from the various equations are suspected to be correlated. Thus, each equation appears to be unrelated to the others; hence the name "seemingly unrelated regressions" has been given to them. For efficient estimates, the two-stage Aitken estimator should be applied to the whole set.

This general approach has also been applied to simultaneous equations systems. The technique of TSLS does not attempt to account for the possibility that the error terms ϵ_D and ϵ_S are correlated. A simultaneous estimating technique that does is called three-stage least squares, or 3SLS. This technique uses TSLS as its first two stages, but only to obtain estimates of the covariance σ_{DS} and the variances of the error terms in each equation. Then the "stacking" routine of Zellner is used to estimate all the coefficients and their standard errors in all the simultaneous equations at once. Most beginners do not use this estimating technique, but it is part of some computer regression packages, so its use is not ruled out.

It is worth pointing out that completely elastic or inelastic supply or demand equations can give rise to recursive models, with the consequent possibility that OLS will be BLUE when used to estimate both demand and supply. To illustrate, take the demand equation 9.9.1 in which quantity demanded is a function of the current price and another variable x. The assumption of a perfectly elastic supply curve implies that the supply price is not a function of the quantity supplied, in the "relevant range" of the quantity and price variables. Thus, the supply equation may be written as:

$$p_t = \delta_2 z_t + \epsilon_{St} \qquad (9.9.7)$$

As long as ϵ_S is not correlated with ϵ_D, equations 9.9.1 and 9.9.7 are considered a recursive model for the purposes of estimation, and OLS will consequently produce BLUE estimates. For solution, the recursive nature of this model is apparent: price in period t is found by equation 9.9.7, and, when substituted into equation 9.9.1, quantity in period t is determined (using estimates of the coefficients and ignoring the error term).

Instead of a perfectly elastic supply curve, suppose that the supply is, for all practical purposes, completely inelastic. This means that, for the time period, only a fixed quantity is available and that no increase in price (in the "relevant range") can increase the amount available. This assumption can be written as the following supply equation:

$$q_t^s = \delta_2 z_t + \epsilon_{St} \qquad (9.9.8)$$

For solution, the quantity comes from equation 9.9.8, and the price is found by solving equation 9.9.1 for it (ignoring the error terms). For estimation, as long as ϵ_S and ϵ_D are assumed to be uncorrelated, equations 9.9.1 and 9.9.8 represent a recursive system for which OLS estimates are BLUE.

Therefore, the researcher can impose priors concerning completely elastic or inelastic supply or demand curves that imply that OLS is the BLU estimator. All such assumptions, of course, should be fully documented and explained.

9.10   Summary

The distinction was made between the structural equations that form the simultaneous equations system and the corresponding reduced-form equations. Each reduced-form equation has as its left-hand variable one of the endogenous variables of the simultaneous equations systems and as its regressors all the predetermined (i.e., exogenous and lagged endogenous) variables of the system. There are m such reduced-form equations for m simultaneous equations.

OLS (ordinary least squares) on the structural equations, called DLS (direct least squares), is biased, asymptotically biased, and inconsistent, the last one being a property caused by its asymptotic biasedness.

An alternative estimator, TSLS (two-stage least squares), is asymptotically unbiased and consistent, the latter generally implying that the variance of the estimator collapses to zero as the mean of the estimator approaches the true parameter value as the sample size approaches infinity. For small samples (to which the property of biasedness refers), the TSLS estimator is biased, as are all simultaneous equations estimators. Thus, situations arise when DLS may be preferred to TSLS, in an MSE (mean square error) sense. Those situations occur when the number of observations is small and/or the degree of correlation between predetermined variables in different simultaneous equations is high.

Even though the t-test is not exact for the TSLS estimators, its use is accurate enough in most circumstances. The biasedness of DLS implies that its t-statistics are not accurate enough to be relied on for testing purposes.

OLS is the appropriate estimating technique for estimating reduced-form equations as long as other maladies, such as autocorrelation or heteroskedasticity, do not apply, because the problem of the correlation of the endogenous variables with the error term is obviated by the exclusion of all endogenous regressors from these equations. Often, researchers estimate the reduced-form equations instead of the structural equations and use the reduced-form equations, for example, for forecasting values of the endogenous variables.

Identification refers to the ability to apply simultaneous equations techniques such as TSLS to a given equation in a simultaneous equations system. A capital-intensive approach to identification is to attempt TSLS estimation on the computer, but the approach usually taken is to examine the equation of interest prior to estimation. The order condition should be checked. It is satisfied—and the equation is (most likely) identified—if the number of predetermined variables in the entire simultaneous equations system is at least as great as the number of slope coefficients to be estimated in the equation of interest. If the order condition is not satisfied, the equation is underidentified, and TSLS is not able to produce any estimates. Researchers in this instance sometimes use DLS, or they respecify the simultaneous equations system in order to achieve identifiability. Although the latter approach is of dubious merit, it usually permits the use of TSLS.

IVE (instrumental variables estimation) is often used to estimate equations that violate Classical Assumption III, and TSLS is an IVE method. The errors-in-the-variables and the distributed lag models may also violate Assumption III. In these cases, many applied researchers apply OLS even though the estimators are inconsistent.

Recursive models are very common, and OLS is ordinarily applied to them. Recursive models contain more than one endogenous variable, but the values of all the variables can be solved for directly by the equation-by-equation application of structural equations instead of via the reduced-form equations as with simultaneous equations. Seemingly unrelated regressions are ones that are not simultaneous, but the error terms from the different equations are correlated. Recursive models may fit into this category of models. The two-stage Aitken estimator is the BLUE (best linear unbiased estimator) for the seemingly unrelated regressions model. This approach can also be applied to a simultaneous equations system if the error terms are suspected to be correlated, and the approach is called 3SLS (three-stage least squares). Other techniques beyond the scope of this text can also be used to account for this type of correlation.

10 Hypothesis Testing and Interval Estimation: Further Results

The first section of this chapter describes a general technique to test hypotheses on two or more coefficients at the same time. The *t*-test, it will be recalled, is a test for a single coefficient, given the other regressors in the model. The *F*-test, described in Chapter 1, tests whether all the slope coefficients are zero simultaneously. Section 10.1 generalizes this test to include tests on subsets of the coefficients. A special *F*-statistic has to be constructed by the researcher, as opposed to the *F*-statistic for the equation furnished by the computer, which is used to test whether all the coefficients are simultaneously zero. This *F*-statistic, however, is relatively easy to calculate, and it usually requires the estimation of two regression equations estimated by OLS (ordinary least squares). In this section, tests are also described on the dummy variable models of Section 2.1, which are important in themselves and also serve to illustrate the application of the general *F*-test.

Section 10.2 discusses other tests, and in particular the Farrar-Glauber test for multicollinearity. The next section describes interval estimates for coefficients instead of the (single-value) point estimates discussed throughout the text. Interval estimates are rarely used in applied econometrics, but prediction intervals, instead of a single predicted value, are sometimes used in forecasting.

Section 10.4 discusses *ex post* forecasting, which involves holding back some sample data from the estimation of the coefficients and then using the estimated equation to predict those data points. Such a procedure has little merit unless the observations held back are of particular importance, in that the estimated equation is supposed to exhibit good predictions for these data if the equation is to be considered acceptable. The final section presents a summary of all the elements of hypothesis testing presented in this book.

10.1   The *F*-Test on More than One Coefficient at a Time

The following illustration introduces hypothesis testing on more than one coefficient at a time and a method for imposing constraints on a regression equation. This method of imposing constraints is essential to the construction of the *F*-test described in this section.

10.1.1   Illustration of Constraints on the Coefficients

Often, production functions (see Section 2.2) such as:

$$Q = AL^\alpha K^\beta e^\epsilon \qquad (10.1.1)$$

where Q is output, L is labor, K is capital, and ϵ is a classical error term, are supposed to exhibit "constant returns to scale": if both L and K increase by one percent, Q increases by one percent. As this production function is written, if both L and K are multiplied by a constant b (such as $b = 1.01$, showing a one-percent increase), output becomes:

$$A(bL)^\alpha(bK)^\beta e^\epsilon = b^{\alpha+\beta}AL^\alpha K^\beta e^\epsilon = b^{\alpha+\beta}Q \qquad (10.1.2)$$

Thus, in order for Q to increase by the same proportion as L and K, the exponent of b must equal unity, or $\alpha + \beta = 1$. If the production function was estimated as is—regressing log (Q) on log (L) and log (K)—probably $\hat{\alpha} + \hat{\beta}$ would not equal the value 1, just because of sampling error. (Recall that $\hat{\alpha}$ and $\hat{\beta}$ can each be any one of a whole range of values, as governed by their sampling distributions. Thus, the sum $\hat{\alpha} + \hat{\beta}$ also has a sampling distribution. Even though in truth $\alpha + \beta = 1$, $\hat{\alpha} + \hat{\beta}$ is not very likely to equal unity.)

Some researchers impose their priors and *assume* that $\alpha + \beta = 1$; they then impose this "constraint" during the estimation procedure. Although there are better ways to impose this constraint to estimate the equation, the method used in the construction of the general *F*-test described below is as follows. Simply solve the constraint for one of the coefficients, e.g., $\alpha = 1 - \beta$, and substitute this expression for α into the (double-log) equation:

$$\log Q = A' + (1 - \beta)\log L + \beta\log K + \epsilon \qquad (10.1.3)$$

Rearrange the equation: pull to the left-hand side those elements that do not need to be estimated—log L—and factor out on the right-hand side those coefficients that need to be estimated—β. (A' is the logarithm of A.) Thus, the "constrained" equation can be estimated as:

$$(\log Q - \log L) = A' + \beta(\log K - \log L) + \epsilon \qquad (10.1.4)$$

That is, $Y^* = \log Q - \log L$ is regressed on $X^* = \log K - \log L$ to obtain an estimate $\hat{\beta}$. Once $\hat{\beta}$ is obtained, the estimate of α is computed as $\hat{\alpha} = 1 - \hat{\beta}$ via the original constraint imposed according to the prior notion of constant returns to scale.

However, instead of simply *imposing* the condition $\alpha + \beta = 1$ on the equation, the researcher may want to *test* whether this assumption is verified by the data. That is, the researcher may want to test the *hypothesis* that $\alpha + \beta = 1$.

10.1.2 The General *F*-Test

This section presents a general technique to conduct tests that involve more than one coefficient at the same time, as in the above example. Briefly, the general approach is as follows. As stressed in Chapter 5, the null hypothesis should be the "strawman," which is opposite to the one that the researcher is interested in accepting, but only at a specified level of confidence, such as 90 or 95 percent. (However, in the illustration in Section 10.1.1, H_0 is $\alpha + \beta = 1$, which may be the hypothesis in which the researcher is interested. This is a violation of the strawman approach, for which there usually is little remedy in this instance.) Under the null hypothesis—that is, assuming the null hypothesis to be true in order to set up the test statistic—M restrictions are implied concerning the coefficients. In general, M turns out to be the number of coefficients the values of which do not have to be estimated under the null hypothesis. In this example, $M = 1$ because only one coefficient (α) is eliminated from the estimating equation when the null hypothesis is assumed to hold. General techniques are shown in Sections 10.1.3 and 10.1.4 that allow the researcher to specify the constrained equation implied by the null hypothesis, a required step in the application of the general *F*-test.

The mechanics of the general testing procedure are as follows. From OLS on the constrained equation, the sum of squared residuals is obtained, call it SSE_M. In this example, SSE_M comes from the OLS estimation of the constrained equation 10.1.4. (If the computer program does not list the sum of squared residuals, it should list the standard error of the equation, SEE. Obtain the SSE by squaring SEE and multiplying the result by $n - K' - 1$, where n is the number of observations and K' is the number of regressors on the right-hand side of the equation, which in equation 10.1.4 is 1.) From the unrestricted regression equation (under H_A), obtain its sum of squared residuals, called SSE. In this example, SSE comes from the OLS estimation of $\log Q$ on $\log L$ and $\log K$. The following special *F*-statistic is then computed:

$$F = \frac{(SSE_M - SSE)/M}{SSE/(n-K-1)} \qquad (10.1.5)$$

where M is the number of restrictions, n is the number of observations, and K is the total number of regressors under H_A (the unrestricted equation). This *F*-statistic has an *F*-distribution with M numerator and $(n-K)-1$ denominator degrees of freedom. Critical values for the *F*-distribution are presented in Statistical Tables A-2 and A-3 at the end of the text, with a table for each level of significance. The numerator degrees of freedom is the column heading and the denominator degrees of freedom is the row heading.

It is always the case that $SSE_M \geq SSE$. That is, imposing restrictions on the coefficients, instead of allowing OLS to select their values, can only increase the residual variance (or the sum of squared residuals). (Recall that OLS selects that combination of values of the coefficients to make the SSE the smallest.) At the extreme, if the unrestricted regression yields exactly the same estimated coefficients as does the restricted regression, then the SSE's are equal, and the *F*-statistic is zero. In this case, H_0 (and its restrictions) is not rejected. The data indicate that these restrictions appear to be correct. But as the difference between the restricted and unrestricted estimated coefficients increases, both for those coefficients that are restricted and for those that are not, the data indicate that the restrictions of the null hypothesis are increasingly likely not to be true. Thus, when F gets large—in particular, when it is greater than the critical value found in the F-table—the null hypothesis is rejected, that is, the hypothesized restrictions are rejected by the test.

The difficult part of this approach to hypothesis testing involves the specification of the restricted equation so that it can be estimated by OLS. As shown in the following two sections, the data input to the computer regression package can usually be easily modified to accommodate the estimation of the restricted equation using the standard OLS estimating routine. As in the production function example, the general procedure is to bring to the left-hand side of the equation all parts on the equation that are assumed to be known (under the restrictions), thus constructing a modified dependent variable; also, some of the regressors may have to be modified. This constructed dependent variable is then regressed on the remaining (and possibly modified) regressors. This general procedure is illustrated for several types of hypotheses in Sections 10.1.3 and 10.1.4.

10.1.3 Compound Hypotheses

One general set of hypotheses involves separate statements on two or more coefficients, to be tested at the same time. These are called compound hypotheses. Consider the following hypotheses:

$$H_0 : \beta_1 = \beta_1^*; \beta_2 = \beta_2^*; \cdots ; \beta_M = \beta_M^*$$
$$H_A : H_0 \text{ is not true}$$

$(10.1.6)$

where the β_k^*'s are constants assigned by the researcher. The regressors have been rearranged so that the first M variables are the ones for which the null hypothesis applies. (The order of the regressors has no effect on OLS estimates.) There are no hypotheses on the remaining $K-M$ coefficients, where $M \leq K$. The restricted regression under the null hypothesis (i.e., assuming it to be true) is:

$$Y_i^* = Y_i - \beta_1^* X_{1i} - \beta_2^* X_{2i} - \cdots - \beta_M^* X_{M,i}$$
$$= \beta_{M+1} X_{M+1,i} + \cdots + \beta_K X_{ki} + \beta_0 + \epsilon$$

$(10.1.7)$

Thus, SSE_M comes from regressing Y^* on $X_{M+1}, X_{M+2}, \ldots, X_K$. (In this chapter, the variables are written in their levels form instead of the usual deviations-from-the-mean form.) Of course, the unrestricted SSE in the F-formula comes from the regression of Y on $X_1, X_2, \ldots, X_K$. In addition to conducting the statistical test, one should compare the estimates generated by the restricted regression with those generated by the unrestricted equation and assess their "reasonableness." If only one equation is to be used, e.g., for simulation, the researcher may have to choose between the restricted and unrestricted equations.

A special case is testing whether all the slope coefficients in the equation are zero in order to examine whether "the whole equation is statistically significant." In this case, $M = K$, and H_0 is $\beta_1^* = \beta_2^* = \cdots = \beta_K^* = 0$. That is, all the regression coefficients (except the constant term) are set equal to zero under the null hypothesis. The F-statistic ordinarily computed by computer regression programs is this particular F-statistic. It has K numerator and $n-K-1$ denominator degrees of freedom.

Another example of a compound hypothesis concerns whether the slope coefficients are altered significantly if they are estimated for a new set of data; for example, the null hypothesis may be that the slope coefficients are the same in two samples, such as before and after a war. The concern is whether a structural shift has occurred from one data set to the other, i.e., whether the coefficients have changed "significantly." Let the two (nonoverlapping) data sets be denoted by superscripts I and II and the combined data set be denoted by the superscript C; then, the hypotheses are

$$H_0 : \beta_0^{I} = \beta_0^{II}; \beta_1^{I} = \beta_1^{II}; \beta_2^{I} = \beta_2^{II}; \cdots; \beta_K^{I} = \beta_K^{II}$$
$$H_A : H_0 \text{ is not true.}$$

$(10.1.8)$

That is, β_1^{I} is the coefficient of X_1 using only data set I; and β_1^{II} is the coefficient of X_1 using only data set II. For the appropriate test, the following F-statistic may be computed:

$$F = \frac{(\text{SSE}^{C} - \text{SSE}^{I} - \text{SSE}^{II})/(K+1)}{(\text{SSE}^{I} + \text{SSE}^{II})/(n + m - 2(K+1))}$$

$(10.1.9)$

where n and m are the number of observations in the two sets of data, respectively, and SSE is the residual sum of squares.[1] The SSEs are found by estimating the regression three times, once with each of the two sets of data (to obtain SSE^{I} and SSE^{II}) and once with the combined (or pooled) data set (to obtain SSE^{C}). This F-statistic is compared with the critical value F_c from the F-table with $K+1$ numerator and $n + m - 2(K+1)$ denominator degrees of freedom. A value of $F > F_c$ leads to the acceptance of H_A. This is often called the Chow test.[2]

In order to reinforce the material both of this section and of Chapter 2, presented here is a dummy variable approach to the Chow test. This approach may be preferred to the traditional approach because it involves estimating only two regression equations instead of three.

Suppose that the regression equation under the null hypothesis of equation 10.1.8 is:

$$Y = \beta_0 + \beta_1 X_1 + \beta_2 X_2 + \epsilon$$

$(10.1.10)$

For reasons that will be made clear, this approach requires the construction of a dummy variable that takes on the value of 0 for data set I and 1 for data set II:

$$D_i = \begin{cases} 0 \text{ for observation } i \text{ in Data Set I} \\ 1 \text{ for observation } i \text{ in Data Set II} \end{cases}$$

$(10.1.11)$

This dummy variable and all its "interaction" terms are constructed and included in the equation. This allows the coefficients to be different under data sets I and II:

$$Y_i = \beta_0 + \beta_0' D_i + \beta_1 X_{1i} + \beta_1'(X_{1i} D_i) + \beta_2 X_{2i} + \beta_2'(X_{2i} D_i) + \epsilon_i \quad (10.1.12)$$

Equation 10.1.12 can now be estimated over the pooled data set, combining the

---

[1] This statistic is appropriate as long as n and $m > K$; otherwise, use the dummy variable approach below.

[2] Gregory C. Chow, "Tests on Equality between Sets of Coefficients in Two Linear Regressions," *Econometrica*, Vol. 28, No. 3, July 1960, pp. 591–605.

observations in data sets I and II. To assess the interpretation of the estimated coefficients and hence the reason for this formulation, assume first that data set II is used. Then $D_i = 1$ and equation 10.1.12 becomes:

$$Y_i = (\beta_0 + \beta_0') + (\beta_1 + \beta_1')X_{1i} + (\beta_2 + \beta_2')X_{2i} + \epsilon_i \qquad (10.1.13)$$

And if data set I is used, equation 10.1.12 becomes equation 10.1.10, the equation which is assumed to hold under the null hypothesis.

Thus, β_0' is the *change* in the intercept term of data set II, compared with data set I. If $\beta_0' = 0$, then both data sets have the identical intercept term, β_0. Similarly, β_1' and β_2' are the changes in the coefficients of X_1 and X_2, respectively, for data set II, compared with data set I. If $\beta_1' = \beta_2' = 0$, then these slope coefficients remain unaltered across the two data sets. Therefore, the null hypothesis (equation 10.1.8) of no change in the coefficients can be translated in this dummy variable framework as:

$$H_0: \beta_0' = \beta_1' = \beta_2' = 0 \qquad (10.1.14)$$

With this formulation, the F-test, equation 10.1.5, can be applied. The restricted SSE_M under the null hypothesis comes from equation 10.1.10 estimated across both data sets, and the unrestricted SSE comes from equation 10.1.12 estimated across both data sets. Thus, the dummy variable approach requires only two regression runs, whereas the more traditional approach to the Chow test requires three. In addition, with the dummy variable approach, one can examine directly the degree to which the individual coefficients vary across data sets (e.g., by examining the coefficients β_1' and β_2' and their t-statistics). Also, dummy variable approaches can be applied to more than two data sets and to overlapping data sets.

10.1.4 Composite Hypotheses

Some hypotheses are amenable to the following general form, in which the null hypothesis is stated as a linear combination of the first M coefficients (again, for convenience of exposition, by rearranging the regressors):

$$H_0 : \delta_0 = \delta_1\beta_1 + \delta_2\beta_2 + \cdots + \delta_M\beta_M$$
$$H_A : H_0 \text{ is not true} \qquad (10.1.15)$$

The δ's are constants specified by the researcher. In this case, it turns out that there is only one restriction implied by H_0. To show this, β_1 under H_0 is stated as a function of the other coefficients (with the proviso that $\delta_1 \neq 0$):

$$\beta_1 = \frac{\delta_0}{\delta_1} - \frac{\delta_2}{\delta_1}\beta_2 - \cdots - \frac{\delta_M}{\delta_1}\beta_M \qquad (10.1.16)$$

Let

$$\gamma_1 = \frac{\delta_0}{\delta_1}, \quad \gamma_2 = \frac{\delta_2}{\delta_1}, \ldots, \gamma_M = \frac{\delta_M}{\delta_1} \qquad (10.1.17)$$

These are known because the δ's are known. This expression for β_1 may be substituted into the unrestricted multiple regression equation to obtain:

$$Y = (\gamma_1 - \gamma_2\beta_2 - \cdots - \gamma_M\beta_M)X_1 + \beta_2 X_2 + \cdots + \beta_K X_K + \beta_0 + \epsilon \quad (10.1.18)$$

or, rearranging terms:

$$Y = \gamma_1 X_1 - \beta_2(\gamma_2 X_1) - \beta_3(\gamma_3 X_1) - \cdots - \beta_M(\gamma_M X_1)$$
$$+ \beta_2 X_2 + \cdots + \beta_K X_K + \beta_0 + \epsilon \quad (10.1.19)$$

Since γ_1 is a known coefficient, $\gamma_1 X_1$ may be moved to the left-hand side of the equation. Since the term $\beta_2\gamma_2 X_1$ contains the unknown parameter β_2, it can be combined with $\beta_2 X_2$ to form the term $\beta_2(X_2 - \gamma_2 X_1)$, where $(X_2 - \gamma_2 X_1)$ is a term of known quantity for each observation, and can be made a regressor. And so on for the other terms. Thus, the restricted equation becomes:

$$Y^* = \beta_2 X_2^* + \beta_3 X_3^* + \cdots + \beta_M X_M^*$$
$$+ \beta_{M+1} X_{M+1} + \cdots + \beta_K X_K + \beta_0 + \epsilon \quad (10.1.20)$$

where

$$Y_i^* = Y_i - \gamma_1 X_{1i}$$
$$X_{2i}^* = X_{2i} - \gamma_2 X_{1i}$$
$$\vdots$$
$$X_{Mi}^* = X_{Mi} - \gamma_M X_{1i}$$
$$(10.1.21)$$

In the application of the F-statistic, there is only one numerator degree of freedom ($M=1$). This is because the linear combination (equation 10.1.15) reduces by one the number of coefficients that have to be estimated. That is, there is one less coefficient to estimate with the restricted form, compared with the unrestricted form.

Most textbooks suggest the use of a special t-test for these particular types of hypotheses. When there is only one numerator degree of freedom, the square root of the F-statistic 10.1.5 becomes a two-sided t-statistic. Thus, one-sided tests can be conducted with this t-statistic using a one-sided level of significance, with $n - K - 1$ degrees of freedom, if H_0 is an inequality. If $t > t_c$, reject H_0.

If there are two separate linear restrictions under the null hypothesis, then two fewer coefficients need to be estimated under H_0 and $M = 2$; and so on for three or more separate linear restrictions tested simultaneously.

As an example, suppose that one wished to test whether one coefficient equals a constant b times another coefficient. Without loss of generality, suppose that the first two coefficients are the ones involved and that the null hypothesis involving the restrictions is $\beta_1 = b\beta_2$. The null hypothesis can be written as:

$$H_0: 0 = \beta_1 - b\beta_2 \quad (10.1.22)$$

so $\delta_0 = 0$, $\delta_1 = 1$, and $\delta_2 = -b$. By using equations 10.1.20 and 10.1.21, the restricted equation can be written as:

$$Y_i^* = Y_i = \beta_2(X_{2i} + bX_{1i}) + \beta_3 X_{3i} + \cdots + \beta_K X_{Ki} + \beta_0 + \epsilon_i \quad (10.1.23)$$

Thus, the first regressor is $X_2^* = X_2 + bX_1$; X_1 is dropped as a separate regressor; and Y remains the same. The SSE_M comes from estimating this restricted equation, and the SSE comes from estimating Y on $X_1, X_2, \ldots, X_K$.

For a second example, suppose that, in the production function example used to motivate this general approach, one wished to test whether the sum of the coefficients equals unity. Then H_0 becomes:

$$H_0: 1 = \beta_1 + \beta_2 \qquad (10.1.24)$$

So $\delta_0 = 1 = \delta_1 = \delta_2$. The restricted equation is:

$$Y_i^* = Y_i - X_{1i} = \beta_2(X_{2i} - X_{1i}) + \beta_3 X_{3i} + \cdots + \beta_K X_{Ki} + \beta_0 + \epsilon_i \qquad (10.1.25)$$

The SSE from this equation (for SSE_M), with the SSE from the unrestricted one, is used in the above F-test (equation 10.1.5).

As mentioned in Section 10.1.1, there is a problem that arises quite often in the application of this particular kind of hypothesis testing, a violation of the strawman approach. As in that example, if this hypothesis (equation 10.1.24) was applied to a double-log version of a production function (with the dependent variable being output, and capital and labor being the two regressors, in logarithmic form), then there is an *unknown* chance of Type II Error if the null hypothesis is accepted. Unfortunately, there is usually no solution to the problem of accepting an explicit value of the sum of coefficients (or any other linear combination). Typically, one performs the standard test on equation 10.1.24 as the null hypothesis, but the documentation should indicate that there is an unknown amount of (Type II) error if the null hypothesis is accepted.

Ordinarily, researchers are not fully confident of the restrictions on the coefficients imposed under the null hypothesis. Instead, they may have some general notions about the likely magnitudes of some of the parameters and may want the estimating technique to assist them in obtaining constrained estimates (but not for hypothesis testing). In this case, they may not wish to rely on the results of the estimation under the restrictions of the null hypothesis. A popular alternative in this case of some uncertainty over the parameter values is Theil and Goldberger's "mixed estimation." Under this approach, the researcher supplies to the (special) computer regression package the most likely values for one or more coefficients and also a type of confidence interval around each best guess, in terms of the likely standard deviation of the estimate. Then, the resulting estimates may differ from the supplied point estimates.

Using any kind of constrained estimation procedure requires the existence of strong priors on the part of the researcher. Whenever any kind of constrained estimation is put forth, the documentation should include the result of applying regression analysis to the unconstrained case. Then readers can judge for themselves the appropriateness and the consequences of applying the priors. Without such documentation, readers are usually left with the feeling that the researcher is trying to deceive them by making the answers come out right when the data or the unconstrained estimating technique does not support the priors.

10.1.5 Tests Based on Dummy Variables

The powerful technique of using zero-one dummy variables as regressors was discussed in Section 2.1. The most important aspect of using them as regressors, as stressed there, is to give them the appropriate set-up and interpretation. Typically, one of the conditions that forms the basis for the dummies is omitted from the equation in order to avoid perfect multicollinearity. Thus, the coefficients of the included dummies are interpreted as the *incremental* effects of the conditions represented by the included dummies, compared with the condition of the omitted dummy.

The types of statistical tests that may be applied to coefficients of dummy variables are derived directly from their interpretation. In this section, various dummy variable models of Section 2.1 are reexamined in terms of possible hypothesis testing.

The first model (equation 2.1.1) explained starting teacher salaries as a function of X_1, which is a dummy variable that takes on the value of unity if the teacher had a Master's degree (and zero otherwise). Thus, the coefficient of X_1, β_1, is interpreted as the expected incremental earnings due to the acquisition of the Master's degree, and it is expected to be positive. Loosely speaking, the focus is on whether a Master's degree is statistically significant in producing higher income. Formally, we can only test for parameter values, not for variables. Thus, the hypotheses are formulated according to the coefficient of X_1. Notationally, setting up H_0 as the strawman:

$$H_0: \beta_1 \leqslant 0$$
$$H_A: \beta_1 > 0$$
$$(10.1.26)$$

If the *t*-statistic is greater than the (one-sided) critical value, H_A is accepted, showing the Master's to have proven of positive benefit to expected income, with 90-percent or so confidence.

If X_1 is defined as unity for a Bachelor's degree and zero for a Master's degree (as in equation 2.1.6), then $\hat{\beta}_1$ would be exactly the opposite sign and of the same absolute magnitude as the estimate $\hat{\beta}_1$ in the case in which X_1 represented the Master's degree. Thus, in this case, the alternative hypothesis would be $\beta_1 < 0$. One would accept the statistical significance of $\hat{\beta}_1$ here if and only if one would accept it when X_1 represented the Master's degree.

In equation 2.1.16, X_1 represents the achievement of the Master's degree, and X_2 represents the accomplishment of half of the requirements for this degree. The omitted condition is the Bachelor's degree. Thus, direct tests are available on whether either the Master's or half through the Masters provides, statistically speaking, more income than the Bachelor's degree. Such tests would be one-sided *t*-tests on $\hat{\beta}_1$ and $\hat{\beta}_2$, respectively. It also may be of interest in this model to test whether the whole Master's degree confers a higher initial income than the completion of half the requirements of the degree. Such a test could be conducted by the composite hypotheses:

$$H_0: \beta_1 \leqslant \beta_2$$
$$H_A: \beta_1 > \beta_2$$
$$(10.1.27)$$

The null hypothesis is equivalent to $0 \leqslant \beta_2 - \beta_1$. For all tests involving inequalities, the maximum amount of Type I Error is controlled by using the border restriction, or $0 = \beta_2 - \beta_1$. Thus, equation 10.1.15 can be used with $\delta_0 = 0$, $\delta_1 = -1$, and $\delta_2 = 1$. (Use the translation of the *F*-statistic to a *t*-statistic as noted in Section 10.1.4 to accomplish the one-sided test.) Alternatively, a direct comparison of half through versus full completion of a Master's can be obtained by defining either the Master's degree or the half-through level as the omitted condition (and including a dummy for the Bachelor's degree), such as in the formulation in equation 2.1.23. Then the *t*-test on the included variable is the appropriate, direct test of whether the incremental earnings are statistically significant.

An important point can be made here in reference to the t-statistics of dummy variables. If half through the Master's does not produce a statistically significant difference in initial income, compared with either the Bachelor's degree or the Master's, then when "half through" is the omitted condition, with the variables X_1 and X_2 representing the Bachelor's and Master's degrees, respectively, the estimated coefficients of X_1 and X_2 will not pass the t-test (their t-statistics will be low). But this does *not* imply that the Master's degree is not important because this has not been tested, under this formulation, in comparison with the Bachelor's degree. Another formulation could be used to test for the statistical significance of the Master's *versus* the Bachelor's degree. But this formulation could be used to test whether the degree structure—Bachelor's, Master's, and half through the Master's—is statistically significant. Such a test would be the standard F-test on whether all the coefficients are different from zero. Furthermore, it does not matter which formulation of the dummy variables is used for this overall test (since all equivalent formulations produce the same F-statistic).

It is appropriate also to emphasize at this time that these tests may show, for example, that a Master's degree, loosely speaking, provides a statistically significant higher initial income than a Bachelor's degree does. Yet the estimated coefficients could show that the initial income of a teacher with a Master's can be expected to be $3 more per year than that of one with a Bachelor's degree! Three dollars would hardly seem "significant" and worth the effort required to obtain the degree. Statistical significance refers to the ability to distinguish between the income levels based not nearly so much on the absolute magnitudes of the average income level, but more on the deviations from those levels as observed in the sample, from one teacher to the next. Thus, in all of econometrics, a clear distinction should be made between "*statistical significance*" and "*significance*." The former may not imply the latter. However, statistical significance is usually necessary before one can say that the data and estimation support a conclusion of significance in absolute magnitude. Otherwise, although the mean incomes may be far apart, there is so much variation in income within each group (Bachelor's and Master's) that the researcher cannot systematically and accurately determine initial income levels on the basis of the type of degree alone.

The techniques described above are equivalent to analysis of variance (ANOVA) tests. ANOVA tests examine whether particular conditions have statistically significant effects on a given variable. All ANOVA tests can be conducted equivalently with regression analysis by using the dummy variable approach. The standard F-test from the regression package is equivalent to an ANOVA F-test in the case in which there are no regressors other than dummy variables.

Seasonal dummies, as in equation 2.1.29, if tested, are usually tested as a group (with an F-test) rather than individually (with a series of t-tests). That is, one would test whether the coefficients of all the seasonal dummies are zero, using the approach of equation 10.1.6, rather than applying t-tests on individual coefficients. (Under the constrained estimating equation, the whole set of seasonal dummies is deleted.) A determination can then be made as to whether the whole set of seasonal dummies should be included. But to exclude some of the seasonal dummies because their estimated coefficients have low t-statistics is not recommended. Although it would appear that a degree of freedom is saved by such a deletion, a degree of freedom has, in fact, been used up in the original estimation. And the final result would smack of the stepwise procedure discussed in Section 6.4.2. Usually, where seasonal dummies are called for, no attempt is made to test even for their collective statistical significance.

Multiplicative dummy variables (or interaction terms), that is, dummy variables multiplied by other variables to form new regressors, can be very useful for hypothesis testing. The stop-time example of Section 2.1 is used here to illustrate how to conduct hypothesis testing with this approach. The variable X_4 of equation 2.1.32 was defined as DX_1, where the dummy variable D is unity if the weight of the shipment is greater than a specified weight w^* and zero otherwise, and X_1 is the shipment weight. The intent of including X_4 as a determinant of stop time is to allow the (slope) coefficient of weight to vary depending on whether the shipment is of large or small weight. (Recall that D is included as a separate regressor in order to allow the constant term to shift when the slope coefficient of X_1 shifts.) Thus, the coefficient of X_4, β_4, represents the amount of difference in the slope coefficient of the weight variable when weight is greater than w^*. Since the slope is expected to be less when weight is greater than w^* (due to an economy in shipment handling), whether the economy exists is tested for by a one-sided t-test on β_4. If its t-statistic is negative and greater in absolute value than the critical value t_c, then the alternative hypothesis is accepted that the slope is less when weight is greater than w^*.

10.2   Other Tests

Numerous other tests have been created for other situations. Among these are tests for normality of the error terms, for multicollinearity, for certain types of specification error, and for the functional form of the regression model. In the opinion of the author, these tests should not be applied at the novice level; however, see below for a description of a test for multicollinearity. The primary focus should be on the development of the appropriate theoretical and applied regression models, and most of the emphasis should be on obtaining "reasonable" coefficient estimates. Quite often, suggested fix-up procedures for various maladies are only subterfuges for searches for a better set of estimated coefficients or for a better statistical fit. In this text, the novice is urged to weigh very carefully the use of the standard GLS corrections for autocorrelation and heteroskedasticity that are so popular at the applied level.

Tests for the normality of the error term are usually not carried out even by competent researchers. Rather, the assumption of normality is a working hypothesis, one of the assumptions that is usually left unquestioned. However, when OLS is applied where the dependent variable is a 0-1 dummy variable, it is known that the error term is not normally distributed. The usual tests of significance (the F- and t-tests) have difficulties but may still serve as useful guides in exploratory work. In this case, more advanced techniques are available (such as probit), but often the coefficient estimates and the relative degree of statistical significance do not change much from the OLS results.

Some tests for functional form or other specification errors are now available, but they are not yet standard tools of most applied econometricians. Until they become more widely used and assessed, their use by the beginner is discouraged.

Testing for multicollinearity is not recommended primarily because of the usually arbitrary approaches that may be taken when multicollinearity is suspected to exist. Some of the approaches include the deletion of regressors, which leads to the problems discussed in Sections 6.2–6.4 of missing relevant variables and irrelevant variables. Multicollinearity is usually thought to be a problem in a particular sample, when the regressors have not exhibited sufficient independent movement to provide accurate estimates of their individual effects on the dependent variable.

There is a popular test for multicollinearity called the Farrar-Glauber test.[3] Actually, it is a series of three tests. The first test is for the general presence of multi-collinearity. A chi-square statistic is computed. If it is greater than the critical value found in the chi-square table (A-8) at the end of the text (for a specified level of significance and for $v = 0.5K(K-1)$ degrees of freedom, where K = number of regressors), then multicollinearity is considered "serious." If this first test finds serious multicollinearity, the second test attempts to locate the regressors causing it. For each regressor, a special F-statistic is computed. (This is not to be confused with the F-statistic ordinarily computed by some computer programs for the estimated coefficients instead of the t-statistic.) If the special F-statistic is greater than the critical value (found in the F-table, for a specified level of significance and $K-1$ numerator and $n-K$ denominator degrees of freedom), then the associated variable is judged to be a contributor to the multicollinearity.

The third Farrar-Glauber test attempts to find the pattern of multicollinearity, to refine the second test. If a special t-statistic computed pairwise for two variables is greater than the critical value (found in the t-table for a specified level of significance, for $n-K$ degrees of freedom), then the pair of regressors are suspected of being the source of, in this case, the collinearity. Quite obviously, this third test does not detect the sources of *multi*collinearity.

A rule of thumb that is sometimes used in place of the entire set of Farrar-Glauber tests is: collinearity between two regressors is considered serious if their simple squared coefficient of correlation, r^2, is greater than the coefficient of determination for the entire equation, R^2. But, to reiterate points made previously, one should avoid testing and correcting for multicollinearity, and also one should not blame multicol-linearity for estimates that do not conform to prior expectations.

10.3   Interval Estimation

Up to this point in the text, the emphasis has been on obtaining "point" estimates of the regression coefficients. As was demonstrated repeatedly, a point estimate obtained with a single sample is only one of a whole range of such estimates that could be

---

[3] D. E. Farrar and R. R. Glauber, "Multicollinearity in Regression Analysis," *Review of Economics and Statistics*, Vol. 49, 1967, pp. 92–107.

obtained from different samples. The approach of hypothesis testing uses this fact to establish, prior to estimation, decision rules on whether a given value (or range) of one or more parameters is compatible with the evidence, as provided by the statistics computed from data from a single sample.

10.3.1   Intervals for Parameters

Interval estimation of parameters is a very closely related procedure to hypothesis testing but it is not often used. It uses the evidence provided by a single sample and, with the knowledge that many samples would produce an entire sampling distribution, establishes an interval around the point estimate within which the researcher can be 95-percent confident (or some other assigned level of confidence) that the true value of the parameter lies. The interval so estimated is called a confidence interval. For regression coefficients, it is always the case that, for a given level of confidence, a confidence interval (a) will encompass the null hypothesis (at least the border condition) whenever the (two-sided) null hypothesis is accepted and (b) will not encompass the null hypothesis whenever the null hypothesis is rejected. The basic reason for these conclusions is that the confidence interval is always made the same length as the region of acceptance of the null hypothesis. Consider the simple model $y_i = \beta x_i + \epsilon_i$, the OLS estimate $\hat{\beta}$, and the two-sided hypotheses:

$$H_0: \beta = \beta*$$
$$H_A: \beta \neq \beta* \qquad (10.3.1)$$

The approach of hypothesis testing is to construct an acceptance region around the value in the null hypothesis $\beta = \beta*$, where $\beta*$ is a value specified by the researcher. The interval is:

$$\beta* \pm s_{\hat{\beta}}\, t_c \qquad (10.3.2)$$

where $s_{\hat{\beta}}$ is the estimated standard error of $\hat{\beta}$ and t_c is the critical value of the t-statistic found in the t-table (A-1) for a (two-sided) level of significance α.

The approach of interval estimation provides a symmetric interval, centered on the estimate obtained in a sample instead of on the null hypothesis value of β, within which the researcher can state with $(1 - \alpha)$ (times 100) percent confidence that the true value of β lies. Such an interval can be constructed if it is assumed that $(\hat{\beta}-\beta)/s_{\hat{\beta}}$ has the t-distribution, which was assumed for equation 10.3.2. Then an interval around $\hat{\beta}$ is constructed within which, say, 90 percent of the time the true value of β lies. The confidence interval is thus:

$$\hat{\beta} \pm s_{\hat{\beta}} t_c \qquad (10.3.3)$$

(This interval has the same formulation for a single coefficient in a multiple regression model: $\hat{\beta}_k + s_{\hat{\beta}_k} t_c$.) By comparing equation 10.3.2 with equation 10.3.3, it is seen that $\hat{\beta}$ lies within the acceptance region if and only if $\beta*$ lies within the confidence interval, because the intervals are of exactly the same length.

Confidence intervals for estimated coefficients are not very commonly used in applied work primarily because hypothesis testing accomplishes enough. Perhaps the most important function provided by presenting interval estimates in the documentation of a regression project is to remind the reader of the elementary yet often forgotten fact that the estimate obtained is subject to a margin of error.

10.3.2 Forecast Intervals

Perhaps the most widely used type of interval estimate is that for predicted or forecast values of the dependent variable, as opposed to the interval estimates for the parameters discussed in Section 10.3.1. Since one of the purposes of regression analysis is to forecast the dependent variable in a systematic, consistent manner, providing a confidence interval is perhaps the easiest way to warn the reader that a sampling distribution exists for the predicted value of y, $\hat{y}$, because sampling distributions apply to the estimated regression coefficients, upon which $\hat{y}$ is based.

A forecast value for Y, Y_F, is found by substituting forecast values for the regressors, X_{Fk}, $k = 1, 2, \ldots, K$:

$$Y_F = \hat{\beta}_0 + \hat{\beta}_1 X_{F1} + \hat{\beta}_2 X_{F2} + \cdots + \hat{\beta}_K X_{FK} \tag{10.3.4}$$

A $(1-\alpha)$ (times 100) percent confidence interval for Y_F is:

$$Y_F \pm s_F t_c \tag{10.3.5}$$

where t_c is the critical value of the t-statistic found in the t-table for $n-K-1$ degrees of freedom (two-sided; that is, α is the probability that both positive and negative values of the t-distribution are outside the interval $-t_c < t < t_c$), and s_F is the estimated standard error of the forecast. Because of the complicated formula for s_F when there are many regressors, the confidence interval is not usually given for Y_F in such models. However, for the single-regressor case, s_F is computed as the positive square root of:

$$s_F^2 = s^2 \left[1 + \frac{1}{n} + \frac{(X_F - \bar{X})^2}{\sum_i (X_i - \bar{X})^2} \right] \tag{10.3.6}$$

where s^2 is the estimated variance of the error term, n is the number of observations in the sample, X_F is the forecast value of the single regressor (X) measured in absolute (not deviation-from-the-mean) terms, $\bar{X}$ is the sample arithmetic average for the regressor, and $\sum_i (X_i - \bar{X})^2 = \sum x_i^2$ (i.e., the sum of the squared deviations of the sample observations from their mean).

An examination of equation 10.3.6 shows that the forecast standard error, s_F, is smaller the closer the forecast value for X, X_F, is to the sample mean $\bar{X}$ upon which the equation is based. The forecast standard error increases as X_F deviates from $\bar{X}$, so the confidence interval widens, as shown in Figure 10.3.1. Forecasting outside the sample range is very common, so researchers should be aware of this phenomenon.

Also, the larger is the sample size, n, used to estimate the equation, the smaller is the confidence interval for Y_F. This is one benefit of greater degrees of freedom. In addition, the more the values of X have fluctuated from their mean in the sample, the smaller the confidence interval is. Wider sample fluctuations in X imply that a number of different situations are incorporated when the regression equation is estimated and that the collinearity between X and the constant term (which has a "variable" of unity) is lessened.

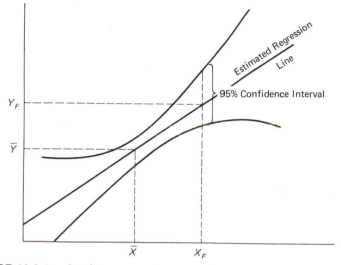

Y_F

$\overline{Y}$

Estimated Regression Line

95% Confidence Interval

$\overline{X}$ X_F

FIGURE 10.3.1   Confidence Interval for Forecast Value of Y (Y_F) Widens as the Forecast Value for X (X_F) Differs from Its Sample Mean ($\overline{X}$)

For reference purposes, the formula for s_F^2 for K regressors is:

$$s_F^2 = s^2 \left\{ 1 + \frac{1}{n} + \frac{1}{s^2} \left[\sum_k (X_{Fk} - \overline{X}_k)^2 s_{\hat{\beta}_k}^2 \right.\right.$$
$$\left.\left. + 2 \sum_{j<k} (X_{Fj} - \overline{X}_j)(X_{Fk} - \overline{X}_k) \,\hat{\text{COV}}(\hat{\beta}_j, \hat{\beta}_k) \right] \right\} \qquad (10.3.7)$$

where X_{Fk} is the forecast value of the kth regressor, and $\hat{\text{COV}}$ ($\hat{\beta}_j, \hat{\beta}_k$) is the estimated covariance of $\hat{\beta}_j$ and $\hat{\beta}_k$. Some computer programs print (as an option) the "estimated variance and covariances of the estimated coefficients," or the "estimated variance-covariance matrix." These can be used in this formula. Even for the two-regressor model, this formula is a bit tedious, and it is not currently standardized on any of the major regression packages.

10.4   *Ex Post* Forecasting

A practice of some econometricians is to withhold some data from the data set used to estimate the regression equation to "validate" the estimated model for this *ex post* set of data. For cross-sectional data, this procedure is suspect since it is usually arbitrary which (and how much) data are withheld from the estimation. For time series, usually the most recent data are withheld under the implicit belief, or so it seems, that, if the estimated equation forecasts well over the most recent period, then it will likely forecast well for the immediate future; i.e., its ability to provide an adequate *ex post* forecast over the withheld data implies that it will provide an adequate *ex ante* forecast for the future. In general, such a procedure is very similar to one in which the equation is estimated using all the data and the residuals for the most recent data periods are examined for reasonableness. In fact, if the *ex post* forecasting procedure is used to select among alternative estimated equations, then the procedure amounts to evaluating equations on the basis of two R^2's (or some other measure(s) of goodness of fit), one for the estimation period (call it R_{EST}^2) and another for the *ex post* forecasting period (call it R_{EXP}^2). The determination of how much data to withhold is usually arbitrary, and it is also usually arbitrary what weights to assign to R_{EXP}^2 *versus* R_{EST}^2. That is, suppose that one form of the equation produces a higher R_{EST}^2 than another but that its R_{EXP}^2 is lower. Selection of the "desired" estimating equation involves another arbitrary assessment on the part of the researcher.

Furthermore, selecting one equation as the "best" one for forecasting, using a criterion of some weighted average of R_{EST}^2 and R_{EXP}^2, is tantamount to using the *ex post* data, correspondingly weighted, in the estimation data set. That is, selecting among equations at least in part on the basis of the *ex post* forecasts implies selecting coefficient estimates on the basis of the *ex post* data. Thus, the *ex post* data indirectly become part of the estimation data set.

Thus, unless the researcher has some extra information that the future (or the prediction interval) will be more like some period in the data set, for most applications there appears to be little reason to exclude data for purposes of estimation.

10.5   Summary of Hypothesis Testing

Chapter 5 developed the notions of hypothesis testing and applied them to testing a single coefficient. Whenever possible, the null hypothesis (H_0) is established as the "strawman," in the sense that the amount of (Type I) error that is expected, by chance, to be made upon rejecting H_0 is kept to some arbitrarily small amount, such as 5 or 10 percent. The 5 or 10 percent is the level of significance and its complement, 95 or 90 percent, is the level of confidence. The decision rule to accept or reject H_0 for a single coefficient is based on the *t*-statistic. A one-sided test is called for when the priors indicate the coefficient to have an expected sign. If the coefficient β is expected to be positive, then the one-sided hypotheses $H_0 : \beta \leq 0$ *versus* $H_A : \beta > 0$ is decided on the basis of the decision rule to accept H_A if $t > t_c$ and reject H_A otherwise. The value of t is computed (by most computer programs) as the estimated coefficient divided by its estimated standard error. The critical value of t, t_c, is found in the *t*-table in Statistical Table A-1 for a specified one-sided level of significance, or confidence. If t turns out to be greater than t_c, then the alternative hypothesis $\beta > 0$ can be accepted with, say, 95-percent confidence that the decision is the correct one (i.e., only 5 percent of the time does the *t*-test have us accept H_A when in fact H_0 is true, just by chance).

Chapter 9 pointed out that the *t*-test is approximately appropriate when applying TSLS (two-stage least squares) on an equation that is part of a simultaneous equations system. Tests on more than one coefficient at a time were discussed in the current chapter. Tests on the values of more than one coefficient, done simultaneously, are called tests on compound hypotheses. Tests on a linear combination of coefficients are called tests on composite hypotheses. Both types of tests can be conducted using the *F*-statistic of equation 10.1.5. The null hypothesis (or its border condition) for each type of test may be viewed as imposing one or more constraints on the multiple linear regression model. Two regressions are estimated, one with and one without the constraints. The F-statistic is formed from the sum of squared residuals from each regression. If the computed F-statistic is greater than the critical value F_c, then the alternative hypothesis is accepted, with a 95-percent or so level of confidence. The critical value for the F-statistic, F_c, is selected by first choosing the desired level of confidence (or significance), and then selecting the appropriate column based on the number of constraints implied by imposing H_0 and then the appropriate row based on the degrees of freedom for the unrestricted regression (see Statistical Tables A-2 and A-3). The F-test can also be used, in conjunction with dummy variables, to test for structural shifts that may occur to behavioral relationships over time or over different samples.

Tests for autocorrelation were discussed in Section 7.2.7. The Durbin-Watson test is the most widely used test for (first-order) autocorrelation of the error term. If the Durbin-Watson statistic, which is usually calculated by the computer regression program, is below the low critical value, d_L, for a given level of significance (which determines which table—A-4, A-5, or A-6—is selected), then the alternative hypothesis of positive autocorrelation is accepted. If the value is greater than the high critical value, d_U, then the null hypothesis of no positive autocorrelation is not rejected. And if the value lies between d_L and d_U, the test is inconclusive. Heuristically, a value of the Durbin-Watson statistic around the value 2 indicates no autocorrelation.

Heteroskedasticity may be tested for in several ways, but the test suggested in Section 8.3 is the Goldfeld-Quandt test. As in testing for autocorrelation, the observations must be given a logical ordering. For autocorrelation, the observations are usually in a time-series sequence. For heteroskedasticity, thought to be more of a problem with cross-section data, the observations have to be ordered according to the magnitude of the variable with which the variance of the error term is suspected to vary. Then the F-statistic for the Goldfeld-Quandt test is computed as the ratio of the sum of squared residuals for the first or last m observations, whichever observation set is suspected of having the higher variance, to that for the last (or first) m observations, while some observations have been excluded from these two sets as a buffer. If the computed F is greater than the critical value, F_c, then the alternative hypothesis of heteroskedasticity is accepted. The F-table is selected according to the desired level of significance (see Statistical Tables A-2 and A-3), and the critical value comes from the m-K row *and* column.

The Farrar-Glauber test for multicollinearity was discussed in Section 10.2. This test attempts to assess whether there is serious multicollinearity and, if there is, what the pattern or source of it is. This test is not recommended for beginners.

Statistical tests are often misused. Perhaps the most blatant misuse by applied researchers is when one estimated coefficient is tested via a t-test only after some regression experiments have been conducted before the test. These regression experiments involve estimating alternative formulations of the model, such as using different functional forms or different regressors. As was illustrated in Section 6.4.2, conducting a t-test, or any other test for that matter, sequentially after other experiments or tests are conducted negates the statistical basis upon which the critical values of the test statistics are founded.

Unfortunately, first-time regression results are usually far from what we would like them to be, and corrective actions of one kind or another are usually called for. These actions are called the ''artistic'' elements of applied regression analysis, and the final chapter is devoted to some of these elements. However, the researcher should be aware of the tenuous nature of the estimated results when a number of regression experiments have to be conducted.

Another point worth making is that the t-test is not appropriate when any one of the classical assumptions is violated. When any one of them is violated, either the numerator or the denominator of the t-statistic, or both, is biased. Thus, for all these reasons, applied researchers should probably rely less on the t-test than appears to be the custom.

11 Artistic Elements of Econometrics

The first section below reviews the properties of the estimators discussed in this text. The "properties" are attributes displayed by the sampling distribution of the estimator, for small or large sample sizes. The primary properties examined in this text are unbiasedness and minimum variance. However, the minimum mean square error criterion was also used throughout the text, starting with Chapter 6. An estimator may exhibit some biasedness but be better in an MSE sense because the estimates generated by its particular formula (or estimation approach) are more likely to be near the true parameter value than those from an unbiased estimator are. In fact, even assuming the classical assumptions (stated in Chapter 4), the ridge estimator of Section 11.5 expressly trades off biasedness for a lower variance in the attempt to obtain an MSE lower than that of OLS, using the identical estimating model. The ridge estimator, the formula for which is different from the OLS formula, attempts to counteract the adverse effects on variance due to multicollinearity.

Section 11.4 below demonstrates a crude method that may be applied to estimate equations that are inherently nonlinear in the parameters. This technique is not recommended, but in some circumstances it may be useful.

Section 11.2 presents a "Regression Mechanic's Guide," which is intended to answer, in summary fashion, the major econometric questions: What can go wrong when estimating an equation? What damage do the various maladies do to OLS estimates? How can the maladies be detected and corrected?

Section 11.3 is a "Regression Mechanic's Checklist," designed to assist first-time users of regression analysis through the various steps of analysis.

The word "mechanic" in both Sections 11.2 and 11.3 is really a double-entendre. Applied econometrics is far from being an exact science, so mechanically applied fix-ups of deficiencies are not appropriate. More times than not, the best planned and executed regression analysis will not produce the expected set of estimated coefficients and the accompanying statistics the first time it is applied. Most likely, something is deficient. When this happens econometrics becomes an art. There is a fine line between curve fitting and searching for the truth by formulating and estimating alternative regression equations or using alternative estimating techniques. Unfortunately, many of the regression results reported in the scholarly literature may very well be fabricated, in the sense that the results shown were strictly a product of chance. What may have happened is that the researchers experimented with a number of models and estimators until they obtained their desired results. Such an approach is not scientific. Many facets, such as the following, often go unreported: which combinations of regressors were tried in other regression experiments? were other definitions of variables used? were certain dummy variables introduced in order to reduce the magnitude of some of the residuals? were other functional forms tried? or were other estimating techniques employed? As was demonstrated in Chapter 6 with a simple stepwise procedure, reported test statistics no longer have their standard interpretation after one or more prior regression experiments have been applied to guide the formulation of the final regression equation. And since the number of possible experiments and the order in which they can be performed are practically endless, it would be extremely difficult to make applied econometrics an exact science.[1]

The core of the problem is that we never know what the true model is. In this text, Monte Carlo simulations were used to evaluate various econometric approaches. Examples of regression analyses from the scholarly literature, on the other hand, can only demonstrate possible estimation approaches to be applied in particular situations. But we never know if these approaches are correct because the true model is never known. When the researcher sets out to investigate a particular problem that involves or uses regression analysis, the literature should be examined critically. Are the reasons put forth for a given regression approach sufficient or appropriate? (Are *any* reasons put forth?) Do any of the techniques applied appear to be ruses for curve fitting? Would alternative approaches, especially different formulations of the model (including different regressors), be more appropriate? These are among the questions that a critical reader should ask, with the knowledge that the writer never saw the true regression model, so the reported results may very well have some flaws. Whether the flaws are major enough has taken up a large portion of the scholarly debate concerning the applied econometrics literature.

11.1   Review of the Properties of the Estimators

Under the classical assumptions, when none of the maladies outlined in the following section applies, OLS (ordinary least squares) estimators of the coefficients in the single-equation model are BLUE (Best, Linear, Unbiased Estimators). They are linear functions of y and thus of the β's in the linear single equation model. They are unbiased; that is, their sampling distributions are centered on the true values of the

---

[1] These points were forcefully made by Thomas Mayer, "Economics as a Hard Science: Realistic Goal or Wishful Thinking?" *Economic Inquiry,* April 1980, pp. 169–78.

parameters. And they are the best estimates, meaning that any other unbiased estimator has a sampling distribution with at least as large a variance, or dispersion, about the central tendency.

Another popular estimating technique is maximum likelihood estimators (MLEs). To use this technique, the probability distribution of the error term must be specified. For the classical *normal* model, MLEs are identical to the OLS coefficient estimators. Thus, MLEs are, in this case, BLUE. In general, MLEs are not unbiased, but they have favorable asymptotic properties (properties that hold when the sample size goes to infinity). Even though econometricians most often deal with small samples, these properties may be somewhat of a comfort. As the sample size becomes ''very large'' (tends toward infinity), the properties possessed by MLEs are: (1) consistency—in a mean square error sense, the MSE tends to zero; (2) asymptotic efficiency—the sampling distribution eventually has the smallest possible variance; and (3) asymptotic normality—the sampling distribution approaches a normal distribution.

MLEs are often applied to complicated situations, especially when one or more of the classical assumptions are violated. The search procedure for correcting for autocorrelation, discussed in Section 7.2.4, is equivalent to an MLE approach. Thus, it has these desirable asymptotic properties. Most applied regression users may apply MLEs, but few are likely to be able to construct a new MLE formula for a new empirical problem, because constructing these estimators is usually a difficult analytic chore.

The TSLS (two-stage least squares) and IV (instrumental variables) estimators for the simultaneous equations model are not in general MLEs although MLEs have been constructed for this model. The TSLS and IV estimators are not unbiased, but they are consistent. For the simultaneous equations problem, unbiased estimators have not been derived, so consistency is normally considered ''the only game in town.'' However, concern over MSE and testing procedures may be relevant and may lead to the choice of DLS (direct least squares) over TSLS in some instances.

The Aitken (or Zellner) two-step estimates for seemingly unrelated regressions are asymptotically more efficient than OLS estimators.

When the various maladies or violations of the classical assumptions apply, as summarized in Section 11.2, the OLS estimators are either biased or inefficient (i.e., their sampling distributions do not have the lowest possible variance of all unbiased estimators). If they are either biased or inefficient, the statistical tests of hypotheses are biased, either toward or against the rejection of the null hypothesis. It is usually impossible to tell *a priori* the direction of the bias in hypothesis testing, even for the inefficiency case. When normality does not hold, the *t*- and *F*-tests no longer apply exactly.

The emphasis in this text is to correct most maladies by correcting, if possible, the specification of the model, e.g., by finding the missing relevant variable or imposing the correct functional form. However, in some cases, it is not possible to do so, and estimation techniques other than OLS may have to be applied. Such techniques discussed in the text are TSLS, the Aitken (or Zellner) two-step procedure, and the GLS approaches for correcting for autocorrelation and heteroskedasticity. The general warning about applying techniques other than OLS instead of fixing up the structure of the equations applies especially to the GLS fix-up procedure for autocorrelation.

With the computer, such corrections are very easily and rather mechanically applied; thus, researchers generally do not investigate the appropriateness of correcting structural deficiencies, although they should seriously consider such an approach.

11.2   A Regression Mechanic's Guide

Table 11.2.1 is a brief summary of the major maladies discussed in this text: what they are, what damage they cause to OLS estimates, how to detect them, and what to do about them. Some of the methods to correct some of the maladies are beyond the scope of this text and are documented in advanced econometric texts.

Reference to further explanation of each item is found in the index. All the classical assumptions are stated in this table, as well as some variants of them. The table is brief, but self-explanatory. For example, the third "malady" is seemingly unrelated regressions. The definition is given in the second column, the consequences *for OLS estimates* in the third column, testing in the fourth, and a corrective procedure in the last column. For seemingly unrelated regressions, no formal test is usually conducted, and the problem is suspected on the basis of a theoretical examination of the equation being estimated that leads to the conclusion that the equation belongs to a set of such equations.

11.3   A Regression Mechanic's Checklist

Table 11.3.1 is a list of possible items to check as the researcher reviews the output from a computer regression package. Not all the items do show up, and some items that show up may not be covered in the table. However, the table can serve as a point of reference; typically, much more analysis and judgment are required than is indicated in the table. In some cases, there are no symbols for the "checkpoint" that is being discussed. Checkpoints are the items that a researcher should look for in reviewing the computer output, such as the signs of the regression coefficients and their t-statistics. The "reference" is a brief explanation of the checkpoint, and the "decision" is the action that may need to be taken if the statistics indicate that something is not adequate. These actions are only suggestive, and their application is among the artistic elements of applied econometrics.

Strict adherence to a set of rules or guidelines is not recommended given the state of the art in econometrics. In the final analysis, applied researchers are nearly always thwarted because they never know for certain what the true model is. The existence of maladies as outlined in Section 11.2 and the element of chance present an effective barrier to the easy application of a set of rules to estimate regression equations.

TABLE 11.2.1

Regression Mechanic's Guide

What Can Go Wrong?	What Is It?	What Are the Consequences for OLS Estimates?	How Can It Be Detected?	How Can It Be Corrected?
1. Linear Dependence among the Regressors (Perfect Multicollinearity)	Some of the regressors are perfectly correlated (occurs most often with inappropriate use of dummy variables).	Regression program will not produce statistics. (Some programs will because of rounding error; then the standard errors are large.)	Regression program will not produce statistics, or, if it does, all the estimated standard errors will be large, even though the R^2 may be high.	Redefine independent variables, or omit one of the variables and interpret the coefficients differently.
2. Simultaneity or "Errors in the Independent Variables" Model	One of the regressors is endogenous, so the regressor and the error term are correlated.	Ordinary least squares gives biased estimates of the coefficients; so do simultaneous equations estimating techniques like TSLS, although they give consistent estimates.	On the basis of theory, usually through analysis of the interaction of supply and demand.	Try ordinary least squares, or specify and estimate a structural model of simultaneous equations, or estimate a reduced-form equation.
3. Seemingly Unrelated Regressions	Error term is correlated with the error term in another equation.	Coefficient estimates are inefficient.	On the basis of theory.	Aitken two-step procedure or 3SLS for simultaneous equations.
4. Autocorrelation	The error terms for different observations are correlated.	The estimates of the coefficients are inefficient. The estimates of the SEE and the standard errors of the estimated coefficients are biased.	Durbin-Watson statistic is different from 2. Can use statistical test on DW, except with the lagged dependent variable as a regressor.	Add appropriate regressors, or change functional form. Make a GLS-type autoregression correction such as CORC.

(continued on following pages)

TABLE 11.2.1 (Continued)

What Can Go Wrong?	What Is It?	What Are the Consequences For OLS Estimates?	How Can It Be Detected?	How Can It Be Corrected?
5. Heteroskedasticity	The variance of the error term is not constant for all observations.	Same as for autocorrelation.	By examining the spread or contraction of the residuals plotted against independent or other variables. A special F-test may be used (the Goldfeld-Quandt test).	Redefine variables such as in percentage change or per capita terms, or apply a GLS correction by dividing all variables (including the constant term) by the square root of the variable (other than the dependent variable—but can use $\hat{Y}$) with which the variance varies. (Add a constant term for estimation.)
6. Multicollinearity	Some of the regressors are (less than perfectly) correlated.	Estimates of the separate effects of the regressors are not reliable, i.e., the estimates lack precision.	Rule of thumb is: when the simple correlation coefficient is greater than R. No universally accepted rule or test is available, although the Farrar-Glauber test is often used.	By better design of experiments, but this may not be possible. Do not modify the functional form unless the theory so indicates. Sometimes elimination of a regressor is useful, but bias is then introduced.
7. Non-Normality	The error terms are not normally distributed.	Estimates of the coefficients may not be efficient. Standard statistical tests are usually only asymptotically appropriate.	Chi-square goodness-of-fit test or the Shapiro and Wilk's W- test. These tests are rarely used.	One usually *assumes* normality. Alternative estimators may be available, such as probit.

8. Specification Error: Inappropriate Formulation of Regression Equation (other than simultaneity).			
a. Suppression of the intercept.	Coefficient estimates and t-statistics are biased.	By examination of the estimated equation.	Intercept term is usually included, since it acts as a "garbage" term for the mean of omitted variables.
b. Omission of a relevant explanatory variable.	To the extent the omitted variable is collinear with the included regressors, coefficient estimates of included regressors are biased and inconsistent, but have lower variance.	On basis of theory, possibly low R^2 or wrong signs of coefficients. Low DW is likely. Advanced tests available.	Include variable, or a proxy or a qualitative variable. Sometimes CORC may lower the bias and the MSE.
c. Misspecification of a variable.	Coefficient estimates are biased and inconsistent.	On basis of theory, and possibly wrong signs of coefficients.	Find a better measure or proxy.
d. Inclusion of an irrelevant variable.	To the extent of collinearity, variance of included coefficients are increased and biased upward.	On basis of theory, or test whether coefficient(s) is statistically significant.	Delete variable if its inclusion is not required by theory, does not change other coefficient estimates, and the $\bar{R}^2$ decreases upon its inclusion (i.e., a "superfluous" variable).
e. Nonlinearity: the functional form is not linear.	Estimates are biased and inconsistent. Possibly misleading interpretation of the coefficients, possibly a poor statistical fit.	On basis of theory, plotting dependent variable against the independent variables, low R^2 and high SEE, DW low. Can use von Neumann Ratio test, or Ramsey test.	Transform the variables to linear regressor terms, or fit a nonlinear form by a nonlinear estimation technique.
f. Incorrect selection of an additive or a multiplicative form for the error term.	Estimates are biased and inconsistent.	On basis of theory. This problem is rarely discovered or treated.	Use correct form and estimate appropriately.

(continued on following page)

267

TABLE 11.2.1 (Continued)

What Can Go Wrong?	What Is It?	What Are the Consequences for OLS Estimates?	How Can It Be Detected?	How Can It Be Corrected?
9. Uncontrolled Type II Error.	In hypothesis testing, the null hypothesis is the one the researcher wants accepted.	Level of error is not known when null hypothesis is accepted (always true).	On basis of theory.	Switch null and alternative hypotheses, but sometimes this is not possible (as when testing $\beta_k = 1$, or with a χ^2 Goodness-of-fit test).

Source: The original version of this table appeared in Henry J. Cassidy and John J. Valentini, ''A Guide to Regression Analysis,'' Research Working Paper No. 27, Office of Economic Research, Federal Home Loan Bank Board, Washington, D.C., November 1972.

TABLE 11.3.1

Regression Mechanic's Checklist

Symbol	Checkpoint	Reference	Decision
N. A.	Data	Check quality of the data relative to their theoretical measurement. Check for data errors in computer printout of the data. Spot check transformations of variables.	Correct any errors. If the quality of the data is poor, may want to avoid regression analysis or to use just OLS.
N. A.	Degrees of freedom	$n - K - 1 > 0$ n = number of observations K = number of regressors	If $n - K - 1 \leq 0$, equation cannot be estimated, and if the degrees of freedom is low, precision is low. In such a case, may want to include more observations or use fewer regressors.
$\hat{\beta}$	Coefficient signs and magnitudes	Compare to expected values.	If they are incorrect for the major regressors, respecify model if appropriate or assess other statistics for possible corrective procedures for various maladies.
t	t-statistic $t_k = \dfrac{\hat{\beta}_k - \beta_k^*}{\hat{\sigma}_{\hat{\beta}_k}}$ (or $(F)^{\frac{1}{2}}$ for each coefficient)	Two-sided test: $H_0: \beta_k = \beta_k^*$ $H_A: \beta_k \neq \beta_k^*$ One-sided test: $H_0: \beta_k \leq \beta_k^*$ $H_A: \beta_k > \beta_k^*$ β_k^* is supplied by the researcher and is zero for the t-statistic supplied by the computer.	Reject H_0 if $|t_k| > t_c$ t_c is the critical value found in the t-table for α level of significance (the column in the table) and $n - K - 1$ degrees of freedom (the row). The estimate must be of the correct sign to accept H_A.

(continued on following pages)

TABLE 11.3.1 (Continued)

Symbol	Checkpoint	Reference	Decision
R^2	Coefficient of Determination	Shows heuristically the degree of overall statistical fit of the model to the data.	If R^2 is too low (lower for cross-section data), may need more model development, but better use F-test below. If too high, such as 0.98, probably have spurious correlation. May want to include "TIME" to detrend the variables, or may want to measure variables as percentage changes or growth rates.
$\bar{R}^2$	R^2 adjusted for degrees of freedom	Same as R^2. Also attempts to show the contribution of an additional regressor.	A regressor is superfluous and may be excluded if theory is unclear as to its inclusion, other coefficients do not change much when it is included, and the $\bar{R}^2$ falls when it is included.
F	F-Statistic	To test $H_0: \beta_1 = \beta_2 = \cdots = \beta_K = 0$ $H_A: H_0$ not true	Reject H_0 if $F > F_c$ where F_c is the critical value found in the F-Table for α level of significance and K numerator (for the column designation in the table) and $n\text{-}K\text{-}1$ denominator (for the row designation) degrees of freedom.
		Can construct special F-statistic to test compound and composite hypotheses.	

TABLE 11.3.1 (Continued)

Symbol	Checkpoint	Reference	Decision
e_i	Residuals	Check for transcription errors.	Correct the data.
		Check for autocorrelation and heteroskedasticity by examining the pattern of the residuals.	If evidence is clear, may want to take appropriate (but not necessarily mechanical) corrective action, or may want to test first.
SEE (or s or $\hat{\sigma}_\epsilon$)	Standard error of the equation	An estimate of σ_ϵ. Compare with $\bar{Y}$ for heuristic measure of overall degree of fit.	Just a heuristic guide to the overall fit.
SST (or TSS)	Total sum of squares	$$SST = \sum_{i=1}^{n} (Y_i - \bar{Y})^2$$	No direct use. Usually found in an "Analysis of Variance" table; used to compute F-statistic.
SSR (or RSS)	Regression sum of squares	$$SSR = \sum_{i=1}^{n} (\hat{Y}_i - \bar{Y})^2$$	Same as above.
SSE (or ESS) (in some references, RSS)	Residual sum of squares	$$SSE = \sum_{i=1}^{n} (Y_i - \hat{Y}_i)^2$$ $$= SEE^2 (n\text{-}K\text{-}1)$$	Same as above. Also used in hypothesis testing.
$\hat{\sigma}_{\hat{\beta}_k}$ (or $s_{\hat{\beta}_k}$)	Standard error of $\hat{\beta}_k$	Used in t-statistic.	A "rule of thumb" is if $\|\hat{\beta}_k\| > 2\hat{\sigma}_{\hat{\beta}_k}$ reject H_0: $\beta_k = 0$, accept H_A: $\beta_k \neq 0$.
BETA	The "BETA coefficient"	Attempts to show relative importance of regressors, adjusted for "standard" movements in the variables.	Highest BETA implies most important variable. Can use t-statistic instead. No measure of relative importance is satisfactory when there is multicollinearity.
R^2 Change or R^2 Delete		Shows the contribution to the R^2 of individual regressors.	Similar to BETA coefficient.

(continued on following pages)

TABLE 11.3.1 (Continued)

Symbol	Checkpoint	Reference	Decision
DW	Durbin-Watson statistic	Tests: H_0: $\rho \leq 0$ $\quad\quad H_A$: $\rho > 0$	Reject H_0 if DW $< d_L$. Accept H_0 if DW $> d_u$. Inconclusive if $d_L \leq$ DW $\leq d_U$ (d_L and d_U are the critical values of the Durbin-Watson statistic found in the Table). See ''Regression Mechanic's Guide'' for correction.
h	Durbin's h-statistic	Test for autocorrelated error term when there are lagged dependent variables.	If $h > N_\alpha$, positive autocorrelation is indicated, where N_α is the critical value found in the Standard Normal Table for α level of significance (A-7).
ρ (or $\hat{\rho}$)	Estimated (first-order) autocorrelation coefficient	Usually the estimate provided by CORC or some other autoregressive fix-up routine.	N.A.
r_{ij}	Coefficient of correlation between regressors X_i and X_j	Examines collinearity.	As a rule of thumb, if $r_{ij}^2 > R^2$, suspect serious multicollinearity. See ''Regression Mechanic's Guide'' for correction, if any.
χ^2 (and other statistics)	Farrar-Glauber test	Examines multicollinearity.	Serious multicollinearity is suspected if χ^2 is greater than the critical value of the chi-squared statistic in the Table for $v = 0.5K$ $(K-1)$ degrees of freedom (K = number of regressors). Other Farrar-Glauber tests to locate the source of the multicollinearity. See ''Regression Mechanic's Guide'' for correction, if any.

TABLE 11.3.1 (Continued)

Symbol	Checkpoint	Reference	Decision
r_{ky}	Simple coefficient of correlation between regressor X_k and Y	Not of much use given the multivariate nature of most regression equations. For a single regressor, $r_{1y}^2 = R^2$, and $\hat{\beta}_1 = r_{1y}\Sigma y_i^2/\Sigma x_i^2$.	N.A.
$r_{ky.1,\ 2,\ ...,\ (k-1),}$ $_{(k+1),\ ...,\ K}$	Partial correlation coefficient between regressor X_k and Y "holding the other regressors constant"	It adjusts r_{ky} for the other regressors, holding them constant as in the concept of $\hat{\beta}_k$. As with all coefficients of correlation, it must lie in the interval $[-1, 1]$.	Sometimes these can be of the opposite sign from $\hat{\beta}_k$. Thus, they sometimes represent additional evidence of a relationship different from that shown by $\hat{\beta}_k$.
N.A.	Stepwise regression	Computes regression equation in steps, adding or deleting regressors according to their relative contribution to the R^2.	Priors should be strong enough not to use it. Biases estimates. Ultimate set of regressors arbitrary. t-test no longer valid. Sometimes justified on the basis of too many regressors that form a "shopping list."
N.A.	Almon lag or polynomial distributed lag	One or more regressors are specified to have a distributed lag effect on Y. This technique imposes constraints on that lag structure in the form of a polynomial.	Avoid its use since it usually represents a "search for fit." If it is used, must specify the length of the lag (L), the degree of the polynomial $(p \leq L)$, and whether "zero constraints" will be applied at the beginning or end of the lag structure, or both.
ARIMA	Integrated autoregressive, moving average process, or Box-Jenkins	Usually applied to a single variable as it relates to its previous values. (Can be applied to the error term and the residuals.)	It may be useful for extrapolation, but it does not "explain" behavior.

11.4   Nonlinear Estimation

Many econometric software firms rent programs that will estimate and solve nonlinear equations and nonlinear systems of equations. *Solution* refers to solving the equation(s) for the dependent or endogenous variable(s) (1) given values of the predetermined variables (exogenous and lagged dependent variables), (2) given estimates of the coefficients, and (3) usually assuming that the error terms are zero. For systems of equations, especially nonlinear ones, such a computer program is invaluable.

In order to solve for the endogenous variables, estimates must be found for the coefficients. Most programs that *estimate* nonlinear equations use the OLS principle of minimizing the sum of the squared residuals.[2] However, this section presents a repetitive application of the standard OLS routine that can be used to estimate a non-linear equation. The method is one of searching for the parameter values that minimize the standard error of the equation, which is the same as minimizing the sum of squared residuals. Take, for example, the following equation, which is nonlinear in the coefficients and not amenable to OLS:

$$y_i = \beta_1 x_{1i}^{\beta_3} + \beta_2 x_{2i}^{\beta_4} + \epsilon_i \qquad (11.4.1)$$

Suppose it is known that β_3 and β_4 are integers between 1 and 11. Then, depending on the accuracy desired, the researcher supplies various values for β_3 and β_4, computes $x_{1i}^{\beta_3}$ and $x_{2i}^{\beta_4}$, forming new variables, and estimates their coefficients β_1 and β_2 by OLS. The researcher searches for that OLS equation with the lowest SEE. Table 11.4.1 is an example of the application of this search technique, showing some of the SEE's so computed.

TABLE 11.4.1

Tabulated SEE's (Standard Errors of the Equation)

| | | Assumed β_4 Values | | | | | |
		4	5	6	7	8	9	10
	1	51.8	11.6	43.1	1.5	36.7	8.0	32.6
	2	51.7	11.4	43.0	2.2	36.6	8.3	32.4
Assumed	3	51.7	11.6	43.0	0.936	36.7	8.0	32.6
β_3	4	51.9	11.6	43.3	2.2	37.0	8.4	32.9
Values	5	51.7	11.6	43.1	0.928*	36.8	8.1	32.8
	6	51.9	11.6	43.3	2.1	37.1	8.5	33.0
	7	51.7	11.6	43.2	1.1	36.9	8.2	32.9

*Minimum SEE

---

[2] This general approach is discussed in Henri Theil, *Principles of Econometrics* (New York: John Wiley and Sons, 1971), pp. 417–423. He claims to have depended on P. J. Dhrymes, "Efficient Estimation of Distributed lags with Autocorrelated Errors," *International Economic Review*, 10, 1969, pp. 47–67.

As may be seen in Table 11.4.1, the regression when $\beta_3 = 5$ and $\beta_4 = 7$ produced the lowest SEE. Note that the SEE has in this instance a tendency to increase and decrease from one regression run to the next. In fact, $\beta_3 = 3$ and $\beta_4 = 7$ produced an SEE almost as low as the minimum. For the selected values $\beta_3 = 5$ and $\beta_4 = 7$, the OLS estimates of β_1 and β_2 are -0.40 and 1.0, respectively.

This illustration was the first simulation of 500 that were performed in a Monte Carlo experiment, in which $\beta_1 = -1$, $\beta_2 = 1$, $\beta_3 = 3$, and $\beta_4 = 7$. Table 11.4.2 shows the mean simulation estimates for these parameters, along with their variances, biases, and MSEs. For this particular case, the OLS search procedure appears to produce relatively unbiased estimates with low variances. Only the estimate of β_3 has bias and a possibly significant variance. Canned nonlinear regression packages give estimates of the standard errors of β_3 and β_4, but such estimates are not generally available for the beginner using the search technique. If finer estimates of β_3 and β_4 are desired, if they were not integers, then smaller increments such as 0.2 could be used about the OLS-search estimates of $\beta_3 = 5$ and $\beta_4 = 7$ found in the rough search of Table 11.4.1. Also, if one of the estimates of β_3 and β_4 had been found to equal unity (i.e., on the border of the assumed interval), either the *a priori* notions of the bounds of β_3 and β_4 should be enforced or the search should take place beyond the specified range.

The data used in this experiment were the same as used in Chapter 7 (with the autocorrelation in the regressors equaling zero). The experiment reported here used data for X_1 and X_2 that had a zero sample correlation. An experiment with values of X_1 and X_2 that had a 0.95 degree of sample correlation produced nearly identical results. (But the estimate of β_3 had, in this case, a larger variance, 0.70, a smaller bias, 0.14, and a larger MSE, 0.72.)

TABLE 11.4.2

Monte Carlo Results for $y = \beta_1 x_1^{\beta_3} + \beta_2 x_2^{\beta_4} + \epsilon$

Coefficient	Assumed True Value	Mean Estimates	Variance	Bias	MSE
β_1	-1	-0.94	0.06	0.06	0.06
β_2	1	1.00	0.00	0.00	0.00
β_3	3	3.22	0.44	0.22	0.49
β_4	7	7.00	0.00	0.00	0.00

In practice, standard computer packages can be used. Data transformations are usually required to set up each regression run. The number of regression runs will be less and the accuracy of the procedure will be improved if priors are established on the ranges of all the coefficients for which no direct OLS estimates are available. Also, be aware that *local* minimum SEE's are possible; search thoroughly for the *global* minimum. (In the example shown in Table 11.4.1., $\beta_3 = 3$ and $\beta_4 = 7$ produced a local minimum because all the SEE's surrounding it were larger. However, the global minimum was for $\beta_3 = 5$ and $\beta_4 = 7$.)

In summary, inherently nonlinear estimation can be carried out by repeated applications of OLS, searching for the minimum sum of squared residuals or standard error of the equation. Given the model, the steps to follow are:

1. Determine possible values for the parameters that will not be estimated by OLS.

2. Determine the degree of accuracy desired for the purpose of specifying the number of values to be used for each parameter specified in step 1.

3. Compute the appropriate transformed regressors as determined by the first two steps.

4. Estimate all the regressions by OLS, using all the combinations of the variables computed in step 3.

Be careful to execute the last step thoroughly because in some cases a minimum SEE will appear that will not be the lowest value for all possible combinations of the inherently nonlinear parameter values.

11.5   Ridge Regression

This final section is more of an extension of regression analysis (along its frontier) than an artistic element of applied econometrics. However, given the current state of art, there are some artistic elements in selecting the ridge estimator instead of the OLS estimator. The type of ridge regressor shown here, however, provides for a unique set of coefficient estimates, whereas many ridge estimators currently in existence do not.

The ridge estimator is first introduced and its rationale explained. Then, some Monte Carlo results are shown that indicate that this particular ridge regressor shows some promise for regression applications.

Consider the two-regressor model:

$$y_i = \beta_1 x_{1i} + \beta_2 x_{2i} + \epsilon_i \qquad (11.5.1)$$

The variables are in deviation-from-the-mean form and ϵ_i is a classical normal error term. The OLS estimator of β_1 may be written as:

$$\hat{\beta}_1 = \frac{\Sigma x_1 y}{\Sigma x_1^2} \left[\frac{1 - r_{12} r_{2y}/r_{1y}}{1 - r_{12}^2} \right] \qquad (11.5.2)$$

where r_{12} is the simple correlation coefficient between x_1 and x_2, and r_{jy} is that between x_j and y. It is known that if r_{12}^2 approaches unity, the variance of β_1 becomes very large. This is epitomized by the factor $1 - r_{12}^2$ in the denominator of equation 11.5.2, which approaches zero when r_{12}^2 approaches unity. (That is, very large positive and negative values of $\hat{\beta}_1$ are then likely because the variance is very large. See also the equations of the variances, equations 4.3.4 and 4.3.5.)

Ridge estimates explicitly introduce bias in order to reduce the variance of the estimates of β_1 (and of β_2), with the intention of reducing the mean square error below that of the OLS estimators. A positive factor k (appropriately scaled) is introduced into the denominator of equation 11.5.2 in order to avoid low values associated with high magnitudes of collinearity between x_1 and x_2. Also, the factor k is introduced in the numerator of equation 11.5.2.

The general ridge estimator is:

$$\beta_1(k) = \frac{\Sigma x_1 y}{\Sigma x_1^2} \left(\frac{1 - r_{12}r_{2y}/r_{1y} + k/\Sigma x_2^2}{1 - r_{12}^2 + k(k+\Sigma x_1^2+\Sigma x_2^2)/(\Sigma x_1^2 \Sigma x_2^2)} \right) \qquad (11.5.3)$$

Thus, a positive value is added to the denominator of equation 10.5.2: $k > 0$, and Σx_1^2 and Σx_2^2 are greater than zero. If $k = 0$, then equation 11.5.3 becomes the OLS estimator, equation 11.5.2.

The major problem with the ridge approach lies in selecting a nonarbitrary, unique value for k. Of course, researchers could select the value of k after searching for that value that produced the desired estimated coefficients. This is curve fitting and should be avoided. Most advocates of ridge regression have offered suggestions on how to select a unique value of k. This section uses one such procedure, suggested by Swamy, Mehta, and Rappoport, called (by them) SMR-II.[3] For completeness, the formula for their suggested selection of k is written here. Let $k = 2s^2/k'$, where s^2 is the variance of the error term as estimated by OLS on equation 10.5.1. Then:

$$k' = (B \pm (B^2 + 4C)^{1/2})/2 \qquad (11.5.4)$$

where

$$B = b_1^2 + b_2^2 - s^2(\Sigma x_1^2 + \Sigma x_2^2)/D \qquad (11.5.5)$$

$$C = \frac{s^2}{D}(b_1^2 \Sigma x_1^2 + b_2^2 \Sigma x_2^2 + 2b_1 b_2 \Sigma x_1 \Sigma x_2 - s^2) \qquad (11.5.6)$$

$$D = \Sigma x_1^2 \Sigma x_2^2 - (\Sigma x_1 x_2)^2 \qquad (11.5.7)$$

and b_1 and b_2 are the OLS estimates of β_1 and β_2.

It turns out that, in general, there is only one value of k' from equation 11.5.4 that is positive (the other solution is negative). Thus, this procedure selects a unique value for k' and hence for k.

Table 11.5.1 reports the results of a limited set of Monte Carlo simulations. The SMR-II ridge estimator performs about as well as the OLS estimator when no collinearity exists between x_1 and x_2, but it performs better for nonzero collinearity, with a lower MSE at the expense of some bias. Individual researchers should assess whether the gain in MSE is worth the bias. It would appear from these results (and others—see Footnote 3) that the SMR-II ridge estimator is worth considering in applications. It should be noted, however, that hypothesis testing is difficult with ridge estimators, given the present state of the art.

---

[3] P.A.V.B. Swamy, J.S. Mehta, and P.N. Rappoport, "Two Methods of Evaluating Hoerl and Kennard's Ridge Regression," *Communications in Statistics: Part A—Theory and Method*, A7(12), 1978, pp. 1133–55. The ridge estimator used here is defined by their equations 27 and 28, with their factor $c_1 = 1$. I thank Dr. Swamy for his assistance with this formulation.

TABLE 11.5.1

Relative MSE and BIAS of a Ridge Estimator

		Ratio of Ridge MSE to OLS MSE	Percentage Bias of Ridge Estimate
	0	1.06	−8%
Degree of Correlation of	0.4	0.86	−7%
X_1 and X_2	0.8	0.66	−12%
(r_{12}^2)	0.9	0.61	−23%
	0.95	0.46	−30%

NOTES: The true model is $y_i = \beta_1 x_{1i} + \beta_2 x_{2i} + \epsilon_i$, where $\beta_1 = 1$, $\beta_2 = 1$, and $\sigma_\epsilon^2 = 1$. The data for x_1 and x_2 were generated from the standard normal distribution having a given degree of correlation (see Chapter 7). The data in the table are for estimates of β_1; similar results apply to estimates of β_2. Twenty observations were used, but similar results apply up through 50 observations. (3000 Monte Carlo drawings were taken.)

Statistical Tables

The following tables present the critical values of various statistics used primarily for hypothesis testing. The primary applications of each statistic are explained and illustrated. The tables are:

Table A-1: The t-Distribution

The t-distribution is applied by regression users primarily to test whether a regression coefficient (say, β_k) is different from a specified number (such as β_k^*). (See Section 10.3 for its use in constructing confidence intervals.) The t-statistic is computed as $t = (\hat{\beta}_k - \beta_k^*)/s_{\hat{\beta}_k}$, where $\hat{\beta}_k$ is the estimate of β_k and $s_{\hat{\beta}_k}$ is its estimated standard error. The computed value of t is compared with the critical value of t, found in the t-table on the opposite page, called t_c. The level of significance of the test is α. To test the one-sided hypotheses:

$$H_0: \ \beta_k \leq \beta_k^*$$
$$H_A: \ \beta_k > \beta_k^*$$

select the column with the desired level of significance, α, for a one-sided test, and find the critical value of t corresponding to the appropriate degrees of freedom, n-K-1, where n is the number of observations and K is the number of regressors. If $t > t_c$, reject H_0 and accept H_A; otherwise, do not reject H_0. For example, for a 5-percent level of significance for 15 degrees of freedom, the critical value of t is 1.753. If the computed t is greater that 1.753, accept H_A. In most applications, β_k^* is zero, so, when the computed t is greater than the critical value 1.753, the coefficient estimate $\hat{\beta}_k$ is said to be statistically significant and positive at the 95-percent level of confidence. (Use $t < -t_c$ to accept $H_A: \beta_k < \beta_k^*$.)

For a two-sided test, find the column with the appropriate two-sided level of significance, as indicated in the table, to obtain the critical value of t. For $\alpha = 0.05$ and 15 degrees of freedom as before, the critical value of t is 2.131. In testing:

$$H_0: \ \beta_k = \beta_k^*$$
$$H_A: \ \beta_k \neq \beta_k^*$$

reject H_0 and accept H_A if:

$$|t| > t_c$$

where $|t|$ is the absolute value of t. In the example, reject H_0 if $-2.131 > t$ or $t > 2.131$. If H_0 is rejected, the estimate $\hat{\beta}_k$ is said to be statistically significant at a 95-percent, two-sided level of confidence.

Some computer programs give F-statistics instead of t-statistics for each estimated regression coefficient. The following procedure is suggested because it makes clear whether the test is one sided or two sided. (Alternatively, the F-table could be used with one numerator degree of freedom.) The critical value of the F-statistic for each estimated coefficient is the square of the t-statistic in the appropriate column and row. For example, for a 2.5-percent, one-sided test (or for a 5-percent, two-sided test) and 20 degrees of freedom (n-K-1=20), the critical value of F is $(2.086)^2 = 4.351$. Then $H_0: \beta_k \leq \beta_k^*$ is rejected in favor of $H_A: \beta_k > \beta_k^*$ if the computed F is greater than 4.351, at the 97.5-percent (one-sided) level of confidence (or at a 95-percent, two-sided level of confidence). Notice that the critical F-value is found in the 5-percent F-table for one numerator and 20 denominator degrees of freedom.

TABLE A-1

Critical Values of the *t*-Distribution

Degrees of Freedom		Level of Significance				
	One Sided: Two Sided:	10% 20%	5% 10%	2.5% 5%	1% 2%	0.5% 1%
1		3.078	6.314	12.706	31.821	63.657
2		1.886	2.920	4.303	6.965	9.925
3		1.638	2.353	3.182	4.541	5.841
4		1.533	2.132	2.776	3.747	4.604
5		1.476	2.015	2.571	3.365	4.032
6		1.440	1.943	2.447	3.143	3.707
7		1.415	1.895	2.365	2.998	3.499
8		1.397	1.860	2.306	2.896	3.355
9		1.383	1.833	2.262	2.821	3.250
10		1.372	1.812	2.228	2.764	3.169
11		1.363	1.796	2.201	2.718	3.106
12		1.356	1.782	2.179	2.681	3.055
13		1.350	1.771	2.160	2.650	3.012
14		1.345	1.761	2.145	2.624	2.977
15		1.341	1.753	2.131	2.602	2.947
16		1.337	1.746	2.120	2.583	2.921
17		1.333	1.740	2.110	2.567	2.898
18		1.330	1.734	2.101	2.552	2.878
19		1.328	1.729	2.093	2.539	2.861
20		1.325	1.725	2.086	2.528	2.845
21		1.323	1.721	2.080	2.518	2.831
22		1.321	1.717	2.074	2.508	2.819
23		1.319	1.714	2.069	2.500	2.807
24		1.318	1.711	2.064	2.492	2.797
25		1.316	1.708	2.060	2.485	2.787
26		1.315	1.706	2.056	2.479	2.779
27		1.314	1.703	2.052	2.473	2.771
28		1.313	1.701	2.048	2.467	2.763
29		1.311	1.699	2.045	2.462	2.756
30		1.310	1.697	2.042	2.457	2.750
(Normal) ∞		1.282	1.645	1.960	2.326	2.576

Source: Reprinted from Table IV in Sir Ronald A. Fisher, *Statistical Methods for Research Workers,* 14th ed. (copyright © 1970, University of Adelaide) with permission of the Macmillan Publishing Company, Inc.

Tables A-2 and A-3: The *F*-Distribution

The following two tables give the critical values for the F-statistic. The first one is for a 5-percent level of significance, and the second one is for a 1-percent level of significance. The F-statistic is used for testing only two-sided alternatives. Its primary use in the text was for testing hypotheses on more than one coefficient at a time (Chapter 10). The F-statistic has two types of "degrees of freedom," one for the numerator, shown in the column heading, and one for the denominator, shown in the row heading. Linear interpolations may be used when the degrees of freedom shown are not exactly the degrees of freedom needed.

As an example of its use, suppose one wished to test whether all the slope coefficients in a regression equation were zero. The hypotheses are:

$$H_0: \beta_1 = \beta_2 = \cdots = \beta_k = 0.$$

$$H_A: H_0 \text{ is not true.}$$

There are K numerator (the number of restrictions implied by the null hypothesis) and n-K-1 denominator degrees of freedom, where K is the number of regressors and n is the number of sample observations of the variables. For $K=5$ and $n=30$, for example, there are 5 numerator and $30-5-1=24$ denominator degrees of freedom. At a 5-percent level of significance, the critical value of F is 2.62. For this particular hypothesis, the F-statistic is the one usually computed by the regression program for the equation (perhaps in an "Analysis of Variance" section of the computer output). Thus, if the computed F is greater than 2.62, H_0 is rejected in favor of H_A, and the equation as a whole is said to be statistically significant at a 95-percent level of confidence. If the computed F is less than 2.62, the null hypothesis of no linear relationship is not rejected.

Critical Values of the F-Statistic: 5-Percent Level of Significance

ν_1 = degrees of freedom for numerator

ν_2 = degrees of freedom for denominator

ν_2 \ ν_1	1	2	3	4	5	6	7	8	9	10	12	15	20	24	30	40	60	120	∞
1	161	200	216	225	230	234	237	239	241	242	244	246	248	249	250	251	252	253	254
2	18.5	19.0	19.2	19.2	19.3	19.3	19.4	19.4	19.4	19.4	19.4	19.4	19.4	19.5	19.5	19.5	19.5	19.5	19.5
3	10.1	9.55	9.28	9.12	9.01	8.94	8.89	8.85	8.81	8.79	8.74	8.70	8.66	8.64	8.62	8.59	8.57	8.55	8.53
4	7.71	6.94	6.59	6.39	6.26	6.16	6.09	6.04	6.00	5.96	5.91	5.86	5.80	5.77	5.75	5.72	5.69	5.66	5.63
5	6.61	5.79	5.41	5.19	5.05	4.95	4.88	4.82	4.77	4.74	4.68	4.62	4.56	4.53	4.50	4.46	4.43	4.40	4.37
6	5.99	5.14	4.76	4.53	4.39	4.28	4.21	4.15	4.10	4.06	4.00	3.94	3.87	3.84	3.81	3.77	3.74	3.70	3.67
7	5.59	4.74	4.35	4.12	3.97	3.87	3.79	3.73	3.68	3.64	3.57	3.51	3.44	3.41	3.38	3.34	3.30	3.27	3.23
8	5.32	4.46	4.07	3.84	3.69	3.58	3.50	3.44	3.39	3.35	3.28	3.22	3.15	3.12	3.08	3.04	3.01	2.97	2.93
9	5.12	4.26	3.86	3.63	3.48	3.37	3.29	3.23	3.18	3.14	3.07	3.01	2.94	2.90	2.86	2.83	2.79	2.75	2.71
10	4.96	4.10	3.71	3.48	3.33	3.22	3.14	3.07	3.02	2.98	2.91	2.85	2.77	2.74	2.70	2.66	2.62	2.58	2.54
11	4.84	3.98	3.59	3.36	3.20	3.09	3.01	2.95	2.90	2.85	2.79	2.72	2.65	2.61	2.57	2.53	2.49	2.45	2.40
12	4.75	3.89	3.49	3.26	3.11	3.00	2.91	2.85	2.80	2.75	2.69	2.62	2.54	2.51	2.47	2.43	2.38	2.34	2.30
13	4.67	3.81	3.41	3.18	3.03	2.92	2.83	2.77	2.71	2.67	2.60	2.53	2.46	2.42	2.38	2.34	2.30	2.25	2.21
14	4.60	3.74	3.34	3.11	2.96	2.85	2.76	2.70	2.65	2.60	2.53	2.46	2.39	2.35	2.31	2.27	2.22	2.18	2.13
15	4.54	3.68	3.29	3.06	2.90	2.79	2.71	2.64	2.59	2.54	2.48	2.40	2.33	2.29	2.25	2.20	2.16	2.11	2.07
16	4.49	3.63	3.24	3.01	2.85	2.74	2.66	2.59	2.54	2.49	2.42	2.35	2.28	2.24	2.19	2.15	2.11	2.06	2.01
17	4.45	3.59	3.20	2.96	2.81	2.70	2.61	2.55	2.49	2.45	2.38	2.31	2.23	2.19	2.15	2.10	2.06	2.01	1.96
18	4.41	3.55	3.16	2.93	2.77	2.66	2.58	2.51	2.46	2.41	2.34	2.27	2.19	2.15	2.11	2.06	2.02	1.97	1.92
19	4.38	3.52	3.13	2.90	2.74	2.63	2.54	2.48	2.42	2.38	2.31	2.23	2.16	2.11	2.07	2.03	1.98	1.93	1.88
20	4.35	3.49	3.10	2.87	2.71	2.60	2.51	2.45	2.39	2.35	2.28	2.20	2.12	2.08	2.04	1.99	1.95	1.90	1.84
21	4.32	3.47	3.07	2.84	2.68	2.57	2.49	2.42	2.37	2.32	2.25	2.18	2.10	2.05	2.01	1.96	1.92	1.87	1.81
22	4.30	3.44	3.05	2.82	2.66	2.55	2.46	2.40	2.34	2.30	2.23	2.15	2.07	2.03	1.98	1.94	1.89	1.84	1.78
23	4.28	3.42	3.03	2.80	2.64	2.53	2.44	2.37	2.32	2.27	2.20	2.13	2.05	2.01	1.96	1.91	1.86	1.81	1.76
24	4.26	3.40	3.01	2.78	2.62	2.51	2.42	2.36	2.30	2.25	2.18	2.11	2.03	1.98	1.94	1.89	1.84	1.79	1.73
25	4.24	3.39	2.99	2.76	2.60	2.49	2.40	2.34	2.28	2.24	2.16	2.09	2.01	1.96	1.92	1.87	1.82	1.77	1.71
30	4.17	3.32	2.92	2.69	2.53	2.42	2.33	2.27	2.21	2.16	2.09	2.01	1.93	1.89	1.84	1.79	1.74	1.68	1.62
40	4.08	3.23	2.84	2.61	2.45	2.34	2.25	2.18	2.12	2.08	2.00	1.92	1.84	1.79	1.74	1.69	1.64	1.58	1.51
60	4.00	3.15	2.76	2.53	2.37	2.25	2.17	2.10	2.04	1.99	1.92	1.84	1.75	1.70	1.65	1.59	1.53	1.47	1.39
120	3.92	3.07	2.68	2.45	2.29	2.18	2.09	2.02	1.96	1.91	1.83	1.75	1.66	1.61	1.55	1.50	1.43	1.35	1.25
∞	3.84	3.00	2.60	2.37	2.21	2.10	2.01	1.94	1.88	1.83	1.75	1.67	1.57	1.52	1.46	1.39	1.32	1.22	1.00

Abridged from M. Merrington and C. M. Thompson, "Tables of percentage points of the inverted beta (F) distribution," *Biometrika*, Vol. 33, 1943, p. 73. By permission of the *Biometrika* trustees.

TABLE A-3

Critical Values of the F-Statistic: 1-Percent Level of Significance

v_1 = degrees of freedom for numerator

v_2	1	2	3	4	5	6	7	8	9	10	12	15	20	24	30	40	60	120	∞
1	4052	5000	5403	5625	5764	5859	5928	5982	6023	6056	6106	6157	6209	6235	6261	6287	6313	6339	6366
2	98.5	99.0	99.2	99.2	99.3	99.3	99.4	99.4	99.4	99.4	99.4	99.4	99.4	99.5	99.5	99.5	99.5	99.5	99.5
3	34.1	30.8	29.5	28.7	28.2	27.9	27.7	27.5	27.3	27.2	27.1	26.9	26.7	26.6	26.5	26.4	26.3	26.2	26.1
4	21.2	18.0	16.7	16.0	15.5	15.2	15.0	14.8	14.7	14.5	14.4	14.2	14.0	13.9	13.8	13.7	13.7	13.6	13.5
5	16.3	13.3	12.1	11.4	11.0	10.7	10.5	10.3	10.2	10.1	9.89	9.72	9.55	9.47	9.38	9.29	9.20	9.11	9.02
6	13.7	10.9	9.78	9.15	8.75	8.47	8.26	8.10	7.98	7.87	7.72	7.56	7.40	7.31	7.23	7.14	7.06	6.97	6.88
7	12.2	9.55	8.45	7.85	7.46	7.19	6.99	6.84	6.72	6.62	6.47	6.31	6.16	6.07	5.99	5.91	5.82	5.74	5.65
8	11.3	8.65	7.59	7.01	6.63	6.37	6.18	6.03	5.91	5.81	5.67	5.52	5.36	5.28	5.20	5.12	5.03	4.95	4.86
9	10.6	8.02	6.99	6.42	6.06	5.80	5.61	5.47	5.35	5.26	5.11	4.96	4.81	4.73	4.65	4.57	4.48	4.40	4.31
10	10.0	7.56	6.55	5.99	5.64	5.39	5.20	5.06	4.94	4.85	4.71	4.56	4.41	4.33	4.25	4.17	4.08	4.00	3.91
11	9.65	7.21	6.22	5.67	5.32	5.07	4.89	4.74	4.63	4.54	4.40	4.25	4.10	4.02	3.94	3.86	3.78	3.69	3.60
12	9.33	6.93	5.95	5.41	5.06	4.82	4.64	4.50	4.39	4.30	4.16	4.01	3.86	3.78	3.70	3.62	3.54	3.45	3.36
13	9.07	6.70	5.74	5.21	4.86	4.62	4.44	4.30	4.19	4.10	3.96	3.82	3.66	3.59	3.51	3.43	3.34	3.25	3.17
14	8.86	6.51	5.56	5.04	4.70	4.46	4.28	4.14	4.03	3.94	3.80	3.66	3.51	3.43	3.35	3.27	3.18	3.09	3.00
15	8.68	6.36	5.42	4.89	4.56	4.32	4.14	4.00	3.89	3.80	3.67	3.52	3.37	3.29	3.21	3.13	3.05	2.96	2.87
16	8.53	6.23	5.29	4.77	4.44	4.20	4.03	3.89	3.78	3.69	3.55	3.41	3.26	3.18	3.10	3.02	2.93	2.84	2.75
17	8.40	6.11	5.19	4.67	4.34	4.10	3.93	3.79	3.68	3.59	3.46	3.31	3.16	3.08	3.00	2.92	2.83	2.75	2.65
18	8.29	6.01	5.09	4.58	4.25	4.01	3.84	3.71	3.60	3.51	3.37	3.23	3.08	3.00	2.92	2.84	2.75	2.66	2.57
19	8.19	5.93	5.01	4.50	4.17	3.94	3.77	3.63	3.52	3.43	3.30	3.15	3.00	2.92	2.84	2.76	2.67	2.58	2.49
20	8.10	5.85	4.94	4.43	4.10	3.87	3.70	3.56	3.46	3.37	3.23	3.09	2.94	2.86	2.78	2.69	2.61	2.52	2.42
21	8.02	5.78	4.87	4.37	4.04	3.81	3.64	3.51	3.40	3.31	3.17	3.03	2.88	2.80	2.72	2.64	2.55	2.46	2.36
22	7.95	5.72	4.82	4.31	3.99	3.76	3.59	3.45	3.35	3.26	3.12	2.98	2.83	2.75	2.67	2.58	2.50	2.40	2.31
23	7.88	5.66	4.76	4.26	3.94	3.71	3.54	3.41	3.30	3.21	3.07	2.93	2.78	2.70	2.62	2.54	2.45	2.35	2.26
24	7.82	5.61	4.72	4.22	3.90	3.67	3.50	3.36	3.26	3.17	3.03	2.89	2.74	2.66	2.58	2.49	2.40	2.31	2.21
25	7.77	5.57	4.68	4.18	3.86	3.63	3.46	3.32	3.22	3.13	2.99	2.85	2.70	2.62	2.53	2.45	2.36	2.27	2.17
30	7.56	5.39	4.51	4.02	3.70	3.47	3.30	3.17	3.07	2.98	2.84	2.70	2.55	2.47	2.39	2.30	2.21	2.11	2.01
40	7.31	5.18	4.31	3.83	3.51	3.29	3.12	2.99	2.89	2.80	2.66	2.52	2.37	2.29	2.20	2.11	2.02	1.92	1.80
60	7.08	4.98	4.13	3.65	3.34	3.12	2.95	2.82	2.72	2.63	2.50	2.35	2.20	2.12	2.03	1.94	1.84	1.73	1.60
120	6.85	4.79	3.95	3.48	3.17	2.96	2.79	2.66	2.56	2.47	2.34	2.19	2.03	1.95	1.86	1.76	1.66	1.53	1.38
∞	6.63	4.61	3.78	3.32	3.02	2.80	2.64	2.51	2.41	2.32	2.18	2.04	1.88	1.79	1.70	1.59	1.47	1.32	1.00

v_2 = degrees of freedom for denominator

Abridged from M. Merrington and C. M. Thompson, "Tables of percentage points of the inverted beta (F) distribution," *Biometrika*, Vol. 33, 1943, p. 73. By permission of the *Biometrika* trustees.

Tables A-4, A-5, and A-6: The Durbin-Watson Statistic

The Durbin-Watson statistic is used to test for first-order autocorrelation in the residuals. First-order autocorrelation is characterized by $\epsilon_t = \rho\epsilon_{t-1} + v_t$, where v_t is a classical normal error term and ϵ_t is the error term found in the regression equation. If $\rho = 0$, then no serial correlation exists. Usually, positive autocorrelation is suspected in time-series models, so the first diagram below demonstrates how to use the critical values of the Durbin-Watson statistics for a one-sided test. For example, with 2 regressors ($k'=2$) and 30 observations ($n=30$), if the computed DW is 1.01, it lies in the rejection region. Thus, the alternative hypothesis of positive autocorrelation is accepted. As another example, if the DW is 1.30, the test is inconclusive; and if the DW is 1.80, the null hypothesis of no autocorrelation is not rejected.

Two-sided tests are conducted as shown in the second diagram. If the critical values are taken from the 5-percent, one-sided table, as in the diagram, then the resulting level of significance is 10 percent, as noted in the heading of the table. For

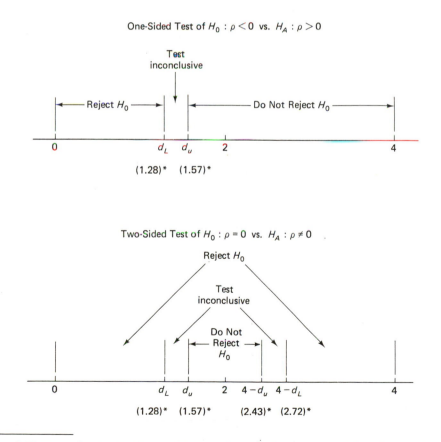

* These are critical values for $n = 30$ observations, $k' = 2$ regressors, and for a 5-percent level of significance. For the two-sided test, it is for a 10-percent level of significance.

example, if the computed DW is 2.50, the test is inconclusive; and if it is 2.80, the alternative hypothesis of autocorrelation is accepted.

Durbin and Watson's tables were constructed for only one to five regressors, for only selected values of the number of observations, n, and for only three levels of significance: 1, 2.5, and 5 percent. However, they tabulated all these numbers (1170 of them) by linearly interpolating from just 39 numbers. Thus, the user may want to make linear interpolations where necessary to obtain critical values of d_L and d_U if they are not found in the table. One might graph d_L as a function of n, for example, in order to interpolate a value of d_L for a value of n not shown. It is possible to obtain approximate values of d_L for more than five regressors by extrapolating a plot of d_L against the number of regressors. Such procedures, while *ad hoc,* may be appropriate as an approximation.

TABLE A-4

Critical Values of the Durbin-Watson Test Statistics d_L and d_U: 5-Percent One-Sided Level of Significance (10-Percent, Two-Sided Level of Significance)

n	$k' = 1$		$k' = 2$		$k' = 3$		$k' = 4$		$k' = 5$	
	d_L	d_U	d_L	d_U	d_L	d_U	d_L	d_U	d_L	d_U
15	1.08	1.36	0.95	1.54	0.82	1.75	0.69	1.97	0.56	2.21
16	1.10	1.37	0.98	1.54	0.86	1.73	0.74	1.93	0.62	2.15
17	1.13	1.38	1.02	1.54	0.90	1.71	0.78	1.90	0.67	2.10
18	1.16	1.39	1.05	1.53	0.93	1.69	0.82	1.87	0.71	2.06
19	1.18	1.40	1.08	1.53	0.97	1.68	0.86	1.85	0.75	2.02
20	1.20	1.41	1.10	1.54	1.00	1.68	0.90	1.83	0.79	1.99
21	1.22	1.42	1.13	1.54	1.03	1.67	0.93	1.81	0.83	1.96
22	1.24	1.43	1.15	1.54	1.05	1.66	0.96	1.80	0.86	1.94
23	1.26	1.44	1.17	1.54	1.08	1.66	0.99	1.79	0.90	1.92
24	1.27	1.45	1.19	1.55	1.10	1.66	1.01	1.78	0.93	1.90
25	1.29	1.45	1.21	1.55	1.12	1.66	1.04	1.77	0.95	1.89
26	1.30	1.46	1.22	1.55	1.14	1.65	1.06	1.76	0.98	1.88
27	1.32	1.47	1.24	1.56	1.16	1.65	1.08	1.76	1.01	1.86
28	1.33	1.48	1.26	1.56	1.18	1.65	1.10	1.75	1.03	1.85
29	1.34	1.48	1.27	1.56	1.20	1.65	1.12	1.74	1.05	1.84
30	1.35	1.49	1.28	1.57	1.21	1.65	1.14	1.74	1.07	1.83
31	1.36	1.50	1.30	1.57	1.23	1.65	1.16	1.74	1.09	1.83
32	1.37	1.50	1.31	1.57	1.24	1.65	1.18	1.73	1.11	1.82
33	1.38	1.51	1.32	1.58	1.26	1.65	1.19	1.73	1.13	1.81
34	1.39	1.51	1.33	1.58	1.27	1.65	1.21	1.73	1.15	1.81
35	1.40	1.52	1.34	1.58	1.28	1.65	1.22	1.73	1.16	1.80
36	1.41	1.52	1.35	1.59	1.29	1.65	1.24	1.73	1.18	1.80
37	1.42	1.53	1.36	1.59	1.31	1.66	1.25	1.72	1.19	1.80
38	1.43	1.54	1.37	1.59	1.32	1.66	1.26	1.72	1.21	1.79
39	1.43	1.54	1.38	1.60	1.33	1.66	1.27	1.72	1.22	1.79
40	1.44	1.54	1.39	1.60	1.34	1.66	1.29	1.72	1.23	1.79
45	1.48	1.57	1.43	1.62	1.38	1.67	1.34	1.72	1.29	1.78
50	1.50	1.59	1.46	1.63	1.42	1.67	1.38	1.72	1.34	1.77
55	1.53	1.60	1.49	1.64	1.45	1.68	1.41	1.72	1.38	1.77
60	1.55	1.62	1.51	1.65	1.48	1.69	1.44	1.73	1.41	1.77
65	1.57	1.63	1.54	1.66	1.50	1.70	1.47	1.73	1.44	1.77
70	1.58	1.64	1.55	1.67	1.52	1.70	1.49	1.74	1.46	1.77
75	1.60	1.65	1.57	1.68	1.54	1.71	1.51	1.74	1.49	1.77
80	1.61	1.66	1.59	1.69	1.56	1.72	1.53	1.74	1.51	1.77
85	1.62	1.67	1.60	1.70	1.57	1.72	1.55	1.75	1.52	1.77
90	1.63	1.68	1.61	1.70	1.59	1.73	1.57	1.75	1.54	1.78
95	1.64	1.69	1.62	1.71	1.60	1.73	1.58	1.75	1.56	1.78
100	1.65	1.69	1.63	1.72	1.61	1.74	1.59	1.76	1.57	1.78

NOTE: n = number of observations; k' = number of explanatory variables, excluding the constant term. It is assumed that the equation contains a constant term.
Source: J. Durbin and G. S. Watson, "Testing for Serial Correlation in Least Squares Regression," *Biometrika*, vol. 38, 1951, pp. 159–77. Reprinted with the permission of the *Biometrika* trustees.

TABLE A-5

Critical Values of the Durbin-Watson Test Statistics of d_L and d_U:
2.5-Percent, One-sided Level of Significance
(5-Percent, Two-Sided Level of Significance)

n	$k' = 1$		$k' = 2$		$k' = 3$		$k' = 4$		$k' = 5$	
	d_L	d_U	d_L	d_U	d_L	d_U	d_L	d_U	d_L	d_U
15	0.95	1.23	0.83	1.40	0.71	1.61	0.59	1.84	0.48	2.09
16	0.98	1.24	0.86	1.40	0.75	1.59	0.64	1.80	0.53	2.03
17	1.01	1.25	0.90	1.40	0.79	1.58	0.68	1.77	0.57	1.98
18	1.03	1.26	0.93	1.40	0.82	1.56	0.72	1.74	0.62	1.93
19	1.06	1.28	0.96	1.41	0.86	1.55	0.76	1.72	0.66	1.90
20	1.08	1.28	0.99	1.41	0.89	1.55	0.79	1.70	0.70	1.87
21	1.10	1.30	1.01	1.41	0.92	1.54	0.83	1.69	0.73	1.84
22	1.12	1.31	1.04	1.42	0.95	1.54	0.86	1.68	0.77	1.82
23	1.14	1.32	1.06	1.42	0.97	1.54	0.89	1.67	0.80	1.80
24	1.16	1.33	1.08	1.43	1.00	1.54	0.91	1.66	0.83	1.79
25	1.18	1.34	1.10	1.43	1.02	1.54	0.94	1.65	0.86	1.77
26	1.19	1.35	1.12	1.44	1.04	1.54	0.96	1.65	0.88	1.76
27	1.21	1.36	1.13	1.44	1.06	1.54	0.99	1.64	0.91	1.75
28	1.22	1.37	1.15	1.45	1.08	1.54	1.01	1.64	0.93	1.74
29	1.24	1.38	1.17	1.45	1.10	1.54	1.03	1.63	0.96	1.73
30	1.25	1.38	1.18	1.46	1.12	1.54	1.05	1.63	0.98	1.73
31	1.26	1.39	1.20	1.47	1.13	1.55	1.07	1.63	1.00	1.72
32	1.27	1.40	1.21	1.47	1.15	1.55	1.08	1.63	1.02	1.71
33	1.28	1.41	1.22	1.48	1.16	1.55	1.10	1.63	1.04	1.71
34	1.29	1.41	1.24	1.48	1.17	1.55	1.12	1.63	1.06	1.70
35	1.30	1.42	1.25	1.48	1.19	1.55	1.13	1.63	1.07	1.70
36	1.31	1.43	1.26	1.49	1.20	1.56	1.15	1.63	1.09	1.70
37	1.32	1.43	1.27	1.49	1.21	1.56	1.16	1.62	1.10	1.70
38	1.33	1.44	1.28	1.50	1.23	1.56	1.17	1.62	1.12	1.70
39	1.34	1.44	1.29	1.50	1.24	1.56	1.19	1.63	1.13	1.69
40	1.35	1.45	1.30	1.51	1.25	1.57	1.20	1.63	1.15	1.69
45	1.39	1.48	1.34	1.53	1.30	1.58	1.25	1.63	1.21	1.69
50	1.42	1.50	1.38	1.54	1.34	1.59	1.30	1.64	1.26	1.69
55	1.45	1.52	1.41	1.56	1.37	1.60	1.33	1.64	1.30	1.69
60	1.47	1.54	1.44	1.57	1.40	1.61	1.37	1.65	1.33	1.69
65	1.49	1.55	1.46	1.59	1.43	1.62	1.40	1.66	1.36	1.69
70	1.51	1.57	1.48	1.60	1.45	1.63	1.42	1.66	1.39	1.70
75	1.53	1.58	1.50	1.61	1.47	1.64	1.45	1.67	1.42	1.70
80	1.54	1.59	1.52	1.62	1.49	1.65	1.47	1.67	1.44	1.70
85	1.56	1.60	1.53	1.63	1.51	1.65	1.49	1.68	1.46	1.71
90	1.57	1.61	1.55	1.64	1.53	1.66	1.50	1.69	1.48	1.71
95	1.58	1.62	1.56	1.65	1.54	1.67	1.52	1.69	1.50	1.71
100	1.59	1.63	1.57	1.65	1.55	1.67	1.53	1.70	1.51	1.72

Source and Notes: See previous table.

TABLE A-6

Critical Values of the Durbin-Watson Test Statistics d_L and d_U:
1-Percent, One-Sided Level of Significance
(2-Percent, Two-Sided Level of Significance)

n	$k' = 1$		$k' = 2$		$k' = 3$		$k' = 4$		$k' = 5$	
	d_L	d_U	d_L	d_U	d_L	d_U	d_L	d_U	d_L	d_U
15	0.81	1.07	0.70	1.25	0.59	1.46	0.49	1.70	0.39	1.96
16	0.84	1.09	0.74	1.25	0.63	1.44	0.53	1.66	0.44	1.90
17	0.87	1.10	0.77	1.25	0.67	1.43	0.57	1.63	0.48	1.85
18	0.90	1.12	0.80	1.26	0.71	1.42	0.61	1.60	0.52	1.80
19	0.93	1.13	0.83	1.26	0.74	1.41	0.65	1.58	0.56	1.77
20	0.95	1.15	0.86	1.27	0.77	1.41	0.68	1.57	0.60	1.74
21	0.97	1.16	0.89	1.27	0.80	1.41	0.72	1.55	0.63	1.71
22	1.00	1.17	0.91	1.28	0.83	1.40	0.75	1.54	0.66	1.69
23	1.02	1.19	0.94	1.29	0.86	1.40	0.77	1.53	0.70	1.67
24	1.04	1.20	0.96	1.30	0.88	1.41	0.80	1.53	0.72	1.66
25	1.05	1.21	0.98	1.30	0.90	1.41	0.83	1.52	0.75	1.65
26	1.07	1.22	1.00	1.31	0.93	1.41	0.85	1.52	0.78	1.64
27	1.09	1.23	1.02	1.32	0.95	1.41	0.88	1.51	0.81	1.63
28	1.10	1.24	1.04	1.32	0.97	1.41	0.90	1.51	0.83	1.62
29	1.12	1.25	1.05	1.33	0.99	1.42	0.92	1.51	0.85	1.61
30	1.13	1.26	1.07	1.34	1.01	1.42	0.94	1.51	0.88	1.61
31	1.15	1.27	1.08	1.34	1.02	1.42	0.96	1.51	0.90	1.60
32	1.16	1.28	1.10	1.35	1.04	1.43	0.98	1.51	0.92	1.60
33	1.17	1.29	1.11	1.36	1.05	1.43	1.00	1.51	0.94	1.59
34	1.18	1.30	1.13	1.36	1.07	1.43	1.01	1.51	0.95	1.59
35	1.19	1.31	1.14	1.37	1.08	1.44	1.03	1.51	0.97	1.59
36	1.21	1.32	1.15	1.38	1.10	1.44	1.04	1.51	0.99	1.59
37	1.22	1.32	1.16	1.38	1.11	1.45	1.06	1.51	1.00	1.59
38	1.23	1.33	1.18	1.39	1.12	1.45	1.07	1.52	1.02	1.58
39	1.24	1.34	1.19	1.39	1.14	1.45	1.09	1.52	1.03	1.58
40	1.25	1.34	1.20	1.40	1.15	1.46	1.10	1.52	1.05	1.58
45	1.29	1.38	1.24	1.42	1.20	1.48	1.16	1.53	1.11	1.58
50	1.32	1.40	1.28	1.45	1.24	1.49	1.20	1.54	1.16	1.59
55	1.36	1.43	1.32	1.47	1.28	1.51	1.25	1.55	1.21	1.59
60	1.38	1.45	1.35	1.48	1.32	1.52	1.28	1.56	1.25	1.60
65	1.41	1.47	1.38	1.50	1.35	1.53	1.31	1.57	1.28	1.61
70	1.43	1.49	1.40	1.52	1.37	1.55	1.34	1.58	1.31	1.61
75	1.45	1.50	1.42	1.53	1.39	1.56	1.37	1.59	1.34	1.62
80	1.47	1.52	1.44	1.54	1.42	1.57	1.39	1.60	1.36	1.62
85	1.48	1.53	1.46	1.55	1.43	1.58	1.41	1.60	1.39	1.63
90	1.50	1.54	1.47	1.56	1.45	1.59	1.43	1.61	1.41	1.64
95	1.51	1.55	1.49	1.57	1.47	1.60	1.45	1.62	1.42	1.64
100	1.52	1.56	1.50	1.58	1.48	1.60	1.46	1.63	1.44	1.65

Source and Notes: See previous table.

Table A-7: The Normal Distribution

The normal distribution is the one usually assumed for the error term in the regression equation. The standard motivation for this assumption was developed in Chapter 3. The body of the table shows the probability (multiply these numbers by 100 to obtain percentages) that a randomly drawn number from the standard normal distribution is greater than or equal to the number identified in the side tabs, called z. The left-hand tab gives z to the first decimal place, and the top tab gives the second decimal place for z. The normal distribution shown in the table is called the standard normal distribution, with a mean of zero and a standard deviation (and variance) of unity.

As an example of the use of the table, the probability that a number drawn randomly from the standard normal distribution is greater than or equal to $z = 1.01$ is 0.1562, or 15.6 percent. This is the number illustrated in the graph.

Any normal variate ϵ with mean μ and standard deviation σ can be converted to the standard normal variate z by the transformation $z = (\epsilon - \mu)/\sigma$. Once the appropriate probabilities are looked up in the table, a translation back to ϵ may be performed by $\epsilon = \sigma z + \mu$. Since the text did not stress the use of the normal distribution by applied regression users, the details of the applications are left to more advanced texts. Only one test was suggested in the text, in Section 7.2.7, testing for autocorrelation when there are lagged dependent variables as regressors. A one-sided level of significance is found in the body of the table, such as 5 percent, or 0.05. The corresponding critical value of z is approximately 1.64. For the h-test for positive autocorrelation, the alternative hypothesis of positive autocorrelation is accepted if the computed z is greater than 1.64 at the 95-percent level of significance.

TABLE A-7

The Normal Distribution

$$Z = \frac{\epsilon - \mu}{\sigma} \quad \text{(Standardized normal)}$$

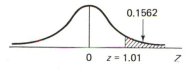

z	.00	.01	.02	.03	.04	.05	.06	.07	.08	.09
0.0	.5000	.4960	.4920	.4880	.4840	.4801	.4761	.4721	.4681	.4641
0.1	.4602	.4562	.4522	.4483	.4443	.4404	.4364	.4325	.4686	.4247
0.2	.4207	.4168	.4129	.4090	.4052	.4013	.3974	.3936	.3897	.3859
0.3	.3821	.3873	.3745	.3707	.3669	.3632	.3594	.3557	.3520	.3483
0.4	.3446	.3409	.3372	.3336	.3300	.3264	.3228	.3192	.3156	.3121
0.5	.3085	.3050	.3015	.2981	.2946	.2912	.2877	.2843	.2810	.2776
0.6	.2743	.2709	.2676	.2643	.2611	.2578	.2546	.2514	.2483	.2451
0.7	.2420	.2389	.2358	.2327	.2296	.2266	.2236	.2206	.2217	.2148
0.8	.2119	.2090	.2061	.2033	.2005	.1977	.1949	.1922	.1894	.1867
0.9	.1841	.1814	.1788	.1762	.1736	.1711	.1685	.1660	.1635	.1611
1.0	.1587	.1562	.1539	.1515	.1492	.1469	.1446	.1423	.1401	.1379
1.1	.1357	.1335	.1314	.1292	.1271	.1251	.1230	.1210	.1190	.1170
1.2	.1151	.1131	.1112	.1093	.1075	.1056	.1038	.1020	.1003	.0985
1.3	.0968	.0951	.0934	.0918	.0901	.0885	.0869	.0853	.0838	.0823
1.4	.0808	.0793	.0778	.0764	.0749	.0735	.0721	.0708	.0694	.0681
1.5	.0668	.0655	.0643	.0630	.0618	.0606	.0594	.0582	.0571	.0559
1.6	.0548	.0537	.0526	.0516	.0505	.0495	.0485	.0475	.0465	.0455
1.7	.0446	.0436	.0427	.0418	.0409	.0401	.0392	.0384	.0375	.0367
1.8	.0359	.0351	.0344	.0366	.0329	.0322	.0314	.0307	.0301	.0294
1.9	.0287	.0281	.0274	.0268	.0262	.0256	.0250	.0244	.0239	.0233
2.0	.0228	.0222	.0217	.0212	.0207	.0202	.0197	.0192	.0188	.0183
2.1	.0179	.0174	.0170	.0166	.0162	.0158	.0154	.0150	.0146	.0143
2.2	.0139	.0136	.0132	.0129	.0125	.0122	.0119	.0116	.0113	.0110
2.3	.0107	.0104	.0102	.0099	.0096	.0094	.0091	.0089	.0087	.0084
2.4	.0082	.0080	.0078	.0075	.0073	.0071	.0069	.0068	.0066	.0064
2.5	.0062	.0060	.0059	.0057	.0055	.0054	.0052	.0051	.0049	.0048
2.6	.0047	.0045	.0044	.0043	.0041	.0040	.0039	.0038	.0037	.0036
2.7	.0035	.0034	.0033	.0032	.0031	.0030	.0029	.0028	.0027	.0026
2.8	.0026	.0025	.0024	.0023	.0023	.0022	.0021	.0020	.0020	.0019
2.9	.0019	.0018	.0018	.0017	.0016	.0016	.0015	.0015	.0014	.0014
3.0	.0013	.0013	.0013	.0012	.0012	.0011	.0011	.0010	.0011	.0010

Source: Based on *Biometrika Tables for Statisticians*, Vol. 1, 3rd ed. (1966), with the permission of the *Biometrika* trustees.
NOTE: The table plots the cumulative probability $Z > z$.

Table A-8: The χ^2 Distribution

The estimate of the variance of the error term was shown in Chapter 4 to be distributed according to a chi-square distribution. Since applied regression users have very little direct use of this distribution, the explanation of this table will be brief. The left-hand tab is the degrees of freedom, and the top tab is the probability that a number drawn randomly from the chi-square distribution is greater than or equal to the number shown in the body of the table in the corresponding column, for given degrees of freedom. For example, the probability is 10 percent that a number drawn randomly from any chi-square distribution will be greater than or equal to 22.3 for 15 degrees of freedom.

TABLE A-8

The χ^2 Distribution

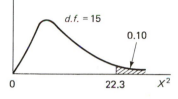

Degrees of Freedom	Probability of a Value at Least as Large as the Table Entry			
	10%	5%	2.5%	1%
1	2.71	3.84	5.02	6.63
2	4.61	5.99	7.38	9.21
3	6.25	7.81	9.35	11.34
4	7.78	9.49	11.14	13.28
5	9.24	11.07	12.83	15.09
6	10.64	12.59	14.45	16.81
7	12.02	14.07	16.01	18.48
8	13.36	15.51	17.53	20.1
9	14.68	16.92	19.02	21.7
10	15.99	18.31	20.5	23.2
11	17.28	19.68	21.9	24.7
12	18.55	21.0	23.3	26.2
13	19.81	22.4	24.7	27.7
14	21.1	23.7	26.1	29.1
15	22.3	25.0	27.5	30.6
16	23.5	26.3	28.8	32.0
17	24.8	27.6	30.2	33.4
18	26.0	28.9	31.5	34.8
19	27.2	30.1	32.9	36.2
20	28.4	31.4	34.2	37.6

Source: See previous table.

Index

F

G